WHY RELIGIONS MATTER

What are religions? Why is it important to understand them?

One answer is that religions and religious believers are extremely bad news: they are deeply involved in conflicts around the globe; they harm people of whom they disapprove; and they often seem irrational.

Another answer claims that they are in fact extremely good news: religious beliefs and practices are universal and so fundamental in human nature that they have led us to great discoveries in our explorations of the cosmos and of who we are. The sciences began as part of that religious exploration.

John Bowker demonstrates that there is truth in both answers and that we need both, in order to understand what religion is and why it matters. He draws on many disciplines – from physics, genetics and the neurosciences to art, anthropology and the history of religions – to show how they shed entirely new light on religion in the modern world.

JOHN BOWKER is an emeritus professor at Gresham College, London. He has also been a Fellow and dean of Trinity College, Cambridge, and Professor of Religious Studies at the universities of Lancaster, Pennsylvania, and North Carolina State. He is the author or editor of more than forty books, including *Problems of Suffering in Religions of the World; The Meanings of Death* (winner of the HarperCollins Book Prize, 1993); *Is God a Virus? Genes, Culture and Religion; The Oxford Dictionary of World Religions; God: A Brief History; Beliefs That Changed the World* and *Knowing the Unknowable: Science and Religions on God and the Universe.*

Why Religions Matter

JOHN BOWKER

CAMBRIDGE
UNIVERSITY PRESS

CAMBRIDGE
UNIVERSITY PRESS

32 Avenue of the Americas, New York, NY 10013-2473, USA

Cambridge University Press is part of the University of Cambridge.

It furthers the University's mission by disseminating knowledge in the pursuit of
education, learning and research at the highest international levels of excellence.

www.cambridge.org
Information on this title: www.cambridge.org/9781107448346

First published 2015

Printed in Great Britain by Clays Ltd, St Ives plc

A catalog record for this publication is available from the British Library.

Library of Congress Cataloging in Publication data
Bowker, John, 1935–
Why religions matter / John Bowker, Gresham College, London.
pages   cm
Includes bibliographical references and index.
ISBN 978-1-107-08511-4 (hardback) – ISBN 978-1-107-44834-6 (pbk.)
1. Religion – Philosophy.   2. Religions.   I. Title.
BL51.B69   2014
200–dc23   2014032790

ISBN 978-1-107-08511-4 Hardback
ISBN 978-1-107-44834-6 Paperback

Contents

Acknowledgements

> My days and strength have lately been much broken; and I never more felt the insufficiency of both than in preparing for the press the following desultory memoranda on a most noble subject.

John Ruskin wrote those words in 1869 (he comes into this book in Chapter 3 savouring 'the kisses kept in amber' of Cardinal Manning). The words apply equally well to myself, so much so that this 'preparation for the press' could not have been completed without the help of many people. I am immensely grateful, in particular, to Peter Barrett, David Bowker, Sarah Brunning, Chip Coakley, Quinton Deeley, Gavin Flood, Tim Hart, Gene Lemcio and Fr. Ben O'Rourke, OSA. My thanks go also to those at Cambridge University Press who helped in so many ways, and in particular to Fred Goykhman, Laura Morris, Alexandra Poreda, Siva Prakash and Elizabeth Shand.

Above all, I owe everything to Margaret, my wife, without whom this book would not exist. With my restricted eyesight, she has been my eyes, correcting, writing and rewriting so much that she is the co-author:

> From you I receive all things
> The reach, the reason and the purpose
> And the love.

For that and for so much more, thank you.

When Ruskin published his book, he wrote that it was the result of thirty-five years of work and reflection. This book draws on an even longer period (my first article was published almost exactly fifty years ago) and it is therefore the consequence of a lifelong attempt to show what religions are and why they remain so important in human life and history. The result is, I guess, a desultory memorandum, but it is a truly noble subject. In the United Kingdom, the academic subject of Religious Studies is being increasingly sidelined at the very moment when it is most needed if we are to succeed in living together in a multicultural society, and in a divided and contested world. I hope that this desultory memorandum will at least indicate why the study and understanding of religions are both fascinating and exciting.

TRANSLITERATION

The transliteration of words from other languages (particularly from Arabic and Sanskrit) is neither academically correct nor consistent. I have not included the diacritical marks because I can no longer see them. I have therefore settled for an approximate anglicised form. Those who know the languages will, I think, recognise the words. A few words correctly transliterated survive when they are in quoted books or texts.

Introduction

*W*HEN MARX AND ENGELS SURVEYED 'THE CONDITION OF THE working class in England' (to quote the title of Engels's own work),[1] their anger was fierce. In *Das Kapital*, Marx made repeated use of reports and statistics describing those conditions. "We misconceive the nature of the communist appeal", wrote Lane Lancaster (p.165), "unless we understand that the moral impetus of that appeal came from the bitter indignation that Marx felt when he contemplated the injustice implied in these figures."

Both Marx and Engels recognised that religious people and religious institutions did much to alleviate the suffering involved in those conditions, but from that it follows (or so it seemed to them) that if the conditions are removed, so too is the need for religion. On that basis Marx arrived at his famous conclusion:

> Religion is the sigh of the oppressed creature, the heart of a heartless world, and the soul of soulless conditions. It is the opiate of the people. The abolition of religion as the illusory happiness of the people is the demand for their real happiness. To call on them to give up their illusions about their condition is to call on them to give up the condition that requires illusions.[2]

The conditions in many parts of the world have changed, but religion has not disappeared. Can secularisation succeed where Marx and Mao failed? The problem in answering that question is that 'secularisation' is a pantechnicon word into which many different and sometimes contradictory meanings have been packed. The claim to secularism is made not just by militant atheists but also by some Christian theologians. In fact, secularisation is not a 'thing', an ideology, as some have suggested, "going about like a roaring lion" seeking what religions it can devour. Secularisation is a word of many meanings reflecting, amongst much else, massive changes in religious practices and beliefs: they include a decline in some, but they also include a growth and an increase in others. 'Secularisation' is certainly not a simple process leading to the abolition of religion.

The abolition of religion, however, has remained very much on the agenda for those associated with people like Richard Dawkins and (in his time) Christopher Hitchens who regard religion as a stupid folly, an irrational survival from the infancy of the human race. As Hitchens put it succinctly (p.64), "Religion comes from the period of human prehistory where nobody ... had the smallest idea what was going on." It is not only stupid, in their opinion, but also dangerous: it is, they observe, religious believers who fly planes into high-rise buildings and who fight against us or each other in different parts of the world.

However, even if that were correct, it would still be immensely important to understand religions much better than most of us do, particularly if we have any interest in the survival of human life as we know it now. Religions can be extremely dangerous: there are among their adherents those who are prepared to kill and destroy with *religious* reasons for doing so. Bal Thackeray, for example, who died in 2012, founded Shiv Sena (Śiva's Army) to defend the integrity of Hindutva[3] against outsiders, initially Communists but later Muslims in particular. He spoke of Muslims as a cancer needing cutting out, and he advocated fighting fire with fire: "Islamic terrorism is growing and Hindu terrorism is the only way to counter it. We need suicide bomb squads to protect India and Hindus."

Or to take another example: the self-proclaimed Islamic State appealed to religious arguments derived from Quran and Hadith (authoritative traditions in Islam) to justify its legitimacy and actions, particularly in relation to the establishing of the Caliphate and its way of pursuing Jihad. Those arguments and the violent actions derived from them were rejected by many other Muslims on specifically religious grounds (i.e., with specifically religious arguments), not by secular denunciations of terrorism.

It is often said that it is not religion but the abuse of religion that does so much damage. For example, on its tenth anniversary, 9/11 was claimed by the speaker on the BBC 'Thought for the Day' to be the result of 'perverted religion gone wild'. The abuse and the exploitation of religion may well be involved, but in all religions there are also reasons and obligations *within the religions themselves* requiring believers to act in those ways in specific circumstances. When Skya analysed how Shinto ultranationalists were able to move Japan so decisively towards total war in Asia and the Pacific in the 1930s and 1940s, he emphasised the paramount importance of their religious beliefs (p.324):

All of them were highly religious people – Shinto fundamentalists – and as such they believed in the core doctrines of Shinto ultranationalism: the divine descent and divinity of the living emperor; the divine origins of the Japanese ethnic group as against the divine natural evolutionary origins of man; and the divine source of political authority stemming from the ancestral deity Amaterasu Omikami. These doctrines were common to all Shinto ultranationalists as much as the crucifixion or resurrection of Jesus Christ is to Christians. Accordingly, for all these radical Shinto ultranationalist theorists, sovereignty resided in the emperor, and no human law was capable of restraining the sovereign emperor.

Beliefs of that kind become politically strong when they are organised into coherent systems. Juergensmeyer has shown how powerfully, since the Second World War, religious beliefs have driven demands for political independence and for the creation of "an indigenous form of religious politics free from the taint of Western culture". Among those beliefs in some particular cases are "the tendency to satanize the United States and to loathe Western civilisation, and the potential to become violent and intolerant".[4] That 'potentiality' now includes the possibility of being armed with weapons of indiscriminate or even mass destruction. For that reason alone we would be wise to understand what religions are and why they have been so important in human life and history. As I put it more than thirty years ago, and long before the invasion of Iraq (1982, p.66),

> The entanglement of religions in virtually all the intransigent problems which confront and threaten us means that we must become more serious in the ways in which we try to understand the power of religious belief both for evil and for good.... One of the most obvious reasons why we seem to drift from one disastrous ineptitude to another is, ironically, that far too few politicians have read Religious Studies at a University. As a result, they literally do not know what they are talking about on almost any of the major international issues. They simply cannot. It is time we began to educate ourselves, not just in economics, or in politics, or in technology, but also in the dynamics of religious belief and continuity, because whether we like it or not, it is religion which still matters more than anything else to most people alive today.

The threats posed by religions, or at least by some religious believers, are extremely real. As I also wrote at the time, if politicians wish to know where the next outbreaks of violence are likely to occur, they should draw on a map of the world the boundaries where religions meet. Iraq is only one example among many of our need to understand religions much more intelligently if we are to have a better chance of living together, with perception and understanding, in a contested and demanding world.

Even so, the threats are *only part of the story*. There are other, far more positive reasons why it is important to understand religions: religions are the source and context of virtually all the achievements and discoveries which people have particularly valued, not just in the past but often still in the present. In this book it becomes clear what at least some of those many achievements and discoveries are. Without an understanding of religions, for example, it is impossible to understand the art of the world, and one chapter looks in more detail at why that is so. Even then it is only one example among many.

It is necessary, therefore, that the severe and often angry criticisms of religion made at the present time are taken seriously, accepting that those criticisms are important and often (though certainly not always) well founded. At the same time, however, it is equally important to see that those criticisms are too blinkered and narrow-minded to be convincing or to have much effect on religions because they fail to take account of the *achievements* of religions – as much in the present as in the past.

The way in which the criticisms and the achievements *belong together* creates the paradox of religions. If it were simply a matter of observing that religious believers do good things and bad things, it would be pointing out the obvious. The paradox arises from the way in which 'the good' may be the reason for at least some of the bad consequences. To give an example, a recent collection of essays has argued that religion does not cause terrorism. Much depends on how 'terrorism' is defined, but on almost any definition it is clear that religious believers do commit acts of violence and terrorism for reasons (sometimes commands) derived from their religion. Among those reasons is the perception that what is of truth and value (to them) in their religion must be defended.[5]

It is, therefore, the fundamental paradox of religions that *both* parts of the story belong together. Both are needed in any attempt to answer the questions of what religions are and of why they matter. What that means in practice we will see in a wide diversity of key areas ranging from genetics and neuroscience to art and ethics, from evolution and biology to philosophy and the miracle of human imagination.

My purpose, therefore, is to make clear why it is so important to understand religions, and to show through particular and extensive examples something of what the study and understanding of religions can involve. It is not possible to explore the examples in the detail they deserve, but they can at least illustrate the diversity of what is involved. It is indeed a basic part of the discipline of Religious Studies to show how the many different parts contribute to the whole.

In that context, there is an underlying focus and theme throughout the whole. It is to apply to the understanding of religion the recent recognition, particularly in the natural sciences, of the connection between cause and constraint.

That may well sound obscure and academic, but it is truly important and even revolutionary in its implications. When in the past people have tried to find the reasons why things happen or how things have come to be as they are or why people behave as they do, they have usually endeavoured to identify the simplest, basic cause. It is an endeavour often summarised as 'the principle of parsimony', or more briefly as Ockham's Razor (to be discussed in more detail later): it is the determination to cut out all superfluous or unlikely suggestions in order to accept the simplest explanation of the data. If, for example, it is claimed that the earth goes round the sun because it needs the exercise, it is wise to excise that as an explanation.

In recent years, however, it has been recognised (especially in physics and biology) that the attempt to identify and settle for a single basic cause can be misleading. That is so because complex behaviours, whether of particles or of people, are brought about, not only by immediate and proximate causes, but also by *networks of constraint* without which those particular complex behaviours could not occur.

The failure to recognise this led in the twentieth century to the widespread ambition of reductionism – the attempt, that is, to reduce complex behaviours to a single and basic cause. An example considered later in this book is the attempt to reduce 'mind' to underlying neural behaviours in the brain, and to reduce those to the behaviour of nerve cells and molecules. That, indeed, was Crick's "astonishing hypothesis" (p.3):

> 'You', your joys and your sorrows, your memories and your ambitions, your sense of personal identity and free will, are in fact no more than the behaviour of a vast assembly of nerve cells and their associated molecules. As Lewis Caroll's Alice might have phrased it: 'You're nothing but a pack of neurons.'

That pursuit of reductionism even led Kendall to modernise the razor: "I wish to propound one principle which is, so to speak, a kind of Occam's *Electric* Razor: we should not invoke any entities or forces to explain mental phenomena if we can achieve an explanation in terms of a possible electronic computer" (Mackay, p.85).

The ambition of that principle cannot be achieved, and we will see different examples of its impossibility. Nevertheless, the reductionist 'quest for cause' continues and has led to what has become known as 'nothing buttery', the now widespread belief that humans are 'nothing but' the most elementary of their constituent parts. But once it is recognised that the quest for cause has to be integrated with the consequences of constraint, it can be seen why that kind of reductionism is both misleading and false. One of the purposes of this book, therefore, is to apply that recognition of the connection between cause and constraint to the understanding of human beliefs and behaviours, including those that are identified as religious.

How that works out in practice is explored in the following chapters in many different ways. It may, therefore, be helpful to indicate the plan and the argument by giving a short summary of the chapters.

After this *Introduction*, Chapter 2 begins with the angry and often passionate criticism of religion and religions. It then explains what the paradox of religions is and how and why it arises, and it begins to show in outline why it is so important and indeed urgent for us to have a much better understanding of religions.

Chapter 3 recognises that today much of the current criticism of religion rests on the widespread assumption that it is science which leads to worthwhile truth in contrast to religion which leads to nonsense. So if we are trying at the present time to understand what religions are and why they matter, the engagement with the sciences in general and with genetics in particular is inevitable. That is so because of the extent to which many of those critics see it as their duty in the name of science to fight against religion. For them, the controlling metaphor of the relationship between science and religion is one of 'warfare'. As Steve Jones, a professor of genetics in London (whose report on the BBC coverage of science is discussed in Chapter 2) put it, 'the battle for your soul rages in your DNA'. On religion he commented (p.14):

> An odd business, religion, and not one – or so it appears – that has much to do with science. To me, it has always seemed no more than a bunch of silly old men in frocks squabbling, often murderously, about who has the best dress designer, but I accept that faith can add real purpose to some people's lives.

Chapter 3 begins by explaining why the model of 'the warfare between science and religion' is seriously wrong, in order to look in more detail at other legitimate ways in which sciences and religions are related. The chapter then illustrates how that can lead to far more constructive and creative understandings of that relationship.

Chapter 4 examines the claim that the conflict between science and religion is inevitable and necessary because religions rely on dogma whereas sciences insist on doubt until observation and evidence establish what is true; the contrast seems complete. But how accurate is that claim?

Chapter 5 recognises that several of those who attack religions in the style of aggressive warfare base their attack on their work in the field of genetics. Their account of religion rests on a belief that the relation of genetics to natural selection and evolution will provide a sufficient explanation of what religions are and why they have come into being. Genes, in their argument, cause and determine those outcomes in biology and culture (including religion) which will assist survival and replication. In that argument there are real strengths but also serious errors, one of which lies in the assumption that there are single causes of complex behaviours.

The error in that assumption leads in Chapter 6 to an examination of the relationship between causes and constraints without which it is impossible to understand human behaviour in general and religions in particular. To take an example from J.Z. Young (p.8), living organisms come into being in the context of invariant constraints (often known as laws) such as those of thermodynamics. Organisms do not create matter or energy and they resist the tendency to dissolution by appropriate expenditures of energy which they obtain from their environment. The constraints of thermodynamics explain many of their behaviours in search of food, but they cannot on their own explain the particular ways in which sustenance is sought, nor even why one food sustains and another does not. There are *additional* constraints that control a lion into its behaviours in pursuit of its prey, and they belong equally to the explanation of that behaviour.

Chapter 7 moves beyond the relationships between the sciences and religions. If we start with religions themselves, we have to begin by attending carefully to what the people involved in the religions believe and do, and that involves trying to understand what they are talking about and what they are actually saying. But that brings us to a basic and fundamental problem: the multitude of languages in the many different religions. Chapter 7 explores what this challenge of translation and interpretation involves in understanding religions.

Religious believers, however, do much more than talk and write. Chapter 8 begins from the point that much religious life is expressed non-verbally, in how people behave and in what they choose to do. Religions offer to people the resources, means and opportunities to live acceptable lives – acceptable, that is, within the tradition involved, and acceptable to the individual, family and social group concerned. In practice this involves 'the internalisation of constraint' leading (amongst much else) to the characterisation of individual lives and of society. Chapter 8 gives examples of what that means in ethics and in art.

Chapter 9 considers the importance in religions of symbols and rituals taking as an example religious understandings of death; it also considers the challenges to those understandings at the present time. It does this with particular reference to ritual as a largely non-verbal way of sharing and expressing beliefs.

Chapter 10 returns to the claim in Chapter 2 that historically "religions are the context in which people began to explore the world around them and to share the consequences of their explorations." The chapter unpacks in more detail what that claim means in practice, and it suggests that religions can be helpfully understood as communities of shared imagination and shared exploration.

From that summary it will be clear that an underlying question throughout is the question of truth. Religions have been able to achieve so much because they are organised systems of ideas, beliefs and practices that have persisted and developed through time. Religions have taken many different forms, but at their heart is a common concern among humans to protect truths that they believe they have received from the past in order to pass them on to the next and subsequent generations.

What are those truths? And are they in fact true? Are they worth defending to the death, as some believe, or should they be confined to what is sometimes disparagingly called 'the dustbin of history'? Those questions lie at the heart of the study and understanding of religions.

In writing this book, I have drawn on my own work including parts of some lectures and articles from the past, but in all cases I have developed and changed them greatly, not least in correcting errors and misjudgements. Many errors surely remain and the process of correction (I hope) goes on. It is a recurrent theme in this book that our judgements usually have to be "approximate, provisional and corrigible", and may well turn out to be wrong, not least from the point of view of future generations. We urgently need each other to work together, not least in the way of correcting each other, if we are to make any progress in understanding religious beliefs and behaviours.

That point came home to me long ago when I was giving a lecture at Oxford. I was attempting to explain an implication of Gödel's theorem when I realised that I had got it wrong. I stopped and said, "I'm extremely sorry, but I've no idea what I'm talking about." A voice from the back said clearly, "That makes two of us." If we are learners together we have some chance of achieving a better understanding.

2

The paradox of religions

I N THE SUMMER OF 2008, *THE INDEPENDENT* RAN A PROMOTION to encourage the better understanding of religion. It was based on a series of short introductions to different religions (published by Oxford University Press) and on my *Oxford Dictionary of World Religions*. I was therefore invited to write two further 'short introductions' to the promotion.

I began these with a reminder of the trenchant and vigorous attacks on religion that were being made at the time by such people as Richard Dawkins, Christopher Hitchens, Sam Harris and Daniel Dennett. The abolition of religion was once again on the agenda. So the questions in which *The Independent* was interested were these: what is the point of taking religions seriously, and why do we need to understand religions? After all, we no longer believe many of the false, not to say absurd, claims made by religions in the past. For example, we no longer believe that the world is balanced on a pile of turtles, or that the sun jumps into a chariot each morning and drives across the sky. Why take seriously the many other religious beliefs that belong to the pre-rational infancy of the human race? Crick's allusion (in the Introduction) to *Alice in Wonderland* may remind us of the White Queen's boast that sometimes she was able to believe as many as six impossible things before breakfast. Religious believers, so we are told by sceptics, multiply six by about six billion and believe them all the time.

So why is it important to understand religions? An immediate answer is that religions are deeply involved in many of the long-running and apparently insoluble conflicts around the world. We have seen this in recent years in Northern Ireland, Cyprus, Bosnia, Kosovo and the Balkans, Chechnya and Dagestan, Palestine/Israel, Iraq, Lebanon, Syria, Iran, Pakistan, Kashmir, Afghanistan, Xizang/Tibet, Xinjiang/Uighur, the Punjab, Sri Lanka, Myanmar/Burma, Nigeria, Sudan and Darfur, Somalia and Eritrea, and now in the rise of the self-styled Islamic State. On 8 December 1992, *The Daily Telegraph* published a cartoon depicting the feet of victims of violence in a morgue, with the tags of identity attached. But instead of the names of the people being written on the tags, the causes of their death were written instead: 'Killed by religious bigots, Bosnia'; 'Killed by religious bigots, N. Ireland'; 'Killed by religious bigots, India'; 'Killed by religious bigots, Iraq'; 'Killed by religious bigots, Azerbaijan'; 'Killed by religious bigots, Auschwitz'; 'Killed by religious bigots, Beirut'; 'Killed by religious bigots, Armenia'.

The recognition that religions are involved in so many dangerous and violent conflicts simply reinforces the attack on religions made by Dawkins, Hitchens and many others. Maybe, they say, we *should* understand the contribution religions make to conflict and terrorism, but then in addition we should never forget all the other damage that religions do: we might think, for example, of how they have treated women or those of whom they disapprove, such as homosexuals and each other. In his book, *God Is Not Great*, Hitchens listed evil things that religions have done – suppressing reason, promoting terrorism, creating "tempests of hatred, bigotry and blood lust"; men-dominated, they control or condemn whole categories of people such as women and homosexuals; they rely on revelations and keep on inventing them, and they condemn the wayward to the torments of everlasting punishment.

There is no doubt that it would be possible to make a much longer list of the evil consequences of religion, as indeed they are listed in many of my own books: one of them, from 1987, is called *Licensed Insanities: Religions and Belief in God in the Contemporary World*. But then we are left with a puzzle: if religions are so evil and so ridiculous, why have they not disappeared long ago? In fact, at the moment, most people alive (more than three-quarters of the world's population) belong to a religion, however much or little they do about it. So the questions persist: if religion does so much damage, why has it not (as H.L.Mencken used to ask[1]) "gone down the chute" long ago? Why do people continue to believe?

WHY RELIGIONS?

The familiar answers given are that people believe because religion consoles them (it is "the opiate of the people"), or because it is wishful thinking (life on earth is "nasty, brutish and short", so let's hope for something better after death), or because it offered pre-scientific explanations (God, not gravity), or because it is even bigger business than the arms trade (and imagine trying to get rid of that!).

To the question why religions persist, other answers are given in the many disciplines that study human behaviour from the individual to the social, from neuroscience and psychology to anthropology and sociology. They take in more specific areas of focus in, for example, politics, economics and gender studies in order to offer explanations of why religions come into being and persist. In his book, *Religion Explained*, Boyer summarised (pp.6*f*) twelve explanations to account for the origins of religion: religion provides explanations (of puzzling natural phenomena, of puzzling experience, of the origins of things, of why there is evil and suffering); religion provides comfort (making mortality less unbearable, allaying anxiety, thereby making for a comfortable world); religion provides social order (holding society together, perpetuating a particular social order, supporting morality); religion is a cognitive illusion (people being superstitious will believe anything, religious concepts are irrefutable, refutation is more difficult than belief).

Further answers can easily be exemplified in the history of religions, and they certainly contribute to the understanding of religion and of what religious beliefs and practices have done throughout human history. Boyer accepted that his twelve explanations are, in his own words, *not that bad* (his own italics). As he put it (p.7), "Each of these 'scenarios' for the origin of religion points to a real and important phenomenon that any theory worth its salt should explain." On the other hand, those twelve reasons for believing are, in Boyer's opinion, so defective that they are not to be taken seriously in a modern world. Belief is, as he puts it (p.344), "a form of mental negligence".

That, however, does not solve the puzzle or answer the question of why, if religions are so absurd, they persist in such strength. What we have to recognise is that religions in the past and still in the present exemplify much more than the consequences of mental negligence. Any explanation of why religion matters to most people alive today has to recognise, not just the evil and the stupidity in religion, but the wisdom and the beauty as well. It has to recognise also, in a much less grudging way, the achievements of religion. Religions are the context in which people, through imagination and technique, have brought into being so much to which we give the highest value, whether in art, architecture, drama, poetry, music, dance, literature, education or even in the natural sciences which began as part of the religious exploration of the cosmos and of human nature within it. The separate word 'scientist' was not even invented until 1834.

At an even more fundamental level, religions have been for millennia (and to a wide extent still are) the social context in which the birth of children and their upbringing have been protected. Or to put it more technically, religions are the earliest systems of which we have evidence in which gene replication and the nurture of children were organised, secured and protected. Obviously, our ancestors did not have our knowledge of genetics, but that is beside the point in terms of evolution and natural selection. In those terms, what matters is the protection and transmission of genetic information into another generation.[2] It is only by passing on genes and looking after children well enough to bring them to maturity that human communities can continue through time – the process summarised as gene replication and the nurture of children.

So how is that process protected? In detail, in many different ways, ranging from tanks and battleships to hospitals, traffic lights and the Highway Code. But in a general way, the process is protected within three different boundaries. The first is the boundary of the cell, the second is the skin, and the third is the culture, including the family, in which we happen to live. Culture is the third defensive skin within which gene replication and the nurture of children are protected.

Religions emerged as cultural systems providing such protection. That protection may be literal and violent. It is an important reason why religions have justified war and conflict. As the anthropologist Jared Diamond has pointed out in his work on traditional societies, "There are many things that these societies do that are wonderful [not least, in his view, in their ways of child-rearing], and there are some things that they do that, to us, seem terrible – like occasionally killing their old people or infants, or persistently making war."[3] Religions have continued to justify war in specific circumstances that religions identify, each in its own way and on its own terms.

Equally, however, the protection may be achieved through the development of organised cooperation and the endorsement of mutual help – and the constant and dynamic connection between religions and altruism is a recurrent theme in this book. Many religions require that their adherents pursue peace and reconciliation after conflict, not as an option if they happen to feel like it, but as an obligation. In the project set up and financed by Gresham College in London (published as *Conflict and Reconciliation: The Contribution of Religions*), experts in major religions showed in detail how they do that, and why, therefore, religions can be a major resource in the pursuit of peace: "Those who regard themselves as belonging to any particular religion are under obligation to put into practice the conditions of adherence, and in all religions the pursuit of reconciliation and peace is a necessary and unequivocal obligation – even though ... the meanings of reconciliation and peace are differently understood" (Bowker 2008, p.17).

That is an important reason why religions have been of such massive importance in maximising and securing what is known in evolutionary terms as 'group selection' (to be discussed in more detail later). It is a fundamental reason why religions as protective systems developed and still frequently maintain strong and identifiable boundaries within which people have a better chance to live securely.

But why *religions*? The truth is that many animals cooperate very closely (flocks of birds, troops of monkeys, shoals of fish, for example) in order to survive and to protect their offspring, but they do not build temples and say their prayers in order to do so.

So why religions? Putting it briefly and in the most general terms, it is because religions have created the many different worlds of imagination, practice and belief in which humans have lived. The word 'imagination' is not chosen lightly: at the heart of Suddendorf's book on what separates us from other animals is his stress on the ability of human minds to imagine scenarios and to travel in imagination in space and time, and even more remarkably to connect imaginations with each other.

No doubt it is possible to imagine evil and false things. *Einbildung* is defined in a Dictionary (Langenscheidt) as 'fancy, imagination, idea, illusion, delusion, hallucination, conceit, presumption'. But a definition does not determine which of the many possibilities we are dealing with, and von Humboldt's comment in a letter remains true: "Die bloße Wirlichkeit wäre unendlich arm ohne den Reiz der Einbildung" (the plain reality of life would be unbearably impoverished without the stimulus of imagination). Religious beliefs and ideas create the stories and the narratives, the rules, the rituals and the organisation of families and societies, that have stimulated the imagination and have guided and controlled humans into particular and characteristic behaviours.

That can be seen clearly in the way in which 'religion, sex and food' are so closely locked together (see Bowker 2007, ch.6). Religions created the narratives and the rules that led (and still do) to behaviours in relation to sex and food that have been rewarded in terms of survival and continuity. For example, they endorsed and celebrated in symbols and rituals the mother (or indeed the Mother)[4] as the source of life in birth and of security in maternal bonding. They have even included the appropriateness in particular circumstances of abstinence and celibacy. In the case of food, they identified the unclean and the clean, 'the forbidden and the permitted' (*haram* and *halal* in Islam).

None of that could be achieved without a shared understanding in each human community of what is going on. It was again the achievement of religions to create a shared understanding in different groups – in a family, for example, or in a community – that could be expressed in action through rituals, and in communication through symbols and language. The communities thus created were extremely different from each other, and those differences continue into the religions as we know and observe them today – a reality that will concern us later in more detail.

This means that religions were and remain decisively important in creating the possibility of cognitive consensus in particular groups. Religions played an immensely important role in human evolution by supplying and sustaining the key metaphors through which people are able to interpret themselves and their circumstances in ways that can be shared. 'The metaphors we live by', as Lakoff and Johnson argued in their book of that name, create, inspire and to a great extent control the ways in which people understand and experience their worlds. Even before 'the age of metaphor', religions had been laying foundations through the invention of communal signs, symbols and actions: they thus recognised also the opportunities in sound that led eventually to language[5] – a recognition that has left its mark particularly on Indian religions.[6] "In the beginning was information," as Dretske put it (p.1), "The word came later." "In the beginning was the Word", says St. John's Gospel; Indians might say, "In the beginning was the Sound." By a careful attention to the sound structure of early languages, it is still possible to eavesdrop on our ancestors in their caves long ago.

As a result, religions were able to offer answers to fundamental questions – those, for example, of Gauguin's famous painting, 'Where have we come from? What are we? Where we going?' Gauguin himself connected the painting with Christianity: the central figure is a reversed image of Rembrandt's study of 'Christ at the Pillar', and in a letter immediately after finishing the painting he wrote (Denvir, p.123), "I have completed a philosophical work on a theme comparable to that of the Gospel."

Not surprisingly, the questions to which religions offer answers extend beyond the personal and individual. They include, for example, questions about the nature and origin of the world which parallel those of Gauguin: where has it come from? What is it? Where is it going? In what is known as 'cultural prolepsis', religions draw vivid pictures and maps of future destiny ranging from destruction and punishment to reward and bliss. So religions frequently tell people what they must do and believe if they are to end up in the latter and not in the former: they remind people that they are accountable and that they live under judgement – hence Harnack's definition of Christianity as "eternal life lived in the midst of time under the eye and by the strength of God."

Many of those answers are given in the form of stories that are told from generation to generation. As Shimamura put it (p.167), "Embedded within every culture are myths that define who we are, where we come from, and what will happen after we die." Religions tell stories that guide and inspire – and often frighten – people in their lives. They provide the great narratives that are now found in sacred texts like the Bible, the Quran or the Epics of India. People take those stories, in whole or in part, into their lives. They internalise them so that they become a part of their own history and the theme of their own biography and of the society in which they live.

The stories thus have a value that is completely obscured if they are assessed as nothing but inaccurate science. It is, therefore, a major part of the study of religion, as we will see, to understand what they are, what role they have played in human life, and how they are to be interpreted now.

The cultural achievements of religion might well seem enough to make religions interesting. But there is more. Religions are the context in which people began to explore the world around them and to share the consequences of their explorations. But they were also given confidence to undertake an even more extraordinary exploration far beyond mere survival. They began to explore the world within them. They discovered what Flood has called 'the truth within' (the title of his book), "the idea that there is a truth within the human person that can be understood or realised through the cultivation of spiritual practices" (p.193).

This means in practice that religions offer specific resources, techniques and objectives through which people can explore the furthest possibilities of human experience, ranging from desolation to ecstasy. They open the way to what Emily Dickinson called 'a brief exhilaration' beyond the power of words to describe (Johnson, p.503). The search and exploration may last a lifetime, as it did for Muso (1275–1351, Kokushi, 'National Teacher', in early Rinzai Zen). After years of meditation, he stumbled one night while walking and put out his hand to steady himself against a wall – but there was no wall there. As he fell headlong he realised complete Enlightenment in a single moment of unforgettable experience. He later wrote (Bowker 2010, p.122):

> Searching, searching for the blue rewarding sky
> I dug deep, deeper in the earth, heavy, alone.
> Then in the night-darkness I grabbed for brick and stone
> And struck the bones of heaven, empty as I.

These explorations have led to a vast range of consequences in experience which form a major part of the attempt to understand the nature and meaning of religion and religions. Those consequences are often summed up as 'religious experience', but that phrase covers so much that it is hard to know what it means. There is no agreement on a definition of religion, let alone of 'religious experience'. It is even a major question whether it is wise to use the word 'religion' in this context on the grounds that it is "an etic category within western intellectual tradition" (Flood, 2012, p.13). The Latin word *religio* is very different in meaning from the word 'religion' as it came to be used from the eighteenth century onwards;[7] and Turner has argued (in a way, however, that can be challenged), that neither he nor anyone else "practises religion": they practise (in his case) Catholicism – or in the case of others, such particular ways of being religious as the Way of the Lotus or of Hanbalite Islam.[8]

Even so, it is clear that there are many specific experiences which occur in religious contexts and which draw on resources that are to be found only in those contexts. There are also many which are given a specifically religious content, meaning and interpretation only in those contexts. For example, the experience of the insertion of thoughts into one's mind, or of alien control of movement, is widely reported across different cultures and periods of history. In many instances they can form symptoms of psychiatric illnesses such as schizophrenia, but in religious settings those experiences are often attributed to possession or inspiration by supernatural agents (such as spirits, demons or God). Experimental studies are beginning to show how cognitive and brain processes can produce experiences of 'alien control', but it is also clear that religious contexts, practices and meanings contribute not only to the occurrence but also to the content and religious significance of experiences of this kind (Deeley *et al.* 2013, 2014; Walsh *et al.* 2014).

The possibility of memorable (though sometimes frightening) 'religious experiences' is a major reason why religions matter so much to so many. It is beyond the scope of this book to describe them or to do more than simply recognise that there are many consistent and predictable experiences which occur within religious contexts, and which religions encourage and teach, while often warning of the dangers in pursuing experience for its own sake. On the other hand, it is certainly important and necessary to consider some of the questions that are asked about the status of those experiences (can they, for example, be reduced to non-specific brain events?) and about what conclusions and explanations can be drawn from them (how reliably, for example, can abductively inferential arguments lead to at least probable conclusions?).

Among those experiences are some which invite or even compel those involved into a recognition of a reality (or at least of what is real for them) as the ground and goal of all life including their own. Ignatius (the sixteenth-century founder of the Jesuits who left in *The Spiritual Exercises* a way of making, as Rahner put it [p.11], "an election or choice, the choice of the means and the concrete way in which Christianity can become a living reality") told a friend of his, Fr. Gonzales, that his long times of prayer and his many visions at Manresa "gave him such a great and lasting strengthening of faith that even if there were no Scripture to teach him these things of faith, he would be ready to die for the faith merely because of what he had seen at that time" (Donceur, p.14). In a different tradition, the Indian, Shankara (c. eighth/ninth century) made a similar claim: "Studying the Scriptures is barren without the experience of Brahman." In China, Xiangyan Zhixian found study so futile that he burned all his books. One day, while hoeing his garden, he heard the crash of a falling tile. Instantly he entered Enlightenment. He later wrote (Bowker 2010, p.122):

> Crash! And all earlier knowing
> Is gone – no effort was needed:
> In an instant the old way of going
> Is clear – with no trace of its track.
>   The rules of sight and hearing are broken,
>   Enlightenment is all: the enlightened have spoken.

Experiences of that kind have evoked a vast vocabulary of words like awe, wonder, ecstasy, peace, insight, meaning, fear and trembling. In ultimate terms the reality to which they point is spoken of as God (or equivalent words) or as Enlightenment (in any of its many forms). Put in words, it sounds dull – prose is, after all, prosaic. Put into life, it is what Danto once called, in his philosophy of Art, 'the transfiguration of the commonplace': it is a poetry that points beyond the sink or the stars or the furthest imaginable limit of any universe. Indeed, there is a surprisingly common experience in which the difference between one's self and the universe is obliterated: there is no sense of the passing of time, and all that remains is a perfect, timeless, undifferentiated consciousness. It is a sense of Absolute Unitary Being, and it is often referred to by its initials as AUB.

Claims to and from religious experience(s) raise immensely searching questions that lie at the heart of the study and understanding of religions. They are well reviewed in Yandell's *The Epistemology of Religious Experience*, which begins with the question, 'Is our task impossible or impolite?'

There are many who reply that it is unnecessary since in their view a true account of all such experience can be reduced to underlying behaviours in the brain. Crick's 'astonishing hypothesis' (see Introduction) was one example. The failure of such hypotheses (to be explored in more detail later) lies in the selection of one elementary level of behaviour (in the case of Crick, that of nerve cells with their associated molecules) as though it alone is fundamental and all-explanatory. But why choose arbitrarily that particular level when it itself depends on the behaviour of lower levels, as, for example, that of the electrons which convey the neural signals? Furthermore, it makes the crass mistake of ignoring the fact that the higher levels to which Crick refers act causatively on those lower levels in what is known as top-down causation – an important point in understanding religions to which we will return.

In the meantime, it is obviously true that neuroscientific research investigates what is happening in the brain when people enter into experiences of any kind, including those that might be described as religious. It is, therefore, a fundamental part of neuroscientific research to establish the correlations between brain events and particular experiences. It is well known, for example, that some people suffering from focal or partial epilepsy experience moments like those described by Dostoevsky in the character of Prince Myshkin in *The Idiot* (II, ch.5) "when his whole heart, and mind, and body, seemed to wake up to vigour and light; when he became filled with joy and hope, and all his anxieties seemed to be swept away for ever." Dostoevsky himself experienced this "unbounded joy and rapture, ecstatic devotion and completest life", and this ecstatic aura is often called 'the Dostoevsky syndrome'. Recent research has shown that the ecstatic aura is associated with the anterior insula in the brain (Picard and Craig), and that a sense of bliss can be induced by electrical stimulation of the anterior insula (Picard *et al.*, 2013).

Correlation, however, does not give a complete account or even explanation of what has happened. Something is *always* happening in the brain in all our thoughts and experiences, since otherwise we would be dead, but to engage in neuroscientific research is the beginning, not the end, of our understanding.

In particular, to know more about what is happening in the brain does not diminish, still less explain exhaustively, the quality or the meaning of the experience – an issue with which Dostoevsky wrestled in that same chapter. The subjective qualities of conscious experience are now usually referred to as qualia (Latin *qualis*, 'being of such a kind'). In Nagel's summary of his own argument (p.736), "Accounting for these features of mental states has been one of the biggest obstacles to materialist solutions to the mind-body problem, because it seems impossible to analyse the subjective character of these phenomena, which are comprehensible only from the point of view of certain types of conscious being, in objective physical terms which are comprehensible to any rational individual independently of his particular sensory faculties."

The brain's activity is increasingly well mapped and researched, but the privacy of the internal experience remains inaccessible to that kind of research. Indeed, it led Susan Greenfield to write an illuminating book called *The Private Brain*. As George Eliot put it much earlier, "Men, like planets, have both a visible and an invisible history."[9] When, for example, the football team you support scores a goal, there are observable (supposing you are wired up to the appropriate equipment) brain events that accompany your experience of delight, but a neuroscientific description of the events does not give an exhaustive account of the experience itself, nor can the quality of the experience be detected in a printout from a scan of the brain. Indeed, the experience in the crowd may be different from the experience of watching the game in front of a TV at home, although both are *caused* by the stimulus of events in the game and are *correlated* with comparable brain events.

The distinction between correlation and cause is crucial, as we will see in debates about the relationship between brain and mind. At the moment, the fundamental points are simply that correlation is not identical with cause, and that contexts are decisively important in the creation of experience, not least in the creation of one experience rather than another. In his book *Zen and the Brain*, Austin explored in great detail many correlations between brain and experience, including near-death experiences and far-death attitudes. After summarising 'a neurological perspective' on those varied experiences, he emphasised (p.452) how important context and personal history are:

> We have every reason to expect that much of their form and content will be coloured by each subject's earlier personal and cultural belief systems. Not surprisingly, cross-cultural studies have revealed the Navajo as then 'seeing a great chief in a beautiful field', a Hindu seeing a death messenger coming to take him away, and the Catholic meeting with the Virgin Mary in a great cathedral.'

No matter, therefore, how varied the realisations of human possibility have been, the fact remains that people in religious contexts have explored the boundaries of their own possibility in ways that have led to extraordinary discoveries, not simply of God or of Enlightenment, but of ways to live in self-sacrificing support of each other. They have also entered into the experience of 'being discovered' – the sense, that is, of an initiative being taken unexpectedly and undeservedly toward themselves in ways that completely change their life.

Those discoveries have driven imagination and technique into the new worlds of shared and organised religion. People have lived and acted on the basis of those discoveries in the human enterprises of prayer, meditation, yoga, art, ritual and many more, and in the care of others in ways that go far beyond kinship altruism.

RELIGIONS AND TRUTH

All those many and very different considerations are a part of the truth about religions – a part that opponents of religion usually gloss over or ignore. The current attacks on religion fail, partly because they never take the trouble to give an accurate account of religions, but even more because they never face the possibility that at least some of the basic and fundamental claims of religion are true.

For those who attack religions, that possibility seems simply ridiculous. Take one look, they say, at the claims of religion and we are back to 36 billion impossible things before breakfast. But questions of truth, particularly in the case of religions, cannot be decided on the basis that some among their claims are clearly false, not to say absurd.

So what is truth? According to Francis Bacon, Pilate would not stay for an answer. Nor, sadly, can we for obvious reasons of space. Nevertheless, we must at least pause in order to recognise that questions of truth, meaning and reference are fundamental in the study of religions and in any attempt to understand what religions are and whether claims made by or about them can be determined to be true or false. There is a widespread assumption, not least among those like Dawkins who attack religions, that science and the scientific method can alone decide what is true (a view known as 'scientism'). Truth is more complicated than that.

Not surprisingly, the evaluation of truth claims has for millennia been a major enterprise among philosophers, not just in the West but also in the East, even though it is possible to discern differences of focus and priority. Thus in the West an emphasis might be on truth and confirmation leading to a specification of those sentences that can be considered true, whereas in India it might be on truth and error leading to a conclusion that all sentences are false.[10]

There are also those who question the whole enterprise. Those who hold what are known as 'deflationary theories of truth' are inclined to go along with Pontius Pilate in the sense that they regard truth as a concept which may be technically useful but which does not serve an essential purpose. To add to a sentence "there are on my hand four fingers and a thumb" the words "it is true that" may give more emphasis, but they do not supply additional information.

On the other hand, we may still wish to evaluate the reasons why in some instances we give that additional emphasis. On what grounds is it justified or unjustified to add the words "it is true that …"? A phrase of that kind is often added to other words, usually to sentences. In the domain of language, it helps to remember, as Tarski observed, that what are true are sentences. Thus what is involved in the assessment of the claim "There are on my hand four fingers and a thumb" is made clearer when it is embedded in a further sentence: "The sentence 'There are on my hand four fingers and a thumb' is true if and only if there are on my hand four fingers and a thumb."

That observation leads to two major ways in which claims to truth are evaluated and judged: the ways of correspondence and of coherence. They answer in different ways the question of how we can decide whether the truth conditions ('if and only if') have been met. Or as we might put it more colloquially, how do we decide whether something is true or not? The most immediate way is to go and take a look. Is it true that there are four fingers and a thumb on your hand? Take a look and count; and that is what is known as empirical verification. If the claim corresponds to your observation, then it is true.

That underlies what is known as a correspondence theory of truth: what is obvious in knowing is what knowing obviously is. At this level, the meaning of truth remains the same, but the methods vary of testing whether or not the truth conditions have been met. In mathematics and logic, for example, the correspondence is established, not by empirical checks, but by formal proofs. In science, correspondence is usually established by empirical techniques and procedures.

Many claims, however, cannot be tested for truth in that way of correspondence. That is the case even in the natural sciences which are commonly (albeit wrongly) thought to rely entirely on observation or on empirical verification. But there is much in the natural sciences that cannot be observed. Did birds evolve from dinosaurs? We cannot go back in time and take a look at the process of evolution. On the other hand, we can take a look at surviving fossils, we can compare genomes and we can also take a look at examples of evolution in the present day. Put them together, and we can see whether the claim about dinosaurs and birds is or is not coherent with the overall picture we have of evolution. And that is a coherence theory of truth.

Oddly, however, those two so-called theories of truth may not actually be 'theories of truth'. Certainly they are theories *about* the nature of truth and they may be the foundation of claims about what truth consists in.[11] Thus correspondence theories may advance no further than a claim that truth is a relationship of correspondence between particular linguistic and non-linguistic items (as, for example, between propositions and facts) without taking up the issue of whether or not they are epistemologically justified.

In practice, however, as Rescher has argued (1973), the two theories appear as theories of justification suggesting how the truth conditions (if and only if) can be met. In other words, they are ways of asking what evidence or what warrants are being offered to support or justify any particular claim.[12] Without warrants for assertions, claims of truth (particularly in the case of coherence) would seem to be negligible. On the other hand, with the possibility of such warrants (even if only in the background), it is clear that truth, both as correspondence and coherence, *can* be told as much through fiction as through fact, as much through a psalm as through a sextant, as much through poetry as through prose. As Basil Grant observed of his brother Rupert, "His reasoning is particularly cold and clear, and invariably leads him wrong. But his poetry comes in abruptly and leads him right" (Chesterton, p.112).

What about religions? Of course religions can accept and indeed emphasise as strongly as empirical scientists that what we think and believe must rest ultimately on what we experience (although they then reflect very divergently on the nature of what experience is, and on the nature of what is claimed to have been experienced). Early Christian theologians summarised the point in a single sentence: *nihil in intellectu quod non fuit prius in sensu*; there is nothing in the intellect that was not first in a sense.[13] They recognised, therefore, that the mind has to address itself to sensory images (*mens convertit se ad phantasmata*), but they equally insisted that on this basis the intellect explores further meaning and truth far beyond the limit of direct sense-experience. They had another elliptical sentence making this point: *mens quodammodo fit omnia non entitative sed intentionaliter*; the mind can in some way become all things, not actually, but by entering into what they are.

That is why religions also attain truth, or what they take truly to be the case, through discernment and insight, and above all through practice and participation. 'Truth by participation' was a part of the devastating critique that Polanyi (1891–1976) made of those (exemplified in his time by linguistic philosophers and logical positivists, in our time by advocates of scientism) who seek to find an absolute and explicit foundation for true sentences and propositions particularly in the sciences.

Having worked as both a scientist and a philosopher, Polanyi knew that that is impossible. To seek knowledge and to seek truth demands what he called "indispensable intellectual powers" and "a passionate participation" on the part of those engaged in the quest.[14] It involves implicit knowledge, and it requires a personal participation to which each person brings a particular cultural and individual history including assumptions that cannot be explicitly formulated. This is the 'tacit knowledge', to use Polanyi's own phrase – the background or domain assumptions, as they are called in more recent sociology – which enables us to make sense of what we are attempting to know. Knowledge is personal (to allude to the title of his best-known work), but it is constrained by the relevant objectivity of what a person is seeking to know. Thus Polanyi claimed as his basic assumption (the italics are his own): "*Scientific knowing consists in discerning gestalten that indicate a true coherence in nature*" (Polanyi, 1969, p.138).

'Tacit knowledge' and 'personal knowledge' led Polanyi to his own understanding of religion and commitment, but 'truth by participation' is not unique to religions. Lovers, poets, therapists, artists, musicians (see Wagner on p.59), to mention only the most obvious, discover what is truly the case through participation – "the extent to which artists not only enter into the reality of what they are portraying in word and painting and become a part of it, but enable the onlooker to do so as well."[15] When the novelist William Thackeray (1811–63) tried to describe how novelists attempt to tell the truth, he compared it to the way in which we learn the truth of other people by participating in their lives:

> And as we judge of a man's character, after long frequenting his society, not by one speech, or by one mood or opinion, or by one day's talk, but by the tenor of his general bearing and conversation; so of a writer, who delivers himself up to you perforce unreservedly, you say, Is he honest? Does he tell the truth in the main? Does he seem actuated by a desire to find out and speak it? Is he a quack, who shams sentiment, or mouths for effect? Does he seek popularity by claptraps or other arts? ... I ask you to believe that this person writing strives to tell the truth. If there is not that, there is nothing.[16]

Religions also evaluate the truth or otherwise of a person's claims and character on the basis of their observable consequence – "By their fruits you will know them." That is at once leading into the domain of pragmatism. Pragmatism as a philosophical approach to truth has taken many forms, but in the case of religion it is particularly associated with William James (1842–1910).

James defined Pragmatism as a way to attain clarity and indeed truth by attending to consequences: "To attain perfect clearness in our thoughts of an object, ... we need only consider what conceivable effects of a practical kind the object may involve." To take his own example, there is no 'essence' of paper that tells us what it is: we can only know the true meaning of 'paper' by observing the uses to which it is put. Concepts and beliefs "become true just in so far as they help us to get into satisfactory relation with other parts of our experience."

If that is so (bearing in mind that many have contested the claims of Pragmatism), it would follow that religious claims and beliefs can only be evaluated in relation to their use in practice and in the coherence of their consequence. Hence in *The Varieties of Religious Experience*, James concluded:

> Both instinctively and for logical reasons, I find it hard to believe that principles can exist which make no difference in facts. But all facts are particular facts, and the whole interest of the question of God's existence seems to me to lie in the consequences for particulars which that existence may be expected to entail. (James, 1922, pp.521f)

There have been many objections to Pragmatism, but we cannot pursue the arguments here. Indeed, it is obvious that this very brief review of issues in relation to truth would not have been much help to Pontius Pilate in answering his question. But it can at least serve as a reminder of how many different ways there are in which questions of meaning and truth can be approached. Clerk Maxwell himself once observed that "scientific truth should be presented in different forms, and should be regarded as equally scientific, whether it appears in the robust form and vivid colouring of a physical illustration, or in the tenuity and paleness of a symbolic expression." In the case of religions, it is clear that the answer to those questions cannot be confined to empirical verification by 'going and taking a look'. Neither God nor Enlightenment, for example, can be inspected by 'going and taking a look'.

But since that is only *one* of the ways in which claims to truth can be made and evaluated, it does not mean (as those critics believe who confine truth to empirical verification) that claims to the reality of God or of Enlightenment cannot be 'true'. In any case, there are strong arguments *based* on observation pointing to the probability that God exists or that states of Enlightenment are attainable. Some of those arguments are closely linked methodologically to the sciences by their use of abductive inference.

In *God: A Very Short Introduction* I have summarised what abductive inference is and why it is as important in the sciences (and in daily life) as it is in reflection on the nature and existence of God. Abductively inferential arguments (which cannot be tested by direct observation) point, not to certainty, but to probability. That is why Niels Bohr could say that the sign of a profound remark is that its negation is equally profound. So in the example given earlier, the proposition that birds evolved from dinosaurs may be abductively inferred as possible, even probable, but it is not certain. Feduccia has argued forcefully against the widely believed claim that spectacular fossil finds in China, including *Sinosauropteryx* ('Chinese dragon feather'), are remains of dinosaurs on the way to becoming birds. The remains, in his view, are those of flightless birds *descended from* birds with flight.

In a comparable way, the proposition 'that God is' may be abductively inferred as probable (see Bowker 2014, pp.22–4), but it is not certain and many reject it: it cannot be confirmed by immediate observation of God.[17] The acceptance of abductive arguments requires commitment and trust, as much in the case of the sciences as in the case of religions.

Those observations are not in any way converting the natural sciences into a matter of opinion, since much is established on the basis of observations and experiments on which abductive arguments themselves depend. Thus it was a human decision in 1961 (constantly under revision) to measure atomic weights according to a standard provided by the carbon isotope C^{12} whose atomic mass was defined as 12, but other numbers relative to that standard were then *constrained* by what occurs in nature ranging from 1.008 for hydrogen to 283.03 for uranium. Nor does it mean that religions can convert themselves into a kind of science as an act of faith. Religious beliefs and propositions remain to be evaluated. Even so, the return of probability to the heart of science (powerfully reinforced in a post-quantum world) is a major irritation to those who think that a claim can only be justified if it corresponds to what it purports to be about. But that is not the only way, even in the sciences, in which claims about putative matters of fact are justified.

Another irritation is that the words or pictures into which religious claims are put are always inadequate. But that is true of science also. No scientist can tell you finally and completely what the universe is. That is why the claims of science, whether justified by correspondence *or* coherence, are approximate, provisional, corrigible (open to correction) and often wrong from a later point of view. Richard Feynman, who shared the Nobel Prize for physics in 1965, used to insist on this point. He wrote in a letter in 1976, "What is not surrounded by uncertainty cannot be the truth" (M.Feynman, p.xvi). At the very start of his introductory lectures on physics he emphasised, as Isaac Newton did before him, that there is in science "an expanding frontier of ignorance":

> Each piece, or part, of the whole of nature is always merely an *approximation* to the complete truth, or the complete truth so far as we know it. In fact, everything we know is only some kind of approximation, because *we know that we do not know all the laws* as yet. Therefore, things must be learned only to be unlearned again or, more likely, to be corrected. (R.Feynman, 2008, p.4)

Nevertheless, the claims of science are extremely accurate and reliable because they are, so to speak, wrong about *something*: the universe is (so far) consistently what it is, even though we can only speak of it corrigibly. Thus Halpern began his recent book, *The Edge of the Universe*, with the even more robust words (p.1):

> Everything that we once believed about the universe is wrong! We thought that most of the material in space was made up of atoms, or at least of visible substances. Wrong! We thought that the expansion of the universe was slowing down – that its growth from the Big Bang was losing steam. Wrong again! We thought that galaxies were fairly evenly spread out and that there were no large regions of space without them.... [W]rong once more!

The language is loose, but it indicates what it means to say that many of the claims of the sciences are approximate, provisional, corrigible and often wrong from a later point of view. So too are many of the claims of religions. No one can tell you finally and completely 'what God is like'. Accounts of God, or of Enlightenment, are approximate, corrigible and may well turn out to be wrong. But they are nevertheless reliable because they are wrong about something (in the case of Enlightenment) or some One (in the case of God).

This means that for most of human history people have had wrong ideas about gravity (Earth's inhalation and exhalation of breath, the collision of atoms, the plan and impetus of a demiurge), but by living in the constant and reliable condition of gravity, and through a long and continuing process of the winnowing of ideas, they have come to characterise the nature of gravity in more profound ways. People have had wrong ideas about God, but by living in the constant condition of God, and through a comparably long and continuing process of winnowing, they have come to know God in more profound ways, not as a patriarchal tyrant, for example, but in the consistent and energising consequence of love.

So when people try to say something about God or about Enlightenment, or when scientists try to say something about the Universe, it is inevitable that they use extremely approximate and corrigible words and pictures. That clearly raises (albeit in a new way) the *als-ob*, as-if, question that intrigued Vaihinger (1852–1933) long ago. When people try to understand reality, they have to make use of assumptions (or, in Vaihinger's term, 'fictions') that may well turn out to be wrong in order to construct their beliefs and experiments: how does it come about that fictions can be the foundation of true or at least reliable conclusions? "How does it happen," to put the question in Vaihinger's own words, "that although in thinking we make use of a falsified reality, *the practical result still proves to be right?*"[18]

Part of the answer lies in the fact that signposts are not the same as that to which they point. The issue is whether the language, however inadequate, points the way to something that is truly the case. That same consideration applies to the language and models of both science and religion. The concerns and practices of sciences and religions are hugely different (however much in important respects they connect and interpenetrate), but they resemble each other in the fact that their languages, their models and their metaphors are necessarily limited and inadequate and are certainly open to error.

That is one reason why not only religions (as the critics of religion have claimed) but also sciences are *equally open to fraud and to deliberate attempts to cheat and deceive*. They are also alike in the ways in which in the past they have produced harmful and disastrous consequences – as they still do.

What has vitiated the debate between 'science and religion', particularly in the public media, has been the assumption that only science tells the truth, and equally the highly selective way in which critics of religion have picked out only what is wrong in the religious case in order to prove how absurd, not to say evil, religions are.

However, by use of that same disastrous methodology we can equally prove 'how wrong, not to say evil', science can be. This defective methodology is so dominant in the accounts given by some scientists of religion that it is worth pausing to show how easily the same methodology can lead to a grotesquely stupid account of science. The attempt to understand 'why religion matters' is completely obscured at the moment by a methodology that attends only to one small part of the evidence and identifies it as the whole – as all that there is to be said.

'SCIENCE IS NOT GREAT'

The point here is fundamental if we hope to arrive at a better understanding of religions. By selecting from the religious world examples of error, fraud and deception, not to mention of wicked and destructive behaviours, the critics of religion are able to mount a vigorous attack on religion, and Christopher Hitchens was able on that basis to call his book *God Is Not Great*.

But by selecting examples from the scientific world, it is just as possible to mount an equally strident attack on science, and no doubt to write a book called *Science Is Not Great*. Goldacre has in fact written a brilliant and hard-hitting book called *Bad Science*, which follows what he calls (p.ix)

> a natural crescendo, from the foolishness of quacks, via the credence they are given in the mainstream media, through the tricks of the £30 billion food supplements industry, the evils of the £300 billion pharmaceuticals industry, the tragedy of science reporting, and on to cases where people have wound up in prison, derided, or dead, simply through the poor understanding of statistics and evidence that pervades our society.

From that it may seem that he is simply attacking the *abuse* of science, but in the chapter entitled 'Is Mainstream Medicine Evil?' he indicates why the answer may well be 'yes'. The chapter ends with the words, "Oh God. Everybody's bad. How did things get so awful?" In 2014 it was reported that the third main cause of death in the developed world is iatrogenesis (Greek *iatros*, physician), deaths caused by medical errors, hospital-acquired infections and reaction to drugs.

It is easy, therefore, to select examples to illustrate why neither science nor religion 'is great'. In both cases it is important to speak out with a loud voice against wrongdoing, fraud and evil. But that is very different from concluding that there is nothing else to be said (and Goldacre certainly does not make that mistake). It is as easy to illustrate defects in the domain of science as it is in the domain of religion, but the conclusion that neither science nor religion 'is great' does not follow. If we adopt that methodology of criticism in the case of science, it immediately becomes clear how utterly misleading, not to say stupid, it is as much in the case of science as it is in the case of religion. If we are ever to understand religions better, it is of paramount importance to get beyond the flawed methodology that, at the moment, dominates the discussion. To see how facile and disastrous that methodology is, let us see, albeit briefly, what the comparable 'case against science' would look like.

The case would begin with the well-known examples of fraud and error in the scientific world. They have often been described,[19] and some have had serious consequences. In 2011, to take only one example, a leading cancer research scientist in the Institute for Genome Sciences and Policy at Duke University in the United States had to resign for what the director of the institute discreetly called "a series of anomalies in data handling, analysis and management"[20]: this led to the retraction of peer-reviewed articles and to the suspension of three clinical trials in one of which the treatment of 111 patients was already under way. Maybe the motives of the scientist were entirely honourable: there may have been a genuine desire to help sick people. But there are many comparable cases in which it is not hard to see that other motivations were at work: career advancement, for example, or the financing of research.

Of course, fraud and cheating in scientific research are supposed to be detected by peer review of published papers, and by replication of results – and together they constitute the so-called gold standard of science. Both of them, however, are becoming increasingly difficult to maintain. The recent case of Jan Hendrik Schön, described by Reich in the book *Plastic Fantastic*, illustrates how easily the peer review process for vetting scientific articles was deceived – as it all too frequently is. Even more recently, in May 2014, *The British Medical Journal* withdrew two articles warning against possible side effects of statins (a major health issue at the time) because, even though the articles had been peer-reviewed, they contained statistical errors. At much the same time (*Nature*, July 2, 2014), Japanese researchers retracted their originally sensational and peer-reviewed claim to convert normal cells into stem cells through chemical stress. There are many such examples, and they led

Lawrence Altman, in an article with the subtitle 'When Peer Review Produces Unsound Science', to conclude:

> The system, known as peer review, is now considered a linchpin of science.... Yet for all its acclaim, the system has long been controversial. Despite its systems of checks and balances, a number of errors, plagiarism and even outright fraud have slipped through it. At the same time, the system has created a kind of Good Housekeeping Seal of Approval that gets stamped on research published in journals.

The point here is clear: the words 'peer review' at the head of an article give the impression that the conclusions have been tested and have passed beyond doubt. This has the disastrous consequence of (amongst much else) enabling politicians to claim that their decisions are 'science-led', since that enables them to evade serious argument and analysis. In fact their decisions are 'politician-led'. Of course one hopes that their decisions will be scientifically informed, just as one hopes that they might be ethically informed, or technologically informed, or economically informed, or even religiously informed. But scientists are human, and their decisions are not made infallible or inerrant by calling them peer-reviewed. What is now being asked is how rigorously the peer review system itself is being exercised, checked and monitored. Given the sheer volume of research papers that are now published,[21] it is not surprising that the peer review system is, to say the least, suspect and defective.

The claim is then made that at least when research is based on experiments, it can be tested by replicating the experiments. But even that is suspect. Clearly not all, and probably not many, claimed results are tested by replication in the peer review system, but it seems reasonable to suppose that in principle they could be. But even that turns out to be doubtful. For example, in an article entitled 'The Truth Wears Off: Is There Something Wrong with the Scientific Method?', Lehrer summarised the widely attested phenomenon of replication decline whereby research results become progressively weaker in subsequent attempts at replication. He took as an example second-generation antipsychotics which began to be marketed in the 1990s. The drugs had been tested on schizophrenics in extensive clinical trials, in all of which the symptoms displayed by schizophrenics had shown a dramatic decrease. One of those drugs became a top-seller, generating more revenue than Prozac did. By 2007 it was reported, from attempted replication of the original published results, that the therapeutic power of the drugs was waning so dramatically that they were no better than the first-generation antipsychotics that had preceded them, and some maintained that they were worse.

Lehrer suggested that an explanation for the decline in replication of initial results lies in the ways in which research is set up, in which it searches for particular results, and in which results are reported selectively when they are published. Drug companies, for example, are extremely reluctant to publish negative results of trials even though members of the public with an interest in the results have been recruited – and even though negative results can be as helpful in science as positive findings are.[22] On the decline in replication, Lehrer concluded:

> Such anomalies demonstrate the slipperiness of empiricism. Although many scientific ideas generate conflicting results and suffer from falling effect sizes, they continue to get cited in the textbooks and drive standard medical practice. Why? Because these ideas seem true. Because they make sense. Because we can't bear to let them go. And this is why the decline effect is so troubling. Not because it reveals the human fallibility of science, in which data are tweaked and beliefs shape perceptions. (Such shortcomings aren't surprising, at least for scientists.) ... The decline effect is troubling because it reminds us how difficult it is to prove anything. We like to pretend that our experiments define the truth for us. But that is often not the case.... When the experiments are done, we still have to choose what to believe.

In an article with an equally forthright title, 'Why Most Published Research Findings Are False', Ioannidis came to an even stronger conclusion and then asked: "Is it unavoidable that most research findings are false, or can we improve the situation? A major problem is that it is impossible to know with 100% certainty what the truth is in any research question. In this regard, the pure 'gold' standard is unattainable."[23] However, he then argued (much as I am arguing throughout this book) that we can nevertheless aim at higher degrees of probability.

The observation that scientific propositions are corrigible and incomplete, and that we may have to settle for degrees of probability, is then frequently evaded by scientists with an appeal to 'the scientific consensus' as though that consensus amounts to what is *in effect* certainty. That is clearly the methodology of Professor Steve Jones who wrote for the BBC Trust a report on impartiality in scientific programmes and reporting.[24] He accepted the position argued in this book that science involves uncertainty and doubt. He then argued that opponents of the scientific consensus on such matters as the effects of the MMR vaccine, herbal medicine and climate change exploit that necessary uncertainty:

> [A]ny concession by the establishment that it is less than certain of the accuracy of its claims – that there is, in other words, room for discussion – is

taken as a statement of surrender. Because so much of science involves uncertainty, it is open to attack from those who have never experienced that sensation. Purity of belief makes it easy for denialists to attract the attention of news organisations but hard for them to balance their ideas against those of the majority. This can lead to undue publicity for views supported by no factual information at all.... In the furore, the crucial point that there is always doubt in science, particularly when it tries to look into the future, and that to be uncertain does not inevitably mean to be wrong, is lost.

The result, according to 'a frequent comment' recorded by Professor Jones, has been that the BBC "does not fully understand the nature of scientific discourse and, as a result, is often guilty of 'false impartiality', of presenting the views of tiny and unqualified minorities as if they have the same weight as the scientific consensus."

Professor Jones is of course right that some opinions and propositions are clearly wrong because there are no warrants (or at least insufficient warrants) to justify them. But a scientific consensus (or what Jones calls 'settled debates') can also be wrong and has often been so in the past. Scientific consensus maintained the existence of (to give 'the standard examples', as I have called them; 2009, p.2) spissitude, phlogiston, caloric, morbid miasma, N-rays and the aether (for another example of scientific consensus being damagingly wrong, see Kelvin in chapter 4).

A striking and more recent example of scientific consensus being, not simply wrong, but aggressively wrong can be seen in the way in which that consensus rejected initially the theory of eukaryotic symbiosis (as an instance of endosymbiosis, meaning roughly that one organism can live symbiotically within another). When its modern-day proponent, Lynn Margulis, died in 2011, the obituary in *The Daily Telegraph* observed:

> At first the idea met with scorn: her findings were rejected by 15 academic journals and grant applications were brusquely rebuffed. The response to one application was: 'Your research is crap. Don't ever bother to apply again.'... Gradually scientists began to accept as a near certainty that the mitochondrion was once a free-living bacterium that invaded another larger bacterium to form a stable symbiotic relationship.... Eventually Lynn Margulis's theory became scientific orthodoxy.[25]

Like the Inquisition (now the Congregation for the Doctrine of the Faith), the defenders of scientific consensus are skilled in the suppression of dissenting views. The cosmologist Hermann Bondi (1919–2005) once offered a paper for publication to the Royal Astronomical Society challenging a consensus and listing mistakes in observations made in the past by members of the Society upholding the consensus. The majority of the Council voted to reject the paper, but Fred Hoyle, a member of the Council, argued that the identified errors all came from peer-reviewed publications, and he asked, "Is a paper to be rejected because its statements are correct?" As Hoyle recalled the occasion, "This argument was having a little success around the table when the President of the Society, W.M. Smart, squirmed in the Chair and exclaimed in an anguished voice, 'Then will somebody propose that this paper be rejected, irrespective of its contents?'"

The abuse of scientific consensus is simply another example of 'scientism', the view that only science and scientific consensus arrive at real truth founded on facts, and that philosophical issues are irrelevant to the work of scientists. If that view seems absurd, it is nevertheless exactly what Professor Jones states:

> Philosophy is of value to science in the way that ornithology is to birds. Most scientists care not at all about what the world's deepest thinkers might say about their profession, but all are aware of belonging to a vast and shared global enterprise which works, more or less, to the same rules. Science is a way of knowledge.

It is ironic that this sentence, and indeed his whole report, contains elementary philosophical errors and formal fallacies. Science is indeed a way of knowledge, but knowledge is not some ripe fruit waiting to drop into the open mouth of unthinking recipients like Professor Jones – 'the banana mentality', as Henry Williamson called it in *Dandelion Days*.[26] The BBC Report has been written by someone who does not seem to know the difference (vital for scientific method) between induction and abduction, nor to be aware of the liberating work in recent years on differentiated induction. Only the BBC Trust (given its membership) would commission a report on impartiality and bias from someone who states that he is biased against careful reflection on the truth or otherwise of his arguments.

If the claim of Professor Jones that most scientists share his contempt for philosophy is true, then the 'case against science' is powerfully reinforced.

If we now add to the list of those defects in scientific methods and procedures a further list of the immense harm and damage that 'science' has done (weapons of war, inventions that led to the virtual enslavement of men, women and children in the Industrial Revolution, indiscriminate animal experimentation, Churchill's 'perverted science' of the Nazis taken even further by Japanese scientists in Mongolia), it is as easy to construct a ranting diatribe against the evils of science as it is to construct a diatribe against the evils of religion.

To do that, however, is, *in both cases*, stupid, fallacious and indeed ridiculous. It becomes even worse than that when the attack is turned into personal abuse – and how easily that can be done has been deliberately illustrated in the preceding discussion. We need to recover courtesy in order to discriminate between what can be *exemplified* and what, if anything, can be inferred and justified as a *generalisation*. In the diatribes against both 'religion' and 'science' it is certainly possible to find examples of what is being described, and in both cases there may well be substance and evidence for the particular claims that are made.

Nevertheless, the diatribes are worthless *in both cases* because the methodology rests on the fallacy of the false identity. It is the fallacy of identifying the part with the whole. The fact that some scientists make mistakes and are wrong, just as some engage in fraud and in deliberate attempts to cheat and to deceive, does not mean that 'science' as a whole is wicked and evil. Nor, of course, does it mean that it has not also achieved immense benefits and engaged in a serious quest for truth. Fraud and error occur in the scientific world, and it is unlikely that all of it has been detected; the peer review system is unquestionably flawed. On the other hand, scientists in general are committed to corrigibility, and *in general* the protocols that act as a constraint in scientific research make it clear how fraud could and should be uncovered and corrected.

In the same way, the fact that some religious believers do hypocritical and wicked things, and the fact that religious structures far too often produce evil consequences, does not mean that 'religion' as a whole is wicked and evil. Nor does it mean, as this chapter has already begun to indicate, that religions have not also achieved immense benefits and engaged in a serious quest for truth.

CORRIGIBILITY AND THE PROTECTED
CIRCLES OF RELIGIONS

There remains, however, a massively important difference between sciences and religions, and it lies in the attitude to corrigibility. Science takes the meaning and practice of corrigibility with unreserved commitment. It is open to correction, no matter how reluctant or obstinate particular individuals may happen to be. When Schrödinger believed that he had created a unified field theory by expanding Einstein's General Theory of Relativity, he told a reporter who had asked him whether he was sure that he was right, "I believe I am right. I shall look an awful fool if I am wrong." But he *was* wrong, as Einstein rapidly pointed out, and the theory was abandoned.[27] His contemporary,

Wolfgang Pauli, scanned the physics of his time for three categories of error: wrong, completely wrong, and not even wrong (i.e., without even the merit to be considered).[28]

Religions have their own criteria and procedures of correction, both of behaviour and of belief, and part of the 'case against religion' lies in the graphic descriptions in religions of its own methods of *ultimate* correction: judgement and punishment after death, and the savagely cruel treatment of dissenters and heretics – although, of course, dissent and heresy are differently identified in different religions. Pauli, having been corrected by Einstein, looked an awful fool; Cranmer, having been corrected by the agents of the Pope, was burned at the stake. It is correction with a vengeance indeed.

So religions may have their own internal procedures of corrigibility, but there is nothing like the same commitment in religions as there is in the sciences to *public and shared* corrigibility (i.e., open to outsiders), particularly when a religion relies on inerrant revelation or unquestioning trust in a guru or teacher. Among religious believers and within religious institutions there is often an extreme reluctance to have their corrigible claims challenged, let alone corrected. The Indian Rationalist Association, to give only one example, has done prodigious work demonstrating how the claimed miracles of religious functionaries in Indian villages have actually been brought about, but the villagers by and large remain unconvinced. In 1989, Narendra Dabholkar founded MANS (Maharashtra Andhashraddha Nirmoolan Samiti, Committee for the Eradication of Blind Faith) in order to fight against superstition and the exploitation of superstition by the so-called 'god-men of India'. On August 20, 2013, he was killed by two 'defenders of the faith' – or more specifically 'defenders of Hindutva' (p.309). As a final irony, Dabholkar's son protested in 2014 that when the police failed to find and arrest his killers, they came under what he called "the spell of irrationality and unscientific temperament": they used, he said, " psychic and occult practices in their search for clues" with a senior police officer hiring "a Hindu Tantrik to commune with the dead."

There are many reasons why public and shared corrigibility is so often vehemently resisted. One among them takes us to the observation that a religion is a circle of shared beliefs, practices, texts, artefacts and the like which act as resources for those who live within it. Within the boundary of any particular circle claims to truth or propriety in belief and behaviour can be tested and assessed, but those tests and assessments cannot usually be made by correspondence with what they purport to be about, but more often by *coherence within the circle*. Criticisms from outside the circle are like tangents that strike the boundary and fly off into irrelevance.

To speak of 'circles' and 'boundaries' is of course to speak metaphorically. The metaphor of a circle draws attention to the ways in which religions (and subsystems within religions) have to be organised to preserve what has been inherited from the past, to implement it in the present and to conserve it for the future. It draws attention also to the fact that the necessary appeal to coherence cannot guarantee unanimity or agreement. In the larger circle of a religion there will be smaller subsystems, or what we might call (to extend the metaphor) 'inner circles', each of which regards itself as legitimate and valid – often exclusively so if it regards itself as the *only* true interpretation.

From even those brief remarks it can be seen how misleading it may be to think of religions under such large and general names as, for example, Judaism, Christianity or Islam. It is often pointed out that the word 'Hinduism' is a European invention of the nineteenth century, and that Indian religion is a family of related but often competing religious systems – or, to retain the metaphor, there are many smaller circles of coherence within the larger circle of Indian religion. The larger and more general names are clearly justified in Wittgenstein's sense of family resemblances,[29] but the fact remains that the smaller circles of coherence within the 'family' may be highly independent. The Constitution of the First Baptist Church of Berwyn, Pennsylvania, used to make a very clear statement of its independence:

> We disavow the position of the World Council of Churches, the National Council of Churches, the National Association of Evangelicals, and any other association or fellowship that would be in sympathy with them. We stand in opposition to the Ecumenical Movement, New Evangelicalism, Interdenominationalism, Protestantism, Neo-Orthodoxy, and cooperative Evangelistic programs between churches and people not alike of precious faith.

Or to give another example: an important movement in Japanese Buddhism is known as Nichiren Shu or Lotus Buddhism. Its founder, Nichiren (1222–82), attacked his 'fellow' Buddhists as corrupters of the truth or Dharma who were thus responsible for the national and political failures of the time. One of his works is called *Rissho ankoku ron, The Establishing of Legitimate Teaching for the Peace of the State.* In it he wrote:

> Alas! Alas! For the last thirty or forty years thousands of people have been bewitched and led far astray. As a result they wander around in the Buddhist way as people without any guide. Would you not expect that the good guardians will be angry when people wander away from Dharma? Is it not

understandable that the evil spirits will seize their chance when they see
people abandon justice and fall in love with evil deeds?

A later follower, Kuonjoin Nisshin (1407–88), believed that the welfare of
the country could only be restored if Nichiren's way of the Lotus were to be
accepted as the true interpretation of Dharma (the teaching of the Buddha),
and if it were to destroy and eradicate all other interpretations. According to
The Righteous Deeds of Nisshin Shonin 6 (see Stone),

> He preached fiercely against other sects, stating that sutras [other than the
> Lotus Sutra] do not lead to the attainment of the Buddha-nature, and he
> made entirely clear that the sin of attacking the [true] Dharma leads to
> the hells.... As a result, men and women who belong to other sects pelted
> him with stones or roof-tiles, and monks and nuns who attacked the true
> Dharma were single-minded in plotting evil against him.

That example of division has been replicated over and over again in the history of religions. It follows that the larger circle of coherence in the case of any
particular religion will supply most of the *criteria* of coherence, but that these
will be appropriated in such individual and ultimately independent ways that
there will always be contest and competition. There will be, so to speak, circles within circles, uneven in size and not necessarily concentric. These 'inner
circles', these subsystems of a religion, may be ferocious in their independence. In the resulting conflicts all the parties involved appeal to coherence in
order to justify themselves, or to repudiate their opponents.

The means that all major religions are deeply and often fiercely divided, not
just from each other, but also within themselves, since judgements of coherence are clearly a matter of opinion: there is no further or additional court
of appeal outside the circle. That is why claims are often made in religions
to a clear (maybe even infallible) authority to which important or at least
divisive matters of opinion should be subject – as, for example, the Pope in
Catholicism, the Quran in Islam and the Lotus Sutra in Nichiren Buddhism.

The appeal to what is in effect non-negotiable authority gives rise to what
is known as 'fundamentalism'. Fundamentalism is an extremely diverse and
complicated phenomenon, and it is not necessarily tied to a text regarded as
Revelation from God. Thus it is certainly possible to identify fundamentalist movements among the varieties of Buddhism of which two in Thailand
were examined by Swearer. In some ways, therefore, it is easier to speak
of 'fundamentalisms' in the plural, unified, if at all, in terms of what they
reject. In Meyer's survey of 'fundamentalism in the modern world', Biblical
fundamentalists are identified by what they are against. They are against:

liberalism, whether in politics, culture or theology; historical criticism of the Bible; any theories of evolution that conflict with a literal understanding of the Biblical creation stories; any dilution of the received faith through recognition of truth in other religions or even among other Christians, or through recognising the independent authority of secular institutions like the United Nations.

Insofar as fundamentalist movements become closed circles, it is irrelevant to observe that the different Scriptures do not all say the same thing and may indeed contradict each other, because within such movements there is only one Scripture revealed by God. Jews have one Scripture; Christians include it in theirs but extend it into a New Testament; in Muslim belief they are both 'People of the Book' who received originally the same Revelation from God, but they have so corrupted it that only the Quran is left as the uncorrupted Revelation.

Such attitudes reinforce the radical divide *between* religions and also *within* religions. Vatican fundamentalists, for example, appeal, not only to the Bible, but also to Papal infallibility, an appeal that Biblical fundamentalists of the kind summarised earlier in this section would certainly reject.

The warrants, however, to justify such claims can be found only within the circles/inner circles in which they are made. Thus the claim to Papal infallibility in matters affecting faith and morals can only be justified by an appeal to its coherence within the highly defined 'inner circle' (in relation to Christianity) of Roman Catholicism. It is not coherent within the 'inner circles' of belief and practice derived from, for example, Luther or Calvin. Catholics and Protestants share many of the family resemblances that characterise 'Christianity', and it belongs to the ecumenical quest to identify and clarify what they are. But the fact nevertheless remains that they do not share them all. Claims about the Papacy are even less coherent in the circles of belief and practice derived from, say, the Buddha or the Quran.

It follows that religions have to rely greatly on coherence in order to justify their claims, but this at once divides them from each other since they do not inhabit the same circles of coherence. Those who maintain and monitor coherence within the circles (usually the hierarchical authorities and those whom they employ for that purpose) are inclined to claim that they alone are in possession of the truth, the whole truth and (provided they do their work of supervision effectively enough) nothing but the truth; as a result, there is a strong and recurrent tendency for 'inner circles' to become *in effect* 'closed circles' in which alone the truth is to be found. That claim, however, as we have seen, can only be made on the basis of coherence within the circle in question: it has no status in the many other circles, let alone outside them.

The metaphor of 'closed circles' is, as we will shortly see, too strong, but for the moment it does at least point to strongly bounded systems in which obedience and conformity are emphasised, and from which nonconformists are excluded. *Extra ecclesiam nulla salus est.*[30]

A classic example within Christianity of 'truth' being defined by coherence in a closed circle of that kind was put forward by John Henry Newman (1801–91), especially in *An Essay on the Development of Christian Doctrine.* On that basis he was able to define Catholicism as the only true religion because he was always able to specify the ways in which other religions (amongst which he included Protestantism) are not coherent with it. In contrast, truth as coherence in a closed circle allowed him to claim that dogma is the mark of true religion, and that religion without dogma is "mere sentiment" (p.66). Coherence in a closed circle also enabled him to claim that all the doctrines in Catholicism are a part of each other and reinforce each other, so that all have to be accepted without question as a matter of "stern logical necessity":

> These [Christian] doctrines are members of one family, and suggestive, or correlative, or confirmatory, or illustrative of each other. One furnishes evidence to another, and all to each of them; if this is proved, that becomes probable; if this and that are both probable, but for different reasons, each adds to the other in its own probability.... You must accept the whole or reject the whole; attenuation does but enfeeble, and amputation mutilate. It is trifling to receive all but something which is as integral as any other portion; and, on the other hand, it is a solemn thing to accept any part, for, before you know where you are, you may be carried on by a stern logical necessity to accept the whole.[31]

Clearly, closed circles of that kind cannot happen by chance. They require boundaries, and those necessary boundaries have to be defined, monitored and maintained. There are many different ways in which that can be done, as the analysis of systems has shown very clearly. It is an obvious reason why there are so many different forms of religious organisation. But looked at as organised systems, it is possible to see how religions deal comparably with particular issues. Thus Harris (J.V.C.) analysed the place of human sexuality in four very different religious systems and concluded (p.271) that "systems theory can be applied in the study of religions", and that "it is possible to explain the deployment of power in religious systems in terms of authority, context and classification" – the classification being one that distinguishes between good-sacred and bad-sacred power.

In systems analysis, a 'boundary' is a means of analysing, both action within a system, and interaction with its environment:

A *boundary* of the system is a closed line placed around certain objects so
that there is less intensity of interaction *across* the line or among objects
outside the line than among objects *within* the closed line. *Less intensity*
means an intensity below some level, this level being a function of the problem under consideration. For example, we might consider communication,
influence or workflow as the interaction variables. (Bobbitt, pp.365ff)

To analyse some systems within religions (and some subsystems within a religious system) in terms of 'a closed circle' is an operational definition: in particular, it draws attention to the extent that a system does or does not allow or
encourage interaction across the boundary of authority and coherence. The
extent to which a religious system (or often community) is closed or relatively
open can often be judged by the function of obedience within the system.

As with all metaphors and analogies, however, the disanalogies are important. It is useful, for example, to regard an egg as a closed system in order to
analyse the embryonic growth within, but it is not a closed system in the strict
thermodynamic sense: an eggshell has to be porous (i.e., open to that extent)
in order that fuel (oxygen) can be taken in through the boundary to drive the
metabolism of the embryonic cells, and carbon dioxide can be discharged.

In the same way, no religious system can be completely closed and isolated
from all interaction with the world beyond itself, true though it is that some
religious systems make a deliberate effort in that direction: the community at
Qumran, for example, Salafi and Wahhabi Islam, the Amish in Pennsylvania,
some forms of Hindu Rashtra, or several indigenous communities in the
Amazon rainforests.

The disanalogy in this case suggests that it may often be wiser to speak of
'protected circles' in the case of religious systems, rather than 'closed circles',
although the fact remains that some are more closely protected than others.
An important difference between different religious systems lies in the degree
to which they are, so to speak, porous – that is, the degree to which interaction is encouraged or forbidden.

In understanding religions, therefore, it can be seen how fundamental
the questions are that arise from the ways in which truth and authority are
related: Who decides, in any particular system, what the truth is in belief
and practice? To what extent can they be changed or challenged within the
system and/or from outside the system? How should dissent and dissenters
be handled?

Those questions are answered in very different ways in the many systems
and subsystems of religions, but in all religions it remains the case that claims
to truth are most frequently tested by coherence within the circle or within

an 'inner circle'. Certainly some religious claims can be justified by correspondence, but many cannot, and in any case, in the end, whatever is claimed
to be the case in any particular religion is accepted or rejected in terms of its
coherence within the circle/inner circle of that religion.

There is no abstract rule to say that tests of coherence must be confined
within the circle of a particular religion, but in any protected circles they usually are. But then a major question is always being asked of religions, and
particularly so in the dramatically new world of IT communication in which
traditional boundaries are dissolved: what is the status of corrections or con-
firmations brought in from outside the circle? In the end, it may remain the
case that their worth or truth can only be justified within the circle; but how
far, if at all, can they be monitored and controlled?

The issue may seem complicated, but it is in fact straightforward: to
what extent should any particular circle seek to be coherent, not just within
itself, but also with claims in the world beyond itself? Take, for example,
the debate between young-earth creationists and theories of evolution.
Creationists of that kind insist on the authority of the Bible or of the Quran
within the inner circle of their understanding of Judaism, or of Christianity,
or of Islam, and they may well have a particular understanding of the nature
of that authority in terms of the inerrancy and infallibility of the Bible or
the Quran. A literal reading of the Bible or of the Quran means that the six
days of creation rule out modern theories of evolution, even if the days are
understood as sequences of time. Counterclaims from outside the circle by
those who pursue what they regard as the abundant evidence for evolution
are ruled out because they are incoherent inside the protected circle of text
literalism.

It is true, of course, that within the protected circle of any text-based religion there are many who reject claims of inerrancy and infallibility while still
emphasising the authority of the text in question. In the simplified slogans of
the day, this is the battle of the conservatives against the liberals, with liberals opening the boundaries of the circle to challenges and insights from the
world outside, and with conservatives believing that liberals, in doing this,
are betraying the faith and subordinating religion to reason.

Conservatives, in contrast, define, not only the boundaries, but also the
content of the circles within which they live. To critics, however, the resulting
protected circle seems indistinguishable from a closed circle, and a closed
circle seems to be identical to the closed mind. Within a circle of that kind it
is easy to define what counts as legitimate or illegitimate, orthodox or heretical, exemplary of the good or of the evil. The definitions of the closed circle
lead to the certainties of the closed mind.

Many humans find a profound satisfaction in the certainty of knowing that they are 'right'. Nevertheless, the questions outside the circle continue to be asked. For example, many religions make claims concerning what has happened historically. Those claims cannot be checked by direct observation, and within the protected circle of a religion there does not have to be a reason why they should be, particularly if that religion is based on texts from the past that are believed to be revealed or inspired, and perhaps therefore are believed to be inerrant – incapable of error. Nevertheless, there may be independent evidence from the past, and that evidence, the warrants for historical assertion, may lie outside the circle of coherence which constitutes a religion. The question will always exist whether surviving evidence from the past is coherent with claims arising within the circle of a religion.

To take an example: the quest for the historical Jesus is not limited to the evidence in the Gospels. On the other hand, for those who believe that the Gospels are part of inerrant revelation, there is no need to look outside the boundary of that particular circle of coherence: the Gospels are the inerrant record of what Jesus said and did. For believers of that kind, coherence within the religious circle will always control challenges from the outside. The responses will then vary enormously, from using external evidence to confirm the religious record to simply denying the truth or relevance of the external evidence.

In this particular case, however, there are many other believers who welcome the insight as well as the corrections that come from outside a less defensively protected circle. That is true, *mutatis mutandis*, in all religions. There are many other ways, in addition to the literalistic, in which revelation (or what is claimed or believed to be revelation) can be understood – hence the conflict *within* religions among those who hold different understandings of what the nature of revelation is and of how it is to be related to life.

The issue of interpretation or of hermeneutics is thus completely fundamental, and there are many in all religions who do not live in the closed circles that religions or sects within religions can become. Even so, the fact will remain that for many believers religious claims can only be justified or challenged within the circle of coherence in which they are made or to which they refer. Let us suppose that someone outside the system, outside the circle, challenges a claim of truth made within the circle: the test for believers can only be the coherence or incoherence of that challenge *within the circle itself.* That is why so much argument amongst believers and between believers and non-believers, and so much dialogue between religions, is ultimately futile. The circles or the inner circles remain isolated because coherence can only be tested according to the criteria within each particular circle.

That leads us to one of the toughest problems in trying to engage in discussion or argument with at least some religious believers. It is what Schimmel has called (as the title of his book), 'the tenacity of unreasonable beliefs'. He wrote (p.7) from personal experience of moving "from [Jewish] Orthodox believer to *apikoros* (heretic), at least as viewed from an Orthodox perspective", in order to understand how and why religious fundamentalists maintain their beliefs "in the face of overwhelming evidence and logical arguments" against them. In a circle of coherence it is easy – and rational – to do so.

CONCLUSION: BOUNDARIES AND BELIEFS

From all this it is easy to see why religions can be so dangerous. Circles have boundaries, and boundaries define who is in and who is out. The boundaries of religions may be literal (an actual land or territory) or they may be metaphorical (the agreed system of belief and practice to which people belong). Either way, if the boundary comes under threat – for example, by an invasion of armies or of conflicting ideas – some people will defend those boundaries to the death.

That is bound to happen because the achievements of religion, in areas ranging from sex to salvation, are so life-giving to believers that at least some of them would rather die than change, let alone lose, them. Those who die in that way may then be highly valued within religions as martyrs or as those who have done what duty or *dharma* requires of them: the basic meaning of the Greek word *marturos* or of the Arabic *shahid* is 'witness'.

So we need to understand religions better, not just because they can be terrifyingly evil and destructive in what they do but also because they are the context in which the finest and ultimately most important possibilities in life are opened up before us – certainly the most far-reaching achievements of mind and spirit, but also of God and Enlightenment as well.

And that is what I have called the paradox of religions: religions are such bad news only because they are such good news. Religions are the vehicle delivering into human life and history the greatest possible treasure, truth and delight, and for that reason people (or at least some people) would rather die than lose or betray them. If necessary, and particularly if a religion demands it, people will not simply be defensive; they will take the fight to those whom they perceive to be the enemy.

So the current attacks on religion are to be welcomed gratefully when they point out instances of folly and wickedness in the religious world. They are in that respect justifiably full of sound and fury. But in the end they are bound to signify nothing because they fail to understand this basic point: religions are such bad news only because they are such good news.

But that is why at least some religious believers will destroy human life as we know it now rather than abandon or betray their belief. The wars of religion were destructive enough in the past, occurring as they have in all religions in all parts of the world. In the present the threat is far more dangerous given that the religious warriors will increasingly have access to nuclear, biological and chemical weapons. Will they use them? That possibility is made more likely by the fact that in most religions there are people who believe (often in graphic detail and with great relish) that the world is going to end in spectacular violence and destruction. If it does so, that will simply confirm the belief.

Can the danger be averted? Probably not. Certainly not unless we make a massive attempt to understand why religions matter so much to their adherents that they will do both good *and* evil in the name of their belief. To enter into that understanding is extremely difficult at the present time when it is assumed so widely, especially in the media, that the sciences alone lead us forward into truth (a view known as 'scientism') while religions lead us backwards into error, and that as a result science must be antagonistic to religion. For E.O. Wilson (to whose work on genetics and group selection we will come in Chapter 5), the word 'antagonistic' is far too mild to describe how, in his view, science must annihilate religion:

> The Armageddon in the conflict between science and religion (if I may be allowed so strong a metaphor) began in earnest during the late twentieth century. It is the attempt by scientists to explain religion to its foundations – not as an independent reality within which humanity struggles to find its place, not as obeisance to a divine Presence, but as a product of evolution by natural selection. (Wilson, 2012, p.255)

Actually, he may *not* be allowed so strong a metaphor, because there is no necessity for conflict of the kind that he and so many others describe. It is true, as we have seen in this chapter, that religions are, in important and fundamental ways, "a product of evolution by natural selection." But that is not all they are. They are indeed the successful context of gene replication and the nurture of children, but as a result they also are the context of immensely important and valuable achievements and discoveries. That does not make them *ipso facto* the enemies of science.

Nevertheless, the fact remains that once the metaphors of warfare and Armageddon are mobilised, it is impossible for religion to be taken seriously because there is no point in even trying to understand it: it is already known to be 'the enemy'. So if we want to understand 'why religions matter' (and it is urgent that we do so), we have to make a start by moving beyond the assumption that 'science' is at war with 'religion'.

That is not to deny that there have been conflicts, and they began "in earnest" long before the late twentieth century. There is no question that in some of them, maybe in many, adherents of religion have defended the indefensible. When, in 1870, T.H. Huxley published his *Lay Sermons, Addresses, and Reviews*, he began it with 'A Prefatory Letter' addressed to John Tyndall. In it he apologised that its phraseology, in some places, was too vigorous, but he asked Tyndall to "recollect that it was written in the heat of our first battles over the Novum Organon of Biology."[32]

Huxley was referring to Darwin's *The Origin of Species*, and he was right to say that some of those battles were necessary and inevitable. Nevertheless, it is wrong to jump from that observation to the conclusion that the metaphor of 'warfare' is the only way in which the relationship between sciences and religions can now be understood. It is certainly a dominant and destructive metaphor at the present time. To make it the controlling metaphor is to miss the many other ways in which sciences and religions are related, and it thus distorts immensely any attempt to understand 'why religions matter' because it defines 'religion' as 'nothing but' the enemy of science. If we hope to 'explain religion to its foundations' as Wilson proposed, or perhaps more realistically to understand 'why religions matter', it is necessary to make a start by looking far more closely at the ways in which the relationship between science and religion can be better understood.

3

Religions and sciences

I Myth and meaning: 'The warfare between science and religion'

I N THAT SAME YEAR, 1870, IN WHICH HUXLEY PUBLISHED HIS *LAY Sermons*, Ruskin published his Oxford lectures, *Lectures on Art*, in which he wrote (IV, §125): "A Spirit does actually exist which teaches the ant her path, the bird her building, and men, in an instinctive and marvellous way, whatever lovely arts and noble deeds are possible to them." Richard Dawkins (one of those who sees himself engaged in a war against religion) exhibits a similar ambition, to find a comprehensive cause of animal behaviour and human culture, but he would reject 'a Spirit' as that cause, just as firmly as his predecessors rejected Bergson's *élan vital*.

There is, however, one point of agreement between Ruskin and Dawkins. Ruskin came to a comparable dislike of institutional religion and religious Orders: in *The Seven Lamps of Architecture* he wrote of Roman Catholicism that "its lying and idolatrous Power is the darkest plague that ever held commission to hurt the Earth", and he denounced 'the Pride of Faith' which, in his view, destroys humanity.[1] It is true that Ruskin retained his 'Religion of Humanity', but during his famous visit to Turin in 1858 (see note 3), he wrote in a letter to C.E.Norton (October 24, 1858) that "to be a first-rate painter – you *mustn't* be pious, but rather a little wicked and entirely a man of the world." He meant by that spending £100 "in grapes, partridges and the opera."[2]

It was in that same year, 1870, that the receding role of religion (or more specifically of Christianity) in society was dramatically illustrated, because it was in that year that the British Parliament passed the Elementary Education Act. Up to that time the extension of national education was almost entirely in the hands of voluntary and mainly Christian societies, not least the National Society which by 1830 had established 3,678 schools.

By 1870, however, it was evident that voluntary societies could not meet the need to make education more widely and nationally available, but the

State could not afford to buy up the schools that they had already established. The Act, therefore, set up the system whose traces can still be seen in the United Kingdom today. Voluntary schools (mainly established and run by the Churches) were allowed to continue and to receive grants-in-aid, but local school boards were established to provide the extra schools that were needed. In Voluntary schools it was accepted, despite the reservations of those like Ruskin who were angered by the consequences of what they regarded as indoctrination, that religious education could continue to be denominational.[3] In Board Schools, however, it was laid down in the so-called Cowper-Temple clause that "no religious catechism or religious formulary which is distinctive of any particular denomination shall be taught."[4]

Christian schools continued, but no longer in so dominant a way, and the Act and its consequences thus illustrate what Matthew Arnold saw (in 'Dover Beach', first published in 1867) as the ebbing tide of the Sea of Faith with its "melancholy, long withdrawing roar". For some, however, the tide was not going out fast enough. They saw the rise of science in the nineteenth century as a powerful challenge to the pretensions of religion. Where Arnold's poem had ended with "confused alarms of struggle and flight where ignorant armies clash by night", they saw the relationship between science and religion as a war of the enlightened *against* the ignorant – hence the titles of two well-known books of the time, *History of the Conflict between Religion and Science* (J.W. Draper, 1874) and *A History of the Warfare of Science with Theology* (A.D. White, 1896).

In 1970, to mark the centenary of that momentous Act, the National Society set up a commission (the so-called Durham Commission) in order to examine what the nature of Religious Education should now be.[5] When the Commission began its work, it seemed realistic to start by recognising the extent to which, during the century after 1870, massive changes had taken place in the Christian understanding of itself as a consequence of the so-called conflict between religion and science. Darwin's *The Origin of Species* had appeared only eleven years earlier than the Act, and it was soon regarded as marking a new stage in the conflict, not least because the length of time required for evolution made destructively impossible those traditional Christian beliefs based on a literal understanding of the Bible's account of the origins and early history of the world. The Report quoted, as an example, Spencer Leeson's description of the destructive consequence for his father when a friend gave him a copy of *The Origin of Species*,[6] but it could, of course, have given many other examples – that of Robert Louis Stevenson, perhaps, who, after he had shared his Darwinian doubts with his father, regretted that his father ceased to whistle in the mornings:

If I had foreseen the real hell of everything since, I think I should have lied, as I have done so often before.... Of course, it is rougher than hell upon my father, but can I help it? They don't see either that my game is not the light-hearted scoffer; that I am not (as they call me) a careless infidel.... I lay in bed this morning awake ... and heard my father go out for the papers; and then I lay and wished – O, if he would only *whistle* when he comes in again! But of course he did not. I have stopped that pipe. (Colvin, 1911)

If the Bible had to be taken literally, then the effects of Darwin could be devastating, epitomised in the famous words of Matthew Arnold:[7]

There is not a creed which is not shaken, not an accredited dogma which is not shown to be questionable, not a received tradition which does not threaten to dissolve. Our religion has materialised itself in the supposed fact; it has attached its emotion to the fact, and now the fact is failing it.

Perhaps, then, the 'men of realities, men of facts and calculations' (as Dickens described Mr. Gradgrind) should be mobilised to fight and overthrow the metaphors and myths on which, so it was claimed, creeds and dogmas rest. Conquest seemed to be the goal of Tyndall in his address to the British Association in 1874 (pp.474f):

The impregnable position of science may be described in a few words. We claim, and we shall wrest from theology, the entire domain of cosmological theory. All schemes and systems which thus infringe upon the domain of science must, *in so far as they do this*, submit to its control, and relinquish all thought of controlling it. Acting otherwise proved disastrous in the past, and it is simply fatuous today.

Tyndall's attack was actually focused more precisely on the necessity to include in the sciences only those explanations which have scientific warrants. At the time, however, it was taken to be an outright declaration of war, particularly when Tyndall appealed to his supporters to have no fear in the conflict with religion (p.474): "Where is the cause of fear? We fought and won our battle even in the Middle Ages; why should we doubt the issue of a conflict now?"

Tyndall's Address has been regarded by many as a nineteenth century's landmark in 'the warfare between science and religion' and more particularly as a consequence of Darwin, in the destruction of the Bible as a historically accurate account of the origins and early history of the world. When, however, the Durham Commission looked more closely, it became clear that there were indeed some who tried to defend the literal truth of the Bible against science in general and Darwin in particular, as there still are. But what was far more striking and impressive was the large number of Christians who welcomed Darwin with gratitude and with something like a sigh of relief.[8] Seas of faith may indeed ebb, but with equal regularity tides rise and return.

Notable among them, as an example, was F.J.A.Hort for whom, as *The Oxford Dictionary of National Biography* puts it, "the year 1871 was an 'annus mirabilis', " not least because he delivered in that year the Hulsean lectures in Cambridge. Hort is particularly well known for his work with Westcott on the text of the Greek New Testament because it began a new era in textual criticism. But his surviving correspondence in Cambridge shows with what enthusiasm and delight he and his friends welcomed Darwin's *The Origin of Species*. Hort knew well the earlier work from the late eighteenth century onwards on the age of the earth, and he knew therefore that the existence of 'worlds before Adam' meant that the account in Genesis could not be literally true.[9] Darwin's work set him free to see the work of creation in the context of a far larger (and longer) view of history in which the evolution of life worked together towards the person of Jesus as the Incarnation of God.

Hort was simply one among many who took that view and welcomed 'the new science'. Many of them, after all, had been educated in the sciences. True, they had been fortunate enough to have their education grounded in the Classics which still remain today (where they survive) the best foundation for clear and accurate thinking in which mistakes cannot be fudged or concealed. One of Hort's students remembered how "*he [Hort] seemed to regard the formation of opinion as a very sacred thing.*" That attention to evidence and argument enabled Hort to begin his career at Cambridge as a scientist, reviewing books for *Annals of Botany* and examining for the Natural Sciences Tripos in 1855.

Examples of that kind made it impossible for the Durham report to take as a starting point an acknowledgement of a nineteenth-century 'warfare between science and theology'. That view, however, is still widely held: it remains a popular and widespread assumption that there is an inevitable conflict between science and religion in which science is the conquering hero. Conflict can of course be exemplified: there are still plenty of people on both sides, those who espouse scientism and those who espouse the inerrancy of texts such as the Quran or the Bible, who continue to 'fight the bad fight'.

But the actual relationship between science and religion is far more complicated and interesting. For a start, we can now see that there is no such 'thing' as science and no such 'thing' as religion to be related. Of course we know roughly what we have in mind when we use those words, but, as we have already seen, Wittgenstein recognised the fatal error in trying to unify diverse but related phenomena under a single definition, and for that reason he introduced his notion of 'family resemblances'.

The point here is a great deal more important than it may seem at first sight. 'Science' takes even more different forms today than it did in the past, and 'religion' equally has taken so many different forms that no one has yet produced a satisfactory definition of what it is.[10]

As a result, it is usually far wiser to speak of 'sciences' and 'religions' rather than 'science' and 'religion'. The different theories and activities which might be described as scientific may, each in their own way, have different ways of being related to the different theories and activities which might be described as religious. There will not be one way, and one way only, in which something called 'science' and something called 'religion' are related.

In recognition of that diversity, Ian Barbour listed four possible types or ways of relationship including conflict:

1. Conflict (not necessarily to the death, as in some understandings of the warfare model, but identifying and probing conflicts on particular issues);
2. Independence (the two enterprises are addressed to such different goals with such different procedures that they are incommensurable);
3. Dialogue (a sufficient acceptance of the worth of each enterprise that a common exploration is valuable of what they are and of what they make of the universe and the human place within it);
4. Integration (the two are different languages about the same subject matter, the universe and the place of humans within it, so that some kind of translation exercise can be fruitful in preserving and transmitting the truth of both).

That list is often quoted, and it is certainly an advance on seeing the relationship as nothing but warfare, but it needs extending. Once we see that we have to think of 'sciences and religions' in the plural, it becomes clear that there are other possibilities.

5. One of them is the contest for authority and power (or for control, as Tyndall put it in his Address). This is discussed in my article 'Science and Religion' (Bowker 1998): "Science shifts the control over life and nature by research in contrast to ritual, and it remedies the evils which afflict us, not by exorcism, but by experiment. Science therefore challenges the exercise of authority and control by religions in areas where it has traditionally obtained."

Three other examples of the relationship are correction, confirmation and extension:

6. Correction: it may seem obvious that particular sciences have often in the past corrected specific propositions about putative matters of fact

which have occurred in particular religions, and they still do so. What is not so obvious is that religions may correct propositions that occur in the sciences; a particular example of this is the way in which the evidence-based understanding of what religions are and do corrects the false metaphor of 'the selfish gene': that is explored in some detail in Chapter 5.

7. Confirmation: some particular findings in a science may be used as a basis for a claim that some particular religious beliefs anticipate the findings of modern science and are thus in a sense confirmed by them. An example (intuitional anthropologies and genetic inheritance) is considered in Chapter 5. On the other hand, the claim to confirmation is clearly open to abuse, as in this example from de Riencourt (Bowker 1998, pp.196f):

> The new picture of the universe disclosed by contemporary physics appears to be largely in accord with Eastern metaphysics ... It might well be that mankind is now on the threshold of a psychological and physiological revolution of a magnitude that will overshadow all the social and political revolutions of our century – made possible by the seemingly incongruous, yet perfectly logical marriage between science and Eastern mysticism's insights.

That example, like many others of the same sort, is unconvincing. To give an earlier, albeit admittedly more secular, example, John Judd (a professor of geology who was a close friend and strong supporter of Charles Darwin) recalled how, in 1871, Matthew Arnold told him:

> 'I cannot understand why you scientific people make such a fuss about Darwin. Why it's all in Lucretius!' On my replying, 'Yes! Lucretius guessed what Darwin proved,' he mischievously rejoined 'Ah! That only shows how much greater Lucretius really was, – for he divined a truth, which Darwin spent a life of labour in groping for.' (Judd, pp.3ff)

Or as we might put it, Darwin sought (over many years) to find warrants for his assertions.

8. Extension through implication: the sciences answer particular questions and achieve remarkable results, but they almost invariably raise further and different questions, some of which can only be answered in other ways, by philosophy, for example, or by religions or by art or by fiction. Chekov, it is true, thought that writers of fiction should not try to *solve* questions (p.88), but should simply *describe* what their characters think and say about such things. He distinguished between solving problems and stating problems correctly – "it is only the second that is obligatory for the artist" (p.100).

But the point of 'extension through implication' is not to solve problems in a scientific way. It is to take further the questions and challenges
raised by that work. What that means can be seen clearly, by way of
example, in the work of Clerk Maxwell (of whom Einstein said that his
"change in the conception of Reality is the most profound and the most
fruitful that physics has experienced since the time of Newton") and
George Eliot. They published their last major works in the same year,
1876, and both were equally clear about where the work of the scientist
ends[11] and where that of "the narrator of human actions" begins. In their
view, each without the other is incomplete, and both are required for
knowledge and understanding – and Maxwell's *Matter and Motion* was
published by the Society for the Promotion of Christian Knowledge.
The way in which a novelist is an observer of 'experiments' is made
clear by George Eliot at the beginning of the Prelude to *Middlemarch* –
which also illustrates the entirely different way in which a novelist
'writes up' the results (1874 p.1; and cf. also the passage from Daniel
Deronda quoted in fn.9, p.310):

> Who that cares much to know the history of man, and how the mys-
> terious mixture behaves under the varying experiments of Time, has
> not dwelt, at least briefly, on the life of Saint Theresa, has not smiled
> with some gentleness at the thought of the little girl walking forth
> one morning hand in hand with her still smaller brother, to go and
> seek martyrdom in the country of the Moors? Out they toddled from
> rugged Avila, wide-eyed and helpless-looking as two fawns, but with
> human hearts, already beating to a national idea; until domestic real-
> ity met them in the shape of uncles, and turned them back from their
> great resolve.

MYTH AND MEANING

The additions to Barbour's list of four open up further ways of understanding the relationship between sciences and religions. The last of them, 'extension through implication', is far removed from the metaphor of warfare and
conflict. It has in fact been a particularly creative way in which sciences
and religions interact, not least in science fiction, art and poetry, but also in
philosophical theology. And yet it has often been overlooked or forgotten in
debates about the relationship between sciences and religions. But what does
it actually mean in practice?

We can at least begin to answer that by looking at one particular example. The example is myth. The focus will be on the powerful way in which

myth has extended the implications of science, particularly in the nineteenth century. Ruskin himself, with whom this chapter began, saw the point about myth being 'extension by implication'. He defined myth as "truths which nothing else could convey." Myth creates a combination of delight and awe "which belongs to the effort of the mind to unweave the riddle, or to the sense it has of there being an infinite power and meaning in the things seen, beyond all that is apparent therein."[12]

In contrast to that, however, the word 'myth' has now acquired a predominantly negative meaning. It is used almost invariably as a synonym for 'false'. The phrase 'the myth of ...' usually precedes a denunciation of something that has been claimed to be true but is now known to be false.[13] 'Urban myth' has become a standard way of referring to an entertaining untruth that has gained widespread credence. It is, for example, widely believed that the invasion by wild parakeets of European cities from London to Rome began when the makers of the film *The African Queen* brought African parakeets to Shepperton Studios and then released them into the wild once the film had been made. The belief, however, is false. Angela Allen, who worked closely, in continuity, with John Houston, stated in an interview for iPM in May 2011 that no birds or animals had been brought from Africa, and that therefore no parakeets had been released: "If you see the film you don't see parakeets flying around." It is, nevertheless, what is now called an 'urban myth', something that is widely believed although it is false.

Myth nevertheless remains an important example of a way in which the human imagination has extended the implications of science. Myth has played a positive and immensely creative part in human history and imagination, and myth has therefore been central to the study of religions in its own right and in related disciplines such as anthropology. But since the word 'myth' has now acquired a predominantly negative meaning, we need to bear in mind the great damage that has been done to the intelligent understanding of religion when religions are associated, or even made synonymous, with that changed and negative understanding.

That illustrates with dramatic clarity how an understanding of the possible relationships between sciences and religions (and indeed of religion itself) is destroyed when the meaning of a word is completely changed. When 'myth' is defined as 'false', it becomes a powerful weapon in the hands of those who wage war against religion because religion is identified with myth and myth is defined as false. That is exactly how Richard Dawkins argues: "No educated person believes the Adam and Eve myth nowadays, but it is surprising how many parents think that it is somehow fun to pass on this falsehood (and others in the same vein) to their children" (Dawkins, 2011, p.28). Not surprisingly he goes on (p.29):

I have sometimes worried about the educational effects of fairytales. Could they be pernicious, leading children down pathways of gullibility towards anti-scientific superstition and religion? Maybe. But could they also be beneficial, in leading children away from static essentialism? And towards a state of mind that is receptive to the dynamics of evolution? I don't know. And, as so often when I don't know the answer to a question, I'd like to find out.

One way for him to find out would be to take the trouble to read at least something of the immense work that has been done during the last hundred years on fairy tales and on the educational consequences for children. Bettelheim, for example, wrote a key book in its time (1976) on 'the meaning and importance of fairy tales' in which he emphasised how decisively important stories (including fairytales and myths) are for children as they grow up in helping them to explore and internalise the possible meanings of their lives:

> If we hope to live not just from moment to moment, but in true consciousness of our existence, then our greatest need and most difficult achievement is to find meaning in our lives.... An understanding of the meaning of one's life is not suddenly acquired at a particular age, nor even when one has reached chronological maturity. On the contrary, gaining a secure understanding of what the meaning of one's life may or ought to be is what constitutes having attained psychological maturity.

On this Sally Goddard Blythe, exploring 'the genius of natural childhood', commented (pp.142, 144):

> Fairytales are not the property of childhood alone but are in a sense the archetypal form of oral narrative upon which so much 'literary' writing is based. Some of the best stories enjoyed by adults fall within the fairytale format. Features of fairy tales are that they usually involve legendary or magical deeds and creatures, are highly fanciful and often contain a hidden moral or explanation.... Thus fairy stories are as much about human destiny and our encounters with 'enchantment' and good and evil in our search for meaning as they are about fairies.... Fairytales are important precisely because, among other things, they use 'make-believe' to teach fundamental principles of moral behaviour.

There is a natural good and a well-winnowed wisdom in storytelling and myth. In that context, myths are connected to facts about ourselves and the imagined worlds in which we live. They extend the imagination by moving deliberately beyond the boundaries of the familiar and the obvious, exactly as Brecht observed of the formality of classical Chinese theatre. The Chinese actor, he wrote (p.131), "wishes to appear alien to the spectator. Alien to the point of arousing surprise. This he manages by seeing himself and his performance as alien. In this way the things he does on stage become astonishing. By this craft everyday things are removed from the realm of the self-evident."

So myths, even though they may contain much that is historically or scientifically incorrect, may also be an expression, in the best language available at the time, of truth that is empirically and evidentially based. Either way, myth is a decisively important vehicle that conveys the meanings of the past into the present where it acts as a powerful (and often coercive) constraint over outcomes in the present, as much in politics and diplomacy as in literature, art and architecture.

Looked at in that way, there is an important sense in which the story of evolution is an immensely powerful myth connecting us to facts about the origins of life and of ourselves. When Halpern, whose strong statement about necessary changes in science was quoted earlier in Chapter 2 invited his readers to travel with him to 'cosmology's extraordinary new frontiers', he used mythological language and references as a way of talking about what is as yet unknown and is certainly beyond the self-evident: "This is a tale of cosmic dragons [the word used in the Fermi Telescope report on gamma radiation], bottomless pits, and looking-glass worlds – of a possible axis of evil and hypothesised portals to hidden realms" (Halpern, pp.5ff).

Myth may therefore be mediating meaning on the basis of both fact and fiction, and may be combining both. A particularly clear example of that is the way in which the myth of the Abominable Snowman or Yeti. What gave rise to the stories? It was suggested that the Yeti was a mistaken sighting of a wild yak or *drong*, but the descriptions of the two did not connect. So, as I asked in my *Alphabet of Animals*, "Does the *chemo*, the Yeti, the abominable snowman, exist?" At the time (2010), Reinhold Messner, who had searched for Yetis for more than ten years, answered both no and yes:

> No, he does not think that there is some hominoid missing link surviving in the Himalayas, ... But yes, there have been encounters with an awesome animal, probably the bear *Ursus arctus*. (Bowker 2010a, p.121)

In 2013, the geneticist, Bryan Sykes, using the techniques of cryozoology, found a match between the DNA of two 'Yeti' hair samples and the DNA of a polar bear jawbone found in Norway. It is likely, therefore, that they shared a common ancestor (or that there has been more recent interbreeding between brown bears and descendants of the polar bear), and that a subspecies of brown bear may still exist in the mountains, sightings of which have evoked the accounts in Tibetan mythology.

To use the word 'myth' as a synonym for 'false', as Dawkins and many others do, obliterates the possibility of mythology being or having been the best or only language with which to speak of what has been observed or experienced. That point was made with great clarity by David Bowker in his article (2011), 'Meteorology and the Ancient Greeks'. Accepting that meteorological phenomena are, in the Homeric epics and in Greek literature in general, "inextricably linked to the activities of various gods", he then observed (p.249):

> On the face of it, this may all seem very unscientific, but it is perhaps unwise to dismiss it as such, since the descriptions of the gods' activities reflect a desire to account for and even predict significant weather events. The Greeks lived in a world which they almost certainly saw as dangerous and frightening, and poetry was a means of communicating ideas and trying to explain the inexplicable ...

The descriptive claims expressed in poetry and myth are as corrigible as any others, and they have indeed often been corrected, but they may well be based on empirical observation, and may equally be communicating important truths in the best available language. The same is true of Aristotle's *Meteorologica*:

> Some will dismiss Aristotle's work as farfetched and wrong in its conclusions. It may be unwise to dismiss it merely on this basis, however. His account is an attempt to offer empirical explanations and thus lays the foundation for further work.... Even these brief glimpses of Aristotle's work show that the study of meteorological observations should be approached with the saying: 'If we have seen so far, it is because we stand on the shoulders of giants' (Bernard of Chartres, 12th century). We owe a debt to Aristotle, as well as the other authors examined in this paper, in that they show the fascination of meteorology for the minds of the ancient Greeks which has in turn inspired future generations and formed the basis for the science of meteorology as we know it today. (pp.250f)

The paramount importance of not equating 'myth' with 'falsehood' lies in the fact that mythology often contains insight and invitation into a wider and more profound understanding of the truth about ourselves and our circumstances. From some other point of view (that of science, for example, or of history) it may be recognised that some or all details are incorrect, but the challenge remains to stretch the imagination and recognise the truth that a myth or a poem or a picture may nevertheless be telling us.

Myth may therefore be a way of exploring and extending the implications of science. When Ruskin read the work of John Tyndall on Alpine glaciers, he connected it with 'Greek myths of cloud and storm', writing a short book with that as part of its title during the course of which he again defined what he meant by 'myth':

> A myth, in its simplest definition, is a story with a meaning attached to it other than it seems to have at first; and the fact that it has such a meaning is generally marked by some of its circumstances being extraordinary, or, in the common use of the word, unnatural. (Ruskin, 1869, p.8; Brecht's word was 'alien')

In Ruskin's time, in the nineteenth century, the word 'myth' had not yet become synonymous with 'false'. By then the attempt to understand the power and importance of myth had had a very long history, during which its virtues and limitations had been threshed out – when, for example, the Romans had to take over the myths of the Greeks; when Christians had to evaluate the myths of Rome; when the pagan gods rose from the dead during the Renaissance; and above all in the nineteenth century, when myth, positively understood, offered the great opportunity to claim that truth can be told as much through fiction as through scientific fact (think how much the novel developed during that century), as much through a poem as through a mathematical proof – indeed, more so, because, as Schelling put it, mythology goes beyond the new physics: "What is every beautiful mythology", he asked, "but a hieroglyphic expression of surrounding nature in a transfiguration of imagination and love?" Phyllis McGinley saw the point more basically when she wrote, "Scratch a myth and find a fact."[14]

Freud was far from being alone in discerning the way in which myth draws out the meaning and implication of what is factually the case. Indeed, David Grene wrote specifically of Oedipus in his introduction to the Theban plays (p.9):

> For Sophocles the myth was the treatment of the generic aspect of human dilemmas. What he made of the myth in his plays was neither history nor the kind of dramatic creation represented by Hamlet or Macbeth. Not history, for in no sense is the uniqueness of the event or the uniqueness of the character important; not drama in the Shakespearean sense, because Sophocles' figures do not have, as Shakespeare's do, the timeless and complete reality in themselves. Behind the figure of Oedipus or Creon stands the tyrant of the legend; and behind the tyrant of the legend, the meaning of all despotic authority. Behind the old Oedipus is the beggar and wanderer of the legend, and behind him the mysterious human combination of opposites – opposites in meaning and in fact.

All this became immensely important in attempts during the nineteenth century to evaluate the worth of the Bible (and the truth of Christianity) in the context of challenges from geohistory and other sciences, particularly when, as we have just seen, the challenges were translated into the metaphor and practice of warfare. The realisation that myth is a vehicle of meaning, and that the word 'myth' is not synonymous with 'false', meant that the apparent dichotomy concerning the Bible of 'either fact or fiction' was destroyed.

Much of that achievement goes back to D.F. Strauss whose *Life of Jesus Critically Examined* was published in 1835. In that year also the first railway was opened in Germany, running twenty kilometres between Firth and Nurnberg. Strauss saw the two events, the book and the railway, as being connected. Enthusing in a letter to a friend about his own first journey on the line, he wrote:

> Five hours in half-an-hour. Impressive significance of the modern miracle, dreamy consciousness during the modern flight. No fear but a feeling of inner kinship between my own principles and that of the discovery.

Strauss recognised that the science which produces steam and engines will set its own limits on what it regards as acceptable or even true, and those limits must be respected. In the Preface to his *Life of Jesus*, he wrote (Zeller, p.103):

> The exegesis of the church of old was based on two presuppositions: first, that the gospels contain a history; and second, that this history was a supernatural one. Rationalism rejected the second of these presuppositions, but only in order to hang on more tenaciously to the first, insisting that these books present plain, though only natural, history. Science cannot remain satisfied with this half-measure. The other presupposition must also be given up, and the investigation must first be made whether in fact, and to what extent, the ground on which we stand in the Gospels is historical.

That seems to be a straightforward capitulation to science. But Strauss, of course, was more subtle. Science may have the right to adjudicate on the truth or otherwise of many factual and empirical propositions. But there is more to life, and the meaning of life, than science. There is also the world of myth.

In arguing this, Strauss seized on Hegel's distinction between 'idea' and 'fact', with 'idea' being transcendence of the fact in the direction of meaning. Religions are the great communities of 'meaning-making', or, to use Strauss's own term, of 'myth-making'. Pure myth *may* have no connection with any event, but equally, myth may arise from events in order to draw out their meaning. Events are not left 'back there' in the past as bare happenings. They are given meaning.

So when Strauss called attention to the primary role of myth in relation to Jesus, he was not denying that there were facts and events which had happened. He was rejecting the approach which tries to sort out scientifically which facts are factual, and then discards everything else as useless fiction or as worthless invention. Clearly something happened in the case of Jesus. But what is more important? The archaeology which attempts to establish the certain details of his biography (which are *in fact* extremely few)? Of course not. Far more important for us, according to Strauss, is to understand the way in which the followers of Jesus used the mythological opportunities of their Bible to convey his significance and importance for them.

The value of myth in that sense became unmistakable in the work of Wagner who specifically linked the indispensable importance of myth to the natural and necessary limits of science. Wagner took poetry and myth to such an extreme that in his view it is the vocation of the artist to produce, in relation to myth, what he called 'the total work of art'. What Wagner meant by the 'total art work' is clearly described in *The Artwork of the Future*. To quote the summary (2.5) of Max Nordau (admittedly antagonistic: "his system calls for criticism in every part"),

> The fundamental thought of the *Artwork of the Future* is this: the first and most original of the arts was that of dancing; its peculiar essence is rhythm, and this has developed into music; music, consisting of rhythm and tone, has raised (Wagner says 'condensed') its phonetic element to speech, and produced the art of poetry; the highest form of poetry is the drama, which for the purpose of stage-construction, and to imitate the natural scene of human action, has associated itself with architecture and painting respectively; finally, sculpture is nothing but the giving permanence to the appearance of the actor in a dead rigid form, while acting is real sculpture in living, flowing movement. Thus all the arts group themselves around the drama, and the latter should unite them naturally ... The effort of true artists must be to win them back to their natural and necessary conjunction with each other. The mutual penetration and fusion of all arts into a single art will produce the genuine work of art.

True to his text, Wagner composed both words and music of his works, including *Parsifal*, and involved himself closely in the design, not only of the sets and costumes, but also of the auditorium itself at Bayreuth. He called Parsifal *Buhnenweihfestspiel*, which might be translated (as it often is) 'sacred festival drama', but in fact is more accurately translated (in relation to Wagner's own intentions) 'festival work to consecrate a stage' – the stage being Bayreuth, and the consecration being for the continuity of Wagner's work.

Wagner did not deny that science has a limited truth to tell, because it is a consequence of what he called, in *The Music of the Future*, "the ineradicable quality of the human perceptive process, which impelled man to the discovery of the laws of causality, and because of which he involuntarily asks himself, in the face of every impressive phenomenon – 'Why is this?'" Far from disappearing into an abstraction of music from the real world in order to produce pure beauty ('art for art's sake', as Pater and others were inclined to say), Wagner argued that the total work of art returns the spectator *to* the real world, and offers much richer answers to the question, 'Why?' p. 15:

> The drama, at the moment of its realistic, scenic presentation awakens in the spectator real participation in the action presented to him; and this is so faithfully imitated from real life (or at least from the possibilities of it), that the sympathetic human feeling passes through such participation into a state of ecstasy which forgets that momentous question 'Why?' and willingly yields itself up to the guidance of those new laws through which music makes itself so strangely intelligible and at the same time – in the deepest sense – gives the only correct answer to that 'Why?'

So there are other and, humanly speaking, far more important questions than physics can possibly answer. What questions? Wagner's operas are the answer. But take *Parsifal* as an example: the major questions are those of suffering and sin. Why do people suffer? How are their sufferings related both to their own past and to the far larger story in which their lives are caught up? And how can we be redeemed from the past? Why does Kundry both help and hinder, the latter often against her will – *Ich helfe nie* (I give no help), she cries scornfully to Gurnemanz (i.1.144); why does Amfortas turn his face to the wall, begging Titurel to resume his role (i.2.26–9: "*Wehe! Wehe mir der Qual!/ Mein Vater, oh! noch einmal/ verrichte du das Amt!/ Lebe, leb und lass mich sterben*", (Woe! Woe to me for my torment! My father, O, just once more resume the sacred duty: live, live, and let me die), and yet he presides at the grail ceremony for the knights? Three times, Parsifal when asked how he came to this '*unerhörtes Werk*', says, *Das weiss ich nicht* (i.1.285ff.; I do not know).

A Newtonian in the nineteenth century would have had confidence that at least in theory he could have answered the question, why has the past brought the present into its present form of existence? He would have thought that a theoretical knowledge of the position and momentum of all the atoms of the universe would have enabled the prediction of all future states. That is exactly the summary made by Huxley of the belief of Tyndall whose description of the conflict between science and theology was quoted earlier:

> A favourite problem of his is – Given the molecular forces in a mutton chop, deduce Hamlet or Faust therefrom. He is confident that the Physics of the Future will solve this easily. (Huxley, 1903, p.231)

In that perspective, however, it is not only the future but also the past that is completely determined. It seems obvious (does it not?) that the past cannot be altered or changed in any way. Agathon, according to Aristotle, had said, "This only is denied, even to God: the power to undo the past."

In contrast, myth, above all the Christian myth of a Redeemer, allows even that to God. And that is Wagner's question which physics cannot answer: how can we be redeemed from the past? How can we, so to speak, re-enter the past and find forgiveness for the harm and the damage we have done? Gurnemanz on Titurel: "*unkund blieb mir, was dorten er gesündigt,/ doch wollt' er büssen nun, ja heilig werden*" (i.1.201f.: I do not know what sin he committed there: he sought atonement for it, yes, holy would he be); Kundry to Parsifal: *Bekentnis/ wird Schuld in Reue enden,/ Erkentnis/ in Sinn die Torheit wenden* (ii.358–61: confession will end guilt in repentance, understanding changes folly into sense); Amfortas longing for the knights to bring him, not the Grail but death, which might be "a small atonement for a sin like mine" (iii.249). And unifying these glimpses of redemption is the concept and the action of what Wagner in *Parsifal* called *Mitleiden*.

Mitleid is usually translated as 'pity' but more literally it means 'suffering with', *cum* and *passio* in the Latin words underlying 'compassion'. Parsifal does not merely pity Amfortas: he enters without evasion into his suffering and shares it, and in that bearing of the same suffering begins to acquire the self-knowledge and the self-understanding which he has previously lacked and which therefore impeded his own redemption; and it is Kundry's kiss – an action of *Mitleid* – which awakens Parsifal after the reality of suffering. That is the single quality of the long-awaited Redeemer, and these are exactly the words central to the Grail scene itself. Amfortas has begged for relief from the torments of hell, and he sees from his pain the vision of redemption:

> The hour draws near:
> A spear of light
> Falls on the holy shrine,
> The covering falls ....
> > Made wise through *Mitleid*
> > The blameless simpleton,
> > Wait for him,
> > The one I summon. (1.ii.234ff.)

Those themes are clearly close to those of Christianity. It might seem to be the case, therefore, that a Wagnerian response to science puts an oblique version of the Christian theme on stage and makes myth a substitute for mass. But Wagner has moved far beyond anything so naive. It is a common question to ask whether *Parsifal* is a Christian work. Superficially it may seem that it is. Wagner himself wrote of *Parsifal* in a letter (September 7, 1865) in answer to his patron Ludwig's question, "Why did it take the kiss of Kundry to convert Parsifal?", and Wagner made a direct appeal to the Christian myth of the Fall:

> You know the serpent in Paradise with its beguiling promise, *eritis sicut Deus scientes bonum et malum* ["You will be as God knowing good and evil"]. Adam and Eve became 'knowing'. They became knowingly aware of sin. The human race had to atone for that consciousness by suffering both shame and misery, until it was redeemed by Christ, when he took upon himself the sins of the world.

So are we, after all this, to conclude that *Parsifal* is fundamentally a Christian work? There have been opposing answers to that question, Beckett, for example, saying 'yes',[15] and Tanner answering emphatically 'no'.[16] Wagner answered both 'yes' and 'no', depending it seems on who it was that asked the question.

But in truth *Parsifal* cannot be 'a Christian work', because to speak in those terms is to miss the point. It is a work, not about Christianity, but about us: and if Christianity, or Buddhism, or Nordic myths, or Grimm's fairytales, or physics, or biology are 'about us', then they lend themselves to any true answer to the questions of 'Why?' and 'How?' which we ask about ourselves. In this way, religious truths, or rather the truths which religious myths may have preserved in the past, are immune from sceptical or positivistic attack. The scientist may understand the world, it is the simpleton who redeems it.

Wagner, therefore, illustrates an entirely different and additional way (additional, that is, to Barbour's four types of relationship) in which sciences and religions can be related: Wagner illustrates the imaginative power of myth in extending the implications of science. He also illustrates another of the great merits of myth: it gives a personality to abstractions so that people can more easily engage with them. The word 'evil' is abstract: when 'evil' is personified as the Devil, it is easier, in terms of human imagination, to fight against "the Devil and all his works." There is much in *Parsifal* to show what that means.

Wagner, however, also illustrates that myth does not become 'true' simply by virtue of being a myth. Myths, if they seem to be making claims without warrant about putative matters of fact, may simply be wrong or misleading, even though they may be good stories. Myth has often been used to construct or to reinforce corrupt political regimes and evil ideologies. Wagner as *bricoleur* in the realms of myth gave precedent for the later attempts by Nazis to create a German and Aryan myth which was not in any way coherent with anything except itself. It was, in other words, a closed circle of the kind that religions all too easily can become.

Wagner's influence on Hitler and the Nazis remains, of course, controversial, but his influence does nevertheless illustrate what can happen when myth is located in the closed circle of a private and self-defining ideology. That is an extremely real danger to which religions need to be far more attentive than they usually are. The use and abuse of myth has led all too often to great evil. Not denying Wagner's "own hateful views on Jews", Michael Burleigh has observed that "the themes of his [Wagner's] operas admit of interpretations which Hitler would have found unsatisfactory" (p.98):

> Hitler's understanding of those operas, which included allegories of doomed bourgeois civilisation and explorations of the power of love and compassion in settings that oscillated between pagan myth and a reworking of medieval Christianity, was as unsophisticated as his grip on Charles Darwin, himself a key influence on Wagner.

So for myth to extend truthfully the meanings and implications of science or of a religious event or symbol or whatever, it is necessary always to ask to what extent it is coherent with other accounts of what it purports to be about. For example, is *Parsifal* coherent with the origins and long history of the Christian Eucharist? Some thought so because they would not eat anything for hours before attending a performance of *Parsifal* on the analogy of people not eating anything before receiving Holy Communion.

THE RELATIONSHIPS BETWEEN SCIENCES AND RELIGIONS

That brief account of the importance of myth in extending by implication the *meanings* of science is simply one example of the entirely different and additional ways in which the relationship of sciences and religions can be explored and understood. It illustrates why that relationship cannot be contained in the single metaphor of 'warfare'. A major and fundamental problem in understanding the relation of religions to sciences is that the different religions of the world, during the course of their long histories, have employed, in different ways and at different times, *all eight* of those styles of relationship just described. They have employed them, not in relation to 'science' as an abstraction, but in relation to whatever the sciences have been as they have encountered or practised them at any particular time.

The consequence is that world religions (and this means in effect *people*, ranging from individuals to authority figures, teachers, and so on) make strategic decisions about what style they believe that they are obliged (by their own faith and understanding) to employ. Those strategies change over time depending on specific and contingent circumstances: there is nothing within religions themselves that dictates which style must be chosen.

And to make matters even more complicated, some or all of the eight strategies may be being adopted in the same religion at the same time – for example, some of its adherents may chose to seek conflict where others seek integration.

Mutatis mutandis, the same is true in the history of science. Out of the possibilities summarised above, the ones that scientists choose in order to describe the relationship between sciences and religions change from time to time, and in any generation, some or all of them may well coexist.

None of this is to deny or to call in question the imperative fact that propositional and conceptual issues are of paramount importance when they arise. In the interests of truth they must never be evaded on the part of religions by a retreat into a closed circle of coherence – nor by a belief on the part of scientists that science *alone* is true. If, in contrast, the boundaries of the circles of coherence are kept open, there are, within the many different ways in which sciences and religions can be related, equally many ways in which they can be, and in my view ought to be, natural and inevitable partners in the service of at least humanity, perhaps also of God.

This means in practice that from the explorations of the sciences and from the explorations of the religions we internalise constraints that control us into shareable opportunities of truth about ourselves and about the universe. In that context we will be able to recover the confidence of those who, like Thomas Traherne (1637–74), lived, not in both worlds at once, but in both worlds as one. That is where the study and understanding of religions in relation to sciences will ultimately lead:

> He that knows the secrets of nature with Albertus Magnus, or the motions of the heavens with Galileo, or the cosmography of the moon with Hevelius, or the body of man with Galen, or the nature of diseases with Hippocrates, or the harmonies in melody with Orpheus, or of poesie with Homer, or of grammar with Lilly, or of whatever else with the greatest artist; he is nothing if he knows them merely for talk or idle speculation, or transient and external use. But he that knows them for value, and knows them his own, shall profit infinitely. And therefore of all kinds of learnings, humanity and divinity are the most excellent. (Traherne, p.134)

Even so, the point can still be made (and often is made) that there is at least one intractable and unvarying point of difference that makes conflict between sciences and religions inevitable. It is the difference of method and attitude that lies (so it is argued) in the way in which the sciences value falsification and doubt, whereas religions rely on dogmatism and on incontestable certainty – and indeed condemn doubt completely. Huxley identified *the consecration of Doubt* as the first great commandment of science in contrast to the Christian *condemnation* of doubt. He made that claim in that same year, 1870, with which this chapter began. In a lecture to the Cambridge YMCA, he claimed that Descartes had established a new golden rule: "Give unqualified assent to no propositions but those the truth of which is so clear and distinct that they cannot be doubted." Short of that, everything must be open to doubt:

> The enunciation of this great first commandment of science consecrated Doubt. It removed Doubt from the seat of penance among the grievous sins to which it had long been condemned, and enthroned it in that high place among the primary duties, which is assigned to it by the scientific conscience of these latter days. (Huxley, 1970, pp.322f)

It is that methodological contrast between dogma and doubt that opens (so it is argued) an impassable divide between 'science' and 'religion'. If that is so, it will tell us something important about religion. But is that argument correct? To answer that we have to ask a further question: Is it the case that religions invariably condemn doubt as 'a grievous sin'?

4

Religions and sciences
II Dogmatism and doubt

*T*HE CONTRAST BETWEEN DOGMATISM AND DOUBT WAS EXPRESSED succinctly by Claude Bernard (1813–78):

> Scholastics or Systematizers never question their starting point, to which they seek to refer everything; they have a proud and intolerant mind, and do not accept contradiction.... The experimenter, on the contrary, who always doubts and who does not believe that he possesses absolute certainty about anything, succeeds in mastering the phenomena which surround him, and in extending his power over nature.... The doubter is a true man of science; he doubts only himself and his interpretations, but he believes in science. (Bernard 1.2)

In more recent times, the same contrast is often made. Sam Harris stated (p.43) that "the problem with religion – as with Nazism, Stalinism, or any other totalitarian mythology – is the problem of dogma itself." To call dogma problematic depends of course on what is meant by the word 'dogma'. In its original Greek context, the word δογμα meant nothing more than an opinion or a belief. It is connected with the verb δοκειν, which means 'to appear' or 'to seem to be the case'. In other words, it meant something far more tentative than our understanding of the word 'dogma'. But from that beginning, the word *dogma* came to mean in Greek a public decree or law or ordinance, something that cannot be contradicted or even argued against.

So the word 'dogma', like the words 'myth' and 'sceptic' (also derived from Greek), has changed and taken on a new meaning. For us the word 'dogmatic' has come to mean 'laying down an opinion in a way not open to argument', and a dogmatist is a person, as Burnyeat once put it (p.27), "with an obstinate and unreasonable attachment to his opinions." As Galbraith observed, "When people are least sure, they are often most dogmatic"; or as Ring Lardner put it more briefly in *The Young Immigrants*: "'Shut up', he explained."

So we arrive at our words 'dogma' and 'dogmatic', meaning in the context of Christianity 'teaching of the Church against which no argument is allowed': dogmatic theology. This is how the certainty of dogma was stated in the Declaration, *Mysterium Ecclesiae*, in 1973:

> As for the meaning of dogmatic formulas, this remains ever true and constant in the Church, even when it is expressed with greater clarity or more developed. The faithful, therefore, must shun the opinion, first, that dogmatic formulas (or some category of them) cannot signify truth in a determinate way, but can only offer changeable approximations to it …; secondly, that these formulas signify the truth only in an indeterminate way, this truth being like a goal that is constantly being sought by means of such approximations. Those who hold such an opinion do not avoid dogmatic relativism and they corrupt the concept of the Church's infallibility relative to the truth to be taught or held in a determinate way.

It was this emphasis on certainty that enabled John Henry Newman to take refuge in dogma from the storms of doubt that raged in the nineteenth century:

> From the age of fifteen, dogma has been the fundamental principle of my religion: I know of no other religion; I cannot enter into the idea of any other sort of religion; religion, as a mere sentiment, is to me a dream and a mockery.[1]

If that is what is meant by 'dogma', then one can see why it is problematic for Harris since it seems to draw a radical and disjunctive contrast between scientific doubt and religious dogmatism. From that radical distinction flow the many definitions of religion which banish it from rational society: "Religion, n. A daughter of Hope and Fear, explaining to Ignorance the nature of the Unknowable";[2] "Religion: see Evildoing";[3] "Surplice –, a white garb, which priests wear when they are humbugging the people" (Piggot, p.140). As Reade expressed it in *The Martyrdom of Man*, when he was describing the Christians of the early Church

> The Christians of that period felt more and did more than those of the present day, not because they were better men but because they believed more; and they believed more because they knew less. Doubt is the offspring of knowledge: 'the savage never doubts at all.'

Reade's book was published in 1872, but the view is now even more widely held that religions rest on dogmatic certainty and unquestioning obedience whereas the sciences make progress by constantly raising questions and doubts. It has become in the media a kind of embedded belief or domain assumption, as we saw earlier, for example, in the report of Steve Jones for the BBC. But is that view correct? How true is it that religions condemn doubt where the sciences commend it? Or conversely, how true is it that the sciences are never dogmatic and that religions never endorse doubt?

THE CONDEMNATION OF DOUBT IN CHRISTIANITY

Looking at religions, however briefly, the disjunctive contrast between dogmatic certainty and scientific doubt seems at first sight to be true. In the case of Christianity it seems particularly obvious because the New Testament records the opinion that doubt is damnable: "Doubt is damnable" according to St. Paul, or at least according to St. Paul according to the Authorised Version of the Bible: "He that doubteth is damned.... "(Romans 14.23). The Vulgate (the official Latin version of the Bible) is equally robust: "...damnatus est". So: he that doubteth is damned. It became a political proverb in nineteenth century America: "He who dallies is a dastard, he who doubts is damned."

If that condemnation of doubt is offered as a generalisation, then it is clearly absurd. Many of our doubts are wise (I doubt if the ice will bear my weight) or entirely reasonable (I doubt whether I can climb Mount Everest). However, Paul was not offering that condemnation as a generalisation. He was writing about a very specific issue: should Gentile Christians, who have freedom to eat any kind of meat, impose this freedom on Jewish Christians who might still be observing the dietary laws?

Or, to put it the other way round, should those Jews who accept that Jesus is the Christos (Messiah), and who are therefore Christians, be condemned if they maintain their sensitivity about clean and unclean food? Paul, in this verse, was arguing that they are only to be condemned if they eat food that *they* regard as unclean, because in that case they would be contradicting their own faith and acting against their own conscience. Paul, therefore, argued, "The one who has doubts is already condemned if he eats, because the eating does not proceed from conviction." And he then added, "Whatever does not proceed from conviction is sin."

It is clear, therefore, that this condemnation of doubt concerns a very specialised form of doubt (whether one should or should not act against conscience), not doubt in general. On the other hand, doubt of at least some kind did remain damnable. That is why, in later Christian tradition, a distinction was made between different kinds of doubt. This can be seen clearly in the *Catechism of the Catholic Church* where a distinction is made between voluntary and involuntary doubt.

According to the Catechism §2087, involuntary doubt refers "to hesitation in believing, difficulty in overcoming objections connected with the faith, or also anxiety aroused by its obscurity." No one can help that kind of doubt arising. Thomas, in Christianity, had sufficient doubts for him to be known as exactly that, doubting Thomas. When Jesus said, "You know the way to the place where I am going", Thomas said, "Lord, we do not know where you are going. How can we know the way?" (John 14.5).

Even more sharply, it was Thomas who doubted whether Jesus could possibly have risen from the dead: "Unless I see the mark of the nails in his hands, and put my finger in the mark of the nails and my hand in his side, I will not believe" (John 22.25–8).

But Thomas did not cease to be an apostle because he doubted, whereas Judas did indeed cease to be an apostle, not because of his doubts, but because of what he did. And Thomas was in any case convinced, and ended up with that cry of faith, 'My Lord and my God'.

Some doubts, therefore, are necessary and inevitable, and they may lead to truth, health and safety. But the Catechism makes it entirely clear that what *is* to be condemned is doubt that is "deliberately cultivated", because at that point it has become *voluntary* doubt. To quote from the Catechism again, "Voluntary doubt about the faith disregards or refuses to hold up as true what God has revealed and the Church proposes for belief."

So the argument of the Catechism is clear: doubt must be condemned whenever it is a refusal of what Scripture and the Church have taught 'beyond all doubt'. On that basis, the Catechism goes on to introduce a third category, obstinate doubt which leads to heresy:

> Heresy is the obstinate post-baptismal denial of some truth which must be believed with divine and catholic faith, or it is likewise an obstinate doubt concerning the same. (§2089)

So doubt of that kind is clearly, to use the language of *1066 and All That*, 'a bad thing'. Nor does this concern only those under the discipline of Rome. Doubt has an equally bad press on the Protestant side. The owner and occupant of John Bunyan's Doubting Castle was Giant Despair. His purpose was to seek the destruction of any pilgrims who become doubtful and who in consequence have, like Christian and Hopeful, lost their way and 'abandoned hope'. Doubt as despair is destructive because it erodes trust in God and it thus 'seeks to destroy his holy pilgrims': "For the doubter, being double-minded and unstable in every way, must not expect to receive anything from the Lord", as it is put in the New Testament in the letter of James (1.7).

The fact that doubts might be destructive does not contradict the point that some doubts are inevitable. In the Christian tradition, therefore, people are encouraged to distinguish between the ordinary doubts of everyday life and radical doubts: the former are disturbing but not destructive, the latter are destructive because they cannot be disturbed. The contrast is well exemplified in the character of Mr Prendergast in Evelyn Waugh's novel, *Decline and Fall*. He was one of the teachers in a lamentable school at Llanabba, in N. Wales. He had been an Anglican vicar in a comfortable living in Worthing, but he had had to resign. Here he tells Paul why he had to leave:

'If things had happened a little differently I should be a rector with my own house and bathroom. I might even have been a rural dean, only'– and Mr Prendergast dropped his voice to a whisper – 'only I had *Doubts* ...'

'Were they as bad as all that?' asked Paul.

'They were insuperable,' said Mr Prendergast; 'that is why I am here now.... You see, it wasn't the ordinary sort of Doubt about Cain's wife or the Old Testament miracles or the consecration of Archbishop Parker. I'd been taught how to explain all those while I was at college. No, it was something deeper than all that. *I couldn't understand why God had made the world at all....* You see how fundamental that is. Once granted the first step, I can see that everything else follows – Tower of Babel, Babylonian captivity, Incarnation, Church, bishops, incense, everything – but what I couldn't see, and what I can't see now, is, *why* did it all begin?' (pp.32f)

It so happens that the question 'why is there something rather than nothing' has been and remains central to both philosophy and theology, despite the assumption of some philosophers and scientists that it is unanswerable and therefore meaningless – a way certainly of evading the question, but it is extremely foolish given the importance of abductive inference in the sciences.[4] Rundle indeed makes the claim (p.vii), "The question, 'Why is there something rather than nothing?', has a strong claim to be philosophy's central, and most perplexing, question." On the other hand, it is equally unwise to assume that it can be answered on the basis of an unchallengeable certainty derived from privileged information – as, for example, in the form of inerrant Revelation received from God. A claim of that kind offers certainty of a privileged kind, and that is what critics of religions in general and of Christianity in particular have taken to be the meaning of dogma.

There is much weight in their criticism, and it needs to be taken seriously. It is, for example, true that much of the construction of Christian thought was based on the unshakable foundation of Scripture taken to be the literal and inerrant Word of God, and it moved into a style in which doubt was an enemy to be overcome. In the twelfth and thirteenth centuries, for example, the great European universities were being established, and in them a new method of argument was being developed, not least among the Scholastics whom Bernard denounced in the quotation with which this chapter began. Scripture was the foundation, and a qualified teacher was known as *doctor/magister in sacra pagina*. Other *paginae* (texts or writings) might be brought in for the purposes of exegesis or correct argument (hence the importance of Aristotle), but the acceptance of the Bible was the unquestioned point of departure. As Persson observed (p.8), it "gave rise to what is perhaps the most characteristic form of instruction in the Middle Ages, and the form preferred by Thomas [Aquinas] himself, namely, the disputation."

The Disputation was a structured and organised form of teaching. From his exposition of a passage in Scripture the master would pose a question. A *quaestio* in this context was defined by Boethius as "a proposition carrying doubt" (*Topica Ciceronis* 1). The questions were then 'disputed' through objections and answers, and the master then gave his determination of the issue, thus formulating the correct understanding of the doctrine involved. The purpose, therefore, was to reach a resolution beyond doubt, and that conclusion was called *determinatio*, the determination.[5]

But if the truth has been 'determined beyond doubt', it leads to dogma in that sense of indubitable (undoubtable) certainty because it offers a true and certain premise from which to develop an argument, a true and certain point of departure from which any number of correct conclusions can be drawn. If two sentences, X and Y, are known dogmatically to be true, the conclusion Z to be drawn from them will also be true.

That is the classic form of a 'syllogism', so called from a Greek word meaning 'to reason', 'to draw a conclusion by reasoning'. The development of syllogistic argument is associated particularly with Aristotle, but it was immensely practised and extended in medieval Christianity, and it seemed a mighty weapon in establishing truth and overcoming doubt. For example,

> All men are mortal;
> I am a man;
> Therefore I am mortal.
>
> God has mercy on all sinners;
> We are sinners;
> Therefore God has mercy on us.

Syllogisms were analysed into different forms, but in general they were believed to fall into the definition of Aristotle as being "discourse in which certain things being posited, something else necessarily follows". Syllogisms are thus an example of what is called a deductive kind of argument. If a particular premise is true, then it is possible to deduce (draw down) equally true conclusions from it. It seems indubitable, an argument that takes us beyond doubt.

But that kind of argument is *not* beyond doubt. As early as Sextus Empiricus (one of the last and greatest of the early Sceptics who lived at the end of the second and the beginning of the third century CE), a basic doubt had been raised about the strength of syllogistic argument. He pointed out that the argument is circular: the conclusion is always implicit in the first step in the premise, so the argument does not tell us anything new, since 'I am mortal' is already contained in the premise, 'All men are mortal'.

Doubts about the certainties of conclusions deduced syllogistically (and about deduction in general) continued to be raised, culminating in the work of Francis Bacon (1561–1626). He is particularly associated with establishing *induction* at the foundations of Western science and philosophy, although there were others before him who argued for induction. Reverting to the syllogism, All men are mortal; I am a man; therefore I am mortal, what happens if the premise, the first step, the first claimed truth, is not itself true? Supposing it is not true that all men are mortal? Yes, no doubt, all the men that we know about have so far died, but what about the day after tomorrow? And what if there are some men of whom we have no knowledge who happen not to have died? How can we be certain that the premise is true? For if the premise is not true, nothing follows from it.

One religious instinct (in this case of some Christians) has been to reply that any premise they put forward must be true because it is derived from infallible and inerrant revelation; or it is derived from the teaching authority of the Church embodied in the Pope. But that cannot be demonstrated. It is an act of faith. In other words, it can only be justified within the circle of Christian coherence – and the instability of that is obvious given that not everyone, and clearly not all Christians, accept those claims about Scripture or about the Pope.

Bacon realised, therefore, that the whole method of searching for and arriving at truth needs to be turned upside down – or inside out: it needs to be taken out of the closed circle of scholastic argument. What is needed, he argued, is not *de*duction, deciding dogmatically on a premise and then deducing conclusions from it, but rather *in*duction, gathering together evidence that will lead into (Latin *in+duco*) truth.

So instead of starting with a premise taken to be self-evidently true and then deducing truth from it – like spiders, as he put it, spinning webs out of their own bodies – the first step is to collect evidence and to allow the evidence to lead to a true conclusion. And Bacon has, of course (though not with strict historical accuracy), often been regarded as the originator of modern scientific method.

THE CONDEMNATION OF DOUBT IN RELIGIONS

Thus far, it surely seems clear that doubt can be regarded in Christianity as destructive and maybe even damnable. But is that true of other religions as well? Only if that is so can the claim be justified that there is a fundamental divide between science and religion because of their contrasting commitments to doubt on the one side and dogma on the other.

It would seem at first sight that that is indeed the case, because if we look by way of example (albeit briefly) at Islam, religions in India, and Buddhism, we find many instances of doubt being condemned with equal vigour.

Of the religions, Islam might be expected to be the most aggressive in its attack on doubt because Islam rests on a belief that the Quran is the complete, final and uncorrupted revelation from God. The 'Mother of the Book', *umm alKitab*, is with God in heaven, and it is simply transmitted through Muhammad without Muhammad interfering in the process at all.

Muslims, therefore, must live within the boundaries and constraints of faith and practice established in the Quran. However, the Quran does not deal with all possible things that might happen, so there have to be interpretations of the Quran in order to apply it to the changing circumstances of life. The first interpreters of the Quran were of course Muhammad and his Companions: their words and actions (and on some issues their silences) were a kind of living commentary on the Quran, they demonstrated in practice how one should live as a Muslim, as one who has entered into a condition of security by giving one's allegiance to God (the fundamental meaning of Islam).

The Traditions (*ahadith*) recording this, known collectively as Hadith, become with the Quran clear guidance and the foundation of Muslim life.[6] They have led to the formation of different codes of practice known collectively as Sharia. These provide for Muslims 'the straight path that leads to the watering place' – the original meaning of the word *sharia*. There are several schools or traditions of Sharia that differ in the details of interpretation. In general, however, they with the Quran enable Muslims to know exactly what they should do and believe. Thus there can be no room for doubt about the meaning and the practice of Islam.

Not surprisingly, therefore, doubt is strongly attacked in the Quran itself. The main word for doubt is *shakkun*, and that word is almost always used

4 DOGMATISM AND DOUBT 73

for the rejection of what God has revealed, or for the failure to accept the messengers of God through whom the eternal Quran is revealed (the point being that God reveals the same Quran through all the chosen messengers or prophets, although the content is related contingently to the circumstances of their time). 10.94 makes this general connection with revelation:

> If you were in doubt [*shakkun*] concerning what we have revealed to you, then ask those who read [or 'recited': the verb is the same root as the word Quran] the Book before you: the Truth [alHaqq] has indeed come to you from your Lord, so do not be among those who hesitate.

Doubt is then condemned when it has been addressed to many of those earlier prophets. The Quran mentions in particular Salih (the prophet sent to the Thamud, 11.65), Joseph (40.36), Moses (11.112, 41.45) and messengers in general (14.10). Inevitably, therefore, it is condemned when it occurs in relation to Muhammad himself (38.7, 42.13).

Doubt is equally condemned when it is addressed, not just to the prophetic message in general, but to one particular part of it, the proclamation of life after death and of the Last Day (10.104; 27.68; 34.20; 44.8). The final condemnation of doubt is that it creates an impassable barrier between what people might desire and what they can in fact obtain, since those who doubt the roadworthiness of a vehicle will never trust themselves to travel in it: "Between them and their desires is placed a barrier ..., for they were indeed in suspicious doubt" (34.54).

There remains one further place where the word *shakkun* occurs, 4.156f.). In its context, that verse is condemning the People of the Book (i.e., the Jews) because (amongst other things) of their false belief:

> They said, Surely we killed the Messiah Jesus, son of Mary, the apostle [or 'messenger', *rasul*] of God, and they did not kill him, and they did not crucify him, but its [or 'his'] likeness [was] to them; and surely those who dispute about it [or 'him'] are full of doubt [*shakkun*] concerning it [or 'him']. They have no knowledge about it [or 'him'] except for following conjecture; and beyond all doubt they did not kill him. But God raised him to himself, and God is mighty, wise. And there are none among the People of the Book except they must believe in him before death, and on the Day of Judgement he will be a witness against them.

The Arabic pronoun may mean either 'it' or 'him'. Since *shakkun* is used elsewhere in the Quran so consistently concerning those who reject God's messengers and their message about life after death, this surely makes it possible that the reference of the pronoun actually shifts between 'him' and 'it', because in that case the doubters are rejecting both the messenger and the message.

In any case, whatever the exact meaning of that passage may be, it reinforces the point that in the Quran, doubt is indeed damnable. In a standard Sunni Muslim text called *Salvation of the Soul and Islamic Devotions*, Muhammad Quasem states that "the physical nature of future life is so strongly emphasized in the Quran and Tradition that its denial is considered as infidelity (*kufr*), which causes eternal damnation" (p.33). He goes on to point out that "faith must be absolutely certain if it is to serve as a means to salvation" (p.34).

So if in Christianity doubt is despair, in Islam doubt is denial. In India doubt is condemned whenever it leads people to stay and dally in the idle pleasures of the world while refusing to move on into truth.

> My old man said, Follow the van,
> Don't dilly-dally on the way ...

The 'van' to be followed in India is Dharma. Dharma in this context means roughly 'the appropriate way to live', the rules and practices that people should follow if they hope through rebirth to attain the goal of *mukti* or *moksha* (release). Those rules and practices are taught in families, and they are also laid out in the many texts of Dharma and illustrated in the great Epics (*Ramayana* and *Mahabharata*) and the Puranas. Many of those works have authority because they are Revelation or are derived from Revelation.

At the root of Indian doubt, therefore, is the refusal to accept any guidance or teaching that might lead to the ultimate goal. In *Bhagavadgita*, a text revered by almost all Indians, Krishna condemns those who waste their time in frivolous argument and who doubt the truth he has been teaching, and he calls them *asuras*, demons or devils:

> Devilish people cannot judge whether to begin some action or to refrain from it. They have no idea what is decent, customary or true. They doubt the reality of the world, or its foundation, or God, or whether the world comes into being through an interacting network of causes. Then by what? By nothing but desire [*kama*]. Committing themselves to this view, these scarcely enlightened lost souls are capable, by their frightening actions, of destroying the world itself which they are in effect seeking to harm. (16.7–9)

Krishna is attacking those who destroy the world because they are so stuck in their condition of doubt that they cannot hear his teaching, and as a result they go on living lives cut loose from true perception and moral foundation. That kind of doubt is about as destructive as it could be, and not surprisingly it is comprehensively condemned. People who persist in that condition of doubt as wilful ignorance are heading for hell. Doubt is damnable: the threefold gateway[7] to hell (*naraka*), as Krishna says (16.21), is wide open before them.

In Christianity, therefore, doubt is despair; in Islam it is denial; in Hinduism it is dalliance. Among Buddhists doubt is distrust and is equally to be condemned. The Buddha went among people after his enlightenment, not in order to convert them to some set of beliefs, but in order to heal their illness. He spoke of himself as a physician whose purpose was simply to diagnose the disease and to indicate the cure. But in the end, people can only heal themselves by accepting the diagnosis and by undertaking the indicated cure.

Basically, that requires an attitude of trust: it is essential to trust the fundamental diagnosis and equally the 'doctors and nurses' who are sent to help you to get better. The 'doctors and nurses' in Buddhism are the gurus and guides who transmit traditions, not just of teaching, but of practice. Doubt in Buddhism is the refusal to trust the teacher. Particularly well known among those teachers in the Japanese Zen tradition is Nicheren (1222–82), who taught:

> If you wish to attain the enlightenment of the Buddha immediately, lay down the banner of pride, cast away the club of resentment and doubt.... After all, when you fall into an abyss, and someone lowers a rope to pull you out, will you hesitate to grab the rope because you doubt the competence of the helper? Has not the Buddha declared, 'I alone am the protector and saviour'? Here is power! Here is the rope! Our hearts ache, our sleeves are soaked with tears until we see face to face the figure of the One who says to us, 'I am your Father'.

It seems clear, therefore, why doubt is condemned in Buddhism. Those who doubt the competence of the physician will not try the cure and will not be healed. Instead, people throw themselves into a proliferation of different religious practices, but they are pointless:

> Neither eating fish only, nor fasting, nor nakedness, nor shaving one's head, nor leaving one's hair uncut, nor matted hair, nor dirt, nor rough skin, nor the worshipping of fire, nor the many pointless penances you can find in the world, nor hymns, nor offerings, nor sacrifice, nor the rituals of the seasons, will ever cleanse people who have not conquered their doubt. (*Samyutta Nikaya* 258)

The teachings of the Buddha are true beyond doubt because he teaches only from his own experience of cure, of enlightenment. That is why in Buddhism doubt is distrust.

In religions, therefore, D definitely stands for doubt and all that goes with it: despair, denial, dalliance, distrust, all adding up to danger. Doubt (to quote Oliver Wendell Holmes), is "a clear and present danger", an enemy. D therefore stands equally for the devil who goes about like a roaring lion seeking whom he may devour. "O thou of little faith, wherefore didst thou doubt?" (Matthew 14.31). Doubt in religions is damnable.

As a result religions tend to end up (as the Roman Catholic Catechism does) saying that some doubts are inevitable, but that radical doubt is bad. In the end, radical doubt must be destructive because it refuses to accept the certainty, the God-given or the Buddha-given authority, of what has been revealed or taught beyond doubt. We therefore end up with the religious endorsement of dogmatic certainty.

THE COMMENDATION OF DOUBT IN PHILOSOPHY AND SCIENCE

So far, therefore, we can certainly illustrate the condemnation of doubt in religions, and it would seem that that part of the contrast between religions and sciences, the *condemnation* as opposed to the *commendation* of doubt, is correct. If we now look at the other side of that contrast, it is equally easy to illustrate the basic and creative importance of doubt in Western philosophy and science. It can be seen as early as the time of Pyrrho, a Greek (second/third century BCE) who was renowned for the establishing of doubt as the foundation of wisdom. We know virtually nothing about him except that he was held (mainly as a result of the advocacy of Timon of Philius) to be the founder of the most widely influential form of scepticism. We now use the word 'scepticism' to mean almost any kind of questioning or doubt. Originally, however, the Greek word *skepsis* meant, to quote the definition in Liddell and Scott, 'viewing, perception by the senses' and 'examination, speculation, consideration, inquiry.'

This means that the early Sceptics were enquirers after knowledge, and that is precisely the reason why doubt became important to them. It was to them fundamental that no one should claim as knowledge something which is uncertain. However, they then observed that when people try to demonstrate that something is certain, it is almost invariably the case that questions and doubts arise.

So they ended up by claiming that very little indeed can be known beyond doubt and with certainty. Our eyes, to take an elementary example, often deceive us. The cover of a book may look red, and so it is for us, but it might not be for someone who is colour-blind, and it might not be for a bat – that is, for some organism with different sensory equipment from our own. The point is that our senses secure much information that is reliable from our point of view, but not necessarily from every point of view, and in any case our senses often deceive us – as one remembers from the many optical illusions that delighted us as children.

If we then move beyond what our senses scan and pick up from the world around us, our uncertainties are even greater. What will happen tomorrow? That is a fairly obvious uncertainty and is the reason why economists have been defined as people who tell you tomorrow why what they predicted yesterday didn't happen today. But even the past is uncertain. There may be records but they do not contain 'the past'. In any case, the memories that people have and the accounts they give of an event in the past differ greatly, as we know very well from the conflicting accounts of witnesses in a court of law.

The early Sceptics, at the foundation of Western science and philosophy, did not conclude from uncertainties of those and other kinds that we are therefore totally ignorant, or that we know nothing at all. In fact, they emphasised that there is a common-sense reliability in everyday life. It is based on what Husserl much later called "appearances in consciousness", or (in their own language) on the consistent presence of *ta phainomena*. On the basis of such *katalepsis* (presentation) or in full *kataleptike phantasia* (presentation able to be apprehended), we build up a reliable basis on which to live our lives.

What Sceptics questioned was the belief (*dogma* in its original sense) that one can move from *katalepsis* to an unquestionably certain conclusion about the real existence and nature of what gives rise to it. There are usually equally forceful (*isotheneia*) and mutually exclusive (*emantiotes ton logon*) conclusions to be drawn from what the senses perceive. On questions of that kind we simply have to suspend judgement (*epoche*, a word also used by Husserl). On that basis it is simpler and wiser to get on with life without waiting to achieve dogmatic certainty.

The Sceptics, therefore, were not arguing for a complete 'scepticism' in our modern sense of the word. What they were arguing for is a different attitude to our knowledge, a more humble acceptance of the fact that we often cannot be certain. That is why it has been pointed out repeatedly that virtually everything we say about anything is approximate, provisional, corrigible (open to correction) and often wrong. They had some great slogans – 'I determine nothing', 'nothing can be apprehended' – but these were not really statements about knowledge. They were statements about their own attitude, their own recognition that we have to live in a world in which doubt is inevitable.

The aim of the Sceptics, therefore, was to live with a much more tolerant good humour. They encouraged us to live with confidence but always with the possibility that we might be wrong. So yes, if you are a fisherman, you have to launch your boat, and no, you cannot be absolutely certain that it will float, or, even if it does, that you will catch some fish. But what the sceptics said is that you don't have to get in a fuss, chasing around for certainty, before you launch your boat. This relaxed and tolerant good humour, this attitude, they called ἀταραξια, freedom from anxiety, knowing your limitations but living calmly within them.

This, then, was the achievement of the Sceptics: from the very outset of Western philosophy and eventually of Western science, they showed why doubt, far from being an enemy, is actually an ally. This enabled people to live confidently, but not to expect, still less to demand, impossible degrees of certainty before they launch their boats. Metrodorus of Chios was a sceptic in the fifth century BCE, and he wrote a work on nature which began with this sentence: "None of us knows anything, not even whether we know anything or not." Despite that, he then went on to write many pages of speculation about the nature of the cosmos.

The Sceptics are thus an early illustration of the claim that sciences and philosophy are on the side of rational reflection and doubt while religions are on the side of irrationality and dogma. For the Sceptics, inquiry and argument are fundamentally worthwhile and valid, so long as it is not expected that anyone can, in any but the most trivial matters, speak the final word. That was profoundly different from the majority attitude among the early Christians, and above all among the Apologists, because Christians believe that they do have the final word, the Word made flesh and speaking still in Scripture.

That name 'apologists' is given to Christian writers in the early centuries of the Church who defended Christianity from the attacks made on it as it spread widely into the Roman Empire. They commended what they thought was good in Christianity, and they condemned what they thought was wrong or immoral in the Empire.

But they did also recognise much that was good in the Empire, especially its inheritance of Greek philosophy, and they were quite prepared to think of Plato as Moses speaking Greek. So where, for example, Greek philosophers commended the natural law, as they often did, the Apologists welcomed that as good: it was the pagan equivalent of the revealed law, both of which point to Jesus as their fulfilment.

But what the Apologists could not, so to speak, 'baptise' in that way was the sceptical tradition because of the way in which that tradition valued the creativity of doubt. For what place has doubt in relation to the certainties of scripture and the blessed assurance of salvation? The answer was, none.

When Tertullian (a second-century theologian and apologist) asked, "What has Athens to do with Jerusalem?", the immediate answer seemed to be, nothing whatsoever, if Athens nurtures a philosophy which endorses doubt.

Not surprisingly, therefore, when the Emperor Justinian in the fifth century gave a new legal status to Christianity as the official religion of the Roman Empire, one of his first acts, in 529, was to close the ancient philosophical schools in Athens – after nearly a thousand years of history. It evoked from Gibbon, in his *Decline and Fall of the Roman Empire*, one of his most savage condemnations of Christian bigotry:

> The Gothic arms were less fatal to the schools of Athens than the establishment of a new religion, whose ministers superseded the exercise of reason, resolved every question by an article of faith, and condemned the infidel or sceptic to eternal flames. In many a volume of laborious controversy they exposed the weakness of the understanding and the corruption of the heart, insulted human nature in the sages of antiquity, and proscribed the spirit of philosophical inquiry, so repugnant to the doctrine, or at least to the temper, of a humble believer. (Dawson IV, p.205)

BEYOND THE WARFARE: BOTH DOUBT AND DOGMA

Thus far it may well seem that the radical contrast is well established between doubt and dogmatism in the case of sciences and religions – the claim and the question with which the last chapter ended and this chapter began. It would therefore seem obvious to conclude (as many do conclude) that science advances through its adherence to doubt resisted all the way by religion through its adherence to dogma. It is possible to exemplify the truth of that both in the past and still in the present.

Nevertheless it turns out to be a vastly inaccurate summary of scientific attitudes to dogma and of religious attitudes to doubt. Scientists can certainly be as much committed to dogmatic certainty as any religious believer, particularly in their refusal of questioning or doubt. Conversely religions can endorse the importance of doubt with as much emphasis as any scientist.

What in fact we observe in the history of religions as also in the history of science and philosophy is a constant but creative tension between securing certainty and yet raising doubts about it. Since, as the Sceptics observed, there is so little of which we can be certain, it is necessary for human wisdom and survival to endorse, not certainty, but doubt. Only when doubt is accepted as the necessary condition in which we all live do we ever take the risk of novelty – the risk, long ago, of moving out of the cave, or even of dropping out of the trees in which our earliest ancestors used to live. If you wait for certainty, you never move. "I respect faith," observed Wilson Mizner, "but doubt is what gets you an education." That is why Bernard, at the beginning of this chapter, drew so strong a contrast between Scholastic certainty and scientific doubt.

But then immediately we seem to get caught in a trap: those who doubt everything the whole time are equally paralysed, they would never risk moving out of the cave in the first place, they would never risk dropping out of the safety of their trees.

The trap is this: we have to remain sceptical in order not to be set in the concrete of our existing certainties; but we cannot live in a constant condition of doubt because if we did so, we would never take a step through a door. Arthur Eddington once observed (p.392) that no scientific or rational person would ever take the risk of stepping through a doorway:

> It is a complicated business. In the first place, I must shove against an atmosphere pressing with a force of fourteen pounds on every square inch of my body, I must make sure of landing on a plank travelling at twenty miles a second round the sun.... I must do this while hanging from a round planet, head outward into space.... Verily it is easier for a camel to pass through the eye of a needle than for a scientific man to pass through a door.

On the other hand, humans through their long history have achieved many *reliabilities* on the basis of which they can build their lives with confidence. The result is a constant and continuing tension in the history of human thought and technology between certainty and doubt. It is a tension that has created a kind of oscillation between scepticism and conviction: we need security and certainty if we are to live with confidence, but we need to doubt and question everything if we are to move into even greater security and wiser truth. We have, therefore, to make daring advances into novelty, but when we get there, we often try to defend the ground we have secured against any further questioning or doubt.

It is that tension between dogmatism and doubt which has been so creative in human thought and imagination, and it can be seen constantly in the history of science and philosophy. A well-known example lies in the work of Isaac Newton and in the way in which it was absorbed into the creation of 'the Newtonian universe'. It was Newton's achievement, building on the foundation of Kepler and Galileo, to explain why tides move and apples fall, and why heavenly bodies move in circles or ellipses, not in straight lines. Before the time of Newton, the nature and effects of gravitation could be observed, but the connection between those observations was unknown. Lying hidden behind disparate and apparently disconnected phenomena (such as Kepler's three laws of planetary motion, and Galileo's laws of motion for bodies on the earth) Newton discerned "the universality of gravitation". As Cushing has put it (p.103)

> Newton was able to take this melange of fragmented facts and partial truths and ferret out a unified set of laws that correctly explained the motion of both heavenly and terrestrial bodies.

In practice, this meant that Newton was establishing certain generalisations from which other *deductions* can be made, and those generalisations are known as Newton's laws. Goodbye doubt. From Newton's laws it seemed as though a complete account could be given of the universe in which there is no room for doubt, and in which, to adapt the remark of Laplace, 'there is no need for the hypothesis of God'.

Where, indeed, in a universe of that kind could God, so to speak, 'get in'? We have already encountered the argument in the nineteenth century that if you knew the position and momentum of every atom at the present moment, you could safely predict the future state of the universe at any time.

It seemed true beyond doubt, and it led to dogmatic certainty. And yet someone did doubt. At the beginning of the twentieth century, the great physicist, Lord Kelvin, delivered his celebrated lecture, 'Nineteenth Century Clouds over the Dynamical Theory of Heat and Light'. Kelvin's lecture described two doubts or 'clouds' about the possibility of giving a complete and final account of the universe in Newtonian terms.

So near, and yet so far, because the two doubts, the two questions which Kelvin refused to evade, were: first, to know how the earth can move without leaving experimental trace through "an elastic solid such as essentially is the luminiferous ether"; and second, to know how to account for the Maxwell-Boltzmann doctrine regarding the partition of energy. Those were unquestionably creative doubts. They led to Einstein and relativity in the one case and quantum mechanics in the other.[8]

Even so, dogmatic certainty about the Newtonian universe led to rearguard endeavours to explain away Kelvin's doubts (see Bowker 1987, pp. 46–9). Lord Rayleigh, a strong supporter of the work of Maxwell and Boltzmann, looked at the destructive effect of Kelvin's 'two clouds' for the ambitions of a Newtonian universe, and said: "What would appear to be wanted is some escape from the destructive simplicity of the general conclusion." On this Kelvin commented:

> The simplest way of arriving at this desired result is to deny the conclusion; and so, in the beginning of the twentieth century to lose sight of a cloud which has obscured the brilliance of the molecular theory of heat and light during the last quarter of the nineteenth century.

Others, however, particularly FitzGerald and Lorentz, made ingenious attempts to provide alternative explanations that might provide the desired escape. But Kelvin's doubts remained, and the new world of twentieth century physics opened up.

The point of that example is that dogmatism as well as doubt can be found amongst scientists, and that the tension between the two is profoundly creative. Thus, to give a different kind of example, it became a matter of dogmatic certainty, far 'beyond doubt' that induction instead of deduction is the empirical foundation of science, since that is the very method that brought those sciences into being. There are still many who believe that science is the only worthwhile kind of knowledge since it rests on empirical observation.

Even that, however, was shown to be open to doubt. Induction itself was doubted in a way that has completely changed the world in which we live. Induction was brought into doubt by a man whom his mother called an "uncommon wake-minded" creature, a man who claimed a few weeks before he died that although he had written "on all sorts of subjects calculated to excite hostility", he had no enemies "except indeed, all the Whigs, all the Tories, and all the Christians."

The man was of course David Hume, in whose shadow subsequent Western philosophy, and especially moral and aesthetic philosophy, has so often been written. It was a truly spectacular achievement, because by his day (he lived from 1711 to 1776), the foundations of modern science had been laid on inductive principles.

And why not? After all, repeated observation establishes that if I push this book I will cause it to move, if I drop this book it will fall, and the laws of motion explain how and why this always happens. But, said Hume, you do not observe 'cause'. What you observe is the conjunction of two events, and you infer the cause, but you never observe it.

Equally, he went on, you can never achieve sufficient, let alone perfect, induction. No matter how many times you observe the conjunction of someone pushing the book and the book moving, it is impossible to be certain that on the next occasion the book will not burst into flames. Induction will never supply the ground for saying that my pushing and the book moving will always happen. All you can say is that there has been a constancy in the conjunction of those events up till now.

Paradoxically, Hume's doubt created a new kind of dogmatic certainty that some kinds of knowledge are beyond us. We can, for example, have opinions about moral values and behaviours, but we do not directly observe them, we impose them on the world. This led to the familiar summary which is now taken for granted in philosophy and ethics, 'You cannot get an ought from an is, you cannot get a value from a fact.' When Captain Aubrey asked Stephen Maturin to explain the difference between moral and natural philosophy (science as it was understood at the beginning of the nineteenth century), Maturin replied: "'Why, natural philosophy is not concerned with ethics, virtues and vices, or metaphysics ... We erect hypotheses, to be sure, some of us to a most stupendous height, but we always hope to sustain them by demonstrable facts in time; these are not the province of the moralist'" (O'Brian p.141).

We now know, from work in current neuroscience, that that way of stating the matter is incorrect and that Hume's underlying assumption about what we observe and how we observe it is wrong (for a summary, see Bowker 2005, pp.38–41, 73ff). We know also that the logic of inference is now analysed in far more sophisticated ways. As a result, we begin to see how we *can* get an ought from an is, and how we *do* get values from facts. But for a long time after Hume, the opposite assumption was a matter of dogmatic certainty, resting as it did on the belief that sentences and propositions can be judged to be true only if they can be verified in some empirical way – on the belief, as we have already seen, that what is obvious in knowing is what knowing obviously is.

For the philosophers known as Logical Positivists, that supplied a criterion 'beyond doubt' which separates true from false propositions: Can the proposition be verified? If I say that there are four fingers and a thumb on my hand, it is easy enough to verify the proposition: take a look and count. If, however, I claim that God has four fingers, or, for that matter, that God does not have four fingers, I cannot verify either proposition, and therefore, those propositions are not simply false; they are meaningless, because God cannot be produced to meet the conditions of truth.

For many years the verification principle was put forward by its proponents with dogmatic and often aggressive certainty. But the verification principle itself was doubted. How, for example, does one verify the proposition that verification is the necessary condition of meaning or truth? Even within the debate itself, Karl Popper pointed out that falsification is more informative than verification. The more you can falsify (doubt) the proposition the more information that proposition is carrying.

That is certainly of great importance in the natural sciences. It is legitimate in science to form a hypothesis (sometimes "to a most stupendous height") and then to try to demonstrate its truth. But it is essential that this process is tested all the way by considering what could possibly contradict or falsify the hypothesis. The more that can be offered that might falsify an idea, the more information it may be carrying. Falsification is a powerfully creative form of doubt.

The purpose of those well-known examples has been to show that dogmatic certainty as well as doubt are equally present in the sciences, and to show also how profoundly creative the unending tension between doubt and certainty has been in Western thought. That can be seen with particular clarity in the work of Descartes (1596–1650), who was both a scientist and a philosopher, and whose ambition is summarised in the phrase 'Cartesian doubt'.

Descartes recognised the value of doubt, but he then asked whether there is anything that lies beyond doubt. In other words, he doubted everything in order to find out whether there is anything at all that cannot be doubted. In Meditation 2 of his *Meditations on First Philosophy*, he reached the one thing that he claimed cannot be doubted – his own existence. I must exist in order to doubt, or to be deceived. And what, essentially, is this 'I'? A *thinking* being: *cogito, ergo sum*. 'I think, therefore I am.'

From that one certainty Descartes then deduced other conclusions. Once again, as with the post-Newtonians, doubt has been used to establish a new kind of certainty and an entirely different foundation for deductive arguments.

But was the one certainty, based on Cartesian doubt, actually certain? Not so, according to Husserl (1859–1938), who threw doubt on Cartesian doubt when he claimed that Descartes's radical doubt was not radical enough: in the claim, 'I think, therefore I am', the conclusion does not follow from the premise: from 'I think', it does not follow that 'therefore, I am'. What does follow? Only, Husserl believed, appearances in consciousness from which our worlds are constructed; and from there we set sail on the oceans of phenomenology, of European existentialism, and of deconstruction and postmodernism – both of which, incidentally, are forms of doubt. The creativity of doubt continues.[9]

The more, however, that that is the case, the wider the divide must surely become if religions have been correctly described as the partisans of certainty and the enemies of doubt – if, that is, doubt is damnable. The accusation against religious believers is that they must necessarily condemn doubt because they claim that their beliefs rest on the privileged foundation of an inerrant revelation or of enlightened teachers or gurus who 'know of what they speak'. As a result, religions are accused of always rejecting anything that denies or calls in question the content of that revealed knowledge. The accusation is that the Inquisition (whose successor still exists, albeit under a different name) will always condemn a Galileo – for we all know, do we not, about Galileo and the Inquisition, and the conflict between faith and science which that episode is taken to represent.

But that also turns out to be a wildly inaccurate oversimplification. In a key article, Finocchiaro (2001) has shown that the two opposing interpretations of 'the Galileo affair' are *equally* oversimplified and misleading – "the approach that interprets the relationship as one of conflict, and the approach that construes the connection as one of harmony." William Shea, in his summary of the issues involved, did not minimise the destructive consequences of the condemnation of Galileo, but he nevertheless concluded that once it is set in its own particular historical context, "Galileo's condemnation was the result of the complex interplay of untoward political circumstances, personal ambitions, and wounded prides."

Galileo himself did not see any necessary conflict. A beneficiary of the doubts raised against deductive arguments, he simply doubted whether deductive arguments could lead to true *empirical* conclusions (except by chance or coincidence). He therefore set out in a different direction in order to answer the questions that concerned him.

One of those for Galileo (*Physics* 7.117–21) was the question of why things move as they do. Both Aristotle and Aquinas had also been interested in that question, but they had approached it as a matter of logical argument rather than observation. Logical argument led Aristotle to believe that anything in motion must have had something to set it in motion. How then did the very first movement happen? There must have been one original initiative, a first beginning to the sequence of all motion. This is how he put it himself:

> Since everything that is in motion must be moved by something – let us take the case in which a thing is in locomotion and is moved by something that is itself in motion, and that by something else, and so on continually – then the series cannot go on to infinity, but there must be some first mover!

It was a logical argument, and it established, not just for Aristotle, but for the early Christian Church, a true premise from which other truths could be derived. There must be an unmoved Mover.

The argument went deeply into the Christian mind and soul because it contrasted the imperfect, mutable and ever-striving world with the immutable and complete perfection of God in whom there is no change at all. It appears, for example, in familiar prayers, as in that of Compline:

> Be present, O merciful God, and protect us through the silent hours of this night, so that we who are wearied by the changes and chances of this fleeting world, may rest upon your eternal changelessness.

It is found also in popular hymns, such as 'Abide With Me':

> Change and decay in all around I see;
> O thou who changest not, abide with me.

'Motion and motion's God' (to quote the title of Buckley's study of this episode in Western thought) seemed to be inextricably linked. Aquinas and
many others, therefore, felt able to deduce from God as the unmoved Mover
the conclusion that God is radically different from all that has been created,
and that everything depends on God for its existence. In that sense, therefore,
God is distinct *from* all things, and yet is *in* all things as the cause is present
in its effect: "God is above all things through perfection in his nature, and yet
God is in all things as being the cause of all things" (*ST* 1a.8.1 ad 1).

For Galileo, there was no point in trying to contradict a deductive theory
like that of Aquinas as though it is untrue. Aquinas's argument is *coherent*
in the protected circle of Christianity (and some Jewish and many Muslim
philosophers argued the same), but it cannot *correspond* to anything that
can be observed. So Galileo spent no time in arguing against Aquinas: he
simply ignored him. Motion, and the reason why things move, might be all
that Aquinas had said. Galileo, in contrast, took round weights and rolled
them down inclined planes in order to 'dilute' the force of gravity so that
the reduced speed of the fall could be measured. After repeated measure-
ments, he was able to formulate the equations of accelerated motion. He
thus found that the velocity of a constantly accelerating object starting from
zero velocity is proportional to the time, and that the distance travelled by
a constantly accelerating body starting from zero velocity is proportional
to the square of the time. In brief, therefore, observation and experiment
displaced deduction.

That was the underlying issue: the scholastic theory of motion may suggest
why things move at all, but Galileo doubted whether it could tell us anything
about the way in which bodies move in space and time, and that was what
Galileo wished to understand. He therefore argued that the universe, if it is
to be understood, can only be understood on its own terms and in its own
language – primarily that of mathematics. In a famous passage, he wrote:

> Philosophy is written in this great book – I mean the universe – which
> stands continually open to our gaze, but it cannot be understood unless one
> first studies the language and the characters in which it is written. It is writ-
> ten in the language of mathematics, and its characters are triangles, circles,
> and other geometrical figures, without which it is humanly impossible to
> understand a single word of it. (*The Assayer* in Drake, pp.237f)

So Galileo admitted that he knew nothing about the ultimate nature of the
forces he was measuring; nothing about the cause of gravitation, or the origin
of the Universe; he deemed it better, as he put it, not to speculate on such high
matters, but to pronounce what he called "that wise, ingenious and modest

sentence, 'I know it not'" – in other words, it is better to remain in doubt than to seek refuge in grand and comprehensive theories that in fact explain nothing about the empirical state of the world.

That is a spectacular illustration of the creativity of doubt. It did not, however, involve any necessary conflict between the Church (upholding the Bible and Aquinas) and Galileo. In fact, Galileo ('Letter to the Grand Duchess Christina', in Finocchiaro 1989, p.96) maintained a principle that he claimed a Cardinal, Cesare Baronio, had taught him: "The purpose of the Holy Spirit is to teach us how to go to heaven, and not how heaven goes."

Conflict, nevertheless, is certain if scripture and the teaching authority of the Church do seem to be claiming to teach 'how heaven goes' and if science then throws doubt on that teaching. Even then, the main issue is not primarily one of 'science' versus 'religion'. It is one of authority and control, as equally of responsibility: it is an example of exactly that different kind of relationship between sciences and religions to which reference has already been made earlier in the book (Chapter 3): if the authority and power of the Church (or an equivalent in other religions) are threatened, that will be the primary concern of the authorities. Of course there are, and no doubt always will be, serious issues, but, as we saw earlier, there are many different strategies that might be chosen in order to address them.

It may, therefore, be more helpful to think of sciences and religions as different narratives (in the rich sense of narrative/narrativism explored by Flood).[10] They are distinguished from each other by the kinds of story they tell and the way they tell them about the subject matter that is of concern and interest to them. They are not, of course, totally divorced from each other. They often include each other, and they constantly overlap and interlock because in the most general sense the subject matter of both includes the cosmos and human nature. Narrative theology, however, always includes its sense that the cosmos is derived from God – and it has strong abductively inferential arguments for doing so. But clearly none of that belongs to the narratives of science since God cannot be an object within the cosmos open to the human investigations that have produced the sciences. So the general fact remains that to engage with God is not to seek additional information about the universe: for that, we go to science.

On the other hand, the investigations of science can certainly be included in narrative theology whenever they are relevant and illuminating – as, for example, I have tried to do in *The Sacred Neuron*, or more specifically in 'God, Spiritual Information, and Downward Causation' (in Harper, pp.479–83). That article looks at the implications of the scientific understanding of downward causation (as, for example, when the feedback loop in a homeostatic system regulates the matrix of transition probabilities and controls future states of the system) for beliefs and behaviours in religious life when it is projected into an acknowledged and hoped-for future (on downward causation, Chapter 6).

There are, therefore, entirely obvious and necessary distinctions, but the narratives of religion and science should never be reduced to rival accounts that have to be judged against each other. Even so, that still leaves open one final part of the initial accusation against religions, namely that they are far removed from the scientific spirit because of their condemnation of doubt and their translation of dogmatism into terror and oppression.

Certainly the continuation of that attitude can easily be found in the religious world: obedience and conformity remain attractive, not just to those who have an inner need to obey and conform (often linked to coherence) but even more to those in authority in religious systems who have an obligation to defend the boundaries of the circles of their own particular religion, and that may well include a condemnation of doubt. Since so many claims within religions are not justified by correspondence, but by coherence and by participation, the necessity to maintain the integrity of the protected circle, and within it the good experience of participation, motivates the defence of coherence and conformity against questioning and doubt. Anger and conflict all too frequently arise when that integrity is questioned or doubted.

All that is true and is often exemplified in religions at the present time. The fact nevertheless remains that within religions, doubt is not invariably condemned. Exactly the opposite. Within religions, doubt can be, and often is, valued as creative. It is not difficult to exemplify in religions the suppression of doubt, but there also exists in religions precisely that creative tension between doubt and certainty that we found in the sciences. That clearly calls into question the caricature of religions as being concerned only with dogmatic certainty.

RELIGIONS AND THE VALUE OF DOUBT

To see what that means in practice, we can look once more at the religions whose condemnation of doubt was summarised at the beginning of this chapter. Within Judaism and Christianity, for example, we have seen that if the Bible is believed to be the infallible and inerrant word of God, then the putative truth of any Jewish or Christian claim can be checked by seeing whether it is or is not coherent with the Bible, and there are many who continue to use the Bible in that way. However, during the nineteenth century it became clear that the Bible is not without error and contradiction: it contains many different writings that are immersed in the history of their times and contain errors of fact. When Colenso, as a Cambridge mathematician who became a bishop, worked out what the numbers in the Pentateuch implied if they were taken to be literal and inerrant, he found that two midwives sufficed for more than 2 million people, that the queue of Israelites before the Tabernacle was nearly 20 miles long, and that each priest had to eat 88 pigeons a day.[11]

As with Lord Kelvin, so here: there were those who fought a fierce rear-guard action. Charles Hodge (1797–1878), a strong defender of the Bible as infallible and inerrant in all matters, including science and history, nevertheless had to admit that errors do exist in the Bible. In his *Systematic Theology* he wrote:[12]

> The errors in matters of fact which sceptics search out bear no proportion to the whole. No sane man would deny that the Parthenon was built of marble, even if here and there a speck of sandstone should be detected in its structure. Not less unreasonable is it to deny the inspiration of such a book as the Bible because one sacred writer says that on one given occasion twenty-four thousand, and another that twenty-three thousand, men were slain.

As, however, the specks of sandstone multiplied, it became inescapably clear that the Bible is a collection of documents compiled over a thousand years and eventually designated as 'the Bible' much later. For those who believe that the works eventually designated 'the Bible' are derived from the initiative and inspiration of God, it is still the case that the books of the Bible are immersed in the history at their time of origin, with all the limitations of knowledge, style and errors in transmission on the one side and all the gains of increased learning, experience and insight on the other.

Since that is so, it is completely impossible to paint over the specks of sandstone and pass them off as marble. In fact, the specks of sandstone are telling us a vital, liberating truth about the Bible: it came into being, not despite the limitations of human knowledge at any given time, not despite the unfolding process of history, but by making use of those limitations and of that process. If it is to be accepted that God is the source of the Bible, it is clear that God did not bypass history and human circumstances but used them in order to help people to mature and come of age by making a name and nature known which people could understand. They found that that unfolding revelation of God invited a response of trust, even in the most appalling circumstances, because it has been tested through time. As a result, people continue to read the Bible in order to encounter God in the words of God and be made a holy people for the worship of God and the service of others.

Doubts about the historical and scientific inerrancy of the Bible have led to a far more perceptive and liberating understanding of how the Bible came into being and of how, therefore, it should be read and interpreted. Those doubts were passionately resisted when they were raised (as by some they still are), but far from being destructive, the doubts set the Bible free to work as an entirely different constraint in the creation of human lives addressed to the love of God and of their neighbour.[13]

Or to give a different example: in the Roman Catholic Church in the nineteenth century, those who came to be described as Modernists accepted a critical understanding of the Bible, and also doubted whether some key parts of traditional teaching could be defended any longer. The Church, in their view, should be open to advances in knowledge and understanding in the modern world. To Leo XIII (Pope 1878–1903) and Pius X (1903–14), claims of that kind were totally incoherent within the protected circle of Catholicism: Modernism was condemned in 1907, and many of the clergy who had participated in that attempt to open the circle were excluded from it – in other words, they were excommunicated.

The tension, however, between doubt and certainty was not removed by those measures, and the creativity of doubt contributed to the reappraisal and development of tradition in the Second Vatican Council. The tension, however, continues, since the status of that Council has been called into question, not least by the Society of St Pius X, the followers of Marcel Lefebvre. Lefebvre thought that the Council had diluted the 'Faith of the Fathers' by following the fashions of modernity, and that the Church should exercise 'constraint' in its sense of control (*An Open Letter to Confused Catholics*, 11):

> It is the current fashion to reject all forms of constraint and to bemoan its influence at certain periods of history. Pope John Paul II, deferring to this fad, deplored the Inquisition during his visit to Spain. But it is only the excesses of the Inquisition that are remembered. What is forgotten is that the Church, in creating the Holy Office (Sanctum Officium Inquisitionis), was fulfilling its duty in protecting souls, and proceeded against those who were trying to falsify the Faith and thus endangering the eternal salvation of everyone. The Inquisition came to the help of heretics themselves, just as one goes to the help of persons who jump into the water to end their lives.

Lefebvre and five other bishops were excommunicated, but Pope Benedict, who shared their concern to defend the protected circle of Vatican authority, lifted the excommunication of the four surviving bishops in 2009. In that context, members of SSPX and those who agree with them may well condemn doubt and insist that conscience as a particular act of practical reason is not an independent tribunal detached from the constraint of Church-defined truth and law. Freedom of conscience, as *Veritatis Splendor* 64 puts it, is freedom *in* the truth, not freedom *from* the truth. On the other hand, John Paul II frequently insisted on the duty and responsibility of all people to search for religious truth and to adhere to it once that truth is discerned.

But that search, as the Vatican II *Declaration on Religious Freedom* insisted, must be open and free since no one can be forced to accept 'the true faith' as the Catholic Church defines it. On that basis the Belgian bishops responded to *Humanae Vitae* (Paul VI's letter on birth control) that "if someone competent in the matter and capable of forming a well-founded judgement – which necessarily supposes sufficient information – after serious investigation before God, reaches different conclusions on certain points, he has the right to follow his convictions in this matter, provided that he remains disposed to continue his investigation."

That insistence, reiterated by Pope Francis, reflects the far more important and fundamental affirmation of doubt in Christian history as a necessity in the human relationship with God. God cannot be known 'beyond doubt' since God is not an object in the universe open to knowledge of that kind. As the French philosopher Simone Weil put it (pp.239f),

> Contact with human creatures is given us through the sense of presence. Contact with God is given us through the sense of absence. Compared with this absence, presence becomes more absent than absence.

It is, therefore, a constant theme in the Christian understanding of the spiritual life that the more people claim to know of God beyond doubt, the further away they are from God. This underlies the so-called *via negativa*, brilliantly summarised by McGinn claiming (p.116) that "the pursuit of the unknowable is an irreducible aspect of the human condition, found throughout the world's religions (and sciences as well).... [T]he mystics remind us that we should also yearn for the higher wisdom that begins by unknowing the known about God and ourselves. Like Abraham, at some stage we must be ready to destroy our idols before setting off on the journey to the promised land."

God therefore remains a constant invitation into exploration and growth (for a fuller account of this, see Bowker 2014), and Christianity is far from being alone in recognising that even though we may conclude *that* God is, we cannot know beyond doubt *what* God is. It is an example of the creativity of doubt which is found in all religions as McGinn observed. The focus of doubt, however, may well be different in different religions, but as an attitude its liberating creativity is recognised.

That is particularly striking in the case of Indian religion because of its realisation that one cannot ever 'believe all one sees'. That is why the word *maya* is so fundamental in Indian thought and religion. *Maya* is a Sanskrit word that is usually translated as 'dream' or 'illusion', but it means much more basically 'supernatural power' or 'magic'. That is what it means in the earliest Indian hymns, the Vedas, where it also carries the connotation of deceit or trickery. However, by the time of *Bhagavadgita*, *maya* has come to mean the power to bring things into their apparent form. If you are a cook, it is *maya* that enables you to turn eggs, flour and milk into a pancake, Thus in *Bhagavadgita* 4.7, Krishna declares that although he is the unborn, changeless Lord of all beings, he assumes human birth through his own *maya* (supernatural power) in every age whenever there is a decline of virtue for the protection of the good and the destruction of the wicked:

> Although I am unborn, being of unchangeable Atman, although I am Ishvara [God] of all creatures, in control of my own manifest nature I come into being through *atmamaya*. I take on existence through the ages for the rescue of the good and the destruction of evil in order to establish Dharma.

Those two meanings of *maya* – power and yet also illusion – became connected because of the belief that the world only exists through the *maya* (power) of Brahman. Brahman can be understood impersonally or as God, but either way Brahman is the unproduced Producer of all things who through the creative power of *maya* brings into being and sustains the transitory universe which humans experience in so many different ways.

The many forms of appearance that we encounter, therefore, exist as a consequence of Brahman, and the purpose of a wise life is to discern the reality of Brahman through (even though ultimately far beyond) the appearances. But the appearances become misleading when we look at them and, instead of discerning Brahman through them, we impose our own ideas on them and get it all wrong (*maya* in the sense of 'illusion'). That is illustrated through many famous examples of how we look at something and claim that it is x, only to find out when we look more carefully, or when we are more fully instructed, that it is not x but y instead. We look at a white shell and think, until we inspect it more closely, that it is silver. Or again, what is thought to be a snake coiled on the path turns out, on closer inspection, to be just a coil of rope. This is how Gaudapada put it:

> A rope not clearly seen in the dark is imagined to be things like a snake or a trickle of water. The Self is misperceived in the same way. But when the rope is seen for what it is, false perceptions are dissolved, and consciousness becomes aware of non-duality with the recognition, This is only

a rope. So it is with the discernment of what the Self is. (*Mandukyakarika* 2.17f)

So in India, people start in ignorance, imposing their own ideas on the world and never seeing what the world truly is. But they then begin to doubt, in the creative sense, the truth or reliability of their ignorant superimpositions. When they begin to realise that they are imposing their own inadequate ideas on appearance, they leave their ignorance behind and discern the truth – the truth that the world is not *in essence* trees and tables and tortoises: in essence, everything is the consequence or the manifestation of Brahman, the unproduced Producer of all things who sustains all things in being but is not wholly contained in any of them. In that sense *maya* as cloak or veil is equivalent to ignorance and illusion: *Brahman satya jagat mithya* – Brahman is real, the world is an illusion.

When people realise *that*, then at once they see Brahman as the only true reality behind the immense variety of all appearances. Even more, they realise that they are not other than that themselves: one's own self (*atman*) is not other than Brahman: *sa va ayam atma brahma*, "He, this *atman*, is most truly Brahman. (*Brihadaranyaka Upanishad* 4.4.5). This fundamental belief is epitomised in the so-called Great Sayings (*mahavakya*) 'you are That'; 'I am Brahman', 'All this indeed is Brahman', and the like. So one of the two great Indian epics, *Ramayana*, records the teaching of Vasishtha:

> The supreme Spirit, unlimited by time and space, of his own will and by the power of his omnipotence, takes upon himself the limited forms of time and space. Know that the world, although appearing as substantial, has nothing substantial in it: it is a void, being merely an appearance created by the images and vagaries of the mind. Know the world to be an enchanted scene, presented by the magic of *maya*.

The world is thus like a conjurer's show, and humans are like children crowding round to see the show, loving to be taken in, but wanting far more in the end to know how the trick is done. How did you do it? How did you do it? How did you do it? *That* is the creativity of Indian doubt, the longing to move from ignorance to knowledge. Sri Ramakrishna, a great teacher of the nineteenth century, said:

> The truth is that God alone is real and all else unreal. People, universe, house, children – all these are like the magic of the magician. The magician strikes his wand and says: 'Come delusion! Come confusion!' Then he says to the audience. 'Open the lid of the pot: see the birds fly into the sky.' But the magician alone is real and his magic unreal. The unreal exists for a second and then vanishes. (Abhedananda, p.787)

It is by recognising why doubt is justified and necessary in a world of this kind that people can begin to move on and see through doubt in both senses of the word 'through': see through it when they realise it is a trick and not the final truth; and see through it as a window that allows them to see the reality of Brahman as the source and goal of life.

There is no access to this release from the seemingly endless process of rebirth except through doubt. Unless people learn to doubt whether the superficially obvious is the final and only truth about the world, they cannot advance into more profound understanding. That is why the discussion of doubt and error is so pervasive in Indian philosophy, where, as Kar concluded (p.121), it is not the object but the *judgement* of error that actually interests the classical philosopher.

In that context, doubt is not the contradiction of certainty but a means of setting it in a wiser perspective (see the discussion of the Sceptics, in chapter 4). In Indian understanding, there is much in life and the universe that can be accepted pragmatically as certain, or at least as consistently reliable. Those fundamental certainties of Indian life are summed up in Dharma. Dharma has many meanings, but in general it means something like 'appropriate behaviour'. There is an ordered and law-governed character to the universe, which is or should be expressed in society and in individual lives. Thus Indian life in ritual and in the organisation of family and social life is highly ordered and not open to contest or doubt. Even so, those certainties have been doubted within India itself. Guru Nanak, for example, cast doubts on the rigidity of the divisions in society and between religions. The result was the organisation of the Sikhs into a separate 'circle of coherence' even though its fundamental claim was to be inclusive. This again is an example of the creativity of doubt in relation to certainty.

Doubt is equally important in Buddhism. Indeed, Buddhism came into being because the Buddha doubted whether some of the fundamental claims being made in Indian religion at the time were true. For example, he accepted the Indian belief that there are appearances in the universe correctly described as gods and goddesses (so that Buddhism is not an atheistic philosophy, as it is sometimes described). On the other hand, he doubted whether claims made about those deities are true: in particular he doubted whether they can be manipulated through the rituals and sacrifices of the brahmins. He accepted the belief that there are long sequences of rebirth through which Karma, the moral law of the universe, works itself out. On the other hand, he doubted the claim that there is a self or soul being reborn: in his view, there is only the long sequence of reappearances without any substantial soul, or atman, being reborn – hence the fundamental Buddhist belief in 'no-soul', *anatman/anatta*.

He accepted that there is an ultimate condition called Nirvana (*nibbana*). On the other hand, he doubted whether it is a state of blissful union with God (*brahmanirvana*): in contrast to *Bhagavadgita*, which describes Nirvana as a candle far removed from a draught, burning with a steady flame, Nirvana is not a place at all, but rather a state in which all interaction with desire and thirst has ceased.

Since doubt lies at the very foundations of Buddhism, it is not surprising that it recurs throughout Buddhist history as an indispensable part of the quest for the final goal. For example, in the form of Buddhism known as Meditation (Chan or Zen) Buddhism, doubt is one of the important conditions of Enlightenment. That at least is what one of the greatest of Zen Buddhist teachers, Dogen, came to realise. Dogen (1200–53) first joined the Tendai tradition in the monastery on Mt. Hiei where all seemed to be going well, but after some years he was suddenly assailed by what he later called 'the Great Doubt', *daigidan*, the great ball of doubt. He therefore went to China to seek instruction in various other traditions.

The problem that faced him can be seen in particular in a tradition of the teaching and practice in Mahayana Buddhism associated with Tathagathagarbha. *Tatha* means 'perfect one', that is, Buddha; *garbha* means 'embryo' or 'womb' or a container of some kind. According to this teaching, the Buddha-nature lies deeply and essentially within all sentient beings. They may look extremely different as, for example, Jack and Jill, or angry and peaceful, or tall and short. But hidden deeply within is the same essential Buddha-nature. By a very rough analogy, we might say that all things we see or experience seem to be vastly different, yet beneath the surface appearances are the same energetic particles in different architectures of appearance. To 'bring the Buddha-nature to birth' and thus to find or reveal it, all defilements and veils of ignorance (whatever obstacles there are that obscure the truth) have to be removed.

The underlying Buddha-nature is known in Japan as Bussho; *bussho-reiko* is defined in Hisao Inagaki's *A Dictionary of Japanese Buddhist Terms* as "the mystic spirituality of the Buddha-nature inherent in each living being". So the wisest purpose of a human life for those who share this understanding is to engage in whatever practices and study will lead them to realise that this is essentially what they are – after all, there is nothing else to be! They too, as a Tibetan text puts it, 'have the Buddha-nature in themselves'. When people realise this, not just with their heads, but with the whole of their being, the path to Enlightenment is clear. The Buddha-nature is the only reality that there is: all else is mere appearance floating about on the surface. To *realise* this is to be Enlightened. Nothing else can be of such great importance, and that is why Buddhist monasteries can be such disciplined places of instruction and learning, helping people, by the internalisation of constraint, to realise this truth.

And that is where Dogen's 'great ball of doubt' hits home: if we already *have* the Buddha-nature, and if we are already endowed with the Buddha-nature, why is such strenuous effort and training necessary to realise it, to attain Enlightenment? Why do we have to struggle so hard to find what we already have? When Dogen began his life as a Tendai monk, he was taught that all forms of Buddhism, whether open or esoteric, believe that sentient beings possess the original Buddha-nature. But if that is so, why do all Buddhas and Bodhisattvas encourage the desire for Enlightenment? And why do they practice asceticism? This question stands at the head of one of his earliest works, *Fukanzazengi*:

> The Way is fundamentally complete and all-inclusive. So how can it depend on practice and realisation? The Dharma vehicle runs freely and without complication, so what need can there be for concentrated effort on the part of humans?

Eventually Dogen found the answer, but only by staying with the doubt, staying with the question. He achieved his answer by a small but all-important shift from what he had first been taught: he had been taught that all sentient beings *have* the Buddha-nature, possess the Buddha-nature hidden within. He realised instead that all sentient beings *are* the Buddha-nature. It is not that there are many people in the world with different appearances and diverse characters, and if you look hard enough you will find that they have the same Buddha-nature inside them. There is not an 'x' to which a Buddha-nature is added; there is only what there is, devoid of any other essential or differentiating characteristics (*shunyata*), despite superficial appearances to the contrary. There is only the Buddha-nature. And since the whole of everything comes and goes, is here today and gone tomorrow, this means that impermanence is itself the Buddha-nature:

> The very impermanence of grass and trees, of woods and forests, is the Buddha-nature. The very impermanence of humans and things, of body and mind, is the Buddha-nature. All things are impermanent because they are the Buddha-nature. Because it is the Buddha-nature, supreme and complete enlightenment is impermanent. Nirvana itself, because it is impermanent, is the Buddha-nature.

Dogen emphasised that to understand this intellectually is interesting, but that to realise it in Enlightenment lies far beyond intellectual understanding.

Enlightenment occurs when we become what we are, nothing other than the Buddha-nature. The opportunity is always present, but not all respond to it even in identical circumstances:

> Consider those who reached enlightenment when they heard the sound of a tile striking a bamboo, or when they saw the cherry blossom in bloom. Does the bamboo sort out the wise from the dull, the enlightened from the ignorant? Does the blossom distinguish between the frivolous and the profound, the stupid from the wise? There are blossoms on the bough year after year, but not all who see them gain enlightenment; bamboos never cease to give off sounds, but not all who hear them gain enlightenment. Only after long study under a trained teacher, combined with much practice, do we grasp what we have struggled to gain – enlightenment and clarity of mind. (*Shobogenzo Zuimonki* 4.5)

There is an obvious danger here that Dogen recognised. It is not enough to hear the teaching and understand it. Dogen insisted that no progress can be made by simply accepting the teaching that is offered. It has to be tested and then put into conscientious practice in order for it to become real in oneself:

> It is of extreme importance in discerning that truth not always to accept the words of the Teachers of old. It is unwise to be constantly suspicious, but it would be a worse mistake to hang on defensively to something that is not trustworthy, and not to question a meaning that demands exploration. (*op cit.*, 4.2)

In that spirit, Dogen even doubted the human interpretation of the experience of time, since there never can be a before or an after in that which is without exception the same Buddha-nature. The implication of this is that being and time cannot be differentiated as though the one can be separated from the other. Both being and time are the one undifferentiated Buddha-nature, so that being is time and time is being *(uji)*. In all things and in all experiences, the Buddha-nature can be realized, especially by not trying to realize it.

When Zen teachers come near to death, they often try to write a verse into which they put their final faith. For Dogen, the final thought that he entrusted to those coming after him was this: we must rest in transience and impermanence and treasure them, for in them we already reach Nirvana. Nirvana is not a goal outside and beyond us. It is already who and where we are. His last verses read:

> From leaf and grass
> beneath the morning sun
> the drops of dew soon pass.
> Calm down, you autumn breath
> restless in the dry fields.

> The world and life and death
> to me resemble – what?
> The moon's slight print
> dropping on dew a hint
> the beak of a bird. (Bowker 2010, p.121)

On that basis, doubt is the condition of truth, much as Unamuno (in an entirely different tradition) wrote in 1907: "La vida es duda, e la fe sin la duda es solo muerte" (life is doubt, and faith without doubt is nothing but death). So important did doubt become in Zen Buddhism that Bankei (1622–93) complained that by his time it was a compulsory part of the syllabus for those in training (*Bankei Zenji goroku* 1a.14): "Zen teachers are telling those in training that unless they can raise 'a great ball of doubt' and then overcome it, they cannot make any progress in Zen." And yet Bankei found that the practice of Zen requires one to be in a constant condition of doubt. As Dumoulin has summarised the point (II, p.312),

> Bankei was acquainted only too well with doubt himself. Although he approached it first from without when struggling with the words about 'bright virtue' that he had met in a Confucian classic, in time he came to know the essence of doubt so deeply that he himself became his own existential doubt.

By doubting the many ways offered in various teachings and methods, Bankei was set free to concentrate on the Unborn Buddha mind (4.2):

> If you simply stay in the Buddha mind, that is all you have to do: that takes care of everything. Why are you constantly going about and thinking up other things to do? There is no need for that: simply dwell in the Unborn.

On a comparable basis, Dogen believed that the major consequence of doubt is to learn what it means to trust. He took the word *ki-e* to summarise the Buddhist way of salvation: *ki* means 'to throw oneself' in the way that a child throws itself into the arms of a parent; *e* means 'to rely upon' in the way that the nation relies on its ruler or government. The Buddha is the parent, the Dharma (true and appropriate teaching) is the Buddhist teaching and the community of those who are always ready to help.

That is doubt leading the way into truth: it is doubt becoming creative in Buddhism. It seems at first sight very far removed from the condemnation of doubt in the Quran (summarized earlier in this chapter). When Rosenthal reviewed the status of doubt in Islam, he concluded (p.300):

> Doubt in whichever way indicated became the true pariah and outcast of Muslim civilisation. It stands for all that is to be shunned like the plague. No

worse fate can befall man than being passed into the sea of doubts and left there to flounder and possibly to drown.

That condemnation seems to be powerfully reinforced in the passage quoted earlier from Muhammad Quasem's book, *Salvation of the Soul and Islamic Devotions*. However, that passage goes on to make it clear that there is a legitimate place for degrees of certainty (pp. 34f):

Faith must be absolutely certain if it is to serve as a means to salvation. Certainty of faith, however, has different degrees. The lowest degree exists when a man fully believes in God, the prophecy of Muhammad and the Last Day by hearing these from an authority. It is in this way that common men form their faith which is sufficient for salvation free from damnation. This salvation, however, is of a low degree, since the certainty of faith is also low. Many Qur'anic verses mean this way of formation of faith. The Prophet was also fully content with people's faith acquired in this way. A more certain faith is generally believed to be that which is formed by way of arguments of theology. This faith, theologians claim, causes a high degree of salvation. The most certain faith is that of a Sufi based on his mystical intuition *(kashf)*. The Sufi's intuitive knowledge of God, prophecy and affairs of the Hereafter is extremely clear and comprehensive. Such knowledge makes his faith most certain, and it is this faith which causes the highest grade of salvation.

So there are different degrees of commitment and faith in Islam. Doubt legitimately enters in as soon as the question is asked, how does one get to these different levels or degrees of faith? The answer in Muslim history has been emphatic: only by personal endeavour, never by accepting things on the authority of others.

That is how doubt in the sense of questioning enters into Islam. One of the major issues in Islam is whether a Muslim should accept anything on the basis of *taqlid*. *Taqlid* is a word that means 'putting a rope on the neck of an animal in order to pull it along', and from that it came to mean 'being pulled along' by others, and hence 'imitation'. The outward appearance of being faithful on the basis of doing without question what you are told to do by others (in effect, simply imitating them) is not Islam. That is why the very first Hadith in alBukhari's Sahih ('Sound') Collection, as well as in anNawawi's quintessential *Forty Hadith*, states from the outset that the worth of any action depends on the intention *(niyya)* with which it is carried out:

Actions are [judged by] intention, and to everyone its worth will be [reckoned] by what he intended. So whoever made a Hijrah for God and his Messenger, his Hijrah will have been for God and his Messenger, but whoever made a Hijrah for a worldly gain, or to take a woman in marriage, his Hijrah will have been for whatever purpose he made the Hijrah.

Of course there are Muslims, particularly among the *ulama*, the trained authorities, who insist that *taqlid*, unquestioning obedience, is necessary. But others maintain that faithful obedience must be with understanding. It was the classic and central issue in Akbar's attempt in the Mughal empire to achieve a better degree of political and religious integration: he distinguished between acts of religious observance that are *taqlidi* and those that can be supported by reason, arguing that those which can be supported by reason can be the basis of a common religion. As Badayuni (who was by no means sympathetic to what Akbar was trying to do) put it at the time (p.211),

> Eventually the observance of the five prayers and the fasts, and everything important was put down as *taqlidi*, that is, not based on reason, and they [Akbar and his supporters] made faith depend on reason, and not on written tradition.

It is true that the reaction against Akbar prevailed, but even so what has been accepted must be tested in experience. That is why Muhammad Quasem could say (above) that the highest degree of faith is that of the Sufis, because they have entered into the direct knowledge of God. The great philosopher alGhazali, renowned in Islam as *hujjat alIslam* ('the Proof of Islam'), explored in great detail why propositional claims have to exhibit the warrants for their assertion if they are to be taken seriously. Consequently, toward the end of his life, he retreated for ten years to the minaret of the Mosque in Damascus in order to test the Sufi way.[14]

So here is doubt being fundamentally creative in Islam: it is doubt about propositions being put forward and then accepted without any foundation in experience – or, in other words, without adequate warrants being offered for them. That is the basis on which Muslims have understood the otherwise puzzling saying of Muhammad, "I am more prone to doubt than Ibrahim/ Abraham." Muhammad was responding to a passage in the Quran (2.260/2) which seems to imply that Ibrahim was doubtful about the resurrection of the dead – exactly the issue which the Quran, as we saw earlier, condemns as most destructive:

> And when Ibrahim said, 'My Lord, show me how you give life to the dead', he said: 'Do you not then believe?' He said, 'But to satisfy my heart.'

It seemed contradictory of the status of Ibrahim and Muhammad as prophets that Ibrahim had deep-seated doubt about the resurrection and that

Muhammad was even more prone to doubt. The later commentators therefore resolved the contradiction by distinguishing between 'necessary knowledge' that cannot be doubted (for example, that triangles have three sides)
and 'knowledge reached through induction' which can and often must be
doubted. They introduced a category of 'unconfirmed propositions' which
are rightly open to doubt even on the part of prophets. The creativity of doubt
was thus extended in Islam even beyond the condemnation of *taqlid*.

CONCLUSION

We can now see that it is an entirely false dichotomy to set on the one side
religions as the guardians of dogmatic certainty, never open to question or
doubt, and on the other side science as the guardian of experimental questioning, always refusing unquestioned dogma. That is an example of the
fallacy of the falsely dichotomous question which so often becomes a substitute for serious discussion in the attacks on religion. It is the fallacy which
assumes that there can only be alternative either-or answers to a question, of
which only one can be right. Thus, 'European Union: triumph or disaster?'
The answer might be both or neither, or much more than both, or indeed one
to the exclusion of the other. In a feast of the fallacy, a publisher (Helix Books)
wrote of *Philosophies of Love*: "The nature of human love is a question that has
long provoked controversy. Is love fleeting or enduring, clearsighted or blind,
possessive or liberating, elevating or degrading?"

In assessing, therefore, the attitudes of sciences and of religions to doubt, it
is important not to keep repeating the fallacy. It is a matter, not of either-or,
but of both-and. This means that although the narratives of religion and science are very different enterprises, addressed to different goals and drawing
on distinct (though not always different) resources, they do nevertheless have
this in common: they are both the consequence of a creative tension between
certainty (which may well be expressed dogmatically) and doubt.

Of course, it is possible to find examples in both sciences and religions
of the opposite, of closed circles of certainty into which no doubt is allowed
to enter. For every Torquemada on the religious side it is possible to find a
Dawkins on the other. It is possible to find fundamentalists, not just among
religious believers, but also among scientists and philosophers who reject
the implications of doubt, as we saw in the example of those scientists at
the end of the nineteenth century who were so committed to the certainties of a Newtonian universe that they resisted for years the implications of
Kelvin's 'two clouds' of doubt. Some philosophers in the twentieth century
were so committed to the certainties of logical positivism and the verification

principle that they dismissed doubts about it, not as false but as meaning-less. Yet in the end, the new physics prevailed and eventually the verification principle was abandoned. A.J. Ayer, a leading exponent of logical positivism, was once asked by Bryan Magee what, in retrospect, he regarded as defective about logical positivism. Ayer replied: "Well, I suppose the most important of the defects was that nearly all of it was false" (Magee, p.107).

In contrast to that, it is clear that doubt has been of paramount impor-tance in the advance of human knowledge and understanding, as much in religions as in sciences. Doubt can, of course, be destructive: it can be a mat-ter of 'deserts and dried-up hopes' as it is put in the exchange in MacNeice's *The Dark Tower* (p.25)[15]; but it can also be profoundly creative, an ally and a friend of truth.

This means that the relationships between 'science' and 'religion' cannot be summarised in terms of a conflict between doubt and dogmatism, despite the persistence with which many books and most TV documentaries continue to do so. Each instance, whether small or large, has to be studied in its own detail.

It so happens that in attention to detail we have been extraordinarily well served in recent decades by historians of science. Reference has already been made to the work of Rudwick in his massive and illuminating study of geohis-tory in the late eighteenth and nineteenth centuries. He concluded the first volume (2005) with these words:

> The great fallacy in the 'conflict thesis' – a fallacy sedulously fostered by those modern commentators who can fairly be described as crusading athe-istic fundamentalists – is that it treats both sides of the supposed conflict as reified and ahistorical entities: 'Science' and 'Religion'. In reality, everything depended, then as now, on when, where, and who ... Literalistic readings of biblical texts had already been widely displaced by historically and cultur-ally sensitive interpretations, often with the intention of uncovering deeper *religious* meaning. On the issue of the earth's timescale there was therefore no significant conflict between geology and Genesis or between geologists and the 'Church' that in reality was far from monolithic. The only conflict – sometimes and locally – was between scientific savants (including those who were religious believers) on the one hand, and specific sections of the wider public on the other.

In understanding religions, therefore, it is important to identify the status and the practice of doubt *in each case*, and with exactly that attention to detail on which Rudwick and all serious scholars insist. It then becomes possible to explore the extent to which any particular protective circle of coherence may in fact *welcome* question or challenge both within and also from outside the circle.

Most of the current attacks on religion achieve the opposite in their unqualified assumption that religions are committed to the intransigent exclusion of all doubt and question, and are therefore necessarily irrational and foolish. Given that the religious world does indeed contain much irrational folly, what is now needed is a far more cooperative attempt to distinguish the dangerously closed mind from the consequences in religions of well-grounded and well-warranted explorations of our human truth and possibility, in which doubt must always and necessarily play its part.

The point that needs urgently to be nurtured and defended, especially in the protected circles of religion, is that doubt is not automatically destructive – indeed, it may be highly constructive and creative. What has been argued here is that the Giant Despair who stands across the path of any pilgrim's progress is not doubt: it is certainty.

What religions have found difficult to handle is the interaction between the two, between doubt and certainty. Nevertheless, it is essential that that interaction is never suppressed. In my book, *The Sense of God*, I wrote at some length about the way in which Matthew Arnold struggled with this. His father, Thomas Arnold, the headmaster of Rugby School, once wrote in a letter that a good man "may be perplexed with doubts all his days; nay, his fears lest the Gospel should not be true, may be stronger than his hopes that it will" (Stanley, p.274). At the very end of his life – indeed, as he was dying – he "dwelt with deep solemnity" on the doubt and then faith of Thomas, "as in his life he had dwelt upon it as the great consolation of doubting but faithful hearts" (p.138).

But even if we recover a wiser understanding of the creative ways in which doubt and certainty interact as much in religions as in sciences, the fact remains that for some scientists the warfare against religion continues. Even Dawkins recognised (in the Preface to the paperback edition of *The God Delusion*, p.15) that there are "subtle and nuanced" forms of religion that would make the world a better place (evoking a bizarre attack on Dawkins for being "a monument to the eternal shallowness of Anglican atheism"[16]), but that did not affect his war against religion.

Fundamental in that campaign has been the belief (not just of Dawkins, but of others whom we have already met in this book) that once the origins of religion have been located in evolution and natural selection, the later accretions of belief and practice can be dismissed as a regrettable (or even worse) episode in human history. On this argument, genes create the social forms of culture, including religions, in ways that enhance the probability of the survival of genetic information; genes thus determine cultural outcomes since otherwise they would be less likely to survive and be selected.

In understanding religions, there is much to be gained from that work, but because it has so often been combined with narrow-mindedly reductionist attacks on religion, it has been resisted or even ignored by those engaged in the study of religions. It has led also to a failure on the part of scientists to realise that a more accurate understanding of religions can illuminate their own work. Seeing, in the next two chapters, why that is so opens the way to a much richer understanding of the complexity of the reasons underlying all human behaviours, including those of religion.

Religions and sciences

III The selfless gene: Genetic determinism and human freedom

*T*HE NORTH SEA CAMP WAS BUILT IN THE PERIOD BETWEEN THE two World Wars as an institution, a Borstal, for young offenders. It was built in Lincolnshire on the edge of the North Sea in order to provide demanding occupation not altogether unlike that of a treadmill: the main work each day was building a long sea wall in order to reclaim land for agriculture.

When I started work on the wall it had reached about 2 miles in distance from the Camp, and about 320 acres had been reclaimed for agriculture. As we worked towards what seemed like Scotland, there were many more miles yet to build. Two men and a digger might have finished it, I guess, in a few months. We still had 'miles to go before we slept' or were released because we were building the wall mainly by hand: we dug mud from the seaward side, shovelled it into a small tipping wagon that was set on rails. We then pushed the wagon to the foot of the wall where a winch pulled it up to the top. Having tipped it out, we then pushed it back to the point where we were digging.

It was, to say the least, hard work, and in winter it was so cold that we were allowed to fall into the pools of sea water only twice a month: to get soaked through meant that you had to return to the Camp to get a change of clothing: to do that too often looked like skiving.

One distinct memory returns: whenever we were walking back to the Camp after a day's work and the sun was setting in winter beauty across the wide marsh, the conversation always turned to death: suicide, life after death, oblivion, the meaning of life in relation to death, and so on. It was so predictable that it was almost invariable. It was as though weariness after work, combined with extreme but fleeting beauty, evoked those conversations. It was my first serious encounter with what has come to be known as 'implicit religion'.[1]

It was also my first serious encounter with the question of how we come to end up in life where we do. How had we come to be that incongruous company of young men ('lads' as they were called in those days) discussing death on the edge of Lincolnshire? Most were there because of a conviction in a court of law. I was there as a volunteer living in Borstal in exactly the same circumstances as everyone else, although it was known that I was not there for the same reason as anybody else since I had not actually been convicted in a court of law. At the outset, therefore, there was a certain amount of physical pressure to see whether I would, as I clearly could, walk out. When that did not happen I would be told about knives hidden under floorboards to see if they were immediately seized. When that did not happen either, life settled down and I got to know people extremely well in the ordinary ways of friendship.

In that way it soon became apparent why those people I came to know well had arrived at the North Sea Camp. The circumstances of their lives had made it virtually inevitable that this would be the outcome. Nor did they have much chance when they were released: at that time, one in three were reconvicted after release. Of course they had made choices and others had chosen differently, but it seemed to me (far too simplistically as it turned out) that they were, in a serious sense, not responsible for what they had done or for what had happened to them. The question therefore became whether they wanted to make the attempt to *acquire responsibility* for themselves so far as that was possible.

What that might mean came home to me on the hills above Usk. At that time the old gaol at Usk was a Borstal, though the daily work was done on a prison farm at Prescoed Camp in the hills above the town. One Christmas I was part of a small working party erecting a post and barbed-wire fence around a field. The weather was so bitterly cold that we were allowed to light a fire, but we were told in no uncertain terms that we were not to cook anything on it. At the break for dinner we went back to a barn where potatoes from the farm were being sorted, the best to be sold, the worst for prison kitchens. When we were about to return to our fence, one of the strongest of our party put a sack of best potatoes under each arm and we disappeared into the mist. We then baked potatoes in our fire.

For the rest of the week on that particular job the conversation kept returning to the potatoes: was it right to steal them? Is it ever right to steal? Should you steal in order to help others in need? Months later I received a letter from the young man who had actually carried off the sacks of potatoes, and had subsequently been released. It ended (exactly as he wrote it): "Last week me mates and me were down by the factories and we saw a window open. They climbed in and they got caught. I didnt. I remembered the potatoes. Ha, ha, ha!"

The way in which he acquired responsibility for himself and for his actions may seem a worthwhile result, and for him it surely was. But I remain uneasy. There were many others in that barn who saw me going off with the stolen potatoes, and with whom the week-long conversation about right and wrong never took place. Maybe from that they were reinforced in some subsequent act for which they were arrested. It is the dilemma from which Borelli never escaped when he went to live among the *scugnizzi* of Naples: to live in complete commitment to, and identification with, people in those circumstances means participating in a great deal that one knows to be wrong. When he was asked whether it was right in law and conscience to have participated completely in their way of life, he replied (West, p.92):

'Much of it was justifiable, yes. Much of it was, shall we say, on the razor edge between right and wrong. But I was committed, you see, I could not turn back. I could only make my own judgement and commit it to the mercy of God. Even so ...'

He broke off and looked down at the palms of his workman's hands.

'Even so?'

'Even so' said Don Borrelli, softly, 'there were many moments when I was a scugnizzo and not a priest.'

Maybe an attempt of that kind to live alongside people in demanding circumstances is naive. Nevertheless, it leads to an entirely different understanding of the reasons why some people end up where they do – in this case, in Borstal. In the case of many of them it seemed, from their circumstances, to be inevitable.

But that conclusion, however compassionate, raises immediate questions about the meaning of the word 'inevitable'. To what extent are humans controlled into thoughts and actions for which they are held to be accountable and responsible when in fact they have had little or no choice? What makes humans act as they do? To what extent are the outcomes in human behaviour inevitable?

Those questions are much debated in philosophy and the sciences, and they are central to the understanding of religions in the context of beliefs about responsibility, accountability and judgement. Religions recognise that individuals are born into circumstances which they did not choose (though in religions that believe in rebirth or reappearance, individuals may have *deserved* particular circumstances) and into a world over which they have little control. It is a world in which the will of God (Qadr in the case of Islam) or of Karma/Kamma is being worked out. In both cases, there are constant questions of the relationship between predestination or inevitability and human independence, autonomy and responsibility. Similar questions arose in Marxism and still arise in the application of genetics to society where they form part of the challenge to religion.

The purpose of this chapter, therefore, is to look at those issues with a particular focus on the strongly deterministic claims made by some geneticists, and also on the ways in which those claims have become the foundation for attacks on the worth and truth of religions. What is often overlooked is that equally strong and deterministic claims (also based on inheritance) have been made in many of the major religions. In general, however, religions have also explored what it means in that context for people to be accountable and to acquire responsibility.

INEVITABILITY AND DETERMINISM

At the time when I was reclaiming land in Lincolnshire, the world was trapped in the Cold War, and the word 'inevitable' was associated with a Marxist understanding of history. While that had a theoretical attraction for some, it was not in the least attractive to those who were aware of the uses to which it had been put under Stalin and Mao Tse-tung (or Mao Zedong, as he would now be known). The consequences of 'inevitability' in those senses are the reason why there is a long chapter on Marxism, including Chinese Marxism, in one of my early books, *Problems of Suffering in Religions of the World* (pp.137–92)

Inevitability, however, could wear other clothes than those of Karl Marx, not least those of social determinism which included the view that social conditioning controls human behaviours into their outcomes. At that time a strong social determinism argued that criminal offenders were the victims of society rather than offenders against it. In that case it would surely be compassionate to treat them sympathetically because they had not chosen the social circumstances into which they were born. In a strong sense, therefore, it was argued that they were 'not responsible'.

It would be hard-hearted in the extreme to reject an argument for compassion and sympathy. Nevertheless, the substance of that argument was wrong because it was oversimplistic. It assumed that social circumstance and conditioning create a single, salient and overriding cause of antisocial behaviour. It thus made the error still frequently repeated that it is possible to identify the cause of complicated behaviours and events, and that having done so it is possible to deal effectively with the cause: tough on crime, tough on the causes of crime.

That may well be desirable, but it overlooks the fact that it is the word 'cause' which leads directly into that error of oversimplification. People and their actions are brought into being by an immensely large *network of constraints*, only a few of which are direct and immediate causes (often referred to as proximate causes). Why that distinction is so important in the study of religions and in understanding why religions matter will become clear in the next chapter.

Back then, in 1959, the point about multiple constraints was already being argued indirectly by Barbara Wootton[2] who claimed that

> few generalisations if any can be made with confidence about those whose behaviour is socially unacceptable, and that not many are applicable even to any one of these. For the popular theories about the delinquency of latchkey children, about social failure repeating itself generation after generation, about the beneficial effects of boys' clubs, of the disastrous consequences of illegitimacy – for these and similar generalisations we have, as yet at any rate, little solid factual evidence.

She even went so far as to conclude: "It seems, therefore, time that we recognised that delinquency or criminality … is not a rational field of discourse. It takes all sorts to make the criminal world." To which we might add that it takes far too many constraints to talk about social determinism.

As a result, she came to the conclusion that what matters most is the attempt we all have to make, as we grow up, to acquire responsibility for ourselves and for our own actions. She was once reported as saying, "We would do better to encourage children from the earliest possible age, however wretched their backgrounds, to believe that they are, or at least soon will be, masters of their fate."[3] That encouragement is futile if there are no opportunities to become master or mistress of anything.[4]

In the event, 'social determinism' did not have much mileage in it, even though it had some influence on planning and political decisions. But there are other forms of inevitability. The one that came to dominate discussion in the second half of the twentieth century was the extent to which genes determine human behaviour. That issue then became crucial, as well as fiercely contested, in debates about the causes and purposes of religious beliefs and behaviours.

Genetic determinism, putting it in its briefest form, is the view that genes build and control organisms in order to replicate themselves (i.e., their information) into another generation. Natural selection weeds out the least able to survive, but genes drive the process and thus determine the outcomes.

According to this widely held opinion, human life and culture are what they are because of the way genes build humans, who in turn develop cultures, including religions, as protective systems in order to enhance their prospects of replicating themselves into another generation. That is why it became fashionable to speak of 'the selfish gene', the title Richard Dawkins gave to his book published in 1976. Of the genes as replicators he wrote (1976, p.21):

> Was there to be any end to the gradual improvement in the techniques and artifices used by the replicators to ensure their own continuance in the world? There would be plenty of time for improvement. What weird engines of self-preservation would the millennia bring forth? Four thousand million years on, what was to be the fate of the ancient replicators? They did not die out, for they are past masters of the survival arts. But do not look for them floating loose in the sea; they gave up that cavalier freedom long ago. Now they swarm in huge colonies, safe inside gigantic lumbering robots, sealed off from the outside world, communicating with it by tortuous indirect routes, manipulating it by remote control. They are in you and in me; they created us, body and mind; and their preservation is the ultimate rationale for our existence. They have come a long way, those replicators. Now they go by the name of genes, and we are their survival machines.

In a new edition of the book in 1989, Dawkins realised that the word 'robots' implied that genes create and control bodies in a mechanistic way to be the instrument of their survival into another generation. Clearly that is wrong. He therefore insisted in the new edition (p.271) that he had used the word 'created', not 'controlled', although he actually used both; and he was still writing in 1996 of "DNA building its robot vehicles to ride around in" (2008, p.270).

Even then, the introduction of the word 'selfish', while good for publicity, made the fundamental mistake of attributing purpose and intention to the gene. By doing so, as Donald Campbell pointed out at the time (1991, p.109), "he confused the unit of retention (the gene) with the unit of selection, and it is only the units of selection to which should be attributed purposes, including selfishness." The genes retain the genetic code, but they are carried in the bodies that the genes and proteins have initiated. Thus some Denisovian and Neanderthal units of retention (i.e., genes) have continued through interbreeding into modern humans, but the units of selection (Denisovian and Neanderthal individuals) have not survived. It is bodies that have to survive long enough for the genetic information to be replicated. Through the process of natural selection, that either does or does not happen. If one wanted to use the word 'selfish', it would have to be used, not of the units of retention, but of the units of selection – those bodies, in other words, that seek, perhaps even selfishly, to survive.

However, by using the word 'selfish' of the gene, Dawkins has attributed to it agency, evaluation and purpose, the latter two of which require some degree of consciousness. But as Calow pointed out long ago (1976, p.120), the genes and the transmission of DNA replication are not so interesting: "The message passing along the communication channels established by the self-replicating systems (from one template to another) was, and still is, basically very dull and very simple – being just 'transmit me.'"

Dawkins, nevertheless, used a word that implied purpose and determination. He claimed that he was not arguing for genetic determinism in a strong sense, but he was clearly arguing for genetic determinism in *some* sense, since genes pursuing their own selfish interest create bodies, and bodies create cultures as defensive 'skins' inside which the genes sit until they can replicate their information into another generation. Genes determine the outcomes which are rewarded by survival in natural selection.

That argument became explicit when Dawkins put forward the view that cultural items are also replicated in units known as 'memes'. On the analogy of genes being replicated from one life to another, and on the further analogy of the infective power of a virus being transmitted from one life to another, he argued that memes are sifted by natural selection so that those which no longer have a survival value go (or should go) to extinction. Among those now dysfunctional memes are, in his view, religious beliefs and God.

The idea of memes has entered into popular language, although it is in fact completely absurd and wrong. It is wrong because there is no analogy at all between the ways in which genes and cultural items are transmitted, nor is there any analogy between a virus and what Dawkins calls "the idea of God" as the god meme. Dawkins, to be charitable, is not a philosopher, and he therefore seems to think that analogy and analogical argument come down to saying that one thing has some sort of resemblance to another. On the basis of his understanding and use of analogy it would be possible to say that the Queen is a bumblebee on the grounds that both are heavy in flight. There are, however, *disanalogies* (never thought about by Dawkins) on the basis of which one can see that there are disjunctive differences between the Queen in an Airbus and a bumblebee on a rose.

SELFISH GENE OR SELFLESS GENE?

Talk of 'the selfish gene' has had disastrous consequences in society and in the human imagination of itself. 'Careless talk costs lives', as we were constantly reminded in the Second World War, and 'the selfish gene' is dangerously careless talk. Just as the phrase 'survival of the fittest' led some (not least the Nazis) to conclude that only the fittest deserve to survive, so 'the selfish gene' has led some to conclude that selfish behaviours are natural. It has long been argued, for example, that the worlds of business and banking have to operate in a Darwinian struggle for survival in which stronger and more ruthless firms survive and weaker ones go to extinction. When Niall Ferguson gave his Reith Lectures in 2012, he called his second lecture 'The Darwinian Economy' (Ferguson, p.3):

> There are indeed more than merely superficial resemblances between a financial market and the natural world as Darwin came to understand it. Like the wild animals of the Serengeti, individuals and firms are in a constant struggle for existence, a contest over finite resources. Natural selection operates, in that any innovation – or mutation, in Nature's terms – will flourish or will die depending on how well it suits its environment.

Although that facile analogy is completely wrong (as, for example, the work of Van Vugt and others has shown: see, e.g., Johnson, D.D.P.), it has been widely influential. By equating Adam Smith's 'invisible hand' (self-interest leads to public benefits) with the Darwinian process, it led to a widespread assumption that selfish behaviours can be pursued because they have genetic endorsement: they are, in other words, 'a natural behaviour' and therefore not to be condemned. One banker, for example, caught up in the Libor scandal, said in a brief interview, "Blame the selfish gene: it makes us behave like that."

In that context, any idea that people should acquire responsibility for themselves and for their society will be regarded as a soft-centred and woolly-minded contradiction of what the selfish gene needs for its survival.

'The selfish gene' has now become a background assumption in popular thinking and in media accounts of evolution. It is, however, grievously mistaken and its consequences are destructive. Survival is not the achievement of a selfish gene, nor is it a result of Nature selecting a 1st XI of survivors. Far from being a consequence of selfish purpose, natural selection is a record or an exhibition of the consequences of gene replication either in success or failure in terms of survival.

From that point of view (the point of view of survival), it would be wiser to drop the word 'selfish' and to speak of 'the rewarded gene' – if one regards survival as a reward. Even that, however, carries its own metaphorical luggage with it, so perhaps the simplest correction would be to speak, not of 'the selfish gene', but rather of 'the selfless gene'. Genes do not have 'a self' that forms plans and purposes in order to ensure survival.

'The selfless gene' is simply an observation of success or failure in replication in the relevant units of selection. The consequences in evolution can then be described and analysed in exactly the same neo-Darwinian way (as a result of mutation, selection and the rest) *except that* we can now move far beyond the false limits imposed by the metaphor of selfishness and can integrate, on a genetic base, the ways in which human individuals, groups and societies have purposefully created the third defensive skin of culture.

That would mean, in effect, an extension of the two levels of selection with which we are familiar. The first is that of the individual organism, but on its own it could not explain why some individuals give up their lives in order to protect others. So the second level is that of group selection in the case of genetically related individuals: kinship-related genes will be replicated if some individuals in the group or family sacrifice their lives to protect others. Kinship altruism of that kind was epitomised in the often-quoted remark of the biologist Haldane: "I'd lay down my life for two brothers or eight cousins" (*New Scientist*, August 8, 1974).

Those kinship groups, however, live, not in isolation, but in wider forms of social association. As Wilson put it (1973, p.631),

> Selection can be said to operate at the group level and deserves to be called group selection, when it affects two or more members of a lineage group as a unit. Just above the level of the individual we can delimit various of these lineage groups: a set of sibs, parents, and their offspring, a close-knit tribe of families related by at least the degree of third cousin, and so on.

What is relatively new in current research is the claim that not only 'close-knit tribes' but other forms of social organisation can form a third level of group selection, a *further* level, known as interpopulation or interdemic selection.

That has been challenged on the grounds that it ignores the unit of retention (the gene) by focusing simply on the different rates at which populations are increased or diminished or even extinguished. That may be interesting in itself, and as such it becomes possible to deploy game theory (provided that the frame problem is ignored) in order to show why altruism can be the best strategy to adopt for the survival of the group. But game theory is only indirectly relevant to evolution unless it can demonstrate the consequence for particular genes that contribute to behaviours that enhance the probability of group survival. In the context of evolution, the altruism of game theory becomes coincidental and perhaps irrelevant to the preservation of the unit of retention (the gene) unless it can be shown that at the level of the unit of selection, there are specific *genetic* contributions to pro-group behaviours on the part of some individuals.

The issue here is *not* that strong groups help individuals to survive, who then as a result have more chances to replicate their genes. That is obviously so, and reference has already been made to the ways in which animals engage in cooperative and altruistic behaviours – even to the extent of the spontaneous altruism that has been observed in apes (see, e.g., Warneken 2009, 2013)

But left like that, gene survival becomes an accidental matter of contingency depending on the history of the group and the strategies it adopts, instead of being a matter of particular selfless genes being rewarded because of their specific contribution to group-supporting individuals in evolutionary history. That is why Dawkins has resisted group selection as a third level of selection, regarding it as a rebranding of kin selection (Dawkins 2013, p.40). Actually, though, it is not. It is a further level of selection in larger populations that protect specific genes leading to group-supporting behaviours in particular individuals.

This means that natural selection operates on more levels than one. This is known as Multi Level Selection (MLS), which integrates the effects of selection at both individual and group levels. MLS seems to be demanded in order to explain some of the major transitions in evolutionary history. An example is the formation of multicellular organisms from groups of cells. Even then the challenge remains to show whether there are *specific genes* that constrain individuals into working for others. The question is exactly as Wilson put it in an interview:

> How well does the group survive vis-à-vis solitary individuals of the same species, and how well does that group produce its own kind? For group selection to happen, all you need is one gene that would cause individuals to come together, and for some of them to be willing to be subordinated and become workers.[5]

It is true that research into the specifically linked and identifiable ways in which group selection can be mapped onto genetics is difficult (the 'one gene' of Wilson), but it has already begun. To give (for reasons of space) only one example, the work of Pearce, Stringer and Dunbar (2013) has looked at brain differences in Neanderthals and AMHs (anatomically modern humans) and asked what implications those differences might have for the fact that one group survived but the other did not.

Earlier studies of the morphological differences between the brains of Neanderthals and AMHs focused on external features and on overall size and shape. This new research explored the distribution and commitment of the interior space in relation to failure in the one case and success (in terms of gene replication) in the other as a consequence over many generations of living and adapting to extremely different circumstances.

The Neanderthals lived in a more northerly ecological setting. They needed, therefore, a larger body size to protect them from the cold, and they also needed eyes that would work best in poor light. In terms of survival, therefore, those genes were rewarded which initiated sufficient structural and neural consequence within the brain to improve those functions – that is, to maintain body size and temperature control, and to maximise sight at low light levels. AMHs, in contrast, remained in Africa in an entirely different ecological setting: it was warmer and the light was better. They faced their own compound of limitations in the savannah, but with smaller bodies and in much better light.

The argument is that in the case of the Neanderthals, those genes (in the process of variation and selection) were rewarded which enhanced the maintenance of greater body mass and better sight in low light levels (i.e., the genes and mutations initiating those consequences were retained into subsequent generations). But AMHs, facing a different compound of limitations with comparably sized brains, were rewarded in terms of gene replication by the use of, so to speak, 'spare space' to increase other brain areas (for example, the parietal lobes), which enabled them to develop social and cooperative behaviours.

There is increasing support for this speculation from research by molecular geneticists on the genomes of extinct humans. Thus, when Pääbo compared DNA in Neanderthals, Denisovans, chimpanzees and modern humans, he found (p.220) that "of the 87 proteins carrying amino-acid changes [in humans], a larger number than expected are expressed in the ventricular zone when neurons of the cerebral cortex are formed during fetal development.... These proteins may thus point to some aspect of cortex development that is unique to modern humans."

The suggestion, therefore, is that gene-based developments in the brain enabled humans to solve a far wider range of ecological and other problems within the compounds of limitation that constrained them. The Neanderthal and Denisovan lines of evolution went to extinction, but the human line was rewarded by its increased individual and social abilities, and thus by the added advantages of group selection. As I put it some years ago (Bowker 1973/1995, p.54).

There were and are many other possibilities of life in the savannah, many other variations on the theme of survival, but the human line represents the rewards offered, not primarily to aggression but to co-operation, not

primarily to territorial imperatives but to territorial exploration. This necessarily is to over-simplify, but it does at least emphasize that the filling-out of
an ecological niche, although it may well be a highly conservative exercise in
which an existing life-way maintains its continuity with only gradual change
as the genetic pool of the better adapted possibilities builds up and becomes
numerically superior (or, if one prefers it, simply survives by having more
opportunities to reproduce itself), the changes in adaptive response can be,
but are not always, dramatic.

That was written forty years ago when genetic research was still in its infancy.
Current research is supplying the warrants for those assertions, as well as for
the recognition of MLS. The differences in neurological organisation that led
to better social organisation in the one case and not in the other are linked
specifically to the genes.

This means that kinship and relatedness are fundamental, but they are not
the only consideration in understanding how genes contribute specifically
to the development of advanced social behaviours of an extremely altruistic
kind. Those behaviours strengthen the group within which they occur, and
it is the strengthening of the group that then gives better protection for the
genes of individual members *including* those group-serving individuals who
carry the relevant genes.

The organisation of groups to protect gene replication and the nurture of
children has taken many different forms, from small (such as families) to
larger (such as tribes and villages) to extremely large (such as nation-states).
Religions are among the earliest of those organised groups of which we have
surviving evidence. It has already been argued that religions are (amongst
much else) a consequence of gene-initiated organisms that have developed
social (and in the human case, uniquely sophisticated) means of protecting
and enhancing the chances among some of its members of gene replication
and the nurture of children.

In the context of religions, signs developed into symbols, routines developed into rituals, sounds developed into language and communication,
words developed into chants and worship, emotions evoked evaluations that
developed into ethics, parental oversight developed into hierarchical authority and control.

Among those and many other developments, one of the truly great
achievements of religion was to extend the extended family. The extended
family made kinship altruism possible (two brothers and eight cousins),
but religions went further. Religions supplied the metaphors and the rituals, the ideas and the imperatives, through which genetic strangers have

been bonded together as members of a single (though metaphorical) family. Eventually many of the major religions came to identify the whole human race as the unit of selection – an *umma* as Muslims speak of it, for example, or the Body of Christ as Christians speak of it in which, according to Paul, we are all members one of another (*Ephesians* 4.25). It is 'the selfless gene', not 'the selfish gene', that has embedded the Golden Rule in all the major religions, albeit in slightly different forms: act towards others as you hope they will act towards you.

By far the most dramatic consequence has been that those groups, in which gene-based cooperative behaviours and organisation flourish, have been rewarded, not just in terms of gene replication and the nurture of children but far more in the vision (and even occasionally in the creation) of compassionate societies.

This means that the *selfless* gene is more rewarded than the *selfish* gene – and the word 'selfless' has actually taken on the additional meaning of a human value. Ironically, if the metaphor of the selfless gene had been adopted from the start, it would have had far more beneficial consequences in the way we imagine how we are and should be related to each other. Think of the difference it would make to society if we were to recognise and reward those many selfless people on whom we all depend. Imagine what society would be like if we put the last before the first and calculated bonuses on that basis.

A final catastrophe created by the aggressive campaign by Dawkins on behalf of the 'selfish gene' is that its obvious errors have distracted attention from the serious work in recent years on the relation between genes and culture. As a result, the many important and often brilliant insights of that work have too rarely been applied to the understanding of religions in general and of gene-culture coevolution in particular.

A further reason why that work was neglected in religious studies arose from the fact that it was associated with 'sociobiology'. Sociobiology is another enterprise which emphasises the genetic control of culture and which therefore offers a reductionist explanation of religion in evolutionary terms. Sociobiology has been thought by its critics to be so limited and controversial in its use of genetics, particularly as it became associated with genetic determinism and 'the selfish gene', that it was hard to take seriously its account of culture and religion. Yet for all its faults, it relied on important research and insights which illuminate the understanding of religion and religions. Is it possible, to adapt an agricultural and religious metaphor, to separate the wheat from the chaff?

GENES, SOCIOBIOLOGY AND RELIGION

From the start, sociobiology was an ambitious programme to establish the biological basis of the social behaviour of animals and humans. Its founder, E.O. Wilson, defined his programme as "the scientific study of the biological basis of all forms of social behaviour in all kinds of organisms, including man." Beyond that, his purpose was "to develop general laws of the evolution and biology of social behaviour, which might then be extended in a disinterested manner to the study of human beings" (Wilson 1978, p.222). In that context, religions are social organisations which have had a value, not because any of their serious claims are true, but because they have helped individuals to survive long enough to replicate their genes into another generation.

In that respect, Wilson and Dawkins regard religions and religious belief in a similar way. Wilson's account of religions is more serious than that of Dawkins, but the early objection remains that sociobiology can only explain religion if it rejects what religion says about itself.

The irony is that there is much in religious belief and history that illustrates and supports some of the basic claims of sociobiology, even though at the same time they draw attention to its limitations. A closer attention to the history of religions might have protected sociobiology from some of its mistakes. Nor is that a trivial point. The past is actually of great importance to sociobiology because it claims to be explaining the past by offering an explanation of the forms that social behaviour has taken. That necessarily includes an understanding of how and why those forms came into being and change through time.

In that case, it is as necessary to pay attention to evidence and data when dealing with the past (for example, in the history of religions) as it is to do so when working on the life cycle of the mosquito. Neither Wilson nor Dawkins do this, although Wilson claims in 'consilience' that everything can be unified in a natural, biologically based explanation.[6] But consilience requires a careful attention to evidence in all the disciplines it seeks to unite, as much in the history of religions as in the history of evolution.

To ask for that same attention to evidence may seem pedantic, but it is far from being so when one remembers how important it is for sociobiology to insist on what Wilson called (1976, p.46), "the psychic unity of mankind." For Wilson, to achieve universal laws of social behaviour linked to genetics, our ancestors must be closely similar to ourselves in the ways in which, under genetic control, they constructed culture, even though the superficial details of all cultures are different. Cultures would then be variations on a stable theme, namely the extent to which cultures defend genetically constructed human nature. Whether that is true about cultures cannot be established without careful examination of evidence from the past of the kind with which historians are familiar.

Wilson attempted to bypass this by proposing 'the thousand year rule'. In contrast to what he called 'the conventional view' (that genetic evolution requires many thousands of years to make a change, and that it has in the human case ceased to be significant since cultural evolution is now virtually the sole agent of change), Wilson argued that a thousand years, or fifty generations, is sufficient for genetic evolution to establish the rules controlling or at the least guiding the construction of culture. As a result, genes and culture work together in co-evolution, with the genes establishing at least some degree of epigenetic bias in virtually every category of cultural behaviour. On the basis of that argument, Wilson claimed that the genes will control culture no matter what form any particular culture may take.

Even if that were so, it would still be important to look at the variations among the examples of cultural and religious co-evolution in great detail in order to know whether, for example, the suggested bias is ever modified or overridden. That cannot be done without a serious attention to the history of religions. The irony here is that there is much in the history of religions which supports some of the basic arguments of sociobiology. The accounts which our ancestors gave of themselves and of their own human nature did not have the benefit of Darwin or Mendel. Their accounts are therefore called 'intuitional anthropologies'. However, those accounts were not wholly intuitional. They were derived from very long-term observations by the human animal of itself and of its environment. They were observations derived from experience.

As a result, even without the benefit of Mendel, major anthropologies, both East and West, concluded that we are affected, not only in appearance, but also in our behaviours, by a heredity transmitted through our parents. In other words, they were able to observe that the consequence of being born from parents went far beyond the shape of the nose or the colour of the eyes. They could observe *that* without difficulty; what they also observed was an evident constraint over behaviour equally derived from ancestry.

The implication of this is not that our ancestors were cryptosociobiologists and that they were saying 'the same thing' as sociobiology, albeit in a different language. That is clearly not so. The reason why there are correlations and points of connection lies much more fundamentally in the fact that there is a common subject matter in human inquiry and reflection – a subject matter which constrains the account that is given of it, however mistaken (from a later point of view) any particular response or description may be.

That common subject matter is the human subject and its universe. There has been no global agreement in the past about the nature of the human subject or about the nature of the universe, as one can see in the immensely different anthropologies and cosmologies in the different religions.[7] The fact that there is a greater consensus in the present about the *latter* (the universe) is simply an illustration that what presents itself evidentially does constrain our account of it: there are instantiating data. Wilson's ambition was to extend the global consensus on the *former*, "on human nature" (to quote the title of one of his books).

What should have encouraged him is precisely the point made earlier, that some major Eastern and Western anthropologies in the past have a close approximation to what is now spoken of as genetic constraint determining cultural outcomes including fundamental religious beliefs and behaviours. To have recognised that would have strengthened Wilson's claim that that he could explain religion 'down to its foundations'.

HEREDITARIAN ANTHROPOLOGIES IN RELIGIOUS TRADITIONS

What then does it mean to say that some major religious traditions recognize that there are constraints, derived from heredity, over the outcomes in social and individual behaviour? It means that religions give accounts of human nature (i.e., religious anthropologies) in which they identify (very differently) the extent to which that nature and its behaviours are already determined, at least to some extent, at or before the moment of birth.

The accounts offered vary greatly, so much so that they were disputed, not just between religions, but also very much within religions. In China, for example, there was a long-running debate about whether humans are innately 'good and evil' – as in the well-known contest between Legalists and Confucianists during the period of the Warring States and the Qin and Han dynasties (475 BCE–220 CE). At that time, as Dien has put it (p.3), "the old order broke down" and "the changes in the social structure were monumental." What had brought about that disorder, and what should be done about it? Had it happened, as the Legalists insisted, because humans are born without any innate sense of good and evil, and need therefore to be strictly controlled by law and sanctions? Or are they born with innate and existing virtues that need simply to be cultivated by education? The outcome at any particular time of the continuing debates in China had immense consequences for the upbringing of children, for education and for the exercise of political authority and control.

The same issue (of the extent to which constraints derived from heredity determine outcomes in social and individual behaviour) is just as fundamental in other religions. We can see at least the outline of this in two brief illustrations, the first in Indian religions, the second in Christianity.

In Indian religions the notion of *karma* or (in Buddhism and in Pali) *kamma* is basic to the understanding of human nature. *Karma* is differently understood in different Indian religions, particularly so among the Jains. However, among Hindus and Buddhists, *karma/kamma*, as a belief, is tied to a corresponding belief that there is either rebirth or continuity (*samsara*) from one form of appearance (e.g., human or animal) to another. *Karma/kamma* asserts that the form or condition of a subsequent appearance and its behaviours is determined at least in part by volitional intentions and/or actions in previous forms of appearance.

What we might call the genetic determinism of that belief is potentially very great because it suggests that some observable behaviours in this life are a result of consequence transmitted through birth. Because of the strong presence of Buddhism in China, the idea of *karma* was used in the debates in China to which reference has just been made. So, for example, Wang Jinmin pointed out how, in the much later debates about the insistence of Wang Yangming (1472–1529) on 'innate knowledge', Yuan Huang (1533–1606) "relied on the belief in karmic retribution that offered something of a compromise between Heaven [Tian] and humankind" (Lou, p.527): on that basis, individuals can, as he put it, "establish their destiny", or, as I have put it earlier, acquire responsibility.

Karma is thus a strong determinant of Indian social life in the sense, to take the most familiar examples, that it reinforces the social system of *varna* (place in society), *jati* (caste) and *ashrama* (the four stages of life).

The 'genetic determination' of individual and social behaviour is thus potentially very strong, and it was indeed made explicit on one occasion by Gandhi, when he was defending the caste system (*Young India*, 29.9.27):

> I believe that just as everyone inherits a particular form so does he inherit the particular characteristics and qualities of his progenitors, and to make this admission is to conserve one's energy. That frank admission if he will act upon it would put a legitimate curb on our ambitions and thereby our energy is set free for extending the field of spiritual research and spiritual evolution. It is the doctrine of *Varnashramadharma* which I have always adopted.

A passage of that kind articulates very clearly the hereditarian component in social determination. But equally it articulates the major issue that sociobiology also has to face: how extensive is the determination?

All religions, including the Indian, address the issue and recognise its paramount importance: to what extent are individuals (and by extension societies) responsible and accountable for their behaviours? If all outcomes are determined, whether by genes or by *karma*, then individuals have no options and cannot be held accountable. On the other hand, is there any way within the boundary of the constraints of genes and *karma* in which they can *acquire* responsibility? – the question raised at the beginning of this chapter and by Wang Jinmin, quoted above.

The Hindu tradition maintains that both sides of the dilemma are correct. Actions are of three kinds, *tamasika, rajasika* and *sattvika. Tamasika* actions are derived from biological necessity; *rajasika* actions are those that come from overruling (*raja*) emotions, as, for example, of rage, hatred or love. People are well aware of these actions, but they are not chosen freely. Indian religions provide the resources and the teaching to gain insight and a degree of control over them, but in themselves they remain unfree.

Sattvika actions, in contrast, are those initiated and undertaken under the constraint of the insight gained. The quest for insight is very much a matter of choice on the part of individuals. In essence, it means that all actions are undertaken with detachment from consequence known as *vairagya* – in other words, things are not done for the sake of some lesser goal, but for the sake of ultimate freedom. The attainment of this detachment is thus believed to undo the consequences of *karma*.

How this works out can be seen quintessentially in *Bhagavadgita*, a text revered by virtually all Hindus, in which *karma* does not have total determination. In addition to the considerations above, it modifies *karma* even further by recognising the help offered by God through *prasada*, unearned generosity, often translated as 'grace'[8].

In general, therefore, Indian religions clearly emphasise that human beings are constituted in such a way that they have the capacity to initiate good or evil actions, even though there are constraints over the present derived from the past. The comparison is often made with the flow of a river through the many channels of a delta to the sea: humans are carried by the flow of *karma*, but some at least have the capacity and the desire to direct their course within the flow into different channels so that they are not simply 'carried along'. This 'capacity' and the ability to undertake it, so fundamental to the whole of Indian religious life and thought, is known technically as *adhikara*: humans are so diverse that not all are willing to undertake this, but for those who can

and do aspire to achieve the goal (known as *sadhakas*), there are many different means and methods open to them, known collectively as *sadhanas*.[9]

But what is the distribution of balance between *karma* and *adhikara*? At
one extreme Radhakrishnan spiritualized the hereditarian determinism into
nonexistence (1948, pp.160–1). But at the other extreme there were certainly
some who drew more deterministic conclusions from the basic data:

> Just as a ball of wool, when thrown on the ground, unwinds itself until it
> comes to an end, so the wise and the foolish travel on equally in *samsara*
> [rebirth] until eventually they reach salvation. (*Samannaphata Sutta* 20–22)

So argued Makkhali, a contemporary of the Buddha, who is known also as
Gosala because, according to the Jains, he was born in a cowshed. His metaphor of a ball rolling down a hillside with a limited, but not wholly determined, range of trajectories is exactly that of Wilson (1978, pp.60–1), which
the biologist C.H.Waddington also uses:

> The developmental topography of human behaviour is enormously
> broader and more complicated [than that of the mosquito], but it is still a
> topography.

In 'The Basic Ideas of Biology' (Waddington, 1968, pp.42–54), Waddington
argued that goal-directed and goal-seeking behaviour is fundamental in
understanding biology and evolution. That was strongly resisted at the time
(and is still resisted by Dawkins) because it seems to imply that such behaviour
is teleological, and that in turn seems to carry with it the biologically impossible Aristotelian associations. For that reason, it is wiser and in fact more
accurate to use the word 'teleonomy' to describe the goal-seeking behaviours
that are common in evolutionary history.[10] Waddington himself preferred to
use the words 'chreod' and 'trajectory', a chreod being "a canalized trajectory
which acts as an attractor for nearby trajectories" – or in other words, it is "the
most general description of the kind of biological process which has been
referred to as 'goal-directed'". It is a good description of Karma understood
in the Indian way.

Makkhali's views were rejected by the Buddha, along with many other
Indian beliefs and practices, including the caste system. But the Buddha did
not refute *karma/kamma*; indeed, he affirmed it, even though he did not
believe that there is a self or soul being reborn.

Once again the determination derived from inheritance is fundamental. The
Buddha's understanding of this can be seen clearly in *Culakammavibhanga
Sutta* (*Majjhima Nikaya* 135). The Buddha was asked why some humans have
short lives and others long, some are sick while others healthy, some are ugly

while others are good-looking, some are humble and poor while others are noble and wealthy, some are stupid while others are wise. To the question why there is this inequality [*hinapanitata*] among human beings the Buddha replied: "Beings are the owners of their *kamma*, they inherit their *kamma*, their *kamma* is closer than their closest relative, their *kamma* is the place where they belong. It is *kamma* that divides beings in terms of their inequalities." The Sutta then analyses particular examples.

It is clear, therefore, that humans are controlled from the past into present outcomes in their behaviour and even appearance. But on the other hand, *kamma* is not wholly deterministic of *all* behaviours and appearances, and *kamma* certainly is not identical with heredity in general, although the two may of course coincide. It is more accurate to say that humans are constrained into their outcome by a very complicated network of constraints that include *kamma*. Consequently it would be as unintelligent to write a book entitled 'the selfish *kamma*' as it is to write a book entitled 'the selfish gene'.

There is in Buddhism an extensive analysis of the many different components of that network of constraint. One such analysis has been discussed earlier. Another, to take only one example, occurs in *Digha Nikaya*. *DN* 3.1.211 states succinctly, "All beings persist through causes, All beings persist through constraints." *DN* 3.1.228 elaborates this aphorism by listing the different constraints and causes as sustenance, interactions, purpose and awareness (of the conditions of reappearance). The network of constraints is thus extended widely.

This means that human beings are constrained into their outcome by heredity *(bijaniyama)* but also by much else. But this network of constraint does not obliterate freedom and responsibility: *it enables it*, and it is thus a sharp example of Stravinsky's claim (in Chapter 6) that constraint is the necessary condition of freedom. It follows that all individuals retain their responsibility and initiative to make what they can, preferably for good, of their state of being as it has come to be in the process of time. They acquire responsibility for the direction of travel towards an ultimate destination. The process itself flows on through other forms of reappearance, although of course there is no self or substance being reborn and going from one existence to another.

The Indian understanding of *karma/kamma* is one example of religions recognising constraint over outcomes being inherited from the past. A second example can be seen in the West, in the Christian understanding of 'original sin', at least in its traducianist forms. Traducianism is the belief that individuals receive their souls from their parents, thus making possible the belief that the original sin of Adam and Eve has been transmitted through birth to all human beings, so that, as Paul put it, "all have sinned and come short of the glory of God" (Romans 3.23). That understanding of the nature of sin is strong in its genealogical and hereditarian emphasis. If it were not so, the Virgin Birth would have nothing like the same significance in later Christianity, since that doctrine carries with it the implication that the birth of Jesus was not held in the same unbroken chain.

Original sin, however, is not aboriginal to Christianity. It is not in the New Testament, and it is virtually impossible to find it in the Apostolic Fathers or in the Apologists of the early centuries. They recognised that sin, however defined, is universal, as did many non-Christians: "Vitia erunt donec homines", as Tacitus put it reflecting on much more than the early Roman emperors (*Histories* 4.74, 'There will be vices as long as there are people'). But universality is not in itself a theory of transmission. What *is* aboriginal in Christianity is the Pauline symmetry between the first Adam in whom death entered the world and the second Adam by whom life is restored, "for as through the disobedience of the one man the many were made sinners, so through the obedience of the one man the many will be made righteous" (Romans 5.19). Paul undoubtedly believed that humans are unable to rescue or exempt themselves from all fault and are therefore in need of rescue or redemption: "The good that I would I do not do; and the evil that I would not, that I do.... Wretched man that I am! Who will rescue me from this body of death?" (Romans 7.19, 24).

But Paul certainly did not articulate what later became the classical doctrine of original sin. The first hints of that appear in Irenaeus (130–c.200), who believed, on the basis of Hebrews 7.9–10, that as Levi was in his ancestor's loins when Melchizedek met him, so all people are seminally connected with Adam and are both the agents and the victims of his transgression. Tertullian (c.160–c.225) then made explicit the traducianist theory, that the whole person, body and soul, is derived from the parents, as opposed to creationism (which holds that the soul is created with and for each new life by God), or to pre-existence, whereby, as Origen maintained, souls are embodied as a punishment intermediate between being a devil and an angel.

Tertullian's view (*De Testimonio Animae* 3) that Adam "infected the whole race by his seed, making it the channel [*traducem*] of damnation" was held also by Cyprian (d.258) who believed, appealing to Psalm 51.5, that the wounds, *vulnera*, of the original sin are transmitted seminally. This means that however much we are constrained in our environment to fault – that is, as Tertullian would have put it, however much we are tempted by the devil – "the evil that exists in the soul ... is antecedent, being derived from the fault of our origin [*ex originis vitio*] and having become in a way natural to us" (*De Anima* 39.41).

But the full expression of this view is associated with Augustine, for whom the whole human race is *massa damnata*. Since we are constrained into this circumstance by the fact of birth, it is clear that here again the hereditarian determination of behaviour is extremely strong – particularly since Augustine distinguished the guilt or *reatus* of original sin, which baptism can remove, and its *actus,* its actualization, which continues and which baptism cannot remove. The genetic determination is indeed so strong that it constrains outcomes even after death in the sense that unbaptized children go to eternal fire with the devil, although they will not suffer so much as adults who have added offences to the guilt.

Not surprisingly, therefore, Augustine appealed to the practice of infant baptism as justifying his view that the inherited fault must be dealt with. Historically, however, Augustine may have got this the wrong way round. Tertullian himself had argued (*De Baptismo* 18.4) that "deferment of baptism is more profitable, in accordance with each person's character and attitude and even age – and especially so as regards children." It is in fact much more probable, as Ferguson concluded on the basis of an analysis of early Christian funerary inscriptions, that "the universal understanding of baptism as for the remission of sins gave impetus to the doctrine of original sin which then in turn became the theological basis for infant baptism" (Ferguson, E., p.45).

But even without that consideration, the extreme emphasis of Augustine was disputed, not only by the so-called semi-Pelagians but even more by the failure of Augustine's ideas in this respect to make any serious impact in the Eastern Church. On the earlier Greek fathers, Kelly observed (p.349):

> The Greek fathers, with their insistence that man's free will remains intact and is the root of actual sinning, have a much more optimistic outlook than the West. It is easy to collect passages from their works which, at any rate in the light of later Orthodoxy, appear to rule out any doctrine of original sin. Both the Gregories, for example, as well as Chrysostom, teach that newly born children are exempt from sin.

The issue and the disagreement remain the same: no one can doubt that at least a measure of consequence is genetically (or, as they would have put it, "seminally") derived; but how consequential is the measure, and how measurable is the consequence? At one extreme in Christian history there is, associated with John Calvin, the strong hereditary determinism (though the actual determinism comes from the purpose of God in dealing with the inherited fault) which is summarized in a catechism, "Certaine Questions and Answeres," bound into the Breeches Bible of 1615:

Question: Why doe men so much vary in matters of religion?

Answere.   Because all have not the like measure of knowledge, neither do all beleeve the Gospel of Christ.

Q.   What is the reason thereof?

A.   Because they onely beleeve the Gospel and doctrine of Christ, which are ordeined unto eternall life.

Q.   Are not all ordeined unto eternall life?

A.   Some are vessels of wrath ordeined unto destruction, as others are vessels of mercy prepared to glory.

Q.   How standeth it with God's justice, that some are appointed unto condemnation?

A.   Very well: because all men have in themselves sinne, which deserveth no lesse ...

At the other extreme is the emphasis, relying on 1 Timothy 2:4, that God wills all people to be saved ("omnes omnino, ut nullus habeatur exceptus," as one of Augustine's opponents put it to him), and that the will of humans may be flawed as a consequence of being conceived and born, but it is not fatally corrupt.

From this follows the view that human behaviour is indeed channelled from the past and from its seminal inheritance, but that it is not fatalistically determined or worthless in its achievements. This is the view particularly associated with Thomas Aquinas, which (as a short-hand and for ease of reference *only*) will be called Thomist, as opposed to Calvinist in emphasis.[11]

CALVINIST AND THOMIST SOCIOBIOLOGY

There is much in the history of religions that supports the argument that successful cultures, above all religions, are effective and well-winnowed units of group selection that protect the survival of genetic information. At the individual level, our ancestors recognised (without the benefit of genetics) that non-negotiable constraints over behaviour are inherited. They did not agree on the extent to which that inheritance is deterministic. In sociobiology we find the same uneasy shifting between a Calvinist and a Thomist emphasis. Dawkins is a clear Calvinist, with his picture of genes constructing "lumbering robots" to ensure their own survival. David Barash (see discussion that follows) is clearly Thomist, and Wilson oscillates between the two.

To put the matter of the extent of genetic determinism in this form may well seem to trivialize it, but it is in truth the most fundamental issue confronting sociobiology and related theories of genetic determinism. It is as much a challenge for those theories as it has been for religions to decide how much of any particular behaviour the genes are supposed to be determining. No one, presumably, doubts that the genes contribute to the construction of what Wilson called the basic capacity to behave, or that they determine explicitly a range of particular outcomes in the human case of which *On Human Nature* gives examples (on 'capacity' see, e.g., pp.2, 33, 56, 58–59, 187).

But do they determine, with the same explicitness, all outcomes? Or is it the case that the human brain (itself constructed from the genes and proteins) is able to organize its own and its body's activity in ways which are not, in all cases, a direct expression of a genetic programme? On how long or short a genetic leash, to ask the decisive question, are cultural innovation and independence held? The difference between short and long leash theories of gene-culture co-evolution (explained in *Is God a Virus?*, ch. 8) means in effect that the longer the leash becomes, the less control the genes exercise. As Stephen Gould put it, "If genes only specify that we are large enough to live in a world of gravitational forces, need to rest our bodies by sleeping, and do not photosynthesize, then the realm of genetic determinism will be relatively uninspiring" (in Caplan, p.345).

Sociobiologists recognize as clearly as anybody else that this is the basic issue. When Wilson observed that "the evidence that human nature is to some extent genetically influenced is in my opinion decisive," one can only reply, 'so it is in virtually everybody else's opinion.' But what do 'to some extent' and 'influenced' actually mean? To continue with Wilson's own words, "The question of interest is no longer whether human social behaviour is genetically determined: it is to what extent" (Wilson 1978, p.19). But so far attempts to answer that question and to "determine the determinism" are mostly vague and rhetorical.

Take Barash's *Sociobiology and Behavior* as an example. Barash is clearly not a Calvinist – he is not a strong genetic determinist. So if the genes do not determine outcomes in social behaviour, what do they do? They provide "blueprints, codes for a range of potential phenotypes"; they supply the *"capacity"* (Barash's italics) to perform "social learning and the passage of traditions"; they create *"susceptibility* to various experiences" and genetic *"tendencies"* as opposed to genetic determinism (pp.41, 286, 125, 287, 226, 284). "Some correlation always exists between genes and behaviour, even human behaviour," but "it may be diffuse and therefore almost entirely dependent upon environmental influences, as in the case of personality" (p.286). So it is likened to "the difference between shooting a bullet at a target and throwing a paper airplane; the paper airplane is acutely sensitive to environmental influences such as wind, and its ultimate path is not entirely predictable by the thrower" (p.287). And finally, applying "a sociobiological approach to human altruism," Barash wrote (p.308):

> Once again, this is not to deny a role for learning or social tradition in medi-ating such behavior; factors of this sort are entirely compatible with under-lying genetically influenced tendencies as well. The value of sociobiology's evolutionary approach is that it allows predictions of possible behavioral universals or at least a common substructure rooted in our biology.

But so what? Barash accepted that human altruism is a more extensive, and therefore a different, behaviour from what is described as altruism in animals or insects, although it includes that behaviour.[12] "Of course," he wrote (p.311), "human altruism is not reserved exclusively for relatives." What then is the exact relevance of sociobiology to the understanding of what human behaviour has become in its cultural extension? Of course it is relevant to our understanding of how the genes (and proteins) contribute to the construction of what Dawkins calls their survival machine; but that is not nearly enough to justify the claim that sociobiology is the new synthesis of behavioural science, or the claim of Trivers: "Sooner or later, political science, law, economics, psychology, psych-iatry, and anthropology will all be branches of sociobiology" (Gould, p.533).

In contrast, Barash, who has rightly seen and avoided the trap of even a restricted genetic determinism, has very much reduced the claim (p.6):

> It may be that social psychology, sociology, and anthropology will also move increasingly toward sociobiology. If so, these disciplines will bring much light with them, and it will be appreciated.

But the only way in which that could happen would be if much greater pre-cision could be established in evaluating the balance between genetic deter-mination and cultural constraint; and that still seems a very distant goal. Indeed, in view of the highly complex interactions involved in gene-culture co-evolution, it may be that the goal is literally unrealizable because human behaviour is much more enabled than determined by the genes.

Sociobiologists, it is true, are inclined to reply that *in principle*, if not yet in practice, they can specify the genetic role. It is worth bearing in mind, therefore, the response of Longuet-Higgins's biologist, in his dialogue con-tributed to the IUBS symposium *Towards a Theoretical Biology* (Waddington, III, 1970):

> Physicist: Surely if we knew all the structures of all the molecules in a cell, we could in principle work out everything about the cell from quantum-statistical-mechanics?

Biologist: Well, for a start, you know as well as I do that when someone says something is possible 'in principle' he really means that it is impossible in practice.

'In practice', Longuet-Higgins argued (p.237), the calculation is impossible because the quantum mechanical calculation on one particular bacterial cell would be incorrect for every other cell, even of the same species.

To make this point is not to hide in a gap of temporary ignorance, which will be closed one day, but to emphasize that the imprecision is inherent as a consequence of *Homo sapiens* being the sort of animal that it is. Thus Barash came to a grand but nevertheless vague conclusion (p.41):

Another way of viewing the interaction of genetics and environment in producing behavior is to recognize that behavior is not contained somehow *within* a gene, waiting to leap out like Athena, fully armored, from the head of Zeus. Rather, genes are blueprints, codes for a range of potential phenotypes. In some cases the specification may be very precise, leaving little room for modification due to learning or other experiences. In others, the blueprint may be so general as to be almost entirely at the disposal of experience. Nonetheless, some restrictions remain: an armadillo can behave only like an armadillo and a zebra must behave like a zebra.

That is unquestionably important. But what does it actually mean to extend the sequence and say that a human must behave like a human? Mascall put the point sharply in *The Importance of Being Human* (p.33):

Living like a gorilla is a very good thing to do if you are a gorilla, and living like an angel is a very good thing to do if you are an angel. And neither of these tasks is very difficult for the being in question. If, however, you are a human being you can achieve true happiness only by living as a human being, and that is a much more difficult task ... It is to be a dweller in both the great realms of creation, the realm of matter and the realm of spirit ... He must be ready to live, not as a disembodied spirit, but as the kind of being ... that he actually is, in a right relationship to God, to his fellow men, and to the material earth which is the basis of his physical life.

The inevitable problem is that sociobiologists like Barash, Wilson and Dawkins cannot engage in conversation with Mascall (or those who argue like him) because for them all talk of "realms of spirit," as opposed to "the psychic unity of mankind," is a kind of outdated rubbish. That presumably is what Wilson meant when he said that we should not look for truth through the prisms of our mythologies: "To understand ... evolutionary history and the contemporary biogram that it produced is to understand in a deeper manner the construction of human nature, to learn what we really are and not just what we hope we are, as viewed through the various prisms of our mythologies."

And yet, to return to the point already made, our ancestors who produced those mythologies necessarily belong to the psychic unity of humanity to which Wilson appealed. In addition, there were among them those who made searching philosophical analyses of the words and ideas through which they reflected on the meaning of their mythologies. The languages of their mythologies and reflections were clearly approximate, provisional, corrigible and often wrong from a later point of view, but they were nevertheless wrong about something (the point already emphasised earlier in the book). Their reflections may often have been expressed in the form of mythologies, but that does not mean they are worthless.

Where the present issues are concerned, they too (or at least some of them) were engaged in issues of mechanism and determination. They concluded with as much realism as a sociobiologist that we do not start life as a completely blank sheet of paper. Yet at the same time they explored with equal realism the possibilities, including the spiritual possibilities, which are enabled in the human form of appearance. They paid far more sensitive attention to human experience (to the widely different experiences of what it actually means to be a human) than is either attempted or reflected in sociobiology of the kind represented by Wilson and Dawkins.

We, in turn, have inherited the results of those explorations and experiences, and we have an even greater opportunity to integrate in our understanding of ourselves and the universe the ways in which constraints are the condition of freedom. As a result, we can now see the way to a far more realistic and hopeful account of human possibility. We are able to return to our humanity a recognition of constraints, not simply as the barrier that they are, but also as opportunity.

Of course it remains the case that constraints may be intransigent and that as a result, the opportunities do not exist or are destroyed. The word 'evil' describes much that happens both within and outside one's self. To recognise and come to terms with that undoubtedly requires considerable cognitive discernment and insight, and it may in some instances require and be helped by cognitive therapy. It may also be helped by the resources in religions (expressed obviously in very different ways) that support discernment and deal with fault and even defeat. It is not easy. Nevertheless, this understanding of the way in which constraints (particularly when recognised) can lead to greater freedom creates the serious possibility of acquiring responsibility for our own selves.

That possibility is itself always constrained in many ways, from inherit-ance at birth to the circumstances (including the cosmos) in which we live. But what we now see with great clarity is that constraints do not reduce us to impotence; still less do they give any warrant for the aggressive reductionism of the last century that still lingers on. At last we see that constraints are the condition of greater freedom, not its contradiction. How that works out and what it means we will see in the next chapter.

6

Religions and sciences

IV Causes and constraints

*T*HE DEBATE ABOUT DETERMINISM AND CAPACITY IN HUMAN behaviour is extremely ancient, and we have looked briefly at some examples of different ways around the world in which the debate was conducted. Genetic determinism introduces its own arguments, but Wilson was well aware that the debate is not a new one. Introducing Caplan's *The Sociobiology Debate*, Wilson wrote (p.xi):

> Caplan has correctly identified the debate as the continuance of the historic conflict created in the social sciences and humanities by the mechanistic examination of human nature through the instruments of conventional biology.

But in that case it would be both wise and illuminating to understand what that debate was, and why and how the mechanistic ambition derived from Newton's laws failed. For it is the failure of 'the mechanistic ambition' that has opened the way to a new understanding of the balance that has to be found between causes and constraints.

There is obviously no space to review the whole, or even a small part, of that debate. But we can at least glimpse what was fundamentally at issue by taking a particular metaphor that once gave focus to the debate.

That may seem at first sight a rather strange way to proceed, but there is a reason for it. Issues of determinism and freedom can rarely be *directly* observed: the relevant arguments have to be inferred, and often therefore they are conducted in terms of comparison so that the unfamiliar can be made more intelligible through the comparison.

That is why metaphor, simile and analogy occur so frequently in religious discourse. But they occur also in scientific discourse, particularly in attempts to 'popularise' science. Think how many were used, at the end of the last chapter alone, by sociobiologists: lumbering robots, held on a leash, shooting bullets and throwing paper airplanes, Athena springing from the head of Zeus, blank sheet of paper. The question, therefore, is fundamental: how do metaphors work in relation to what they purport to be about? To take the particular example advanced by Dawkins and considered briefly in the previous chapter, the notion of 'memes' is offered as an analogy, but when he and his followers ignore the disanalogies, the sleight of hand becomes an affront to human reason.

If, then, we are to engage in what Wilson called (p.133) "the continuance of the historic conflict", we need to look with great care and in detail at the metaphors and analogies that people use and have used in the past, in order to be clear how much weight they will bear. When Wilson proposed consilience (p.315) as a way to insight and understanding (and consilience is clearly essential for the study of religions), he observed that it involves, not just what he called 'facts', but also 'fact-based theory'. In other words, it involves *method*, and that is why it is important to look, not just at what Dawkins and Wilson argue, but also at *how* they argue – in this case, by the use of analogy and metaphor.

Returning, therefore, to "the historic conflict" that arose from the ambition to extend Newtonian mechanism to human nature and behaviour, we will look at the way in which a powerful metaphor was frequently employed to focus the central issue in the eighteenth and nineteenth centuries in the debate derived from Wilson's 'Newtonian mechanism'. The issue was the extent to which humans can be understood as machines. The metaphor was taken from a musical device known as 'the Aeolian harp'. Through that example we can see the strength of a metaphor in focusing an issue, but we can see also the paramount importance of recognising the disanalogies as well. The implications of this will lead us in the second half of this chapter to consider more carefully the importance of constraint in relation to cause when trying to understand human behaviour in general and religions in particular.

THE AEOLIAN HARP

The Aeolian harp is so called because Aeolus was the Greek god of the wind. The Aeolian harp is an instrument played without human hand. It is played, in other words, by the wind when the harp is hung in a window. The strings are tuned to the same note, but the strings are of a different thickness and therefore vibrate differently when the wind blows obliquely over them. William Jones described its sound in 1781 (W. Stevens, pp.70ff):

> If we consider the quality of its harmony, it very much resembles that of a
> chorus of voices at a distance; with all the expressions of the *forte,* the *piano,*

and the *swell*; in a word, its harmony is more like to what we might imagine the aerial sounds of magic and enchantment to be, than to artificial music – we may call it, without a metaphor, the music of inspiration.

It is the music also of sorcery since it is played by no visible human hand; and according to tradition, that is why Saint Dunstan was thrown into a cesspit. Despite the suspicion in which it was held, the harp reappears in respectable circles at least by 1650, when the astonishingly prolific Athanasius Kircher designed a mechanised and automated version, a water-driven *aeolia camera*. To judge from the illustrations in his work, *Misurgia Universalis* (II, p.311), it worked either with a water wheel driving a variable shaft which would then, by means of pistons, pump bellows up and down in order to drive wind through the harp, or by compressing air by the raising of the level of water in airtight containers.

By 1784, the more ordinary Aeolian harp was so well known that Matthew Young could state (p.170):

> This pleasing instrument, which has been reputed by some to be a modern discovery, was in truth the invention of Kircher ... It is an instrument so universally known, that it may well be presumed unnecessary to give any account either of its construction, or the manner of using it.

Actually, though, there were some ways of using the Aeolian harp of which Young, as a bishop, would surely have disapproved. Ferdinand Count Fathom, in Tobias Smollett's novel of that name (1753), used "the stream of melody" from an Aeolian harp, "more ravishingly delightful than the song of Philomel, the warbling brook, and all the concert of the wood," in order to seduce Celinda in a forest hut. Not surprisingly, perhaps, Curt Sachs commented (p.402):

> The supernatural, ghostly sound of these chords, changing, increasing and fading away with the wind, without any player or any artificial contrivance, was wholly romantic. Between 1780 and 1860, therefore, Aeolian harps were much in favour in parks, on roofs and on ruins of medieval castles, especially in Germany and England.

But the harp was not hanging simply on the roofs of romantic castles; it was hanging very firmly in the romantic imagination. From the very start of the romantic protests against materialism, against Isaac Newton's sleep,[1] the Aeolian harp became a focus for the divisive issue of whether a mechanistic account does tell us "what human beings really are" or whether that description of the human machine and its construction leaves us far short of what constitutes the human case.

Exactly then as now, there was no shortage of those who, like Wilson, derided "the prisms of our mythologies." The most explicit was Thomas Love Peacock, who laid into what he regarded as the extravagances of English and German romanticism with an invective hardly matched even in the socio-biology debate. Peacock knew nothing about genes, of course, but what was at stake was the same then as now, the extent to which human behaviour is controlled or constrained into its outcome by the way in which the human machine is constructed.

Peacock attacked what he called "the degenerate fry of modern rhyme-sters" because in his view they were not sufficiently aware that only modern science can tell us what the meaning and value of life really are. Their fault, in other words, lay in their adherence to poetry "as if it were still what it was in the Homeric age, the all-in-all of intellectual progression, and as if there were no such things in existence as mathematicians, astronomers, chemists, moralists, metaphysicians, historians, politicians, and political economists" (p.20). The result, according to Peacock, had been a divorce between poetry and life.

The people most responsible for bringing about the divorce, in Peacock's view, were the Lake Poets. It is true that Wordsworth in *Lyrical Ballads* made a deliberate attempt to return to the language and passions of the people. In his own words ('Preface to the Lyrical Ballads'), " I have chosen subjects from common life, and endeavoured to bring my language near to the real language of men." The results, however, would scarcely have met Peacock's criticisms and in some instances cannot possibly count as successful poetry: consider the first versions of 'Simon Lee' and 'The Thorn'.

The way in which the Lake Poets had in Peacock's view created a divorce between the poetic imagination and the scientific explorations of nature, including human nature, anticipates an early version of the famous 'two cultures', to which Wilson also referred with an ambition similar to that of Peacock (Wilson 1978, pp.ix–x):

> I became more persuaded than ever [after the publication of *Sociobiology*] that the time has at last arrived to close the famous gap between the two cultures, and that general sociobiology, which is simply the extension of population biology and evolutionary theory to social organization, is the appropriate instrument for the effort.

Peacock wrote (pp.15f) with a comparably prosaic literal-mindedness, and with a venom comparable to that of Dawkins:

> We know that there are no Dryads in Hyde-park nor Naiads in the Regent's canal ... While the historian and the philosopher are advancing

in, and accelerating, the progress of knowledge, the poet is wallowing in the rubbish of departed ignorance, and raking up the ashes of dead savages to find gewgaws and rattles for the grown if babies of the age. Mr. Scott digs up the poachers and cattle stealers of the ancient border, Lord Byron cruises for thieves and pirates on the shores of the Morea and among the Greek islands ... Mr. Wordsworth picks up village legends from old women and sextons, and Mr. Coleridge, to the valuable information acquired from similar sources, superadds the dreams of crazy theologians and the mysticisms of German metaphysics, and favours the world with visions in verse, in which the quadruple elements of sexton, old woman, Jeremy Taylor, and Emanuel Kant are harmonized into a delicious poetical compound.

But what was at stake in 'the mysticisms of German metaphysics', and the reason why Coleridge turned not only to Kant but to Friedrich Schelling and others, was what I have called, in *The Sense of God* (see especially ch. 1, 'Explaining Human Behaviour'), the rapidly developing dilemma of individual meaning or of individual significance. That dilemma, in this particular period, was a consequence of the ambition, on the part at least of some, to extend to human nature those Newtonian mechanistic principles which had proved so exhilaratingly successful in explaining fundamental phenomena in the natural universe. The ambition, to put it the other way round, was to include human nature within the natural order and to account for the phenomena exhibited in that nature by the same laws and principles that are found throughout the natural order in general.

Thus whereas Descartes had argued that all animals are 'machines' but that humans are an exception, de La Mettrie responded, in *The Natural History of the Soul* (1745), by denying any distinction between animals and humans. In that work he obliterated the distinction by maintaining that animals are not machines because they also think and feel. However, three years later, by a subtle inversion whose consequences were almost as profound intellectually as the inversion whereby Karl Marx stood Hegel on his head, La Mettrie argued (Bussey p.135) that the distinction between men and animals is still to be obliterated but now for a different reason. Both animals and humans are machines but the sort of machines which think and feel:

Man is but an animal, or a collection of springs which wind each other up ... Wherefore the soul is but a principle of motion or a material and sensible part of the brain, which can be regarded, without fear of error, as the mainspring of the whole machine.

It is not unlike the strongly mechanistic opening of Wilson's *On Human Nature* (p.1):

> If the brain is a machine of ten billion nerve cells and the mind can some-how [*sic*] be explained as the summed activity of a finite number of chemical and electrical reactions, boundaries limit the human prospect – we are bio-logical and our souls cannot fly free.

So we arrive at *l'homme machine*. The unity of living organisms is absolute. As La Mettrie put it, "Man is not moulded from a costlier clay; nature has used but one dough, and has merely varied the leaven." Indeed, La Mettrie (p.100) went so far as to suggest that a young ape might be educated much as Amman had educated deaf mutes, provided one chose for the experiment "an ape with the most intelligent face, and the one which, in a thousand little ways, best lived up to its look of intelligence." In that case the ape "would no longer be a wild man, or a defective man, but he would be a perfect man, a little gentle-man, with as much matter or muscle as we have, for thinking and profiting by his education" (p.103). From that speculation and from Lord Monboddo's belief that the Orang Outang was not an ape but a variety of the human spe-cies whose lack of language could be remedied by education, Peacock derived his splendid fantasy, *Melincourt*, in which an educated ape is elected to the House of Commons.

The antireligious and antitheological implications of all this are unmis-takeable and were explicitly articulated by La Mettrie, although even in eighteenth-century France he hedged a little and attributed the most extreme statement of the view that "the universe will never be happy until it is athe-istic" to a friend of his, whom he described (p.103) as "a wretch – cet *abom-inable* Homme." So despite his claims that human faculties summarised in imagination are not diminished in worth, the whole thrust of the argument is that the correspondence between animals and humans is legitimate and observable, and that even morality is not a distinctive human possession. He therefore wrote in conclusion (p.149):

> Convinced that in spite of the protests of his vanity, he is but a machine or an animal, the materialist will not maltreat his kind ..., and following the natural law, given to all animals, he will not wish to do to others what he would not wish them to do to him.

This Isaianic vision of the wolf lying down with the lamb, or of a pack of wolves restraining their conduct altruistically by appeal to the Golden Rule, seems somewhat remote from the world in which lambs live. That, however, does not obscure the real thrust and purpose of La Mettrie's argument: it is to unify all phenomena under single principles or laws of explanation, with nothing distinctively human to escape the net (p.149):

> Let us then boldly conclude that man is a mechanism, and that in the whole universe there is but a single substance differently modified ... Such is my system, or rather the truth, unless I am much deceived. It is short and simple. Dispute it now who will.

It is that kind of argument which creates the dilemma of individual significance. What is the virtue or the value of the 'modification', overplus, in human performance and character? There is certainly a difference of degree between animals and humans, but is the difference of such proportion that it amounts to a difference of kind? As Hegel put it, looking for an escape from the bondage of materialism, and identifying one of the three moments of civil society as the system of needs (p.127):

> An animal's needs and its ways and means of satisfying them are both alike restricted in scope. Though man is subject to this restriction too, yet at the same time he evinces his transcendence of it and his universality, first by the multiplication of needs and means of satisfying them, and secondly, by the differentiation and division of concrete need into single parts and aspects which in turn become different needs, particularized and more abstract.

The same point can be put in more colloquial and familiar terms. Let us accept for the sake of argument that a thousand of La Mettrie's apes, with a thousand typewriters, would, in a thousand years, produce the works of Shakespeare. But would they recognize and share the qualitative nature of their achievement, and would they reinforce and inspire their subsequent lives by reference to what they had produced? The German metaphysicians, whose mysticism Peacock disliked, had recognized more acutely than most the seriousness of the issue and the complete inadequacy of a naive Newtonian materialism to account for the qualitative consequence and mental function of brain behaviour. That is why such figures as Coleridge and Thomas Carlyle relied so heavily on them, if not in detail, at least as an encouragement and as an inspiration – as what we might call now 'a background assumption'. For them scientific and materialistic reason cannot tell the whole tale. Instead, they were "living riotously," as Carlyle once put it (consoling himself for the loss of his first love, Margaret Henderson), "with Schiller, Goethe and the rest" (Hanson, p.34).

Coleridge did not begin his serious study of Kant until his three-year visit to the Lake District between 1800 and 1803.[2] Already by 1801 he was able to write to Thomas Poole (Griggs p.173): "I turn at times half reluctantly from Leibniz or Kant even, to read a smoking new newspaper – such a *purus putus* metaphysician am I become."

Less than ten years before, while still an undergraduate at Jesus College, Cambridge, Coleridge had been overwhelmed by the persuasive power of David Hartley's *Observations on Man,* published in 1749. Hartley was another of those who were attempting to construct a Newtonian and mechanistic system bringing all phenomena, including all human phenomena, into a single frame of explanation or analysis. As Bate put it (p.12),

> It was precisely this systematic inclusiveness that appealed to Coleridge. It seemed to explain everything, from the most elementary physiological facts to the highest states of consciousness, benevolence, and religious apprehension.

It was, we might say, the sociobiology of its day.

Coleridge's enthusiasm for iconoclastic novelty is familiar to anyone who has been an undergraduate – taken to an extreme, perhaps, by Coleridge, who called his first son Hartley. But in later years he saw with increasing clarity that a Newtonian materialism, bringing all phenomena within its single scope, did not do justice and could not do justice to the creativity of the mind in initiating, in observing and in reflecting on its own activity (who or what initiates, observes and reflects?). Referring specifically to Hartley's system, Coleridge wrote in *Biographia Literaria* (p.62):

> Whether any other philosophy be possible but the mechanical, and again, whether the mechanical system can have any claim to be called philosophy, are questions for another place. It is, however, certain that as long as we deny the former and affirm the latter, we must bewilder ourselves, whenever we would pierce into the adyta[3] of causations.

Why must we remain bewildered? Because, Coleridge answered (p.68), the *explicandum* becomes the *explicans*:

> The will, and with the will all acts of thought and attention, are parts and products of this blind mechanism, instead of being distinct powers whose function it is to control, determine and modify the phantasmal chaos of association. The soul becomes a mere *ens logicum;* for as a real separable being, it would be more worthless and ludicrous than the grimalkins in the cat-harpsichord described in the *Spectator.* For these did form a part of the process; but in Hartley's scheme the soul is present only to be pinched or stroked, while the very squeals or purring are produced by an agency wholly independent and alien … Accordingly this *caput mortuum* of the Hartleian process has been rejected by his followers, and the consciousness

considered as a result, as a tune, the common product of the breeze and the harp.

Here at last the Aeolian harp returns to the scene; and here also we can see why Geoffrey Grigson called the Aeolian harp "really the prime romantic image" (p.342). The question is utterly simple and divisive: are we an instrument hanging in the wind, played by the mechanistic laws which govern the falling of an apple – or, to put it in other words, played by the genes which programme us? Such an instrument produces ethereal and ravishing sound, unique and unrepeatable, on each occasion, but it is ultimately passive to the forces which evoke its utterance. Or are we constructed in such a way that even within the mechanism we are able to initiate our own programme of music and composition? In that case we would be active in harnessing the forces which have made our utterance possible, as the religious imagination insists.

Within a year of leaving Cambridge, Coleridge had married and moved to Clevedon, and there, in 1795, he wrote 'The Aeolian Harp', in which exactly this conflict is expressed. Coleridge at this stage was still very much more on the materialist side, although it was a kind of spiritualized materialism; indeed, Schrickx has argued that we can be more precise and say that it was a neoplatonic spiritualism of a Cambridge kind. Coleridge, in this early poem, gets no further. He edges cautiously towards a more explicit pantheism, but he puts it very hypothetically:

> And what if all of animated nature
> Be but organic harps diversely framed,
> That tremble into thought, as o'er them sweeps
> Plastic and vast, one intellectual breeze,
> At once the Soul of each, and God of all?

At this stage Coleridge drew back from the edge and put into the mouth of his newlywed wife "a mild reproof" against "these shapings of the unregenerate mind." But of course the real issue which ran on into the rest of Coleridge's life was not orthodoxy versus speculation, but how to account for the creativity of human life. Are we the harp or the harpist?

That is exactly the point of a letter by Robert Burns in which the image of the Aeolian harp again sharpens the issue (Cushing, pp.504f.):

> We know nothing or next to nothing, of the structure of our souls, so we cannot account for those seeming caprices in them, that one should be particularly pleased with this thing, or struck with that, which on minds of a different cast, makes no extraordinary impression. I have some favourite flowers in spring, among which are the mountain-daisy, the harebell, the

foxglove, the wild-brier rose, the budding birch, and the hoary hawthorn, that I view and hang over with particular delight. I never hear the loud solitary whistle of the curlew in a summer noon, or the wild mixing cadence of a troop of gray plover in an autumnal morning, without feeling an elevation of soul like the enthusiasm of devotion or poetry ... Are we a piece of machinery, which, like the Aeolian harp, passive, takes the impression of the passing accident; or do these workings argue something within us above the trodden clod?

Exactly the same issue, focused on the Aeolian harp, became the foundation of Shelley's *Defence of Poetry* (p.26) against the sallies of Peacock:

> Poetry, in a general sense, may be defined to be 'the expression of the imagination': and poetry is connate with the origin of man. Man is an instrument over which a series of external and internal impressions are driven, like the alternations of an ever-changing wind over an Aeolian lyre, which move it by their motion to ever-changing melody.

The words 'Aeolian lyre' here are very precise, because in what appears to be the first draft of this essay Shelley originally wrote the word 'lute'.[4] So thus far in the argument, by the change of instrument from 'lute' to 'Aeolian lyre', Shelley has constructed a thoroughgoing Hartleian, mechanistic argument, which is very similar – indeed, it is formally identical – to an argument put forward in sociobiology: humans are driven from behind (by Newtonian laws in the one case, by the genes and by their necessity to inhabit bodies and environments appropriate for their survival in the other), but this does not diminish the accidental beauty of human achievement; it is simply that nothing further, such as mind or God, should be inferred from it.

Shelley, however, did not leave the argument at that point. His own experience of himself – to say nothing of the reported and observed experience of such friends as Keats and Southey – drove him on to make exactly that statement of the issue which occurred also in the letter by Burns. Shelley continued (p.27):

> But there is a principle within the human being, and perhaps within all sentient beings, which acts otherwise than in the lyre, and produces not melody, but harmony, by an internal adjustment of the sounds or motions thus excited to the impressions which excite them. It is as if the lyre could accommodate its chords to the motions of that which strikes them, in a determined proportion of sound; even as the musician can accommodate his voice to the sound of the lyre.

There is thus a deep uncertainty in Coleridge and Shelley, focused on the harp: on the one side, the materialist arguments are of course strong – Coleridge had been converted by them in Cambridge. The new materialist synthesis, attempting to embrace all phenomena and all other forms of inquiry into its scope, was undoubtedly attractive: it was, after all, 'the latest thing'.

On the other side, however, it was turning out for them as poets and people of imagination to be a Procrustean bed. William Blake, with his usual intuitive vision, had seen the point at much the same time, when he protested, in his famous letter to Thomas Butts in 1802, *not* against Newton's genius but against Newton's sleep. The edge of his protest was against a *single* vision, that is, against seeing the world in one way only:

> With Angels planted in Hawthorn bowers
> And God himself in the passing hours,
> With Silver Angels across my way
> And Golden Demons that none can stay ...
> What to others a trifle appears
> Fills me full of smiles or tears;
> For double the vision my Eyes do see,
> And a double vision is always with me.
> With my inward *Eye* 'tis an old man grey;
> With my outward, a Thistle across my way ...
> May God us keep
> From Single vision and Newton's sleep. (Keynes pp.817f)[5]

This is the very root and sustenance of what is referred to as the Romantic movement. Coleridge wrote:[6]

> Believe me, Southey! a metaphysical solution, that does not instantly *tell you* something in the heart is grievously to be suspected as apocryphal. I almost think that ideas *never* recall ideas, so far as they are ideas, any more than leaves in a forest create each other's motion. The breeze it is that runs through them – it is the soul, the state of feeling.

Here yet again the breeze is blowing strongly, just as it does through the poems of Wordsworth:

> O there is blessing in this gentle breeze
> That blows from the green fields and from the clouds
> And from the sky ...

Those are the opening words of the original version of *The Prelude*; and before long, the Aeolian harp makes its appearance (ll.101–7):

> It was a splendid evening, and my soul
> Did once again make trial of the strength
> Restored to her afresh; nor did she want

> Aeolian visitations; but the harp
> Was soon defrauded, and the banded host
> Of harmony dispersed in straggling sounds
> And lastly utter silence.

Here Wordsworth would seem to be on the side of those who regard humans as passive instruments. But just before this, in lines 41–47, he wrote strongly of "the correspondent breeze" within the human subject, a creativity which acts within the mind as the breeze acts upon the body.[7]

What the so-called Romantics were concerned to defend was what we may deliberately call 'inspiration' – deliberately because of the Latin words *in-spiro* (I breathe in or into). Coleridge did not need to doubt that we are 'an ingenious mechanical contrivance', so long as he remembered, as he did, that we are contrivances of a quite extraordinary kind with 'emergent properties' that certainly transcend 'mechanism'. The difference of degree does emphatically amount to a difference of kind. The human contrivance means that no two of those 'contrivances' respond identically to identical phenomena: one eye works much the same as another; but no two eyes see the same thing, even when they look at the same object.

That was the point of Blake's protest. To materialists the individual vision and its interpretation in the mind are epiphenomena; to poets the hardware (of muscle, tissue, bone, etc.) are the space vehicle in which they are launched into beauty and those other eternal values that are not limited by the contingent circumstance of their instantiation.

That was why Coleridge denounced the ambition of Hartley and other materialists like Priestley, Godwin and Tooke who wished to remove the ambiguities and imprecision of poetic language and to subordinate all language to science – to make language itself, as Priestley put it, "an abstract science". Poetry and the Aeolian harp became the focus for a resistance to scientism in general and materialism in particular. The issue remains the same in the resistance to Dawkins, Wilson and their followers, even though the details are very different. Then as now, what is at stake is an adequate account of human nature. The issue is exactly as Hamilton put it in his analysis of 'language and the radical tradition' in Coleridge (p.98):

> Poetry, self-consciously ideal, challenges the pretensions to adequacy of any systematic description of human nature. Coleridge criticizes radical theories which explain progress as though human nature was an easily understood mechanism. In contrast to these closed theories of human nature, he argued for an element in our progress beyond the reach of scientific vocabulary.

The fundamental issue remains, as it did for Coleridge, whether we are played by the programme or whether we are programmed in such a way that we take important control of the transactions of energy in this system. Is it inevitable, to return to the Lincolnshire marshes, that some end up in Borstal, or can we, within whatever it is that constrains our particular lives, *acquire* responsibility and direction?

The centrality of that question has led religions and philosophies to explore what it is within the human case that is the subject of its own experiences and the agent of its actions, evoking the languages of consciousness, mind, self, soul, spirit, atman and the rest (languages, incidentally, that cannot be identified with centres of coordination in the brain if and when these are located[8]). In trying to answer that question it becomes indispensably necessary to understand that constraints, whether in genes or in society, are *not* deterministic: they are the necessary condition of freedom. This means, as we will now go on to see, that Wilson was right to observe that we are biological, but completely wrong to conclude that our souls cannot fly free. It is precisely because we are enabled by so many biological constraints that our souls become evident as an emergent property and are very much set free to fly.

CAUSES AND CONSTRAINTS: THE SINGER AND THE SONG

It follows, therefore, that this long pursuit of the Aeolian harp is far from having been an exercise in the archaeology of knowledge and nothing more. It has been a reminder (as much to religious believers as to scientists) of the extreme care that is needed in the use of metaphors, similes and analogies. 'Memes' and 'Aeolian harps' can focus and illuminate debates, but when they are not recognised for what they are (as has happened in the case of 'memes'), they become destructively misleading.

It has been a reminder also that the issues raised by sociobiology and genetic determinism do not originate with sociobiology and the discovery of the genes. They are part of the long human exploration of itself and of its own nature and possibility focused on the question of the extent to which we are free and responsible or are compelled and determined in our behaviours.

The alternatives in the debate (free or compelled, responsible or determined) have been expressed over the centuries in many ways, of which the most frequent in recent years has been the question, nature or nurture. Sharp alternatives are attractive, but they should nevertheless alert us to the fact that they entice us into one of the most common fallacies in human argument – the fallacy of the falsely dichotomous question (defined earlier).

That fallacy dominates the arguments of those like Wilson and Dawkins who give an overwhelmingly decisive role to genes in the construction and control of human life because they assume that if one answer (their own) is correct, any alternatives must be wrong. If genes create and control human life and behaviours, no other proposed answer has any contribution to make by way of explaining cause: the most it can do is illustrate and reinforce what they take to be the correct answer. That is why, as we saw, Dawkins rejected MLS (Multi Level Selection).

The underlying error here that leads straight into the fallacy is the assumption that there can only be single causes of complex events. The assumption is that if genes make a decisive and causative contribution (as they do) to the way humans exist and behave, then other proposed 'causes' are at best secondary, contingent and ornamental. What is known as 'causal closure' draws a boundary around what amounts to a closed circle of explanation – and we will return shortly to the damaging consequences of causal closure exercised in that way.

In fact, nothing that happens is brought about by a single cause, but only by a complicated cooperation of causes. It is true that when we are trying to understand how or why something has happened, we usually prefer to select and concentrate on only one cause among the many. We need, nevertheless, always to bear in mind that nothing ever is 'the sole cause' of anything; or to put it the other way round, there are many causes of even the simplest occurrence or event, as we can see in what I have called elsewhere 'the Flashman philosophy of history':[9]

> You'll have heard it said that the British Empire was acquired in a fit of absence of mind – one of those smart Oscarish squibs that sounds well but is thoroughly fat-headed. *Presence* of mind, if you like – and countless other things, such as greed and Christianity, decency and villainy, policy and lunacy, deep design and blind chance, pride and trade, blunder and curiosity, passion, ignorance, chivalry and expediency, honest pursuit of right, and determination to keep the bloody Frogs out. And often as not, such things came tumbling together, and when the dust had settled, there we were....

This means that if we want to find out the reasons why anything has come into being as it has, or why anything has happened as it has, it is far wiser not to seek the cause but to specify the constraints. It may of course seem a pedantic and even trivial point, but it can have dramatic and divisive importance in social policies and actions. In *The Sacred Neuron* (pp.101f), I gave as an example the way in which the isolation of 'cause' in contrast to the specification of constraints has vitiated the debate about whether the watching of violent videos and the participation in violent media games have an influ-ence on behaviours, especially those of young people.[10] Those who sup-port the sale of such games and videos defend it on the grounds that, as the director-general of ELSPA put it in 2004 (rejecting the claim by the parents of a fourteen-year-old boy that the older boy who murdered him had been obsessed with a game, 'Manhunt', in which players are rewarded for inflicting the most brutal deaths they can), "There is no substantive evidence in this case to link this tragic event to the fact he was playing a game." That defence rests on the extreme difficulty of establishing a direct link between a particu-lar video that an offender has seen and a particular act of violence as the sin-gle and explicit cause. If, however, we look at the constraints that have been internalised and have controlled a person into an act of violence, obsession with extreme violence in video games may, as one among other constraints, have played a causative part – not, of course, *inevitably*, because this is not a matter of determinism. Many people watch violent films, but extremely few of them translate them into real life.

The point, therefore, needs to be emphasised: when we are studying any phenomena, including human phenomena, at some point it is always appropriate to ask to what extent we can discern and specify the constraints which have controlled this particular event or outcome into its eventuality – namely, the appearance which is presenting itself evidentially as an instan-tiating datum.

Whether we wish to know why one boy murders another, or why Caesar crossed the Rubicon, or why an apple falls, or why coal burns and stones do not, we are always asking, at least in part, what the constraints are which have controlled these eventualities into their outcomes, namely the way in which they have instantiated themselves as data, pressing themselves on our attention and calling out for an explanation or for an account to be given of themselves.

Clearly at some levels – and certainly in the case of Caesar – the account is complicated by self-organisation or intentionality: "The cause is in my will", as Shakespeare's Caesar says of himself.[11] Intentionality is itself constrained, but it also acts as a constraint, one among many others. It is, of course, never pos-sible to specify *all* the constraints in any particular instance. Nevertheless, the *concern* with constraint remains fundamental in any account of behaviour.

In ordinary usage the word 'constraint' sounds restrictive and negative, as, for example, when we speak of holding dangerous people under constraint. The same may be true in more technical usage. For example, for a physi-cist a constraint is an external limitation generally expressed in terms of a set of fixed parameters worked into the equations of motion in such a way that motion is only free within the limits of the constraint. In that context, a constraint can best be regarded, as the biologist Pattee has argued (pp.260f), "as an alternative description which generally ignores selected microscopic degrees of freedom in order to achieve a simplification in predicting or explaining the motion."

This means, however, that although the notion of constraint is indeed restrictive, it is also in its realisation extremely liberating *precisely because* it is restrictive. That is the main thrust of Pattee's argument in an article whose title ('Physical Theories of Biological Coordination') makes clear that he was exploring the difference between explanations in physics and in biology (p.256):

> Biological organisation is manifestly different from the order of the non-living world, and the study of biology is largely the search for the nature of this difference.

In the case of biology, the fundamental observation is that the elaboration and multiplication of constraints, far from reducing the freedom of behaviour, actually enables it (p.256):

> Co-ordination in biological organisms takes the form of hierarchical control levels which at each level provide greater and greater freedom or adaptability for the whole organism by selectively adding more and more constraints to its component parts.

From this it follows that "the imposition of new constraints results in some corresponding freedom in the behaviour of the organism" (p.260). Of course, there remains at the same time a restrictive sense of constraint. Unless limits and constraints are set on the transformations of energy in a universe of this kind, there would be either chaos or perfect equilibrium in which nothing can happen. Nevertheless, it also remains true that constraint is the condition of freedom. That is why there is in cybernetics a simple but profound principle which states: "When a constraint exists, advantage can usually be taken of it" (Ashby p.130).

That principle occurs in cybernetics because cybernetics characteristically envisages a set of possibilities much wider than the actual, and then asks why and how a particular case under examination has been constrained into occurring as it does. Looking at this in a wider context and connecting constraint with the laws of nature, Ashby then argued:

> [T]he existence of any invariant over a set of phenomena implies a constraint, for its existence implies that the full range of variety does not occur. The general theory of invariants is thus a part of the theory of constraints.

Further, as every law of nature implies the existence of an invariant, it follows that *every law of nature is a constraint.*

The crucial point of this observation is that if there were unlimited degrees of freedom (or what, as we will see shortly, Stravinsky called "unrestricted freedom" and de la Mare called "illimitable" freedom), then organisations of energy, constructions of particles, atoms and molecules, would not be possible. Elaborate networks of constraint, running down eventually into the laws of motion, set the conditions and boundaries that allow the different constructions of energy. The advantage of the word 'constraint' is that it includes both the active (most naturally associated with the idea of cause) and the passive conditions that have controlled an eventuality into its outcome, into its being whatever it is that presents itself evidentially and as an instantiating datum to an observer.

As I argued in *A Year to Live*, there is an important consequence of this understanding of constraint: the more complex the organisation of an organism is, the more complex and elaborate is the network of constraint which allows its possibility. Thus the human is brought into its evident and characteristic appearance and form by a far more elaborate network of constraint than that which produces a rockweed kelp or an amoeba.

At the level of biology, therefore, the elaboration of constraint, far from restricting freedom, actually increases it. Far more degrees of freedom and choice are open to a human than are open to a rockweed kelp. We can therefore put forward a second principle that applies in many circumstances and not just in biology: the greater the constraints, the greater the opportunities (freedom in that sense) may become. Most snakes, for example, are constrained (in the sense of restricted) by their lack of large teeth and the limited size of their mouth opening or 'gape' to swallowing their food whole. But that created the opportunity for some snakes (e.g., *Gerada prevostiana* and *Forddonia leucobalia*) to devise ways of catching and consuming crabs much larger than their 'gape-size' by devising ways of tearing their prey in pieces: they thus extended their chance of survival by identifying new sources of food beyond the initial and inherited constraint. Constraint is initially restrictive, but it creates opportunity.

That principle is vastly extended in the human case because the brain (an immensely elaborate product of high degrees of constraint) is not only sensitive to its environment but also has developed language with which it can think about and communicate its sensitivities.

The neat trick in the human case is the realisation (who or what realises?) that if constraints are recognised and *internalised*, the degrees of freedom can be dramatically increased. The most elementary example of this is the way in which we are prepared to accept initial restrictions on freedom in order to learn some skill which will, eventually, liberate us into freedoms which would otherwise be unobtainable: think of the constraints which you accept (or which are imposed on you) if you set out to learn French, physics, football or the flute. If, in that last instance, you accept and internalise the constraints of scales and notation and fingering, and accept the restrictions on your use of time in order to practise, you will eventually be liberated into the far greater freedom of playing what music you will, and of writing your own music.

Of course, not even this is a matter which belongs simply to our desire that it may be so. There are, for example, limitations of competence which lie very deep; and since the genes build the proteins which build the structures of the brain which prepare us for our behaviours, it is clear that there is a genetic contribution to basic competence. Equally, someone who has lost both arms in an accident cannot play the flute – but even in cases of that kind, human ingenuity often finds ways to make the impossible possible.

Nevertheless, the fundamental point remains true: constraints, while they may initially restrict our freedom, and while they will always make some things impossible, are the necessary condition of *greater* freedom; and where such constraints are understood, they can be taken advantage of, as all the massive advances in technology make abundantly clear. The necessary virtue of constraint for the freedom of human creativity is exactly as Stravinsky put it in his Harvard lectures on *Poetics of Music*, insisting on the necessity for order and discipline in the composition of music (pp. 61–65, 76):

> So here we are, whether we like it or not, in the realm of necessity. And yet which of us has ever heard talk of art as other than a realm of freedom? ... Well, in art as in everything else, one can build only upon a resisting foundation: whatever constantly gives way to pressure, constantly renders movement impossible.
>
> My freedom thus consists in my moving about within the narrow frame that I have assigned myself for each one of my undertakings.
>
> I shall go even further: my freedom will be so much the greater and more meaningful the more narrowly I limit my field of action and the more I surround myself with obstacles. Whatever diminishes constraint, diminishes strength. The more constraints one imposes, the more one frees one's self of the chains that shackle the spirit....
>
> Let us take the best example: the fugue, a pure form in which the music means nothing outside itself. Doesn't the fugue imply the composer's submission to the rules? And is it not within those strictures that he finds the

full flowering of his freedom as the creator? Strength, says Leonardo da Vinci, is born of constraint and dies in freedom.

In another example, the poet Walter de la Mare asked (p.136) how the highly constraining rules that govern the composition of sonnets can produce such extraordinary beauty:

> The problem remains. Why has this metrical structure of fourteen arbitrarily rhymed ten-syllabled lines proved so pregnant and fruitful a means of expressing all that man cares for most in life – in love, in Nature, in the divine? ... Every work of art, epic to nursery-rhyme, cathedral to ivory box, masterpiece of painting or sculpture to a scrap of embroidery or Bewick wood-cut; every science, every game even, has as it were a frame and certain laws separating it from the illimitable.

In a comparably creative way genes and proteins act as constraints, delimiting what would otherwise be chaotic, but it does not follow that they negate human freedom, nor does it follow that they are the only significant *cause* of human life and behaviour. They are a part of elaborate networks of constraints which produce the miracle of human freedoms.

That is resisted by those who believe that it belongs to the paradigm of scientific method to reduce explanation to the least that is necessary, as Crick did in his reductionist account of humans (in the Introduction). And there is, of course, a legitimate (but too often misused) scientific interest in doing that: it is the concern not to multiply explanations beyond those that are sufficient to account for what needs to be explained – a concern epitomised in Ockham's Razor, to which we will return.

What is known as 'causal closure' (cf. Hamilton's 'closed theory' p.144) excludes what is regarded as unnecessary, false or frivolous. Thus, as an example, materialists exclude mind or mental initiatives as causative in human behaviours. It seems to be the case that my intention to make a cup of tea leads me to fill the kettle and switch it on, but materialists claim that those thoughts and intentions can be translated into physical events in the brain. Thus Dennett, a leading advocate of causal closure of that materialist kind, states his position with clarity (p.33):

> The prevailing wisdom, variously expressed and argued for, is *materialism*: there is only one sort of stuff, namely *matter* – the physical stuff of physics, chemistry, and physiology – and the mind is somehow nothing but a physical phenomenon. In short, the mind is the brain. According to materialists, we can (in principle!) account for every mental phenomenon using the same physical principles, laws and raw materials that suffice to explain radioactivity, continental drift, photosynthesis, reproduction, nutrition, and growth.

We have already seen (p.129) the caustic comment of a scientist (a physicist), Longuet-Higgins, on what scientists, or in this case a philosopher, claim can be done 'in principle'. It is certainly the case that human desires, intentions, purposes, fears and so on are always correlated with activity in the brain, but correlation is not the same as identity, and correlation does not mean that the mind (the agency initiating those mental activities) is not in itself, and of its own initiative, causative, because clearly it is. Causal closure undertaken to exclude mind and mental initiative as causative among the networks of constraint is robustly attractive, but in this instance (as actually in many others) it is false.

The causal closure exercised by Wilson and Dawkins in favour of genetic explanation may seem equally robust and attractive, but it too is misleading and false. It is, on the other hand, not surprising. Life being short, we normally (and scientifically) specify, when we are trying to explain why or how something has happened, only the immediate or proximate causes: if I push this book and it moves on the table, the cause is that I pushed it. Nevertheless, that 'event' is controlled into its outcome by a far wider network of constraints including the laws of motion, as a result of which the book moves and does not fly off into outer space. But clearly we do not have time, nor is it necessary, to specify among the constraints (or causes) the laws of motion. We therefore specify those constraints which are immediate (or proximate) to this outcome, to this event or eventuality. We leave the others, many of which are passive and are simply securing the boundary of possibility, unspecified as domain assumptions. The advantage of the word 'constraint' is that it includes both active and passive conditions which control an eventuality into its outcome.

What we decide to specify is therefore a *choice*, depending usually on what it is that we want to explain or understand. Thus we do not usually specify 'natural selection' as a constraint when explaining many events in biology and zoology (i.e., it is left as a domain assumption), but in explaining the long neck of a giraffe we certainly do specify it.

Where the study of religion and theology are concerned, we have to recognise that something like that is true also of God. For a theist, we are always in the condition of God, much as on this planet we are always in the condition of gravity or of natural selection. Thus God is always a constraint over the outcomes of the universe, the primary cause sustaining and operating through the secondary causes in the entire network of constraints.

Thus the meaning of creation is not that God brings something into being and then lets it work things out on its own. The meaning of creation is also preservation, as in the prayer of Humble Thanksgiving: "Almighty God, ... we bless thee for our creation, preservation, and all the blessings of this life." As Aquinas put it in a more detached way, God as Creator "is the cause not only of becoming but of being" (*De Potentia* 3.7). Creation means that everything created (everything, that is, apart from God who creates) depends entirely on God for its existence for as long as it exists: "Just as it depends on God's will for things to come into being, so also it depends on God's will that they are preserved in being. For God does not preserve them in being in any other way than by constantly giving them being. So if God withdrew that action from them they would return to not existing" (*ST* 9.1).

There is nothing, therefore, that can escape from the constraint of God without ceasing to exist. Nevertheless, it is clearly unnecessary to specify God as constraint on every occasion when we want to explain some particular outcome. The primary cause is exercised through the secondary causalities in the created order on which in general we focus our attention. However, there are occasions when we do specify God as a relevant constraint – those events, for example, which are claimed as miracles or as answers to prayer (whether such claims are justified is another matter: on the meaning of the word 'miracles', see Bowker 2014 p. 11). Even then, such events or occasions are only a particular way in which the primary and constant constraint of God is brought to bear, much as the constant constraint of gravity is brought to bear in particular outcomes like bowling a cricket ball or sending a rocket to the moon.

That understanding of the relationship between primary and secondary causation is totally different from introducing God into the gaps of explanation. It is simply that the universal (domain assumption) constraint of God *has* to be specified if an adequate account is to be given of some particular events or eventualities – just as the long neck of a giraffe cannot be explained adequately without specifying natural selection within the entire network of constraints. Even then, natural selection is not an *active* cause: natural selection does not actually produce or actively select anything: it is simply the context and the record of what has survived. That is why Darwin himself wished (within a year of the publication of *The Origin of Species*) that he had used the phrase 'natural preservation'. He wrote to Lyell: "Talking of 'Natural Selection', if I had to commence *de novo*, I would have used 'natural preservation'; for I find men like Harvey of Dublin cannot understand me."[12]

God, however, is not merely the record of what goes on (although religions, in pre-scientific language, have certainly recognised the truth in that). God, to be what God has traditionally been believed to be, is the creator and interactive sustainer as a constant constraint of all that is. In more traditional language, Aquinas (*S.T.* 104 ad 4), having distinguished 'being' from 'becoming', wrote, "The preservation of things by God does not take place by new actions, but by a continuation of the activity by which he confers existence, an activity which is outside change and time." To illustrate this, Aquinas used the analogy of the coming into being of instances of light relying on the constant activity of the sun.

By a more recent analogy, to say that the constraint of God is effective constantly (and not in the gaps of occasional interference) can be seen in what is known as 'downward causation' or 'top-down causation' (to which reference has already been made). When that was misunderstood by some to imply the counterintuitive suggestion that the future causes events in the present, other names were proposed: for example, environment-system interaction (Drees), or whole-part influence (Peacocke 1989).

The alternative names show that what brings about the misunderstanding is, yet again, the word 'cause' or 'causation'. Downward *constraint*, however, simply means that, in a system taken as a whole, eventualities are controlled into new and often surprising outcomes within, and as a consequence of, the total boundary conditions that obtain. A familiar example is the way in which "order out of chaos", as Prigogine and Stengers (1984) called it, appears in open dissipative systems far from equilibrium, which tend to self-organise toward the same states, even though they start from different initial states. Familiar instances can be observed when large-scale patterns are produced despite the fact that the motions of the units are random. In the Bénard-Mangoni effect, for example, a fluid heated uniformly from below moves from the random Brownian motion of its molecules to the production of a regular pattern of convection cells on the surface.

In examples of that kind the point is that the micro-level events or behaviours (which have their own proximate or immediate constraints/causes) cannot account *on their own* for the sudden shift into what is observed to be happening. Those outcomes occur because they are constrained, not only by the immediate and proximate, but also by the whole system. It is the state of the whole system that constrains in a causative way what the component parts actually do.

Prigogine and Stengers then extended the application of this to such fundamental questions as the emergence of order in biological evolution, the problem of evolution versus entropy, and thus more particularly the maintenance of structures (for example, of genetic material) through the erosive processes of time, and they also applied it to the human systems of social and economic organisation.

To apply it further to the understanding of God as the constant constraint over the universe in a comparable whole-part relationship is to show how God is constantly effective and indeed causative without overruling or abrogating the regularities that are referred to as 'the laws of nature'. The system is drawn into its outcomes by the overall constraint of God. Particular events or eventualities can be understood as a consequence of God, but they are brought about by secondary agents. By the internalisation of the constraint of God people find themselves drawn into new and unpredictable patterns and configurations of relatedness, not simply to each other in the transfigurations of love but also to God from whom the first initiative comes.

It then becomes fundamental in understanding why religions matter so much to so many people that they are enabled to become as an act of consent or of will the agents of God in extending the domain and the consequence of love. To live in the constant condition of God is to live, in more traditional language, deliberately and reflectively in the presence and in the order of God. There are many ways in which that can be done, and religions are maps and guides to the different ways in which it can happen, but it always involves for secondary agents an alignment of will and intention with the primary cause of God. To give an example from Christianity, Fénelon wrote (Whiston p. 8):

> Whoever goes forward in the presence of God in the most trivial matters ceases not to perform God's work, although he appears to do nothing important or serious. I suppose that we are always in the order of God and that we are following God's rules for our condition in doing these trivial things. Most people, when they wish to be converted or reformed, expect to fill their lives with especially difficult and unusual acts, far more than to purify their intentions and to mortify their natural inclinations in the most usual acts of their condition. In this they often badly deceive themselves. It would be much more valuable for them to change their actions less, and to change more rather the disposition which makes them act.

To understand the constraint of God in that way does not make it necessary or even desirable to specify that constraint on every occasion. To repeat the point: in the ordinary business of life, and especially in the business of offering scientific explanations, we do not have time to specify all the constraints that have controlled an eventuality into its outcome, into its being what it is. Therefore, in explaining any phenomenon, we choose from the whole range of actual constraints those that relate most closely and immediately to our concern and leave the others as an unspoken or domain assumption.

In making those choices, recognition of what is known as 'the frame problem' is a paramount necessity.[13] The frame problem in artificial intelligence research and in computer programming means that unless all possible options and their consequences are narrowed down, the optimal solution will never be found: without being supplied with the equivalent of 'innate knowledge', a computer cannot make progress in an algorithmic search procedure, since if all options are genuinely options, even the most powerful computer simply cannot work through all the near-infinite possibilities. It is why, conversely, computers can be programmed to play chess so well, because the rules create the frame within which the multiple options can be rapidly reviewed.

The implication of this is that in any particular circumstance we have to limit the specification of constraints to those that seem most directly relevant. The fact always and necessarily remains that we do have to choose. If, as loss adjusters for an insurance firm, we ask, 'What caused that fire?', we are unlikely to specify, 'the presence of oxygen'. Yet, if we are seeking to explain the outbreak of fire in an unmanned space capsule, we will undoubtedly want to include the presence of oxygen in the specification of constraints.

So how do we choose? It is at this point that a version of Ockham's razor is usually wielded. The words attributed to him are *entia non sunt multiplicanda praeter* [or *sine*] *necessitatem* (though that form of words is later), or in Isaac Newton's version (p.398), "Nature is pleased with simplicity, and affects not the pomp of superfluous causes." On that basis, Ockham's razor is often summarised loosely in the form 'where one explanation will do, don't multiply explanations.'

Summaries of that kind, however, pay insufficient attention to the words *praeter necessitatem* and 'superfluous': how do we *decide* what belongs to the category of the 'beyond necessity' or of the superfluous? In fact, Ockham's razor, far from being a shortcut to the aggressive reductionism of a Dawkins, is nothing more than a methodological strategy based on a bias in favour of simplicity (hence its name *lex parsimoniae*) in the construction of theories. It has been taken to be a mark of truth, but as Nancy Cartwright observed (Honderich, p.827), "that makes sense only if one believes that nature *is* simple, and will appear so through the filter of theory and language." So Ockham's razor has virtue only so long as you do not use it to cut off your own head. As I put it in *Is God a Virus?* (p.104),

> Where additional constraints must be specified in order to account for an eventuality, nothing is gained by insisting, in the name of Ockham, on only one. A better principle is this: be sufficiently, but not recklessly, generous in the specification of constraints; or at least otherwise be modest in what you claim to be 'the true and only explanation'.

That principle was recognised and expressed with great clarity by Blumberg (himself a Nobel prize winner "for his discoveries concerning new mechanisms for the origin and dissemination of infectious diseases") when he emphasised (p.xi) the fact that different choices about the specification of constraints have to be made in different sciences, and that the choices depend on what one is trying to understand or explain:

> My experience is that, in medicine, where observational science is crucial, the complexities of a phenomenon can be understood, at least in part, by repeated observations of the whole organism or a population of organisms under a wide range of circumstances; all the variables are retained and as many as possible are examined. For example, in studies of disease, it is possible to build up a knowledge of the effects of a large number of variables on the host, genetic susceptibilities to the disease, and outside factors which interact with each other, the host, and the environment. By contrast, in the reductionist approach, traditionally found in physics, chemistry, and molecular biology, experiments are designed to simplify the study of a natural phenomenon by the elimination of all but a few variables, and explanation is in terms of the most fundamental units.

For about the last hundred years there has been an overriding ambition to find 'single explanations' of complex phenomena, but that has proved to be impossible because it has ignored (or reduced to insignificance) the causative contribution of multiple constraints. Unless the *relevant* constraints are *integrated*, the ambition will be frustrated. Multiple constraints were recognised, of course, but too often they were thought to be an interim necessity until a simpler and more fundamental solution of the problem could be found. A clear example of that, still in the field of medical research, can be seen in Bellak's attempt to explain schizophrenia:

> So far, no convincing single explanation of the etiology or pathogenesis of schizophrenia has been produced. Bellak's attempt to find an answer has been formulated in the 'ego-psychological *multiplefactor psychosomatic theory of schizophrenia*', wherein schizophrenia is seen as a syndrome caused by different aetiological factors and pathogenic pathways.

The danger of seeking single and simple explanations of complexity are now well recognised in serious science. For example, the authors of articles in *Nature Genetics* publishing the results of research on links between genes and particular medical outcomes, rarely claim that they have found *the* single cause. Instead, they use words like 'influence', 'association', 'correlation', 'susceptibility'. Indeed, a recent publication of research on schizophrenia (Ripke *et al.*), based on a gene-wide association study, identified thirteen new risk loci for schizophrenia and concluded that "common genetic variation has an important role in the aetiology of schizophrenia." It did not conclude that the genetic variation *causes* schizophrenia. In contrast, the disaster of so much of the popularisation of the sciences in recent years, brilliant though much of it is, has been the imposition of the reductionist approach on complexity where it is completely inappropriate and misleading.

There is no abstract rule outside the subject matter that we are attempting to understand which dictates or controls the constraints that we choose. Some that are offered are clearly irrelevant, frivolous or absurd, not least when people insist for religious reasons that revelation must contradict science if they seem to be in conflict. Equally, 'choice' is often the wrong word, since we so often make use of certain reasons without giving the matter much or indeed any thought. In other words, we operate our modes of explanation from well-tried precommitments which sometimes take the form of prejudice – as is obvious in the case of Dawkins.

For those in contrast who can recognise their own prejudice and make some effort to set it aside (or as Husserl put it, 'bracket it out'), what has to be decided in each case is how far the specification of constraints has to be taken in order to give an adequate or satisfactory account of cause. As Miller summarized the point,[14]

> When is a description of causes helping to bring about something informative and thorough enough to explain its occurrence? No general answer seems right – and this is the first step toward the right answer.... In some cases, a standard requiring a list of causes sufficient under the circumstances is too weak. But in other cases, a standard requiring a list of causes sufficient in themselves is too strong. We need a compromise between these two extremes.

The compromise (if that is the right word) is extremely simple: it is to move from cause to constraint, because only in that way can we resist the temptation to define causal closure in such a narrow and reductionist way that it excludes genuinely causative contributions to observable outcomes. Only in that way can we recognise how causality works in and between the many layers of complexity.

That is exactly the point made by Ellis in his article in *Nature* entitled 'Physics, Complexity and Causality'. In that article, he raised the question why the laws of physics, although they explain much of the world around us, do not provide what he calls "the realistic description of causality in truly complex hierarchical structures" – moving, say, from quantum theory illuminating the physical basis of the periodic table and the nature of chemical bonding, to molecular biology showing how complex molecules underlie the development and functioning of living organisms, to neurosciences revealing the functioning of the brain.

In that hierarchy of complexity, each level links to the one above, and particle physics underlies them all. So if cause and explanation *could* be taken down to the level of physics, as a thoroughgoing reductionist operating causal closure would propose, then nineteenth-century mechanism might yet prove to be the final truth.

It is, however, a simple statement of fact, as Ellis put it, that "today's physics has nothing to say about the intentionality that has resulted in the existence of objects like buildings, books, computers, teaspoons, even though this intentionality is clearly causally effective." He therefore concluded that "even if we had a satisfactory fundamental physics 'theory of everything', this situation would remain unchanged." So he asked the question:

> Is it plausible that quantum fluctuations in the inflationary era in the very early Universe – the source of the perturbations at the time of decoupling – implied the future inevitability of the Mona Lisa and Einstein's theory of relativity? Those fluctuations are supposed to have been random, which by definition means without purpose or meaning.

'Purpose' and 'meaning' are introduced as emergent properties in the higher levels of the hierarchy of complexity, and particularly in the human brain, and they act in supervenient ways that are causative:

> Brain functioning is causally affected by abstractions, such as the value of money, the rules of chess and the theory of the laser. These abstractions are realised as brain states in individuals, but are not equivalent to them – so Maxwell's theory of electromagnetism is not the same as any individual's brain state. Although such concepts are causally effective, they are not themselves physical variables. Consequently physics *per se* cannot causally determine the outcome of human creativity; rather it creates the 'possibility space' to allow human intelligence to function autonomously.

Ellis, therefore, issued a challenge:

> The challenge to physics is to develop a realistic description of causality in truly complex hierarchical structures, where a top-down causation and memory effects allow autonomous higher levels in order to emerge with genuine causal powers. So far, attempts to relate physics to complexity – such as the reaction-diffusion equation, chaos theory, the renormalisation group, complexity theory – take us only a small step on this road.

What I am suggesting is that what he calls 'the challenge' – that is, the relation of physics to complexity – will never be met by an attempt to unify explanation in one cause or set of causes located in physics, nor at the other extreme will it be avoided by seeking a 'man of the gaps' who escapes from the laws of physics altogether.

The challenge will be met by recognising the causal power not just of physics but of other linked but independent constraints located in the emerging consequences of physics in chemistry, biology, psychology, sociology and so on, and by giving sufficient weight to the fact that the constraints play their autonomous part in controlling possible eventualities – what Ellis calls 'the possibility space' – into their outcomes. Among those constraints are those of mind, purpose and intentionality ("the cause is in my will", p.316). By using the language of constraint, rather than the language of cause, we counteract the competitive paranoia of reductionism particularly when it masquerades in the deceitful guise of causal closure.

Once this is applied to the relation between sciences and religions, the immediate advantage is striking: it means that constraints derived from the scientific and the religious domains can be considered together for their salience and relevance, just as constraints derived from physics and from human intentionality can be considered together. The constraints from each domain are extremely different, and always, therefore, we have to be on guard against the introduction of frivolous or false constraints. That *can* be a tense and contested matter: astrology and horoscopes have been so in the recent past. However, it certainly means, as we have just seen, that God (properly and not defectively considered; the distinction is a major theme in Bowker 2014) cannot be excluded from the network of constraints.

No doubt the human recognition of God is, like other human possibilities, genetically enabled. But its truth, its beauty and its virtue are neither contained nor diminished in the genetic constraints that help to make it possible, nor are they contained or diminished in the observation that they are correlated with particular activities in the brain. God, or WXYZ, or some referential word is required in order to make communicable and thus available to others those experiences of relatedness which are a consequence of attending to their possibility in the modes of attentiveness, intentionality and brain behaviour which we refer to by such words as prayer, worship, meditation and contemplation.

Religions can thus accept that we are, in all our potentialities, tunes sung by the genes – and proteins. Religions have long since recognised the strength of those inherited constraints, as we saw in the previous chapter, although inevitably they have talked about them and dealt with them in pre-scientific languages.

What religions have also recognised and defended (not least against quasi-scientific reductionism) is the fact that those constraints have created in the human case the ability to recognise what the constraints are and increasingly to understand them, and also on that basis to move far beyond them into freedom – and they have had much to say about how that freedom should and should not be exercised. The fact that genes and proteins build us consistently in highly constrained ways does not contradict our freedom: it creates it. And that is why humans are able to acquire responsibility on the basis of insight if they so choose and (if necessary) they are helped to do so, no matter how abject (as Freud would have put it) their points of departure may be.

A further point of equally paramount importance in understanding religions is that religions have identified other, highly specific constraints which, if internalised, lead to Enlightenment or to God. The internalisation of constraint is, in all religions, a matter of spiritual order and discipline, even though it has led to searching debates about the relation between grace and effort. That in itself contributes to the paradox of religions since religions are systems that identify, teach and transmit those liberating constraints. The constraints have to be protected because otherwise they may be plundered or made use of in such idiosyncratic ways that they become something entirely different – as indeed happens constantly in the history of religions.

So yet again, this takes us to the heart of the paradox of religions. Religions offer the constraints which, if internalised, can lead to consequences that otherwise will not occur in anything like the same way. They lead ultimately to God or to Enlightenment however they are defined. Not surprisingly, therefore, religions, or subsystems within religions, identify the constraints that need to be internalised (the equivalent of learning the notes and practising the scales in music), and they describe and offer the practices, including education, through which those constraints can be internalised. Religions, or subsystems within religions, then organise the means through which the nature and content of those constraints are protected and preserved: they have developed in many different ways the monitoring and controlling of the process of internalisation, both as it happens at any particular moment in time and also as it passes from generation to generation.

As a result, religions, or subsystems within religions, frequently (but not inevitably) tend to become protected circles within which the content and the internalisation of identified constraints can be monitored and controlled. In protected systems of that kind, it is inevitable that at least some authority figures will regard the maintaining of the system as their paramount responsibility leading to a preference for a system as closed as possible with strong boundaries that they can monitor and control. In that perspective the transcendence of the system *as a consequence* of the internalisation of constraint can actually be seen as a threat – hence the persecution of heretics and dissenters (or their equivalent in other religions).

It is this that creates the paradox: the purpose of the internalisation of constraint is to enable people to attain goals and to become what otherwise they could never be. It is to set them free into what Paul called 'the glorious freedom of the children of God' (Romans 8.21). Constraint is the necessary condition of freedom, not just in Christianity, but in other religions as well: the point of the protected or even closed circle is to make it possible for people to transcend it. That, however, is extremely disturbing, often unbearably so, for those in authority who see it as their responsibility to monitor and maintain the boundary of the circle *as an end in itself.* The resulting tension in religions and in education between authority and freedom is excellently summarised in the symposium edited by Gates.

Religions, therefore, supply and make available the constraints which, if internalised, lead to many different kinds of freedom in the composition of life, including ultimately those of Enlightenment and of God. On that basis, theistic religions know through long experience that because humans are tunes sung by the genes, there exists the possibility of composing their own music and of becoming tunes sung by God.

That too is a very ancient theme. Neither the fact that it is even more ancient than the theme of 'seminal constraint', nor the fact that it is expressed in corrigible (often poetic) language, makes it untrue or unimportant. John Donne wrote on his own death ('Hymn to God in My Sickness'):

> Since I am coming to that Holy Room
> Where, with Thy quire of Saints for evermore
> I shall be made Thy Music; as I come
> I tune the instrument here at the door,
> And what I must do then – think here before.

But it is a contemporary theme as well, as in this poem by Abercrombie:

> For love doth use us for a sound of song,
>   And love's meaning our life wields,
> Making our souls like syllables to throng
>   His tunes of exultation.
>
> Down the blind speed of a fatal world we fly,
>   As rain blown along earth's fields;
> Yet are we god-desiring liturgy,
>   Sung songs of adoration;
>
> Yea, made of chance and all a labouring strife,
>   We go charged with a strong flame;
> For as a language love hath seized on life
>   His burning heart to story.

Like that poem by Abercrombie, many of the poems or other reflections on this theme accept the strength of hereditarian constraint. And yet, exactly as the Buddha knew in his own case and asserted on behalf of others, they know also that we are constructed in such a way that we have both the possibility and the responsibility to change our course within the flow of the stream. The song cannot escape its origins, nor has it any reason to do so, but by the internalisation of constraints it is set free to become its own original singing, as Francis Thompson wrote (p.25):

> Pierce where thou wilt the springing thought in me,
> And there thy pictured countenance lies enfurled,
> As in the cut fern lies the imaged tree.
> This poor song that sings of thee,
> This fragile song, is but a curled
> Shell outgathered from thy sea,
> And murmurous still of its nativity.

At last, therefore, we are able to see how wrong it is to claim that genes determine and control human life and behaviour to such an extent that they are the sufficient explanation of all that happens in the human case, including culture and religion. Such claims miss the point that the more the genes constrain the construction of human beings, the greater are the resulting degrees of freedom which humans are then able to exercise and enjoy – including the freedom to turn back on what might be advantageous for gene replication and contradict it. This creates the clear possibility that with cognitive insight (maybe with the help of cognitive therapy) people can acquire responsibility even in circumstances like prison or Borstal where the immediate constraints are severe and restrictive. It also creates a social and moral imperative to make that acquisition of responsibility feasible.

These last chapters have shown that we can find points of connection between the genetic determination of behaviour in sociobiology and the realism with which at least some of our ancestors assessed the constraints derived from heredity delimiting the possibilities of action and behaviour. All the more reason, therefore, to pay equal attention to the serious and realistic ways in which they explored and assessed the immense range of possible behaviours that those same constraints have enabled, and that have led (amongst much else) to the worlds of religious belief and experience.

Certainly our ancestors came to many conclusions that we would have good grounds for regarding as false. The tenacity (as Schimmel described it, p.42) with which some religious believers and institutions continue to defend those false conclusions and regard them as incorrigible is a major problem in the relation between religions and the non-religious world. But our ancestors are not proved, for that reason, to have been wrong about everything. Wilson may well be correct that "neurobiology cannot be learned at the feet of a guru", but then *satori* cannot be learned, still less attained, at the feet of a neurobiologist.

From all this we can see that the sciences (in this case genetics) and the religions have much to offer to each other. We are in desperate need of a new and restated anthropology which signs an armistice and receives with gratitude all that is now offered to it. Yet all too often, and certainly in the case of Wilson and Dawkins, the relation between the sciences and the religions has been stated in yet another example of a false dichotomy: either science or religion. Here again it should be a case of both-and. What is needed in the relation between sciences and religions is a far more cooperative phenomenology – a critical but also more patient listening to the reports which come in of the far range of what humans are capable of experiencing, of being and of becoming. All of that the genes and proteins enable, and some parts (for example, certain genetically inherited diseases) they dictate. But in general they *prepare* us for behaviours without determining them – and what that vital point about 'preparation' means we will look at in the final chapter.

Without that more cooperative phenomenology, scientists will be tempted to imagine that science alone supplies 'the true explanation' of all that is, while conversely poets will be compelled to be protestant, instead of more often celebrating and making more human the vastly new vision of the universe which has opened up in the post-Einsteinian and post-Darwinian perspective.[15]

But is a more cooperative phenomenology possible? Certainly. It depends, however, on a costly (at least in terms of time) commitment to understanding: understanding on the part of those who are not scientists of at least the implications of the sciences, and understanding of the religions not least by those who at present hold them in contempt. There will still be disjunctively serious arguments and issues between them, but in the context of the construction of a more integrated phenomenology, they will be handled in a different way.

The problem is, of course, that neither of those ways of understanding is easy. In the case of religions, there is a preliminary, but nevertheless formidable, problem in trying to understand them. In religions people speak, write and think in a multitude of different languages. So the immediate and unavoidable question for those trying to understand why religions matter so much to so many is this: how do we enter the Tower of Babel with any hope or confidence that we can comprehend what is going on inside?

7

Understanding religions

I Issues of translation and interpretation

*W*E HAVE JUST SEEN THAT THE WORD 'CONSTRAINTS' MAY WELL sound restrictive, as indeed it is when constraints mark the boundaries of the possible or the permissible. But constraints, even when doing that, can also open the way to far greater freedoms of action: those who stop at the fence on the edge of a cliff are more likely to survive and do other things than those who try to walk on air.

Constraints can thus be the necessary condition of freedom, not its contradiction. In the case of human thought and behaviour, they act as markers that guide or control people into their characteristic ways of thinking, speaking and acting. Some (for example, the so-called 'laws of nature') are external and are simply the context in which people live. But many are internalised by individuals and become a part of their memory and experience in ways that characterise who they are, what they think and how they behave.

Constraints of that kind are extremely diverse and come (sometimes but not always consciously) from many sources, ranging from family to education, from peer-group approval to manuals and media. In the case of religions, the constraints are many and diverse, but some of the most important are derived from texts or from teachers that are believed to have authority. They may, for example, come from 'sacred texts' of the kind described in my *The Message and the Book* where the status and use of those texts are also discussed. Here it is sufficient to observe that when the content of a text or the guidance of a teacher is internalised, it can act as a powerful constraint over the outcomes in life.

It does not follow that the process of internalisation among believers in any religion leads to conformity in belief and behaviour. Far from it. Even when people in a religion recognise the same basic text(s) or teacher as the source of challenging or inspiring or legitimising constraints, there are many serious disagreements among them.

At the most elementary level, they may not agree on what the actual text is since there may be many different versions of the same text. Before the invention of printing (earlier in China than in the West), texts were copied by scribes in successive generations, leading to many variants. Even in the case of the Quran, where an agreed text was standardised very early on (under the third Caliph Uthman) and scribal transmission was not the issue, many variants have survived.[1] Uthman ordered all other copies to be destroyed, but the text can still be read in different ways because certain different consonants in Arabic look the same until diacritical marks are added (for example, *s* and *sh*, *t* and *th*, *d* and *dh*). Something similar is true also of Chinese before Qin Shihuangdi (r221–206 BCE) unified the script. Each of many characters could be read with different meanings, as Holloway commented in the introduction to his edition of *Xing zi ming chu* (p.x): "[A] large percentage of the characters can be read in two ways. Some can be read in three or four ways in Chinese, meaning that crafting an English translation was nothing less than a nightmare."

Beyond those issues, there are more searching disagreements about how texts recognised as authoritative should be understood or applied. Among particular groups there may well be degrees of consensus, but there is no absolute agreement on what the (or a) text means or on how it should be applied. The impossibility of agreement arises for two main reasons: first, texts are usually made up of words that are not self-explanatory and need interpretation; second, there is no agreement in any religion on how they should be interpreted or on what those words mean – despite attempts on the part of some in each religion to insist that there is.

For those trying to understand religions, those difficulties are exacerbated by the fact that the texts appear in an immense variety of different languages and scripts. We are therefore faced with some extremely challenging questions: what are the texts? How have they come into being and what has been their history? What status or authority do they have? What are the possible meanings of those texts? How can we gain access to those texts if they are in languages that we do not happen to know – how much, in other words, can we rely on translations?

Where the meaning and interpretation of texts is concerned, there have been in recent years dramatic advances, particularly in the deconstructed world of postmodernism, based on a recognition that there is no single 'meaning' of a text on which all must (or even can) agree. In contrast to the view that there is 'a meaning' of a text that the reader or interpreter can, with patience, tease out and identify, postmodernists affirm a vast diversity of meanings that depend on the interest and point of view of the reader. That observation has given rise to many different ways of reading texts – to the ideological, for example, or to feminist and womanist readings; and it has given rise also to serious and illuminating academic disciplines with somewhat formidable and perhaps off-putting names like 'reader/reception criticism', 'audience criticism', 'rhetorical criticism', 'semiotic transference analysis' and the like. When Fowler provided a guide or 'grand index' to postmodernist interpretation, he did so in a series of contrasts. The postmodern, he claimed (p.21) is

> an increasing recognition that reading and interpretation is always interested, never disinterested; always significantly subjective, never completely objective; always committed and therefore always political, never uncommitted and apolitical; always historically-bound, never ahistorical. The modernists' dream of disinterested, objective, distanced, abstract truth is fading rapidly.

The problems of understanding and interpretation may, however, be far more local and immediate, as we are likely to discover if we go on holiday to a foreign land: how do we understand and how do we communicate with people who speak a different language from our own? Those problems of language, communication and translation are a fundamental challenge in our attempts to understand religions. They came home to me personally many years ago in a dramatic way when I was standing in a marketplace in Nigeria with two small pamphlets in my hand, *Duties in Connection with Unlawful Assemblies and Riots*, and *Duties in Aid of the Civil Power*.

I was, like other young men at the time, doing National Service in the Army. Most of the time was spent in preparing for the independence of Nigeria, and that could of course include dealing with 'unlawful assemblies and riots'. Those of us who had to do that were haunted by the ghost of General Dyer and Amritsar – that episode in 1919 when protestors were driven into the Jallianwalla Bagh, a square in which there was only one entrance or exit. The troops under General Dyer came into the entrance, and General Dyer then ordered the protesters to disperse, warning them that if they did not do so the troops would open fire. Since the soldiers were standing in the only exit, the protesters could not disperse, and nearly 400 were killed.

The event was called by Winston Churchill "a monstrous event, an event which stands in singular and sinister isolation." The British Army was determined that it should remain in isolation and should never be repeated. That was why we were issued with the two small booklets containing the rules to be followed scrupulously when dealing with a riot: a bugle must be blown to alert the rioters to the presence of troops, interpreters must explain at least three times to the rioters that they must disperse or else be fired on, and above all else minimum force must be used: "The degree of force to be used is to be just so much as, and no more than, is essential to deal with the immediate situation" (*Duties in Connection* ..., p.13). To get this wrong was to be liable for a court martial.

So I faced a mob of Muslims and animists fighting over a donkey – why, I did not know. In a state of near panic about getting it wrong, I went through the rules, blowing bugles and telling the crowd through a loudspeaker in as many local languages as I could, "Disperse three times or I will fire". While I was doing this, the crowd pulled the donkey apart limb from limb.

As I stood there, looking at the hatred and anger in those faces, I decided what I wanted to do, if possible, with my working life: I wanted to understand why people, and especially religious people, hate each other so much. There are many sciences of animal and human behaviour, as well as much work in sociology, which contribute to that understanding. But prior to them all is the problem of languages. How can one hope to understand what other people think and believe if, because of their different language, one does not know what they mean? That again came home to me in Africa: there used to be a young Muslim, Tukuru, working each day on his own near the company office, and I used to hear him passing the time by talking aloud. At first I had no idea what he was talking about, and I thought (naive cultural assumption) that he was simply talking to himself. But as I gradually learned Hausa, I came to realise that he was talking all the time to God.

The Tower of Babel, the multitude of different languages in the world, is thus the fundamental problem in trying to understand religions and religious people. We can try to learn at least some languages, but no one can learn them all. At some stage, therefore, we have to rely on interpreters and translators.

The immediate problem is that all translation *is* interpretation. And here at once we are dealing, not with a remote academic problem, but with communication in everything from education and health to politics and global economics. Summits and conferences rely on interpreters, and while their skills are fantastic, they undoubtedly make mistakes. At an early stage of the negotiations leading to the independence of India and the establishing of Pakistan, Jinnah (speaking English) insisted that Muslims must be apart from a Hindu state, but he was interpreted as saying that Muslims must be a part of a Hindu state. In 2008, the Israeli deputy minister of defence, Matan Vilnai, was attacked worldwide when he was reported by Reuters to have said that the Palestinians in Gaza were bringing upon themselves a bigger Holocaust. He was understood to have been threatening genocide. In fact he used the Hebrew word *shoah*, 'disaster'. The confusion arose because *haShoah*, *the* Disaster, is a common name for the Holocaust. The translation had not noticed the absence of the definite article.

At a more individual level, mistakes occur in health and justice. To give an example in the case of health: about 50 million people in the United States speak at home a language other than English, of whom about 19 million are limited in English proficiency and need an interpreter when they meet a physician. Research by Dr Glenn Flores showed that there are, on average, thirty-one mistakes of interpretation at each such meeting (Flores 2003). Counterclaims were made that this was less than one word in every one hundred spoken (Abadia-Brown), but Flores pointed out that even one mistranslated word can have disastrous results. The consequence of mistranslating *intoxicado* as 'intoxicated' led to a hospital having to pay a settlement of $71 million for malpractice (Flores 2006).

To give an example in the case of justice: in 2008, *The Herald* (May 24) reported that "Scotland could be seeing miscarriages of justice because sheriff clerks and procurators fiscal are using unqualified linguists as interpreters for migrant defendants and witnesses in the courts." In response, professional translators formed the Scottish Interpreters and Translators Association, but were soon complaining that they were not being employed and that the use of inadequate translators was still leading to miscarriages of justice (McCaughlin 2009). When the UK Ministry of Justice outsourced to a private company the contract for providing court interpreters, the result was described by the Parliamentary Justice committee as "shambolic". As a result, to give only one example, in 2013, an unqualified man stood in for his wife and translated questions to the accused, not in Punjabi, but in a language no one in the court could identify.

So even small mistakes in translation can have extensive and serious consequences. Even worse are deliberate mistranslations in pursuit of what often appears to be profit or sensation. To give a recent example: Dr Glenn Shepard, an ethnobotanist and medical anthropologist, accused the makers of a reality TV show about an Amazon tribe, the Matsigenka (called Machigenga by the programme) of reaching "new depths of irresponsibility". Few viewers would know the indigenous language, but he did. He listed absurd and tendentious mistranslations, and he then argued that the programme "is rife with egregious mistranslations and outright falsifications" designed to portray the Matsigenka as "mean and savage people" (Shepard, p.18).

These issues of translation and interpretation appear in all walks of life, and sometimes they may be matters of life and death. On the beach at Dunkirk, Robert Harling tried to get French soldiers to understand what they must do if he was to rescue them, but they were hostile because they could not understand him: he found himself cursing "the folly of language that in crisis can still keep men unfamiliar with their friends."

The relevance of this to those who are trying to understand religions is obvious. Much of religious belief is expressed non-verbally, in gestures, rituals, signs, architecture and so on. But much of it is expressed through words, and of those words many are captured in texts that are regarded as sacred or holy.[2] There is much more to the understanding of religions than the study of texts, as we will see, but the question nevertheless remains: how can we understand religions without understanding their revered and authoritative texts? That raises a specific question for those who study religions in colleges and universities: is it necessary for students to have some knowledge of the languages of the religions they are studying, or can the religions and their texts be understood through translations?

That question would not arise so seriously if we could devise effective methods of machine-translation, so that a text in one language can be immediately reproduced in another. But, as we will see, that cannot be done. It is so difficult that we cannot yet imagine how it could be done. So the next and unavoidable question then arises: why is translation so difficult? The answer to that question takes us at once into hermeneutics – a fundamental issue in understanding religions as we have already seen.

HERMENEUTICS

The word 'hermeneutics' is said to come from Hermes, the Greek messenger of the gods. It refers, therefore, to the problems and issues that are involved in the transmission of meaning from one speaker to another, as well as from text or symbol to reader or hearer. At the heart of hermeneutics is the question: Whose meaning is the meaning of the meaning? In my book *Is God a Virus?* (pp.250–1) I addressed this question through the examples of the New Testament and Shakespeare. Thus when we ask the question, 'What does this passage in the New Testament mean?', we immediately have to ask, 'Whose meaning are we looking for?' Are we looking for the meaning the original author intended to convey, or that of the Church community that associated it with other documents into what became the canonical New Testament, or of the Biblical commentary, or of the preacher, or of the individual who reads the text, or, in a theological perspective, of God?

In a comparable way, when we ask for the meaning of a play such as *The Merchant of Venice,* are we asking what Shakespeare meant when he wrote the text, or what critics of the play through the ages have made of the text, or what a producer of the play at the National Theatre sees in the text, or what you as an individual find in the text when you see or read the play, or some combination of them all.

What we have to realize in reading a text, whether of Scripture or of Shakespeare (or of any other kind), is that the text offers, not one single 'meaning', but rather the opportunities of meaning and interpretation. John Barton once produced *The Merchant of Venice* with two different actors, Patrick Stewart and David Suchet, playing the part of Shylock in close succession. John Barton said of this experience:

> "Basically I gave Patrick and David the same directions and made the same points, both in detail and in general, yet the result was utterly different and individual."

How could that come about? Clearly because the two actors 'read' the play and the character differently, and the difference created in consequence, not just a different style, but a different interpretation and therefore meaning of the text. In Halio's summary (p.36):

> Consider the question of Shylock's Jewishness. How 'Jewish' is he, that is, how much should the fact of his Jewishness be emphasized in performance? Patrick Stewart argues that Shylock's Jewishness is irrelevant, a distraction when emphasized; he is essentially an alien, an outsider who happens to be a Jew ... David Suchet cannot agree. For him, Shylock is an outsider because he is a Jew ... Although both actors concur that the play is not anti-Semitic (despite the anti-Semitism it contains), they recognize that in the latter part of the twentieth century this aspect cannot be ignored; it must be reckoned with. That each of them did so in quite different ways leading to quite different performances indicates the richness of the character and the possibilities for interpretation.

'Opportunities of meaning', 'possibilities for interpretation' – those are the all-important phrases. It might not be particularly important if the differences of meaning and interpretation were a matter simply of taste. Often, however, the issues can be of huge importance – and that is especially so in the case of religions.

Take, for example, two Greek words in Paul's letter to the Romans, ἐφ᾿ ᾧ. The words occur in a sentence (5.12) in which Paul was expressing how death entered into the world and how, through the grace of God and of one man, Jesus Christ, the sentence of death has been annulled. But what Paul 'meant' depends on the meaning of those two Greek words – an issue of such seriousness that it contributed to the division between Catholics and Protestants at the Reformation. So what do the words ἐφ᾿ ᾧ mean? Fitzmyer, in his commentary on Romans, lists eleven different possible meanings, each one of which affects the divisive issue. As he put it with mild understatement, "The meaning of the phrase has been much debated through the centuries."

Clearly, therefore, in approaching the study of religions we have to face from the outset the question of how much and to what level it is possible to understand religions through translations of their texts, whether in written or spoken form.

It may seem a rather remote question, but in fact it is absolutely fundamental and at the same time extremely complicated. What, then, are the issues, and how can we deal with them?

THE PROBLEMS OF TRANSLATION AND THE
STUDY OF RELIGIONS

The first and unavoidable point is, of course, to recognize how difficult translation is. If translation were a matter of substituting a word or sentence in one language for an equivalent word or phrase in another, there would be no problem. Replacements of that kind are known technically as 'semiotic transformations', as in this brief definition of Ludskanov:

> Semiotic transformations are the replacements of the signs encoding a message by signs of another code, preserving (so far as possible in the face of entropy) invariant information with respect to a given system of reference.

The basic problems for translation arise from the last words of that sentence, 'with respect to a given system of reference'. It is that, more than anything else, which makes it impossible to make direct and unequivocal replacements from one language to another in any but the most elementary circumstances, and those certainly do not obtain in religious texts. A brief illustration of the point was made by Cornford commenting on Jowett's nineteenth-century translation of a particular sentence in Plato's *Republic*:

> One who opened Jowett's version at random and lighted on the statement that the best guardian for a man's 'virtue' is 'philosophy tempered with music' might run away with the idea that in order to avoid irregular relations with women, he had better play the violin in the intervals of studying metaphysics. (Cornford in Jowett, p.vf)

But that recognition of the impossibility of successful translation (defining 'success' as the transfer of a source language [SL] text into a target language [TL] without loss) is nothing new. Shelley made perhaps the most famous statement of the point in his *Defence of Poetry* against Peacock (pp.33f):

Hence the vanity of translation; it were as wise to cast a violet into a crucible that you might discover the formal principle of its colour and odour, as seek to transfuse from one language into another the creations of a poet. The plant must spring again from its seed, or it will bear no flower – and this is the burthen of the curse of Babel.

It is the point also that came home to Clarence Day as he reached the conclusion that God cannot possibly speak French after he observed the emasculation of robust religious concepts when they are translated into that language (pp.78f):

> In my English Bible, David was a fine Anglo-Saxon type, 'a youth, ruddy and of a fair countenance'. In the French, he was a revolting little snip from the boulevards, 'un enfant blond, et d'une belle figure'. Where my Bible spoke of 'leviathan' the French said 'le crocodile'. . ., and where mine said, 'Behold now behemoth', they said 'Voici l'hippopotame'.
>
> Instead of the children of Israel fearing lest the Lord should be worth, the French said *les enfants d'Israel* were afraid lest *le Seigneur* should be *irrité*. This word *irrité* appeared everywhere in the French version. It wasn't only the Lord. Cain was *tres irrité*. Moise (which seemed to me a very jaunty way of referring to Moses) was *irrité* again and again. Everybody was *irrité*. When my regular Bible, the real one, impressively described men as 'wroth', their anger seemed to have something stately and solemn about it. If they were full of mere irritation the whole time, they were more like the Day family.

However, there was *one* compensation in the possibility that God might actually understand French. One verse which Day had always disliked was the sentence in the Sermon on the Mount, "Blessed are the meek, for they shall inherit the earth". To him, Uriah Heep typified the meek:

> The meek were a snivelling, despicable, and uncomfortable lot. But in poring over the French Bible one evening, I had found to my delight that some daring Frenchman had altered this passage and had changed the Sermon on the Mount into something that a fellow could stand. 'Heureux les debonnaires', he had represented Jesus as saying, 'car ils hériteront de la terre'. The debonair! That was more like it! I cheerfully jumped into bed.

The basic point, then, is inescapable: there cannot be a single *correct* translation from one language to another – or to put it more technically, translation cannot adequately transfer the force and meaning of the original, whatever that might have been, without loss (or entropy). In those circumstances, the argument seems irresistible, that it is simply not possible to undertake the study of religions in translation.

But that point, about the impossibility of adequate translation, cuts both ways: for by what superhuman feat of intelligence do we suppose that *we* gain access to an original meaning of a text, or to a better understanding of a text, by attending to it in its original language, when we know that other translators necessarily fail? Since *all* translation is inadequate, perhaps we would do better to rely on *skilled* translators rather than on unskilled translators such as ourselves?

So the perfectly correct observation (that all translation is approximate) does not actually resolve the issue of whether we should abandon translations and attend to the texts in their original languages. What we need to know is *how* approximate or imprecise the possibilities of translation are. Is the burden of Babel really as great as Shelley supposed? What *are* the problems involved in translation? And *do* they suggest that we would be wiser to rely more on skilled translation than on our own (usually) unskilled efforts when we are trying to understand religions?

THE PROBLEMS OF CULTURAL RELATIVITY

The basic problem confronting us has been expressed in many different ways, but it was put forward with particular vigour by Ogden and Richards in 1923, in their book, *The Meaning of Meaning*. In that book they tried to exorcise what they called 'word magic' – by which they meant the view that there is some inherent, natural connection between words and their meanings – that a house is a house, or a man is a man; or in other words, that the meaning of a word is somehow locked up *within* the word. Their own example was the English saying, 'The Divine is rightly so called', as though divinity is actually locked up in the word.

But if an inherent independent meaning is *not* somehow locked up within the word, then of course a translator cannot look for the houseness of a house locked up within the word *maison* or the word *haus,* but has to decipher the determination of those sounds or symbols within the use and culture of the people who employ them. A French house is by no means the same entity as a German house.

This immediately suggests that our own personal knowledge of a language is in itself no guarantee of gaining access to the *meaning* of a text – indeed, a translation or even a paraphrase by someone more familiar with the history and culture of the people involved might actually catch and convey the contextualized sense of what is going on in a text just as well as our own attention to the original language – perhaps even better. Indeed, without a knowledge of the context, translation is sometimes impossible. Eithne Webster once asked of this sentence in the obituary of the Nawab of Pataudi, 'He once turned Trueman, who was bowling at full pace, off his stumps for four down to long leg', "Is this a winning entry for this year's most untranslatable sentence?"[3]

The emphasis on context is a direct consequence of the shift from a realist to a relativist view of language which became associated particularly with what is known as 'the Sapir/Whorf hypothesis'. In contrast to the view of language that it mirrors and reflects an independent reality which it describes (so that, roughly speaking, we can translate from one language to another with reasonable confidence, because all our languages have to do with the same reality which is independent of language), the Sapir/Whorf hypothesis made the point that languages are part and parcel of our total picturing activities. This means that they are certainly not in any simple one-to-one relationship with an independent 'out-thereness', which 'is what it is'. On the contrary, our constructed world views are powerful for us but are always culturally, historically and linguistically dependent. If there is any independence which pre-exists us, it is the cultural circumstance in which we were born, of which language is a part. Consequently Sapir argued (Hoijer, p.92):

> Language is a guide to 'social reality'... It is quite an illusion to imagine that one adjusts to reality essentially without the use of language and that language is merely an incidental means of solving specific problems of communication or reflection. The fact of the matter is that the 'real world' is to a large extent unconsciously built up on the language habits of the group ...The worlds in which different societies live are distinct worlds, not merely the same world with different labels attached.

This means that the language of any particular group, or for that matter religion, cannot be decoded in a simple one-to-one correspondence with our own by reference to an independent objectivity which they are both attempting to describe: another language can only be decoded – insofar as it ever can be – by reference to its own context of meaning and apprehension. To put it now in Whorf's words (p.213),

> The categories and types that we isolate from the world of phenomena we do not find there because they stare every observer in the face; on the contrary, the world is presented in a kaleidoscopic flux of impressions which has to be organized by our minds – and this means largely by the linguistic systems in our minds.... We are thus introduced to a new principle of relativity, which holds that all observers are not led by the same physical evidence to the same picture of the universe, unless their linguistic backgrounds are similar.

What, then, a text *means* is not a simple function of decoding a sequence of words and of re-presenting them in a parallel sequence of words, like the original (pre-IT) Unicode system, which was devised in 1896 in order to deprive the submarine telegraph companies of revenue. Under the Unicode system, a single word in a telegram stands for an entire sentence. Thus 'duodecim' represents a message about a sick person, 'Passed a sleepless night, and is feverish this morning'. The word 'annosus' means 'Confined yesterday, twins, both dead, mother not expected to live' (*Unicode*, pp.121, 41). Here one can pass from code to sentence or from sentence to code because they are deliberately devised to represent each other.

But languages are not in that relation to each other. It is rarely possible to look up a word in the dictionary of one language and be certain what it means in another. Take Hava's *Arabic-English Dictionary*: for the word *jawn* it offers the following (p.106): "Black, white. Light red. Day. Intensely black (horse)." Or again, for the word *chal* it offers (p.192): "Huge mountain. A camel. The banner of a prince. Shroud. Fancy. Black stallion. Owner of a thing. Self-magnified. Caliphate. Lonely place. Opinion. Suspicion. Bachelor. Good manager. Horse's bit. Liberal man. Weak-bodied, weak-hearted man. Free from suspicion. Imaginative man."

The point is that words do not have simple, single meanings. More than sixty years ago work started on an official and comprehensive dictionary of Sanskrit with English definitions. By 2003, the team involved had got halfway through the letter 'A' and was expecting to take another eighteen years to complete the letter 'A'. After that there are another forty-three letters in the Sanskrit alphabet.

Given, therefore, that languages are a social and cultural artefact, it is not surprising that words are rarely in a simple one-to-one correspondence with each other in different languages. If they *were*, the problems of machine translation would have been solved long ago – indeed, there could scarcely have been any problems. But that is exactly the point: it proved relatively easy to produce a mechanical dictionary in which linguistic items – not just single words but groups of words as well – could be processed independently and converted into corresponding items in another language. But the step from there to mechanical *translation* has proved impossible to take, because the *context* of a word (even in a much narrower sense of context than that employed by Sapir and Whorf and their successors) is as decisive for intelligibility as the word itself. Oettinger produced the first mechanical dictionary in 1954, but a mere nine years later he was reporting (p.18):

> The major problem of selecting an appropriate target correspondent for a source word on the basis of context remains unsolved, as does the related

one of establishing a unique syntactic structure for a sentence that human readers find unambiguous.

Consequently, it is possible to look up the word *gida* in a Hausa dictionary and discover that it 'means' house, *maison, haus, oikos*, or whatever; but what any of those words *means*, in the stronger associative sense, in any particular English, French, German or Greek utterance *cannot* be attained by the ability or the skill simply to look the word up in the relevant dictionary. It was a point that came home famously to Samuel Butler when, as a young schoolboy, he concluded that Mr Hall's shepherd was an energetic man who always slept with his face downwards. He came to that conclusion because he was relying on a dictionary to translate the words, "pastor ignavus dormit supinus":

> The sentence was translated in the old Eton grammar, 'The idle shepherd sleeps with his face upwards.' I took this, when a child, as an interesting fact in natural history, and believed I could always now distinguish an idle from an industrious shepherd by observing whether he slept with his face downwards or upwards. I was sure that Frick, Mr Vincent Hall's shepherd, always slept with his face downwards, but if you really wanted to know about a shepherd you must watch. (p.219)

The implications of all this were made even more precise by the philosopher Quine. Quine conceded that at a very rudimentary level direct translation is feasible. In his "newly discovered tribe whose language is without known affinities", a linguist has to learn the language directly "by observing what the natives say under observed circumstances, encountered or contrived" (p.2).

His first steps seem straightforward enough: when there appears on the scene what he in his own language calls 'a rabbit', the natives consistently make the same sound when they point at this object in the environment. Therefore, conceded Quine,

> I will grant that the linguist may establish instructively, beyond reasonable doubt, that a certain heathen expression is one to which natives can be prompted to assent by the presence of a rabbit, or reasonable *facsimile*, and not otherwise. The linguist is then warranted in according the native expression the cautious translation 'There's a rabbit', 'There we have a rabbit', 'lo! a rabbit', 'lo! rabbithood again', insofar as the differences among these English sentences are counted irrelevant.

On that basis Quine accepted that "this much translation can be objective, however exotic the tribe: it recognizes the native expression as in effect a rabbit-heralding sentence".

But that is extremely elementary, and is scarcely a beginning in understanding the complexity of language uses which occur when the natives are not preoccupied with heralding rabbits for the benefit of the comparative linguist. Even the next step is problematic:

> Given that a native sentence says that a so-and-so is present, and given also that the sentence is true when and only when a rabbit is present, it by no means follows that the so-and-so are rabbits. They might be all the various temporal segments of rabbits. They might be all the integral or undetached parts of rabbits. In order to decide among these alternatives we need to be able to ask more than whether a so-and-so is present. We need to be able to ask whether this is the same so-and-so as that, and whether one so-and-so is present or two. We need something like the apparatus of identity and quantification; hence far more than we are in a position to avail ourselves of in a language in which our high point as of even date is rabbit-announcing.

No doubt even that could gradually be adduced. But the problems do not end there: indeed, they compound. As Quine put it (pp.11, 25),

> The case is yet worse: we do not even have evidence for taking the native expression as of the form 'A so-and-so is present'; it could as well be construed with an abstract singular term, as meaning that rabbithood is locally manifested. Better just 'Rabbiteth' like 'Raineth'.

There is no need to pursue the argument further. Quine concluded:

> We could know the necessary and sufficient stimulatory conditions of every possible act of utterance, in a foreign language, and still not know how to determine what objects the speakers of that language believe in ... The obstacle to correlating conceptual schemes is not that there is anything ineffable about language or culture, near or remote. The whole truth about the most outlandish linguistic behaviour is just as accessible to us, in our current Western conceptual scheme, as are other chapters of zoology. The obstacle is only that any one intercultural correlation of words and phrases, and hence of theories, will be just one among various empirically admissible correlations, whether it is suggested by historical gradations or by unaided analogy; there is nothing for such a correlation to be uniquely right or wrong about.

Those arguments have, of course, moved on, but the early proposals show why a translation, or even a paraphrase made by someone knowing the original context of the text, may well help students and others to catch its meaning far more than their own attention to the original language.

There is a practical question here: putting it in terms of current jargon, the question is whether, in attempts at translation, literal equivalence is more important than dynamic equivalence. It sounds remotely academic, but it has become a serious conflict in, for example, the Roman Catholic Church over the official English version of the Order of the Mass, the Missal. In 1998, the International Commission on English in the Liturgy (ICEL) completed a revised translation of the English Missal, and it was approved by bishops' conferences. In 2000, Pope John Paul II announced a revised edition of the Roman Missal to be in the future the basis for new translations. In 2001, the Congregation for Divine Worship (CDW) issued *Liturgiam Authenticam* distinguishing 'sacred vernacular' (to be used in translations) from ordinary speech. In 2002, CDW rejected ICEL's translation, and the twelve-member Vox Clara was appointed by the Vatican to oversee ICEL's work. In 2010, Vox Clara/CDW made more than 10,000 changes to ICEL's translation, and its version was authorised.

In that way adherence to the 'sacred vernacular' (i.e., Latin) through as literal an equivalence as possible was made far more important than the English that people now understand and use. That seemed to many the wrong way to go. Sara Maitland, arguing as a Catholic that "the liturgy should empower us to go out and proclaim the Good News", observed: "One problem I find with the new translation of the liturgy is that it uses so much insider jargon. 'Consubstantial', 'chalice', 'dewful', 'we may merit to be co-heirs'; none of this language is going to play well in our daily lives, at work, in the pub, in our own homes."[4]

The seriousness of the issue can be seen, by way of example, in the vote of the US Bishops' conference on whether to accept the revised Vox Clara/CDW translation. An opponent, Bishop Trautman, claimed that "the new translation 'is slavish' in its overly literal translation of the original Latin." He was reported as saying:[5]

> Insisting that translators should be guided by the Second Vatican Council's Constitution on the Sacred Liturgy, *Sacrosanctum Concilium*, that stipulated the use of vernacular rather than 'sacred' language, he said that the average Catholic would not understand words like 'ineffable', 'consubstantial', 'incarnate', 'inviolate', 'oblation', 'ignominy', 'precursor', 'suffused' and 'unvanquished'. Using such words, he said, could lead to a 'pastoral disaster'... The new translation's 'give kind admittance to your kingdom', that replaces the current wording in Eucharistic Prayer 3, 'welcome into your kingdom our departed brothers and sisters', he said called to mind 'a ticket-taker at the door'.

This issue is even more familiar in the continuing parallel productions of *both* translations *and* paraphrases of the New Testament, and particularly of Paul's letters; and it has at times been an issue in the Churches whether a paraphrase (such as that of J.B. Phillips, the Cockney Bible of Mike Coles or the Strine Bible in Australia) could or should be read in public services, or whether a more literal translation should be used. It was perhaps a similar uneasiness (about not tampering with a pure original) which led to the synagogue practice of reading the Hebrew text of Tanach (the Jewish Bible) and following it with, not an Aramaic *translation*, but an Aramaic *paraphrase* or (as they called it) targum: the purpose was to protect the 'sacred text' in its original language and then to convey the sense to Aramaic speakers who no longer understood Hebrew.[6]

The basic point, then, is that a translation, no matter how literally intended, cannot deliver an innocent original into our hands, because all words are relative to the networks of cultural and individual assumption which alone create and guarantee the languages; and the words in turn work back on our assumptions and delimit the possible ways in which we can see and interpret our experience.

It follows from this that those who seek to understand a text and who rely on a translation are not necessarily worse off than those who make their own translation: both are still faced by the far more demanding task of seeking to understand the cultural and the contingent constraints which controlled that particular utterance into its outcome; and both are still faced by the problem of deciding what the words are capable of meaning.

WHOSE MEANING IS THE MEANING OF THE MEANING?

This at once brings us into another labyrinth of problems to which reference has already been made: meaning in relation to *what?* To the author's intention? There was a famous occasion once, when T.S. Eliot was reading his poems in public, and one of those present asked him, 'But what is the meaning of the line, "Lady, three white leopards sat under a juniper-tree"?' After a long pause, he said, 'What I mean is, "Lady, three white leopards sat under a juniper tree"'.

The point is equally clear in Dylan Thomas's vigorous response to an attempt by Edith Sitwell (as reported in Maud, p.21) to say what one of his poems 'meant':

Miss Edith Sitwell's analysis (wrote Dylan Thomas) ... of the lines

> The atlas-eater with a jaw for news
> Bit out the mandrake with tomorrow's scream
> Altar-wise by owl-light

seems to me very vague. She says the lines refer to 'the violent speed and the sensation loving craze of modern life'. She doesn't take the literal meaning: that a world-devouring ghost creature bit out the horror of tomorrow from a gentleman's loins.

Thomas then drove the point home by adding the comment: "This poem is a particular incident in a particular adventure, not a general elliptical deprecation of this 'horrible, crazy, speed-life'."

So even if we suppose that the translator is concerned with the representation of meaning, even in a broad, contextual sense, we still have to ask: meaning in relation to what? To the writer's original intention when he or she put pen to paper or stylus to clay? That is of the highest possible importance in trying to establish what the words may once have meant, but it rarely helps us to understand the meaning of the words in subsequent religious history: what shall it profit a man if he gain the original meaning of a sentence and lose the use of that sentence in the religious life of a community or a tradition?

Take this familiar sentence: *weheamin baAdonai wayyahsheblah lo zedhaqah* (Genesis 15.6). We can learn Hebrew and we can transpose those words into English as, 'And he believed in the Lord; and he counted it to him for righteousness'. We can then, no doubt, spend a lifetime trying to determine more securely what those words were originally intended to convey and what constrained them into being written or recited in the first place. But what has that to do with the subsequent use of those words among the Jews in evaluating *zekut aboth* (should it be 'on account of the fathers' or more strongly 'the merit of the fathers'?), or with the meaning of those words for Paul, or for the subsequent evaluation of Judaism by Christianity? The answer is, very little indeed – if anything: the meaning of those words for Paul, as part of a revealed utterance from God, is not in the least constrained by what those words might have meant to an original writer. New Testament writers frequently apply texts from the Bible (Tanach) to Jesus that have an entirely different sense in their original context, in any understanding of the Hebrew in that original context. On what grounds, then, can we possibly suppose that the *sine qua non* of religious studies is an attempt to disentangle what a text originally meant at the time and to the person when it was written?

Perhaps, one might reply, if not Hebrew then Greek: if our interest is in Paul then we must surely be able to translate *dikaiosune*. But again the same point comes back: we know that *dikaiosune* has been translated as 'righteousness'; but what does it *mean* in the context of Paul's life and letters? It may be more important to know German than Greek to participate in *that* discussion.

But the problems for religious translation go even deeper than that. Many religious 'texts' were in origin composed and transmitted orally. The meaning of such texts may well depend on inflection or on tone of voice. Jakobson offered an illustration in miniature of this, when he recalled how a Russian actor, trained by Stanislavsky in Moscow, was required by Stanislavsky to take the phrase *Segodnja večerom*, 'this evening', and to speak it with forty different expressions, to convey forty different emotional situations – and to do it in such a way that an audience could identify the situations from the tone of voice. Jakobson then repeated the test in a research programme which he was conducting, and the actor listed fifty situations and taped fifty corresponding 'messages'. According to Jakobson, "Most of the messages were correctly and circumstantially decoded by Moscovite listeners" (de George, p.91).

So the meaning of a sentence can depend very much on the tone of voice, and it may well be impossible to pick that up without a knowledge of the original language in question. The point is particularly important in languages that depend on tone in order to indicate the sense of what, in print or writing, would appear to be identical letters or characters. Jay Matthews recalled his experience in learning Chinese (p.17):

> Many years ago my first Chinese professor began her first class by handing out mimeographed copies of a complicated story about a man who ate stone lions. Below the English version we found, to our horror, the same story rendered in Romanized Chinese. It went 'Shih Shih Shih Shih Shih Shih Shih...' and so on, an entire story told with one sound. The only way even a Chinese could make sense of it, without seeing the actual Chinese characters, was to hear it read with each sound given one of the four Chinese tones, which are (roughly) high, rising, low or falling. A few students in that class did not return the next day.

Tone of voice, therefore, may affect greatly the meaning of a word or sentence. Consider this example from Tanach (the Jewish Bible): the Book of Amos records how Amos, having come from the South to declaim against the Northern kingdom, was confronted by Amaziah, the priest of Bethel, and was told by Amaziah to stop prophesying in the North where he does not belong, and to return to his own land. Amos replies (7.14): "*lo nabhi anoki welo ben nabhi anoki.*" He then continues, "But I was a herdsman ... and Yahweh took me as I followed the flock, and said to me, Go, prophesy."

In the transliterated sentence, there is no verb 'to be'; so what could the sentence mean? Literally it means, 'Not a prophet I and not a son of a prophet I'. If we supply the verb 'to be' in its possible different tenses, it can mean, 'I was not a prophet and I was not a son of a prophet, but God made me one';

that is, *you* may think that I don't have the credentials of a prophet entitled to prophesy here, but I certainly do because I got them directly from God. Or it could mean: 'I am not a prophet and I am not the son of a prophet'; that is, I have nothing to do with *your* understanding of a prophet, but nevertheless I have a right to prophesy here. Or it could mean, 'I will not be a prophet and I will not be the son of a prophet': I will never meet your criterion of a prophet, but the fact remains that God has made me one.

All of those give a different emphasis to the reply of Amos, but in different ways they all accept that Amos is making a negative statement in order to draw a strong contrast between *his* understanding of what makes a prophet (entitled to speak out in Bethel) and Amaziah's.

But now consider that Hebrew has no written or printed punctuation: it is therefore possible, by altering the stress and tone of the voice, to change a sentence from a statement to a question: *lo nabhi anoki? welo ben nabhi anoki?* Not a prophet I? Not a son of a prophet I? I most certainly am. From being a strong negative, the tone of voice, which changes the sentence into a question, also changes the sentence into a strong affirmative. The sentence may thus be an example of the *lo*-interrogative, a construction which is scarcely ever picked up in translations of the Bible. Nevertheless there are other examples in Tanach in which what is usually *translated* as a negative can actually be a strong affirmative, depending entirely on the tone of voice.[7]

It is easy to see how that rather precise example can be generalized – as indeed it was in the pioneering work of such people as Milman Parry, Lord, Ong and Vansina, all of whom made the point that the oral transmission of material creates its own constraint over utterance (and thus over interpretation), to which we have virtually no access through a subsequently printed text. As Lord put it (p.129),

> The art of narrative song was perfected, and I use the word advisedly, long before the advent of writing. It had no need of stylus or brush to become a complete artistic and literary medium. Even its geniuses were not straining their bonds, longing to be freed from its captivity, eager for the liberation by writing. When writing was introduced, epic singers, again even the most brilliant among them, did not realize its 'possibilities' and did not rush to avail themselves of it. Perhaps they were wiser than we, because one cannot write song. One cannot lead Proteus captive; to bind him is to destroy him ... The two techniques [oral and writing] are, I submit, contradictory and mutually exclusive. Once the oral technique is lost, it is never regained.

Perhaps that is why, when the Clown in *The Winter's Tale* asks Autolycus whether in his 'parcels' for sale there are any ballads, Mopsa, the shepherdess, at once cries out, "Pray now, buy some: I love a ballad in print a' life; for then we are sure they are true" (iv. 3). It is a point similarly seized on by Ong in his claim that "Sound is a special sensory key to interiority"; and he unpacked the implications of that by arguing (p.117 referring to Carothers p.311):

> Sound is more real or existential than other sense objects, despite the fact that it is also more evanescent ... Cultures which do not reduce words to space but know them only as oral-aural phenomena, in actuality or in the imagination, naturally regard words as more powerful than do literate cultures. Words *are* powerful ... Only with writing, and particularly with the phonetic alphabet, do words readily appear to be disengaged from non-verbal actuality to the extent to which the technological man today commonly takes them to be ... The greater reality of words and sound is seen also in the further paradox that sound conveys meaning more powerfully and accurately than sight. If words are written, they are on the whole far more likely to be misunderstood than spoken words are. The psychiatrist, J. C. Carothers ... puts it this way: 'Few people fail to communicate their messages and much of themselves in speech, whereas writings, unless produced by one with literary gifts, carry little of the writer and are interpreted far more according to the reader's understanding or prejudice.'

The claim being made here complicates the already ferocious problems of translation: narratives passed on by oral transmission become different entities when they are written down. In cases of that kind, to what extent should translators bear in mind the oral precursor? Where religions are concerned, the importance of storytelling is so fundamental that 'religion as story' was once proposed as a foundation for the study of religions (see Wiggins). The importance of 'word' and 'story' in religious life was strongly emphasised in the report of the Anglican Doctrine Commission, *Believing in the Church*, which pointed out that what is mainly found in the Bible is not explicit formulation of doctrine but narrative.

It is true that postmodernism and deconstruction have challenged – even derided – the place of 'narratives'. But what in fact has been challenged is not the importance of narrative in human life and society, but the claim that some, or even only one, narrative is privileged above others. What have been challenged, in other words, are the so-called meta-narratives. Even in a postmodernist world of deconstruction, the creative and constraining importance of the public and private narratives of religion are unaffected unless they are combined with that claim of privilege.

So the basic point remains. Reading a story in a translation is one thing; listening to it spoken in its original language is another. I first and suddenly began to understand Homer in a different way when, long ago, the school day began with a period once a week during which Homer was read aloud in its original Greek.

TEXT AND TRANSLATION IN RELIGIOUS STUDIES

The challenges of translation occur, as we have seen, in many aspects of life, but they present particular problems for the study of religion in colleges and universities. So we return to the question: if, as George Borrow put it, translations are at best an echo of the original, is it not desirable or perhaps even necessary for those studying a religion to understand its language, even if only at a rudimentary level? During the 1960s, there was a debate in the Faculty of Divinity at Cambridge about whether the study of one or other of the Biblical languages, Hebrew or Greek, should continue to be compulsory. At the meeting to decide the issue it was argued that *both* were necessary, and that Latin and German were equally indispensable in order to study the Christian tradition. As I said at the time, it resembled the moment in 1907 when a decision had to be made about how many new Dreadnought battleships should be built. Churchill later recalled (*The World Crisis*), "A curious and characteristic solution was reached. The Admiralty had demanded six ships; the economists offered four; and we finally compromised on eight."

Compulsion of that kind is clearly unrealistic. So should we therefore come to the opposite conclusion? If translation is a difficult exercise requiring a serious competence, might we not be wiser to entrust ourselves to translators whose knowledge of the languages in question is far better than our own? Translations and paraphrases made by others are at least as likely to indicate possible ranges of meaning as are our own efforts at translation which (to revert to George Borrow) may be a very distant echo indeed. Perhaps, therefore, a student's understanding of what religion is will be very much *hindered* by learning languages, not enhanced – not least since there must be at least thirty major religious languages to learn.

That argument can be put much more positively: translations can convey the sense of an original in exciting ways. Keats is not alone in looking into a translation (in his case Chapman's Homer) and feeling like "some watcher of the skies/ When a new planet swims into his ken". Indeed, Keats was *not* alone when he first looked into Chapman's Homer: he was spending the evening with Cowden Clarke, to whom a folio edition of Chapman's translation had recently been lent. Together they began to read aloud episodes and passages which they remembered from Pope's translation: "One scene",

Clarke recalled, many years later, "I could not fail to introduce to him – the shipwreck of Ulysses ...

> 'Then forth he came, his both knees falt'ring, both
> His strong hands hanging down, and all with froth
> His cheeks and nostrils flowing, voice and breath
> Spent to all use, and down he sank to death.
> The sea had soak'd his heart through.'

And as Clarke read, he was rewarded, as he put it later, by one of Keats's 'delighted stares'. We all know the consequence: at daybreak, Keats walked home through the city of London, and within two hours of reaching home he had finished the sonnet which, in a sense, unlocked his life to poetry.[8]

The 'delighted stare' can often be evoked by a translation – even in the unlikely circumstance of a Religious Studies' classroom; and I can see no justification for supposing that there is something educationally inferior in evoking through translation, not only the delighted stare, but the creative response which occurred in Keats' case.

The point is that it depends on what you want – what you want to see as a consequence of the educational exercise. There are goals in any education, whether in Religious Studies or anything else, and the issue of translation cannot be discussed in abstraction from the determination of the goals which are believed to be worth aiming at. Even if a goal is that students should understand the meaning of a text, still it does not follow that they themselves should be required or advised to learn the language in question: as we have seen, what is involved in 'understanding' and 'meaning' does not follow so simply. Keats himself grasped the issue of meaning in his original version of his famous sonnet, as one can see from the manuscript in the Harvard Keats Collection: lines 7 and 8 read originally: "Yet could I never judge what men could mean, Till I heard Chapman speak out loud and bold." Later he corrected it to become:

> "Yet did I never breathe its pure serene
> Till I heard Chapman speak out loud and bold."

Atmosphere, rather than meaning: maybe. But now we come to the other side of the argument, because Keats is raising here another issue, the issue of judgement – "yet could I never *judge* what men could mean". It is all very well appealing to the fact that we can never be sure that we have actually understood anything in another language, but the other fact remains that there is *something* to be understood imperfectly. How can Keats or anybody else be sure that he is 'breathing its pure serene', without some check on the original – and Keats, after all, knew no Greek? Latin was another matter: Keats started to translate *The Aeneid* when he was ten and completed it by the time he was sixteen. It was from Lemprière's *Classical Mythology* that he absorbed the Greek mythology that proved so essential for his poetry.

The issue here is a matter of judgement. The argument is clear that we cannot know 'what the text means' as though that were a single and simple issue, nor can we know for certain 'what the text meant' because we cannot gain access either to its own original context or to the author's intention. We have to accept that all translations are approximate, provisional, corrigible and imperfect. That is true of the translations of even the most expert linguists, and certainly of those that we make for ourselves. But there are degrees and degrees of approximation; and if we do not give to our students *some* knowledge of language, how can they judge between the various translations on offer? Quis custodiet custodes? Or as we might put it more appropriately, Quomodo iudicantur iudices?

The point here is that major issues of interpretation and understanding turn on judgements about the possible meanings of the original text. Translations have to choose one possibility, but they cannot usually indicate what the other possibilities are, or what has led to the one possibility that has been chosen. One example of the importance of this (of two Greek words in Paul's letter to the Romans) has already been given (p.171).

Another example goes down to a single letter, the letter ل (l) in Arabic. The issue arises from the practical question of whether – and if so, to what extent – intercession for others is allowed in the Quran (see Bowker 1966). The general view of the Quran is that each soul acquires on the Day of Judgement exactly what it has earned, in terms of a balance between the good and the evil which it has done. No intercession can help to tip the balance. But then the Quran, in several passages, seems to allow an exception: "no intercession *illa laman* it is allowed by God". The preposition ل in Arabic, like the dative in Latin and Greek, can mean 'to' or 'for': so this phrase can mean that intercession is efficacious either *to* whom God allows it, which can then be taken to be restricted to Muhammad who becomes *the* intercessor *par excellence*; or it means that it is efficacious *for* whom God allows it, which immediately opens up the scope of intercession extensively, as Shia Muslims in particular appreciate. The judgement concerning which of the two is correct is of extensive consequence in the practice of Muslim life, and it is equally important if we are trying to understand the Quranic picture of human nature and its destiny. Translations have to make that judgement, but without a knowledge of Arabic, the general reader cannot judge what is at issue except with the help of footnotes.

The importance of this is not confined to texts containing issues of major importance. It always obtains since, to repeat the point again, there are often many justifiable translations of the same text. Not surprisingly, translation *itself* carries with it cultural assumptions which create and control it. Consider Edward Harwood's translation of the New Testament (1768). His endeavour was

> to Cloathe the genuine ideas and doctrines of the Apostles with that Propriety and perspicuity in which they themselves would have exhibited them had they now lived and written in our language.

How successful was he? This is the opening of his version of the Parable of the Prodigal Son:

> A gentleman of a splendid family and opulent fortune had two sons. One day the younger approached his father, and begged him in the most importunate and soothing terms to make a partition of his effects betwixt himself and his elder brother. The indulgent father, overcome by his blandishments, immediately divided all his fortunes betwixt them.

Tucker commented on this (in Dorsch, p.109):

> Needless to say, the bluntness of the Authorized Version which tells how the young man 'would fain have filled his belly with the husks that the swine did eat' is too much for Dr Harwood – 'he envied even the swine the husks which he saw them greedily devour – and would willingly have allayed with these the dire sensations he felt.'

Dr Johnson read this, and when he found that 'Jesus wept' had become 'Jesus burst into a flood of tears', he threw the book down exclaiming 'Puppy'.

Maybe it seems a trivial point, but it becomes extremely serious when translators use their translations to advance their own point of view. 'Tendentious translations', as they are known, are not surprising among rival religious groups making use of the same text.[9] In the case of early Christianity, striking examples were gathered by C.S.C. Williams, and Epp showed how one of the two main text traditions of the Book of Acts (Codex Bezae) has heightened the anti-Jewish emphasis.

Tendentious translations are not confined to the religions. They are, in fact, extremely common. To take only one example: some years ago Bettelheim analysed the way in which the English translators of Freud's work on psychoanalysis tried to make him sound more 'scientific', leading Bettelheim to the conclusion that "the English translations of Freud's writings are seriously defective in important respects and have led to erroneous conclusions, not only about Freud the man but also about psychoanalysis."[10]

Thus Freud's pronouns *das Ich und das Es* (to quote the title of his book) lost all their German associations and became 'ego' and 'id', with 'superego' for *Uberich*. *Die Seele*, which might most naturally be translated 'the soul', meant for Freud the way in which individuals appropriate their own histories and live their own personal lives. But 'soul' had far too many religious associations for Freud's translators, so they rendered it instead (usually) as 'mind', a complete misrepresentation of what Freud intended.

Comparable attempts by translators to make humanistic vocabularies more 'scientific' have now become widespread. They reflect the way in which, as Seidler has claimed recently, the everyday languages of personal relationship, so common among Jewish philosophers, have been abandoned by those who pursue the more detached and 'scientific' analysis of language as the proper task of philosophers. To put it in his own words (p.108),

> Within an Enlightenment vision of modernity, we have generally learned to dispose of a language of soul that is often confined to the religious sphere. Within a Cartesian tradition, we have learned to think of the mind, reason and consciousness where we might once have spoken more easily of the soul. We learn to wonder about the relationship between mind and body as a defining issue within 'modern philosophy', and assume that this expresses whatever was meaningful in the relationship between 'soul' and 'body'.

The point here is simple and profound: *all* translations, including our own, are constrained by cultural context and indeed by the biography, purpose and competence of the translator.

That, however, simply reinforces the argument that we cannot make *judgements* about a translation or about competing translations without some knowledge of the original language. We can know that some translations are wrong (that the word *maison* means 'hippopotamus'), but it is usually impossible to say that a translation is right.[11] Therefore, we have to make corrigible judgements about probability or even possibility. No doubt those judgements are as culturally embedded as the original text, but we cannot make judgements of that kind without a knowledge of the relevant languages.

CONCLUSION

We are thus left with a dilemma. We need to understand religions, maybe for their own sake, perhaps to live more peacefully together in multifaith communities, certainly in order to address more effectively some of the most threatening and dangerous conflicts in the world.

That, however, cannot be done without understanding the languages of the different religions. There are in the world about 7,000 languages spoken (and many religious texts are in languages no longer spoken). Even cutting them down to those that are most widely spoken or used, no one can learn them all. It is hard enough to learn the languages together with their related dialects within a single group (say, Chinese, Indian or Semitic). If the purpose is to understand situations of conflict, then many conflicts involve more than one group of languages.

We therefore have to rely on interpreters and translations in order to understand the religions of the world. But translation carries with it all the many problems reviewed in this chapter. So the difficulty is this: we know that translations are approximate and in that sense unreliable, and yet at the same time we know that no individual can learn all the languages necessary to make a judgement on the quality of available translations.

Common sense, therefore, says that we have to trust each other: we have to trust the translations of others, just as scientists have to trust the experiments of others. It is one criterion of scientific truth that experiments should be repeatable, but scientists cannot possibly repeat all the experiments on which they rely.

There is, however, a major difference. Translations cannot be trustworthy in the way that repeatable experiments hope to be. However much we trust the translations of others, we know, for all the reasons given earlier in this chapter, that no translation is perfect. We do not even know what the word 'perfect' could mean in that context. We can, of course, look at more than one translation and make comparisons, but even then we have to live with the fact that translations, like so many other of our judgements, are approximate, provisional and corrigible.

So the fundamental question persists: granted that all translations are approximate, how does one judge between them if one cannot refer to the text in its original language? To what extent can one rely on translations made by others if one cannot make judgements about them based on at least a limited knowledge of the languages involved? The answer depends on goals, levels and priorities. They are clearly different for politicians, doctors, economists, those engaged in business and those engaged in Religious Studies.

In all those cases, there are thresholds and levels of attainment that are related to the purposes and requirements of those involved. Much academic research is completely impossible without a knowledge of the relevant languages, but we are not looking for primary schoolchildren to learn Greek in order to enact the Christmas story. What we need to be clear about are the limits imposed on the levels of insight and understanding by the *absence* of language: in all cases, there will be loss, however much there may also be compensatory gain, not least because there will be more time to do other things.

Even so, it is equally important to remember that translations vary greatly. Judgements are necessarily involved because some translations are a great deal more probable than others. If we wish or need to decide on degrees of probability, then it is necessary that those who are teaching or undertaking the serious study of religions should know the languages of the religions that most concern them.

If that is too large a demand, it is still worth attempting to reach the level of what may be called a 'translation knowledge' of languages. That means, in effect, knowing a language to the level of being able to follow what a translation is translating, and of being able to check words and phrases in a dictionary. That does at least allow some judgements to be made about the translations on offer. We have to live with the fact that translations are approximate, provisional, corrigible and may actually be wrong, but the fact remains that some are a great deal more probable than others. What is urgent, therefore, is to find ways in which by sharing possibilities with each other we can move towards the more probable. Here, for sure, that 'way of exchange' known as the Internet will transform the field entirely.

In this chapter we have looked at the fundamental importance of texts in understanding religions. Through the reading and hearing of texts, people internalise constraints that control or guide their lives into particular outcomes. But texts are only one part of religious belief and practice, and it is essential not to give them such an isolated status that the non-verbal expressions of religion are lost sight of. Constraints are internalised from many other different sources, and they lead to decisively important outcomes in belief and behaviour. That can be seen most obviously in the practice of daily life, but it can be seen also in art.

Understanding religions

II Being religiously human: The internalisation
of constraint in ethics and art

IN RECENT YEARS IT HAS BECOME AN ISSUE WHETHER TO MAKE A
start in understanding religions with the beliefs that characterise each
religion, or with the practices – with what religious believers and religious
institutions actually commend and do in practice. Thus it is often pointed out
that Christianity is unusual in its focus on beliefs epitomised in an emphasis
on Creeds, hence also on orthodoxy. In contrast, the emphasis in other religions, so it is claimed, is on the practices that will lead to particular goals: the
goals may, for example, be related to the learning and practice of particular
forms of meditation (as, e.g., in *samatha-bhavana* and *vipassana-bhavana* for
Buddhists, p.288, *sadhana* for Hindus, p.123), or to the observing of rules and
laws (as in Torah for Jews or Sharia for Muslims). It has therefore been argued
that in order to understand religions we need to observe what is done (and
what is required to be done) in practice far more than we need to analyse the
nature and cogency of beliefs.

On that basis, to give an example, the anthropologist Whitehouse has proposed two 'divergent modes of religiosity' (to quote the subtitle of his book):
the 'doctrinal' and the 'imagistic'.[1] His argument is that "modes of religiosity
constitute tendencies towards particular patterns of codification, transmission, cognitive processing, and political association" (p.1):

> The imagistic mode consists of the tendency, within certain small-scale
> or regionally fragmented ritual traditions and cults, for revelations to be
> transmitted through sporadic collective action, evoking multivocal iconic
> imagery, encoded in memory as distinct episodes, and producing highly
> cohesive and particularistic social ties. By contrast, the doctrinal mode of
> religiosity consists of the tendency, within many regional and world reli-
> gions, for revelations to be codified as a body of doctrines, transmitted
> through routinized forms of worship, memorized as part of one's 'general
> knowledge', and producing large, anonymous communities.

In fact, once again, we are drifting onto the lee shore of the falsely dichotomous question. Whitehouse was certainly aware of this because he wrote (p.1),
"These fundamentally contrasting dynamics are often to be found within a
single religious tradition, where they may be associated more or less strongly
with different categories or strata of religious adherents."

So it is not a case of either-or, either orthodoxy or orthopraxy, but of both-
and. Creeds do indeed have an important status in Christianity because of
the emergence of Christianity in the Roman Empire, the relation of baptism
to the death and resurrection of Christ, and the understanding of *symbolum*
as 'password' in the Roman army; but that has not made Christianity less
concerned with particular practices, not least those of prayer and meditation
(e.g., *The Spiritual Exercises*, p.16). Conversely, religions concerned with practical goals or with the observance of laws are founded on particular beliefs
even if those are often (though certainly not always) left as domain assumptions. Wensinck, after all, gave as a title to his study of *'aqida* in early Islam
the title *The Muslim Creed*, followed sixty years later by Montgomery Watt's
Islamic Creeds.[2] At the very least they presuppose traditions of teaching that
have frequently been captured in authoritative texts as described in my *The
Message the Book*.

Although, therefore, the supposed disjunction between beliefs and practices is easily overstated, what does remain important is the fact that beliefs
do not *have* to be expressed in words, whether of creeds or of texts or of any
other form. Religious beliefs as well as behaviours are very often expressed in
non-verbal forms of practice – for example, in contemplation, or single-point-
edness of mind, or rituals, or the creation of symbols and signs, or in art.

Or in the actions of life from day to day. The expression of beliefs in practice
is not confined to actions that belong identifiably to a particular religion – as,
for example, in sacrifice or yoga or rituals. Far more fundamentally, the practice of religion is seen in everyday life and in the ways in which people act on
the basis of the constraints that they have internalised and made their own.

The internalisation of constraints derived from religions may result in lives
of admirable holiness, beauty and service, but it is not automatically so: the
outcomes are not necessarily desirable or good. The opinions of Mencken and
Pascal to the contrary have already been quoted. It means that any attempt to
study and understand religions through the ways in which believers put their
beliefs into practice has to keep a careful eye on hypocrisy, the ever-present
ghost that haunts the religious world.

The point here is that the participants in a religious system are offered from
the system resources to be internalised, at least in part, and expressed in the
outcome of life – or should be, if the participant is not to be hypocritical in

his or her allegiance: 'A what, my good sir?' demanded Mr Pecksniff when Anthony Chuzzlewit told him bluntly not to be a hypocrite.

> 'A what, my good sir?' ... 'A hypocrite.' 'Charity, my dear,' said Mr Pecksniff. 'When I take my chamber candlestick tonight, remind me to be more than usually particular in praying for Mr Anthony Chuzzlewit, who has done me an injustice.'

As I pointed out in 'Religions as Systems' (in *Believing in the Church*, pp.159–89), the real harm in hypocrisy lies neither in the prayer nor in the candlestick. If we all waited to pray until we were free of fault, the word 'prayer' would cease to exist in any human language. The real harm lies in the distinction in the nature of hypocrisy which Chuzzlewit made later on, when he encountered Pecksniff in the stagecoach, and when Pecksniff protested that while he may be a hypocrite, he is certainly not a brute:

> 'Pooh, pooh!' said the old man. 'What signifies that word, Pecksniff? Hypocrite! Why, we are all hypocrites. We were all hypocrites t'other day.... The only difference between you and the rest was – shall I tell you the difference between you and the rest now, Pecksniff?' 'If you please, my good sir; if you please.' 'Why, the annoying quality in you is,' said the old man, 'that you never have a confederate or partner in your juggling; you would deceive everybody, even those who practise the same art; and have a way with you, as if you – he, he, he! – as if you really believed yourself.'

HYPOCRISY AND CHARACTER

Religions are of course well aware of human fault and failure, and they have far larger vocabularies of fault than the word 'hypocrisy' alone. There are, for example, more than 100 words in the Quran for human sin, offence and failure. "'We all have flaws,' said the Duke of Coffin Castle, 'And mine is being wicked.'" (Thurber, p.79).

Religions obviously confront and deal with sin and evil, but they do so in very different ways – so much so that in consequence they give strikingly different accounts of human nature. But on one thing they are agreed: to try to evade or conceal fault through hypocrisy is itself a part of that evil, especially when it leads to tragic consequences. That has been all too clear in the Vatican attempt to protect priests and religious who committed sexual abuse. The determination, shared for years by cardinals and bishops, to protect the system and its authority completely overwhelmed their human and moral obligation to protect the innocent and deal effectively with the offenders. On repeated occasions, they (and spokesmen for the Vatican) gave the impression that, like Mr Pecksniff, they really believed themselves.

But that immediately alerts us to the fact that the structures of religious systems can themselves produce evil consequences: protecting "the system and its authority" can all too easily become an end in itself. If individual believers do bad things and are at fault, each system has its own ways of dealing with the matter – and religions have much to say about penitence, forgiveness and reconciliation. As a result, a defence of the *system* frequently put forward is that in any barrel of apples there are always bound to be a few rotten apples.

But that 'defence', if such it is, does not address the fact that the organisation and institutional structure of religions (or at least of some groups within religions) actually produce damaging and destructive consequences: they are often hierarchical and unaccountable except to themselves – and maybe to a very much higher authority.

Clearly one can accept that in any barrel of apples there are likely to be some rotten apples, but what if the whole barrel seems to be designed to make the apples go rotten? That surely was illustrated in the structure of the Vatican and the Papal Curia as they defended the institution in the face of the child abuse that took place within the protected circle of the Church. The United Nations Committee on the Rights of the Child was still reporting as late as 2014 (§26) that "in dealing with allegations of child sexual abuse, the Holy See has consistently placed the preservation of the reputation of the Church and the protection of the perpetrators above children's best interests, as observed by several national commissions of inquiry."

The recognition of structural fault and the subversions of 'hypocrisy' is simply to reiterate the point that the internalisation of constraints does not produce automatic or inevitable consequences. Even more serious than hypocrisy is the ease with which some people can live parallel and apparently disconnected lives, with internalised constraints producing consistent outcomes in public while having no effect on particular private behaviours.

So the human appropriation and expression of religious resources or inputs is nothing like so simple or mechanical as the input, storage, retrieval and output system of a constructed information processor like a computer. It is perfectly accurate – and, with reference to many social and psychological issues, is extremely helpful – to regard the human form of energy transaction as an information-processing system. But the complexity and 'regular irregularity' (effective rule-breaking) with which this is done in the human case creates the awkward reality of diverse character – awkward, that is, from the point of view of the system or design theorist, or from the point of view of those who believe that the brain is 'nothing but' a computer, but not from the viewpoint of the artist, the poet or the person who has to live.[3]

So the internalisation of religious constraints is not like putting a coin in a machine in the hope that it will produce (if it is working) a high-energy drink. It is not like throwing petrol on a fire, nor is it even like taking a medicine where the consequences are not inevitable, but they are at least known and tested. The consequence in the religious case is not cure but character: a life becomes characterised by the extent to which the constraints are internalised and given expression in practice. "By their fruits you will know them."

Here, yet again, the paradox of religions returns, because each religion, or more often each subsystem of any religion, makes clear what those 'fruits' – that is, what those behaviours and practices – should be. There is thus an unending tension between those, on the one hand, who monitor and evaluate acts according to rules and norms, and those, on the other hand, who evaluate the character that people make manifest in what they do and how they live. It is the classic tension between 'act moralities' and 'virtue moralities'. Should the authority figures in any religion or subsystem of a religion insist on acts that conform to the rules, or should they look for the transformation of character in the direction of the ultimate goals? It is exactly the same issue that individuals have to face in forming their own judgements and actions, and the consequences are made manifest in their lives.

That tension is graphically illustrated in the contrast between Pope Benedict XVI and his successor Pope Francis. *Both* (not surprisingly) endorse and in a sense take for granted the protected circle of Roman Catholicism under the authority of the Pope mediated through the Vatican and the Bishops of the Church. For Benedict the priority was to defend the circle by excluding dissent (even to the extent of silencing what Curran called 'loyal dissent')[4] and endorsing conformity and obedience (even to the extent of trying to bring back the highly conservative SSPX, the followers of Lefebvre). For Francis the priority is, not to abandon the constraints of the circle, but to endorse the freedoms in thought and action that the constraints enable. In his interview with Spadaro he accepted that his authoritarian way of making decisions in the past had led to him being called ultraconservative, but he then said, "We must not reduce the Church to a nest protecting mediocrity."

That tension, between protecting the system and endorsing the freedom to which it is supposed to lead, is a direct consequence of the paradox of religions: should the authority figures be maintaining the boundaries of the system and monitoring the internalisation of constraints in the form of rules, or should they be endorsing the new life to which it is supposed to lead? That conflict between 'act' and 'virtue' moralities can be seen in this example:

> Consider the reaction to the recent case in Israel when an Orthodox Jew in Tel Aviv was told by rabbis to divorce his wife after she had been raped. They both wanted to stay together, not least to bring up their nine children. The man was a *cohen*, a descendant of the Temple priests, and therefore must, according to Torah, divorce his wife if she is raped. There is a let-out clause; when she reports what has happened, he must declare to her, 'I do not believe you', but this man had failed to do that. This ruling had warrant on the basis of an act morality derived from the authoritative source of Torah, but to the protesters, it seemed to contradict the character of a society that attends to the circumstances of the people involved in particular issues. (Bowker, 'Morality', pp.25f)

This, then, is the dilemma, the schism between act morality and virtue morality, between fact morality and agent morality, between issue morality and character morality, between morality independent of the agent's community and history and morality as the consequence of context.

It is true that religions throughout the world have tried to cut through the dilemma by appealing to what in one tradition (the Christian) is called 'natural law'. Putting together the words 'natural' and 'law' can be misleading in the extreme. To some it suggests that 'natural law' yields objective moral judgements because it is embedded in the objective 'laws of nature'. That, however, is a mistake because the nature of the 'laws of nature' is not unambiguous, as Trefil makes clear (p.xxix):

> The laws of nature are not always called 'laws'. Scientists haven't always concerned themselves overmuch with terminological precision, and a law is just as likely to be known as a 'theory', a 'rule', a 'model', or a 'principle', or, reflecting the fact that laws are often stated in the language of mathematics, as a 'relation' or an 'equation'. I suspect that whether or not something is called a law has more to do with quirks of history than with the logic of the sciences.

It is a mistake, therefore, to suppose that regularities in the natural order lead to an objectivity in moral judgements which can then masquerade under the name 'natural law'. That understanding is often found in authoritarian religious systems, but it is mistaken. In contrast, the basic claim of 'Natural Law' (using that phrase as a short-hand) is that people endowed with reason can work out rationally what they should and should not do as they live with each other in a universe of this kind in which the norms of natural and good behaviour can be observed. Since rationality is a universal human competence, its exercise in discernment of this kind should result in objective ethical judgements on which all rational people can agree.

That argument rests on the claim that reason can discern, from the way in which human nature and the universe are constituted, what its constituent parts are for. Reason can discern to what end or ends, specific to their nature, they are directed that lead to their good or proper fulfillment. Thus the end or good purpose of food is to sustain health and life, and an end or good of human nature is to live healthily: the natural law governing eating and drinking is to do so in order to promote health and life, and not, for example, to gratify greed.

Natural Law, therefore, implies that what is right or wrong is related to whatever it is that helps humans and their context in the universe to attain their true end and thus to flourish. The word 'flourish' goes back to the Greek *eudaimonia* (used by Aristotle in advancing an argument of this kind), so that human flourishing as a goal in the rational discernment of what is good is usually referred to as 'eudaimonic' – sometimes now translated as 'happiness'. Thus, as McCoy summarised the point in relation to Aquinas (p.6), "For Aquinas, flourishing and true happiness are the same thing; so the first question of ethics asks about what makes human beings genuinely and lastingly happy."

Natural Law as a rational exercise does not have to appeal to any religious reason to justify it – to the command of God, for example. It can be an expression of rational consensus as it is in such documents as the UN Universal Declaration on Human Rights. It may still then be argued that Natural Law is the objectively good order established by God as the Creator of the universe and of human nature within it. The point may also be added that human reason often fails to make that discernment of the good, and that God has consequently given guidance or command to humans in Revelation. But the concept of Natural Law does not depend on those additions.

Religions, nevertheless, can readily connect Natural Law to their beliefs about God or about the Universe, and equivalent arguments can, for example, be found in relation to Dharma in India (especially in its connection with the Vedic *ṛta*), to Dao and to Tian in China, and to Shen-tao in Japan. But the consequences and applications of the argument are extremely different. They do not have the same understanding, either of human nature or of what constitutes happiness and flourishing. The result is that there is no objective agreement about what Natural Law means in practice, as the detailed and immensely helpful Trialogue of Emon, Levering and Novak (looking at Natural Law in Judaism, Christianity and Islam) makes clear.

This means that appeals to the natural good and to the eudaimonic, whether or not connected to God as Creator, cannot assume that there is general and objective agreement on what 'the good' and 'happiness' are without addressing far more profoundly the ontological question of what sort of thing the goodness of a good life is. Nor can they assume that human nature is sufficiently invariant across the world (in very different cultures and forms of society) to justify the claim that it will lead to objective moral judgements.

Certainly there are universal norms (remembering that norms are statistical): humans normally have two eyes and similar satisfaction systems in the brain. They are prepared normatively by genes and proteins for characteristically human features and behaviours (see further chapter 10), but they are prepared in such a way that appearances and behaviours are immensely diverse. So as Miller put it (p.544), "the fixed elements that we discover must be substantial enough to do some useful work in this role. It is not enough to be told that all human beings use language and die without adequate supplies of food; we must have richer information about, for instance, people's characteristic motives and capacities."

In detail, it is obvious that Dharma, the Dao and Shen-tao (to mention only those examples given above) have very different understandings of human nature and of what counts as 'the good' to be pursued in a moral life and its judgements. Reason does not deliver objective agreement. The UN Committee on the Rights of the Child is based on the *Universal* Declaration on Human Rights, but it is not universal: the Vatican itself has not signed up to all its requirements – and the UN Committee, in the Report quoted earlier, specifically appealed to it to do so. What was eudaimonic for Aristotle is very different from what it might be for us, and even he recognised that there is disagreement about it: "Concerning the eudaimonic, people cannot agree what it is, and the ordinary people [*hoi polloi*] do not agree with the wise [*hoi sophoi*]" (*Ethics* 1.2).

None of this is to deny the worth and the urgency of attempting to construct rational consensus, as in the Declaration on Human Rights. But such constructions are not objectively certain, and even under the title of Natural Law and connected to Revelation, they cannot be inflexibly applied. Thus it used to be argued in the Catholic Church until recently (and by some still is) that "the primary natural end of marriage is, in the economy of nature, the birth and rearing of offspring. Its essential properties and laws must therefore be determined with a view to this end" (Cronin, p.155). From that it was argued that sexual intercourse must be open to the possibility of conception so that artificial contraception must never be used, homosexual acts are intrinsically evil and "the marriage-contract must be regarded as lasting as long as is required for the rearing of children." Divorce is prohibited because "marriage, even as an institution of nature, must be regarded as lasting almost to the end of the lives of the parents, the age at which the last child will have been fully reared."

No doubt a 'primary natural end of marriage' is (to quote the phrase used earlier) gene replication and the nurture of children, but that does not make it the only and exclusive end of marriage. There are many other natural ends of marriage belonging to human good and contributing to human flourishing, including pleasure, satisfaction and bonding ("the mutual society, help, and comfort that the one ought to have of the other" as BCP puts it), and including also the good of each partner and each child – particularly if 'the eudaimonic' is translated as 'happiness'.

This has led to an inevitable conflict in Roman Catholic Christianity: by isolating only one 'natural' good in the act of sexual intercourse and ignoring others, artificial contraception is forbidden and homosexual acts are 'unnatural' and 'intrinsically evil'. Clearly not all Catholics, and certainly not all Christians, agree. According to Woodhead's survey of Catholics in 2013, only 9 per cent said that they would feel guilty using contraceptives and 44 per cent thought that same-sex couples should be allowed to get married (35 per cent thought that same-sex marriage is right).

It is not the case, therefore, that appeals to Natural Law locate an assured objectivity in ethics, nor does it resolve the inevitable tension between maintaining the system and endorsing the liberating consequences to which the system is supposed to lead. Of course the two can and often do belong together: together they can create the greater freedom to which the internalisation of constraint leads in so many of the different enterprises of human life.

Nevertheless, the practical working out in religions of where the priority and the emphasis should lie creates not just tension but serious and passionate conflict. Recently, Keenan has surveyed the history of Catholic moral theology in the twentieth century, showing how the Catholic tradition has moved from a detailed definition in textbooks and manuals of what people should do, to a rediscovery of casuistry – that is to say, to an exploration of particular cases in the contexts in which particular people find themselves, and with reference to their circumstances, intentions and consciences: his subtitle is 'from confessing sins to liberating consciences'.

It hardly needs to be said that the reaction of Vatican Catholics is not sympathetic. The primacy of conscience is not in question. In a radio broadcast in 1952 (23 March), Pius XII said, "Conscience is the innermost secret nucleus in man. It is there that he takes refuge with his spiritual faculties in absolute solitude alone with himself and his God. Conscience is a sanctu-ary on the threshold of which all must halt, even, in the case of a child, his father and mother." But the exercise of conscience is only valid *provided* con-science is informed by the teaching authority of the Church. As the *Catholic Encyclopedia* puts it (Stravinkas, p.251):

> Modern understandings of conscience have tendencies to absolutize con-science and to make it totally autonomous and unrestricted, but these ten-dencies are opposed by both Aquinas and the Church. The Second Vatican Council resisted this tendency, holding that authentic conscience had to be formed in accord with the dictates of 'right reason' and the authentic moral teachings of the Church.

But here, yet again, it is important not to turn those sides of the dilemma or schism into the fallacy of a falsely dichotomous question. In trying to under-stand the ways in which belief is related to practice (in this example, the way in which morality is exercised in religions), it is not a question of *either* norms/obedience *or* characterised decisions/personal responsibility, it is a question of both-and. Constraints will often be expressed as norms or rules, but their internalisation is not an end in itself: it leads (or should lead) to a characterisation of life applying the rules with insight far beyond conformity. It is hard for the structures of religious organisation to recognise that, still less to allow it, but in its proper exercise it is one of the most profound reasons why religions matter.

ART AND TRADITION

The consequences of the internalisation of constraints derived from religious beliefs can to some extent be observed in ethical decisions as also in the life-long forming of character, in the characteristic ways in which a person lives and acts. The internalisation of those constraints can be seen (literally seen) even more directly in religious art where exactly the same tension obtains between constraint and freedom: constraints derived from a particular reli-gion often lead in art to conformity and repetition, but they can lead also to freedom and innovation in a creativity that lies far beyond the boundaries of conformity.

That is an important reason why art is such an illuminating point of entry into the understanding of religions. In some courses in Religious Studies the 'set text' is visual, not verbal, and that is not surprising when one remem-bers the original and fundamental relationship between performing arts and ritual.

To say, however, that art is a good point of entry to the study and under-standing of religions is to raise immediately the familiar question: What is art? And that raises the further question: How is religious art in particular related to art and the arts in general?

They are not easy questions. To begin to answer them we need to start where so much art, especially from the past, is now collected and secured. We need to walk into an art gallery containing art from the past, and there, hanging on the walls, we are likely to see works of art from different parts of the world. Without much difficulty we will be able to distinguish the differ-ent kinds of art. Art from China is recognisably different from African art, or from Indian art, or from European art, or from Aboriginal art, and so on, just as they are easily distinguishable from each other. It is even possible to distinguish Chinese from Japanese art, although that may require a trained eye. Each civilisation has produced its own characteristic art which, in many cases, is instantly recognisable and different from any other. How does it come about that the different styles of art are so consistent and persistent through time that it is easy to distinguish them from each other?

In a general way it is because the great works of the world's art belong to traditions and civilisations each of which has its own character and history. They may interact, but each of them retains its own history and identity. The values and beliefs of any civilisation are reflected and expressed in its art. Maquet, looking at 'art as anthropologist', emphasised how deeply aesthetic objects are integrated in the particular cultures where they have been made (p. 241):

> Aesthetic forms are among the ideational configurations of the culture of which they are a part. They are influenced by the processes of production and are responsive to institutions and other societal networks. In a word, aesthetic objects are deeply cultural.

Of course, beliefs and values develop and change through time, but there is nevertheless impressive continuity in the art of any civilisation from one gen-eration to another. So the traditions not only differ from each other, but also each of them has retained its own characteristic forms and styles, and they continue with great stability through time.

That stability is brought about through a wide variety of constraints: the training by one generation of another, patronage, the availability of materials, and so on. But more important than any of these has been the relation of art and artists to the beliefs and values that a particular civilisation wishes to sus-tain. Beliefs in particular have exercised a powerful constraint over the kind of art that is produced, both in general and in particular detail.[5] In the past and often still in the present, religions have been vehicles that have carried those beliefs and values through time.

That is an important reason why religious beliefs have been fundamental and profound in the creation of art, and to a great extent still are. It is true that the huge inheritance of the world's art gives delight and pleasure to countless billions of people, many of whom do not share the beliefs that underlie it. Nevertheless, the beliefs are important, not just for artists, but also for those who wish to understand the world's art.

This means that the question 'What is art?' is closely related to a more practical question, 'Why do people create it?' Even that is a dauntingly large question, so it may be more helpful to make a start by putting a more limited question to yourself. Supposing someone asks you, 'Why do you paint pictures?'; there are many different answers that you might give. One might be that you never do anything of the kind. But supposing you *have* done so, then you might say something like 'because I enjoy it'; 'because I like creating things of beauty'; 'because I like helping others to see and feel the experience of beauty'; 'because I like expressing ideas that cannot be put into words'; 'because I make a living by selling my pictures'; 'because someone has asked me or paid me to do so'; 'because I have been taught to do so and I like to use my skills'; 'because it is a way of coming close to God or to Enlightenment'; 'because it is a way of helping others to come close to God or to Enlightenment'. The artist Paul Nash was once asked why he painted a particular landscape, and he replied with the same answer given by Mallory when he was asked why he climbed a mountain: "Because it is there."

All those answers (and there are many others) have helped to create the vast body of art that humans have brought into being through thousands of years. And the word 'art' includes much more than painting. It includes such things as music, sewing, sculpture, drama, making plates and throwing pots. Nor is that variety surprising when one considers what the word 'art' originally meant, since it includes virtually everything that humans create.

THE MEANING OF 'ART'

The English words 'art', 'artist' or the equivalent words in other languages such as 'artiste', 'arte' or 'artista' come from the Latin *ars* (in the genitive, *artis*). That word was used originally to describe skill in joining things together, or skill in undertaking some trade or work with one's hands, or with one's head. It was used, for example, of skill in public speaking or rhetoric. It was used to translate the Greek word *techne*, the word that has come into English in terms like 'technology' or 'technique'.

The basic meaning of 'art' as skill can be seen in other languages not derived from Latin. For example, the German word for 'art' is *Kunst*. It is a noun from the verb *können*, which comes from the old Teutonic word, 'to know how', 'to be able', and it appears also in the English 'I can'. *Kunst*, like *ars*, meant originally the skill or competence to do something, hence the German proverb: "Es gehört Kunst zum Apfelbraten" (as also in the French "Même pour faire cuire des pommes,/ Encore faut-il savoir comme"). Only much later, from about the seventeenth century onward, was the word applied to the skill to produce works of beauty – or of art in the modern sense.

A similar development from 'skill' to 'art' can be seen in other languages. For example, the Sanskrit word *śilpa* can be used to translate 'art', but far more extensively it means 'skill', 'technique' and 'craft', as well as 'rite', 'ritual' and 'creation'. In Arabic the root *swr* is used in words denoting the ability to measure or shape something exactly; on that basis the verb *sawwara* means 'he painted a picture', while the noun *sura* means both 'a shape' and 'a picture'.

In China also 'art' began as a practical skill. The origins of the Chinese character for art, *yi*, can be found in the oracle bone inscriptions (ca 2000 BCE) where it was written to represent a man holding a plant and planting it. Therefore the earliest dictionary defines *yi* as 'planting'. The character was then extended to describe the skill of planting in a way as beautiful as the clouds above. Hence the character developed from the skill of planting and cultivating to other skills in writing and in other arts, and then finally to the standards that apply when these things are done well.

In a comparable way the Latin word *ars* occurs in many phrases describing the skill or the technique that humans use for a wide range of purposes – for example, *ars musica, ars gymnastica, ars duellica* (the skill of warfare) and *ars amatoria* (the title of a famous poem by Ovid, the skill of seduction).

In fact, the word *ars* was applied to so many different skills and techniques that Cicero, a leading Roman statesman and writer in the first century BCE, summed up the meaning of the word (*de Natura Deorum*, 2.22): *ars maxime proprium creare et gignere*; "It is above all the true nature of art to create and to bring to birth."

In that case, virtually anything that humans produce outside the boundary of the human body can count as art. That is why the first examples of art are constantly pushed back by archaeologists to an ever earlier date. Once it was thought that our ancestors were first becoming artists in the caves of Lascaux about 15,000 years ago. Then the more recent discoveries in the Fumane and Danube caves pushed the date back by another 3,000 or 4,000 years. After that there were found in the Blombos caves in South Africa pieces of ochre, on which were inscribed, with care and purpose, lattice patterns, and they are at least 70,000 years old.

Even more sensational has been the exploration of other caves at Daraki-Chattan in central India: there, cut into the walls, are dramatically older incisions, hundreds of so-called petroglyphs, deliberate patterns of circular indentations; and these are claimed to be something like two or three times as old again – some date them even earlier than that.

Lattice patterns and circular incisions! And can you not imagine our ancestors standing there in a semicircle in front of them, and saying in a puzzled voice, 'Yes, but is it art?'

Is it art? It is a question that the experts tell us we should no longer ask. Surely by now we understand that art is determined, not by definition, but by decision on the part of the artist – or even, on the part of the observer. As poetry is said to be created by those who decide not to write to the end of the line (to quote the child's essay, 'Poetry is the stuff in books that doesn't quite reach the margin'), so, we are often told, art is now created by those who produce an artefact and decide not to put it in a frame.

That is exactly what has happened to Western art during the twentieth century and at the beginning of the twenty-first. Art has reverted to its infancy and to the definition of Cicero, and as a result it has become virtually any kind of production – endorsed by Picasso when he declared, "Creation is all."[6] The long-established traditions of what counts as art, whether in music or in painting or in any other way, have been broken, thus opening the way to the immense variety of experiments with which we have become familiar.

For a time, those experiments were summarised as 'the shock of the new', but that was rapidly displaced by 'the shock of the now', of which Collings wrote (p.225):

> Art now has meanings by the bucketful and anyone can get them, at least after an initial puzzlement, because meanings that can't be got straightaway have been banished by artists. And the adventure now is for artists ceaselessly to seek out any obvious or inane meanings that might have been overlooked since obviousness became the new thing, whenever it was, the 80s maybe.

This means that where people used to ask the question 'What is art?', the new question has become 'When is art?' To that question we now give the answer, 'Always' – or at least, whenever someone has "created and brought to birth" something outside the boundary of the human body, something that did not previously exist. That might be anything, ranging from wrapping the

Reichstag in Berlin (Christo and Jeanne-Claude, 1995) to suspending basket-balls in water (Jeff Koons, 'The Equilibrium Tanks', 1985). That is why the Italian artist, Piero Manzoni, was able, in 1961, to exhibit 'Merda d'artista', the excretion from his own body, as a work of art (see Collings, pp.208f).

Using the word 'art' in that way is to go back to the origins of the word. It is giving the name of 'art' to anything that is made, anything that is produced outside the boundary of the body. On that definition, there is no difference between art and artefact, between the Turners bequeathed to the Tate and the confusions of an unmade bed. Petroglyphs and patterns, products of chimpan-zees and of children, all qualify as art, or at least have been claimed to do so.

Monkeys and other primates can produce consequences that look like the intended effects of modern art. However, there remains a distinction between intention and reception. Historically, as we have just seen, art emerged as a skill used well, and skill is developed, not by chance, but by training, and training involves the internalisation of constraint. It is the internalisation of constraint that opens the way to innovation and creativity beyond the unin-tended marks of paint. Lenain concluded his book on *Monkey Painting* with that distinction (pp.183f):

> A monkey painting is not a work of art. We can grasp this rationally, but cannot *see* it. Our eye remains attached to the painting as a product. Our ability to attach the formal structure of monkey paintings to something as specific as a creation whose typically simian motivation is familiar to us does not mean that we can dismiss the aesthetic effects of duration, pres-ence, formal ideality – in short, the illusion of a work of art. It is useless trying to remind ourselves that the forms are nothing more than gestures made visible, and that from the animal's point of view they are devoid of interest. In spite of everything our glance will grant them the same weight as any other work of art.

It would seem, therefore, that art is in the eye of the beholder because it is a human decision to regard any particular artefact as art, although it can equally well distinguish between accident and intention. The question therefore still remains how and why, among the immense number of things that humans make 'outside the boundary of the body', humans have come to recognise that some are so different that they have evoked the word 'art' on which accidental productions are parasitic. The answer is that to some objects there has been applied the equivalent of a 'value added tax'. It is a value added difference which has evoked the word and history of 'art' since it is usefully applied to some works but not to all.

It is the addition of value that takes art beyond competence. All the higher primates, including humans, are competent to produce things outside the boundary of the body. But what *we* are able to do, and what this one particular primate *alone* can do, is produce works deliberately that invade (through the senses) the brains and bodies of others in ways that evoke and sustain the vocabularies of approval, of satisfaction, of appreciation, of value.

All that must seem extremely straightforward. But in fact it has become increasingly a matter of conflict and division. The conflict began long ago when the arbiters of art felt it necessary to *define* what those added values actually are, and what therefore counts as 'art'. For example, it was that attempt at the definition of value, and of how it must appear in all works of art, which produced in Europe the Salon and the Academy art of the nineteenth century, against which such a vigorous and long-running protest has subsequently been made. From Blake's 'War of the Pictures' down to the Turner Prize, the protest has been against the repetitive art of conformity that evoked from Heine his description of the Louvre in 1833 as "a multi-coloured yawn". Heine dismissed the exhibition with the words (Windfuhr, p.53), "There were about four and a half thousand paintings on show without really any single work of quality among them."

Beyond and after the boredom and the yawn lies the far more serious process of deconstructing the received codes of value in art. After the Enlightenment in the eighteenth century, the highest and overriding value was given in Europe and the New World to supporting (or at least tolerating) the freedom of individuals to pursue their own lives within the boundary of law. In other words, the highest value was given to diversity and not to doctrine, to choice and not to conformity. In Liberation Theology it is said that there must be a preferential option for the poor. In the West there has been, from the eighteenth century onward, a preferential option for options.

The resulting deconstruction of existing conventions and codes led to the kaleidoscope of modern art – so much so that innovation became the new and overriding value. The excitement of the protest has produced the variety in which the brilliant has proved hard to distinguish from the absurd. The preferential option for options is unmistakable. What has turned out to be a mistake is the way in which the original protest against too narrow a definition of value has become confused with a protest against value itself.

ART AND THE WORLD AROUND US: THE RESPONSES OF EMOTION AND REASON

If art were simply a matter of skill and competence, then everything could indeed count as art. If the value added to skill and competence were a matter simply of convention, then art would rapidly decline into imitation, as it has so often done. The all-important 'value added difference' arises, neither in skill and competence nor in imitation, but in a two-way traffic between ourselves as human beings and the world around us.

In one direction we invade the world with imagination and insight, and we create it in the images of our sciences, our play, our art, our poetry, our stories, and so on. But in the other direction, the world invades us. Our brains and bodies are sensitive to the world around us. Human brains receive signals from the outside world through our various senses – especially, in the case of art, through our eyes, or, in the case of music, through our ears, or, in the case of ballet or of a rock concert, through both at once. We respond by liking (or disliking) what we see and hear, and that is the beginning of art.

In an excellent introduction to the developing field of neuroaesthetics, Shimamura surveys the answers now being given to the question of "what happens when we experience a work of art." In his own words (p.25), "Throughout this book, we will consider the beholder's experience in terms of how the mind and brain interpret art works." In a short section on neuroscience he draws attention (p.22) to the way in which fMRI scanning "has completely changed psychological science. Now we can readily relate mental processes to brain activity"; and in the book he explores those correlations. But by concentrating on mind and interpretation he pays less attention to the extensive research that has been done on the more immediate responses in the brain that lie at the foundation of our aesthetic (and other) judgements.

That research is summarised briefly in my *The Sacred Neuron*. Putting it even more briefly and oversimplifying it, the process is this: signals from the outside world reach a small part of the brain known (from the Latin, because it is almond-shaped) as the amygdala. The amygdala (or more accurately the amygdaloid complex) is a kind of command centre from which, in particular circumstances, our emotional and muscular responses are initiated.

Thus in a situation of danger, the emotion of fear and an appropriate muscular response (such as running away) are initiated. In other situations other responses are initiated, such as delight or disgust or any other of our many emotions and feelings. They contribute fundamentally to the construction of our values and to the many evaluations we make of things or people or events, whether, for example, they are good or evil, beautiful or ugly, exciting or dull, safe or dangerous.

It used to be thought until very recently, and particularly since the time of Hume, that our rationality or reason ('mind and interpretation') enters in only *after* our emotional response in order to weigh up what our evaluations should be. For many centuries, it has been thought that our judgements and evaluations are based first on the engagement of our emotions and feelings, followed only then by rational reflection and consideration.

We now know that that is wrong. We also know that the ways in which this used to be summarised ('You can't get an ought from an is', 'You can't get a value from a fact') are equally wrong *as a generalisation.*[7] From recent research in the neurosciences it has become increasingly clear that our emotions are not at work on their own in separation from our rationality and reason. Sometimes they may be, but far more often they work together in the forming of moral, aesthetic, religious and other judgements. This is a consequence of the different ways in which the brain processes the kind of information on the basis of which our evaluations are made.

The first way is by receiving signals and sending them immediately from the thalamus to the amygdala by a shortcut route so that our responses are initiated at once. This is vital (literally, life-saving) in situations of great danger. If you see a dog about to attack you, you are right to be afraid, and the amygdala initiates at once an appropriate response, namely feeling afraid and running away (or hitting it with a stick, or whatever might defend you). In the case of fear (the best researched of our emotions so far), many animals share with us this short-cut route because it helps them and us to survive longer and therefore to pass on our genes to another generation. It is the reason why Charles Darwin visited the London Zoo in order to show that he could overcome rationally his emotion of fear and failed to do so. His work on evolution had led him to believe that our emotions have helped us to survive. But then surely, as rational creatures, we ought to be able to put ourselves in a dangerous situation and then by willpower to control our feelings and responses. Reason should have control over emotion. But could he do it?

> I put my face close to the thick glass-plate in front of a puff-adder in the Zoological Gardens, with the firm determination of not starting back if the snake struck at me; but, as soon as the blow was struck, my resolution went for nothing, and I jumped a yard or two backwards with astonishing rapidity. My will and reason were powerless against the imagination of a danger which had never been experienced.

The point here is that if you actually stop to think about it, you may stop thinking altogether, because the danger, if it is real, gets you. As Remarque put it of his experience of being under artillery shelling on the Western Front in 1916 (p.43),

> With the first rumble of shellfire, one part of our being hurls itself back a thousand years. An animal instinct awakens in us, and it directs and protects us. It is not conscious, it is far quicker, far more accurate and far more

reliable than conscious thought ... If you had relied on thought, you would have been so many pieces of meat by now. It was something else, some prescient, unconscious awareness inside us, that threw us down and saved us without our realising. But for this, there would long since have been not a single man left alive between Flanders and the Vosges.

The second way in which the brain processes the kind of information on the basis of which our evaluations are made is by receiving signals and sending them to the amygdala by a longer route, via specialised areas in the cortex, so that they arrive at the amygdala *combined with* a rational evaluation of what is actually going on, and in this our memories and life experience play a major part. Thus you realise that the dog is rushing towards you, not to attack you, but to greet you – and you know this from your memory and experience of recognising the difference between greeting (tail wagging) and attack (teeth bared in a snarl).

Something like that happens when we look at a work of art. We may respond immediately to signals transmitted by the shortcut route by saying, 'That's marvellous', or 'That's terrible'. But far more often, the signals go via the cortex so that our reason gets involved, along with our memory, experience and intelligence, and we make what is still an emotional evaluation, but *combined with* our reason and rationality. Vasari (p.238) recorded of Andrea del Verrocchio that "when he came to die in the hospital they brought him a badly made crucifix, but he bade them to take the ugly thing away and instead bring him one made by Donatello, insisting that if they didn't do so he would die in despair, he so detested the sight of bad works of art."

This means that when people say, 'I don't know much about art but I do know what I like', they are fundamentally right, although they are often told by experts that they are wrong to say this. The reason why they are right is because all art depends on the satisfaction it triggers in the human brain.

But they are wrong if they think that the appreciation of art rests on the shortcut route alone. Some art does indeed rely on that immediate, shortcut satisfaction to produce its effect, but it results in what Ruskin called "tinsel and glitter"[8] and what Henry Moore called "the affected and sentimental prettiness sold for church decoration in church art shops." It produced in Salon art "the appalling monotony" of what Henry James used to call "the conscientious nude".[9] The effect may be immediately pleasing, but it rapidly wears off. It has nothing more to say to us, and after seeing it more than a few times, it becomes boring – the very word that Heine used and that Stendhal also used even earlier writing of the 'Salon of 1824', when he called for a rebellion against the definition of 'good art' in terms of imitating the classical art of the ancient Greeks (Holt, p.40):

We are at the dawn of a revolution in the Fine Arts. The huge pictures composed of thirty nude figures inspired by antique statues, and the heavy tragedies in verse in five acts, are, without a doubt, very respectable works; but in spite of all that may be said in their favour, they have begun to be a little boring. If the painting of the 'Rape of the Sabines' were to appear today, we would find that its figures were without passion, and that in any country it is absurd to march off to battle with no clothes on.

A century later, when the rebellion was well under way, the Swiss artist Cingria called that kind of 'shortcut' art 'diabolical' (Griffiths p.18):

There is a truly diabolical art which consists of aping beauty. This art gains the approval of almost all the Christian public, by a certain prettiness, by a poetic appearance, by a surface polish which conceals, from insensitive, lazy eyes, a complete absence of life, intelligence and beauty ... This art is all lies.

The point is that to rely *only* on the shortcut route to our feelings and emotions does not produce enduring art. That is so because 'what we like' ('I know what I like') is vastly extended and enriched when we *do* know something about art: memory, education and knowledge are integrated with emotion and feeling to produce an entirely different satisfaction. As Samuel Johnson observed of poetry (p.121), "Poetry is the art of uniting pleasure with truth, by calling imagination to the help of reason." It is on that basis that we can evaluate works of art and can distinguish between those that are superficial and those that have enduring value – works that come to be recognised as 'great' art. In the words of Shimamura (p.191), "Art can be construed as thinking with feeling."

That observation is by no means confined to visible arts alone. In the case of music, for example, Rosen, has made exactly the same point with detailed illustrations in his book, *Music and Sentiment* (p.ix):

Understanding music in the most basic sense simply means enjoying it when you hear it ['I know what I like']. It is true that with music that is unfamiliar and seems alien at first hearing, this requires a few repeated experiences of it and, indeed, a certain amount of goodwill to risk new sensations. It is, nevertheless, rare that specialized knowledge is required for the spontaneous enjoyment that is the reason for the existence of music. However, specialized study can bring rewards by allowing us to comprehend why we take pleasure in hearing what we appreciate best, and can enlighten us on the way music acts upon us to provide delight.

What, therefore, has happened since the time of Cicero is that the meaning of the word 'art' has changed completely as people have used their skill and competence, not just to fight and seduce each other, but to produce works which evoke from their creators and from those who see them the emotional and rational vocabularies of satisfaction, including the satisfaction of beauty.

Those vocabularies are necessarily embedded deeply in the human brain and body. The relatively new field of neuroaesthetics has therefore taken us far beyond the elementary observations summarised above. Even so, those observations have already transformed our understanding of the ways in which we register and evaluate the difference between such things as good and evil, up and down, truth and falsehood, beauty and ugliness. As John Drinkwater put it in 'A Prayer' (p.18),

> We know the hemlock from the rose,
> The pure from stained,
> The noble from the base.

ART AND VALUES: THE CONTRIBUTION OF CONDUCIVE PROPERTIES

When we make those evaluations, what are the values that we look for and recognise? What are the values which are added and which turn some but not all human artefacts into art? There is no quick answer to that, because there are so many of them. To list them would be to write an alphabet of things or attitudes that we value, ranging from anger and adoration to yearning and zeal. And in fact it turns out that it is usually destructive of art even to try to list them. When attempts were made in the past to define exactly what values a picture or a sculpture or a building (or whatever) must include in order to be judged 'good', the results were inevitably a long and boring procession of 'more of the same'.

That is why Stendhal protested against the way in which, in Europe, rules were derived from the classical art of Greece and Rome and were applied to all art if it was to be accepted and exhibited in the Salons and Academies of Art. It was from this 'Salon art' and from what many regarded as the prison camp of those rules (D.H. Lawrence's "barbed-wire entanglement"[10]) that the Great Escape was made into twentieth-century art.

That escape, however, becomes destructive and contemptuous of our humanity if its rebellion against the definition of value becomes a rebellion *against values* themselves. For the fact remains that humans, given the brains and bodies they happen to have, continue to evaluate works as good or bad, beautiful or ugly, engaging or boring, likeable or unlikeable, on the basis of satisfactions (or dissatisfactions) in the brain, in which rationality (including memory, education and experience) is as much involved as emotion and feeling.

The values vary from one civilisation to another, and they may change through the course of time. That is an important reason why the word 'art' has changed its reference and meaning constantly through the long history of human enterprise. The changes and contrasts are important, but so is persistence through the process of change.

It is, therefore, as true today as it has ever been that art is one of the most important ways in which humans share with each other the values they hold in common. How do artists do this? Partly by technique and training. But also by putting into the works they produce features that create an appropriate response in those who see them. As a result, those who look at works of art can recognise (or at least respond to) the values in them, and can feel and understand them for themselves.

The features which do this are known technically as 'conducive properties' – in other words, they are features in works of art that lead (Latin *duco*, 'I lead') from themselves to the minds of those who see them, and they then create (or *can* create) an appropriate response. It sounds complicated, but it is familiar to everyone in the way in which conducive properties in erotic art (or for that matter in pornography) can lead to sexual arousal.

Conducive properties are equally familiar in the skills of advertising because an advertisement is designed with particular conducive properties in order to lead people to a desired outcome – to buy a particular product, for example, or to change their behaviour in some way. Often the image will be reinforced by a short and memorable catchphrase or slogan, such as, 'My Goodness, my Guinness' or 'Keep death off the road' or the earlier example (p.111), 'Careless talk costs lives'. In introducing his book, *20th Century Advertising*, Saunders wrote (p.7):

> Advertising is the world's most powerful industry. More powerful now than at any time in history. It can help put governments in power, or oust them. It can make a company's – or country's – fortune. And it can change public opinion.... During the course of the century some of these advertising messages reached virtually every individual on earth.

The conducive properties in an advertisement are thus designed to lead those who see the advert to a particular response of feeling and understanding, with a result intended by the advertiser. Not surprisingly, conducive properties are used in advertising in the domains of economics and politics in order to gain control over others – to achieve, in Foucault's words, "control by stimulation" (p.58).

That is why conducive properties are so obvious in the art of propaganda, in the relation between 'art and power', to quote the title of an exhibition (at the Hayward Gallery, London, in 1995) of art under the interwar dictators.[11] The way in which the dictators used conducive properties in art and architecture (and indeed advertising) to achieve their political goals required what Schultze-Naumberg called in 1932 *Kampf um die Kunst*,[12] the battle *for* art, the elimination of any art thought to be subversive.

In the case of Hitler, who had "a personal hatred of art criticism" (Spotts, p.31), it led directly to the contrasting exhibitions in 1937 of, on the one side *Grosse Deutsche Kunstausstellung* (the Great German Art Exhibition), and on the other *Entarte Kunst* (Degenerate Art). As Schultze-Naumberg put it at the time (p.5), "A life-and-death struggle is taking place in art, just as it is in the realm of politics. And the battle for art has to be fought with the same seriousness and determination as the battle for political power."[13]

A similar (but not the same[14]) struggle took place in the Soviet Union. Sjeklocha and Mead began their book on *Unofficial Art in the Soviet Union* with a quotation from Plekhanov: "There is no force on earth which could say to art, 'You must take this and not another direction.'" Stalin disagreed and believed that a strongly committed, proletarian culture was part of the revolution. By 1934 (the date of the First All Union Congress of Soviet Writers), Stalin was instructing writers to be "engineers of human souls" by standing "with both feet on the ground of real life."

Given the recognition and effectiveness of conducive properties in political propaganda, it is not surprising that conducive properties are of fundamental importance in religious art. They may operate in the same ways as they do in advertising and propaganda. Religions have a long history of advertisement and propaganda, and they even have their own equivalent to slogans: 'Jesus lives'; 'Allahu akbar'; 'Namu Amida butsu'; 'Tat tvam asi'; 'Hare Krishna, Hare Krishna'; 'Om mani padme hum', and the many mantras which are so important in Asian religions. There is also in religious art a deliberate use of conducive properties to evoke a desired response, including on occasion an erotic response.

But the use and nature of conducive properties in religious art go far beyond anything to do with advertising, propaganda and the evocation of elementary emotion. At their most profound, they convey the essence of what they purport to be about. They do not simply portray or illustrate what is claimed to be true or real; they bring that truth and reality into being and convey them into our experience as a real presence.

Equally, the images in religious art often work in two directions. Most advertising works with its conducive properties *from* the image *to* those who look at it in order to produce the outcome that the advertiser intends, and much religious art works with its conducive properties in a comparable way, in order to evoke an appropriate (and often a desired) outcome.

But it also works the other way around. Works of religious art lead those who see them back in the other direction in order to relate them to what the images purport to be about, and they therefore evoke and sustain particular responses which are important in religious life.

RECIPROCATING IMAGES IN INDIAN ART

That reciprocal interaction can be seen with particular clarity in Indian art. It is a fundamental purpose of Indian art to evoke worship and to celebrate and give expression to the divine energy which creates, sustains and in the end destroys the entire universe. But equally its purpose is to bring into union with the divine those who participate in that art in a way that connects them with the divine energy. Art is thus a part of the whole process of that creative energy through which Brahman, understood as the unproduced Producer of all that is, produces through *maya* all appearances.

Among those appearances are the many Gods and Goddesses who play various and essential parts in the unfolding process of the universe. Above all, they offer, in contrast to Brahman, a manifest form that humans can approach in worship and prayer. As an early ritual text puts it (*Vishnu Samhita* 29.55–7),

> Without a form, how can one contemplate God? On what will the mind focus? If there is nothing to which the mind can attach itself, it will drift away from meditation and slip into a state of sleep. The wise, therefore, will focus on some form.

The Gods and Goddesses are manifestations of Brahman (of That which alone truly is), who then make *themselves* manifest in forms through which the faithful can approach them and can learn to worship and revere them. They become manifest in many different ways of which *avatara* is distinctively important. The word *avatara* means basically 'descent', but in effect it means (to use Gonda's word, 1961) *Erscheinung* or 'manifestation'. Gods and Goddesses become manifest in living forms, both animal and human, and supremely (in terms of devotion for many Hindus) in Krishna and Shiva – and that is why *avatara* is often loosely paraphrased as 'incarnation'.

That may, however, be misleading, since the underlying Latin *in carne* is far too narrow for the Indian understanding of *avatara*, since Gods and Goddesses also become manifest in the form of images or temple sculptures, and the word *arcavatara* (one of the five forms of Vishnu) is used of sculptures and images of that kind. That is why so much Indian art creates those carvings and images as an act of adoration, and they bring into being exactly those conducive properties that evoke the appropriate response. An image is known as *murti* (embodiment), and there are very careful rules and rituals which control how images are made, together with a formal ceremony of consecration and of 'bringing to life' (*pratiṣṭhapana*).

The divine thus becomes a real presence during the act of worship, and the enlivened images are treated with great reverence, but they are not regarded *as* the God or Goddess, even when they are regarded as vehicles *of* the real presence of the Deity. Indeed, in village worship, the small clay image through which the divine has become really present is, at the end of the worship, simply thrown away and broken. In Indian art and worship, the signpost is not confused with that to which it points. It is always pointing beyond itself to the final and ultimate truth that cannot be contained in words or images.

An important purpose, therefore, of Indian art is to connect participants with the ways in which Gods and Goddesses have made themselves manifest in the world. The Gods or Goddesses can be recognised by the specific symbols or objects or gestures associated with them, and through them connection can be made with the divine and cosmic energies by means of which the universe is created, sustained and destroyed.

In that context, it is not surprising that dance and drama are fundamental forms of Indian art. Indeed, a basic and key text (*Cittasutra* in *Visnudharmottara Purana*) describing the constraints that control Indian art into its outcomes states quite simply (3.2.4), "It is not possible to understand the rules of painting without understanding dance." Stories of Gods and Goddesses are danced and enacted in the many Indian festivals, and they are told also in a variety of different ways, not least in the great Indian epics, *Mahabharata* and *Ramayana*, and in the vast anthologies called Puranas. They are told as well in every home and village where the storyteller is a revered figure.[15] They are told also through painting and sculpture, not least in the carvings which are so abundant on the walls of Indian temples.

The point of this, however, is not simply to tell stories or to relate what the Gods and Goddesses have done. The real point is to unite people with the object of their devotion.[16] A vital way in which that is done is by the arousing of the emotions and memories which are appropriate for the occasion – or which are being experienced by the participants in the original story, including those of the Gods and Goddesses. Each of these combined 'feelings and memories' is known as *rasa*. It is the Indian understanding of *rasa* that epitomises the reciprocal interactions of religious art.

Rasa is a word that means basically 'sap' or 'juice' or 'essence'. It is the intrinsic quality which belongs to any true work of art and to the human response to it, whether it is of sculpture or of dance or of painting or of any other kind. It may seem to be equivalent to a straightforward response of emotions and feelings, but as we saw earlier, the emotions cannot, except in extreme circumstances, be isolated in that way. *Rasa*, therefore, is much more complex and profound because it seeks to involve the whole person, reason as well as emotions, memory as well as feelings, and that is why (according to Bharata's *Natyasastra*, an authoritative work of c. fourth century CE on the rules governing dance), there are eight *rasas* embedded in human experience, each of which has its associated colour. *Visnudharmottara* (c. fourth–fifth centuries, an appendix to *Visnupurana*, dealing extensively with the goals and methods of Indian painting) adds a ninth *rasa*, *santa*, calm and peace, whose colour is the colour of the moon.

A 'true' work of art is one in which the diverse qualities are present (*rasavat*, imbued with *rasa*) and which may lead the viewer or participant (*rasika*) into a state of union with the divine, a state of utter bliss known as *rasananda*. It is a two-way interaction.

Every work of art should thus attempt both to convey and to evoke the recognition, mood and feeling appropriate to what is being displayed, or to the story that is being enacted or told, and it should lead those who see it or hear it into the real presence of God. That is particularly the case with drama and dance, because it is easier to dance a story than to tell it in a sculpture. Even so, temple friezes often tell the sequence of a story, and many Indian miniature paintings originated in series of continuous paintings, even though the sequences have frequently now been broken up.

Just as much, therefore, as in drama and dance, it was expected that a carving or a sculpture would be a dynamic work through which the divine energy would break out into the world. A temple and its carvings "are not 'all that God is', but the bearer of God's life (*jiva*), so that through them the unknowable can begin to be known" (Bowker 2009, p.16). It was a feature that the French sculptor Rodin admired from afar, regarding a carving of the dancing Siva as the finest work that had ever translated energy into an image.

All this is gathered together in the paramount form of art in India, the Temple. All the arts play their part in the creation of Temples and in what happens within and around them. The goal of the conducive properties in a Temple is to form a union between the worshipper and God. As Kramisch put it in her 'Introduction to the *Visnudharmottara*' (p.272),

> This common basis of architecture, sculpture, and painting – it was shown that it primarily underlies dancing – at times is responsible for a fusion of

the various disciplines of sculpture and painting, for a desperate attempt at visualising what perhaps is beyond visualisation.

Indian art exemplifies with great power the two-way interaction that conducive properties in the context of religion bring into being. The same is equally true of other religions, although the goals and the conducive properties in different religions are, as one would expect, extremely varied. The actual conducive properties deployed in any particular work of art will also vary because they are directed toward specific goals related to particular possibilities in human perception. When, for example, the conducive properties are those of threat or denunciation, they may evoke 'fear and trembling' and they may even produce prudential changes in behaviour. But what produces 'fear and trembling' is differently identified and described in each religion.

Far more often, however, religious art is invitation. It is invitation to those who see it or handle it or enact it to enter into relationship with whoever or whatever it purports to be about. This is most literally the case in architecture, and in *Knowing the Unknowable* (pp.16–21) I have shown how that literal 'entering' happens in Indian temple architecture and also in the Gothic Revival of the nineteenth century, through "the dim religious light of impressiveness and solemnity".

To give another example, art as invitation is equally unmistakeable in the different ways in which religious art encourages visualisation. Visualisation may be a fairly basic practice of trying to imagine or envisage oneself in some particular circumstance or place. For example, prayer in relation to the Bible may involve imagining oneself within the scene as one of the participants. At an extreme, Merkabah contemplation in Judaism may take one so close to the vision of God that it was restricted to only those who had received the highest training: it is that kind of visualisation that underlies the experience of Saul on the road to Damascus (see Bowker 1971).

Visualisation of a different kind is important in Asian religions. In India, for example, the diagrams known as *yantras* and *mandalas* are created to help worshippers to approach through visualisation the Deity, and each Deity has his or her own Yantra. Even the word *darshana*, often translated 'worship', comes from a root, *dṛś*, meaning 'looking at', or 'viewing'.

Another striking example occurs in Tantra and in Tibet where its consequences in art are direct and where also it exemplifies for Flood what he means by 'the truth within' (p.2):

The idea of the truth within can be captured in the image of the Tibetan Buddhist practitioner who meditates upon the external ritual diagram or *mandala*, then closes her eyes and visualizes the diagram in the mind's eye.

This eidetic image becomes the focus of practice and its intensification opens out an inner world where the realization of Buddhahood can be found.

Since the purpose of tantra in Tibet is to attain Enlightenment by realising for oneself the Buddha-nature, that necessarily involves realising the Buddha-nature in any and ultimately all of its forms, including those which seem in terms of their superficial representation in art or sculpture to be horrific and terrifying – the forms in which everything that is hostile to Enlightenment confronts us both within and without. That certainly is how Maraini described them in his book *Secret Tibet* (pp.50f):

> At the entrance are hung the decomposing bodies of bears, wild dogs, yaks, and snakes, stuffed with straw, to frighten away the evil spirits who might desire to pass the threshold. The carcasses fall to pieces, and the whole place is as disgusting as a space under a flight of stairs with us would be if it were full of rubbish covered with cobwebs, of ancient umbrellas that belonged to great-grand-father, and fragments of bedraggled fur that had been worn by a dead aunt ... Pictures of the gods are painted on the walls. At first sight you would say they are demons, monsters, infernal beings. They are, however, good spirits, protectors, who assume these terrifying shapes to combat the invisible forces of evil ... [It is a] dark, dusty pocket of stale air ... containing greasy, skinless carcasses, with terrifying gods painted on the walls riding monsters, wearing diadems of skulls and necklaces of human heads, and holding in their hands blood-filled skulls as cups.

Maraini as an outsider could not understand what he was looking at. Tibetans certainly can. The visualisation of the archetypal deities, whether of terrifying violence or of sublime peace, enables the yogi or the yogini to confront the worst and the best of their own nature and to pass beyond it into the condition beyond all differentiating characteristics, the Buddha-nature. Those forms of art are the means through which people can visualise what they represent, and can then realise, not theoretically but in fact, that they are not other than the Buddha-nature.

Visualisation is simply one example of the way in which religious beliefs and practices create, not just the content, but also the form of distinctive art as, for example, in stained glass and calligraphy. In the case of Tibet, to continue with that example, they create *tangkas*. The walls of Tibetan monasteries are frequently covered with murals and with painted pictures, often of a vast size, to assist with instruction as well as visualisation. But these could not be moved, so the Tibetans produced portable equivalents, *tangkas*, 'a thing that one unrolls', so that meditation and teaching are not dependent on place. In the same way the fundamental Indian practice of making *mandalas* was given a distinctive Tibetan content and form.

Much religious art, therefore, is not intended to work in one direction only, from the object to the observer. It works with a kind of interactive reflex making the observer into a participant. Examples occur in every religion – in Hindu images and Temples as we have just seen, in Christian icons, Muslim calligraphy, the expression of 'The Dreaming' (*wongar/djugurba/alcheringa*[17]) among native Australians: those who bring that art into being will often point at it and say, 'This is my Dreaming'.

This interactive participation means that the conducive properties in religious art lead those who see them back into the image in order to draw them deeper into their spiritual and religious life. Religious art of this kind becomes a designed and carefully constructed bridge connecting the living to the ancestors and earth to heaven, or enabling the transition from ignorance to Enlightenment.

It is of course possible to look at that art without any understanding of what is involved, much as Maraini looked at what he saw in Tibet. One might still be impressed or moved or revolted by what one sees. But to move beyond the immediate but superficial 'I know what I like', it is essential to understand the system of beliefs and practices in which it is embedded.

BELIEFS AND THE CHARACTERISATION OF RELIGIOUS ART

Because works of art are able to deal so fundamentally with the externalised expression and sharing of imagination and values, it is not surprising that so much of the world's art has come into being in the context of religions. Religions are the organised systems in which human imaginations and values, including specifically *religious* values, have been identified, coded, protected and shared. As Denis asked the question in 1890 (Chipp, p.100),

> What is great art if not the disguise of natural objects with their vulgar sensations by icons that are sacred, magical and commanding? Is it hieratic simplicity of the Buddhas; or of monks transformed by the aesthetic sense of a religious race? Compare a lion in nature to the lions of Khorsabad: which of them forces one to his knees?

Religions have been able to do this because they are also the systems in which the most profound and life-changing beliefs and practices have been sustained. Those beliefs and practices have given a different shape and style to the many different societies, both small and large, throughout the world. They *characterise* these societies in profound ways – that is, they give a recognisable and distinct character to them.

Differences between societies are brought into being by a wide network of constraints, including such fundamental constraints as those of climate, geography and resources. But among the constraints are those of religious beliefs and practices, and those beliefs and practices are very far from being the same in all religions. Superficially, they may look similar, in the sense that many religions look to God as the source and the goal of life, others hold out the goals of Enlightenment and of release from the otherwise endless cycle of rebirth and reappearance. But the ways are very different indeed in which different religions *characterise* the nature of God and what is required in order to reach God now and in life beyond death, or in which they *characterise* the paths and procedures that will lead to Enlightenment.

These characteristic beliefs and practices, combined with the different histories that each religion has had, make up a large part of the content and subject matter of religious art. This means that each religion (and each of the many smaller groups which make up any religion) has its own characteristic memories, beliefs and practices, and it is those which constrain and produce the distinctively different art of the different religions.

What that means in practice is clearly exemplified in the way in which characteristic Chinese beliefs and practices produced the recognisably distinct form and content of Chinese art. In Bowker (2005, pp.56ff) *mimesis*, 'the representation of reality', is examined as a conducive property. It is recognised and used in both China and the West but it produces entirely different kinds of art in each tradition. In contrast to Holman Hunt and the pre-Raphaelites, the artist Jing Hao (ninth/tenth century, author of the widely used guide, *Notes on Brushwork*) wrote:

> Painting is to paint, to estimate the shapes of things and really obtain them, to estimate the beauty of things and reach it, to estimate the reality of things and grasp it. One should not take outward beauty for reality. He who does not understand this mystery will not obtain the truth, even though his pictures may contain likeness.

There are, of course, many other examples of fundamental religious beliefs acting as constraints that produce recognisably characteristic art. Thus in Islam it is forbidden to produce pictorial representations of human beings, partly because it might lead to idolatry, partly also because God alone can give life to creation. That prohibition comes from the Quran which is believed by Muslims to be *the* revelation of God's Word and the only one not to have been corrupted. That belief, combined with the prohibition, led to a paramount emphasis on Calligraphy. In his introduction to Islamic calligraphy, Safadi wrote (p.31) that "the Quran, which is the word of God and touches every aspect of Muslim life, has always been an object of devotion and the focus for the artistic genius of Islam. This not only elevated calligraphy to the level of a sacramental art, but made the many hundreds of exquisite Quran copies which were produced the best documentary evidence of the art itself."

Calligraphy is equally fundamental in Meditation Buddhism (Chan and Zen Buddhism), but it is entirely different in practice because it is related to very different beliefs. Zen teaches that every sentient being, including oneself, is a manifestation of the Buddha-nature. The underlying Buddha-nature is what it is: it has no differentiating characteristics, and that is what is meant by *shunyata*, often translated as 'the void' or 'emptiness'. Zen exists in order to help people to realise that they are not other than the Buddha-nature. Of course in our ignorance we experience ourselves as being real and different from each other, just as birds and animals and other sentient beings that we see or touch or sense in any way seem to be both real and very different. Yet in fact it is the same Buddha-nature that underlies them all: the appearances are simply different ways in which the Buddha-nature manifests itself – just as we might say that it is energy that underlies and manifests itself in all different forms of appearance. Since there are 'no differentiating characteristics', it follows that in all living beings without exception the Buddha-nature can be discerned.

It is that belief which creates the many different forms of Zen art. They are simply different ways of entering into that truth. The internalisation of that truth leads to Enlightenment (*satori*). The forms of Zen art are thus ways of entering into the Buddha-nature, whether as artist or as observer, and that is why the main forms of Zen art involve participation, as in Zen gardens, Chado (the way of tea), Kado (the way of flowers) and Calligraphy. Loori therefore commented (Addiss p.2):

> This art was not representational or iconographic. It did not inspire faith or facilitate liturgy or contemplation. It did not function to deepen the devotees' experience of religion. It was not used in worship ceremonies or as a part of prayer. Its only purpose was to point to the nature of reality. It suggested a new way of seeing and a new way of being that cut to the core of what it meant to be human and fully alive. To this day, Zen art touches artists and audiences deeply. It expresses the ineffable as it helps to transform the way we see ourselves in the world.

Calligraphy, therefore, in Zen art (*zenga*) is completely different from Calligraphy in Islam. In Zen it becomes a way in which one enters into the undifferentiated Buddha-nature. Even the preparation of the ink and brushes for Calligraphy is a part of this. Although the words chosen were often sayings of the great masters, or their poems, the writing or painting itself had to be entirely spontaneous, and there could be no corrections, since they would be visible at once on the absorbent paper that was used.

So the beliefs of Zen create characteristically different forms of art, and they create different content also. That can be seen specifically in the *enso*. The *enso* is the simplest and yet the most profound statement of Zen. It is a line, preferably painted with a single stroke of the brush, forming a roughly circular shape. Usually, though not invariably, the beginning and the end of the line meet in order to emphasise the fundamental truth of *shunyata*: it is empty and all content has escaped, because in Zen belief there is nothing in existence except the Buddha-nature. Since, however, no 'rules' control the painting of the *enso*, some artists did not paint the *enso* in a single unbroken line. Bankei, for example, sometimes made two separate lines come close to meeting in a curving embrace, suggesting both emptiness and the work necessary for completion.

The painting of the *enso* may take many years to learn because, although it is in itself a way of meditation, it can also be the attainment of Enlightenment (*satori*). Almost always the *enso* is integrated with calligraphy. The script may be a koan, or a quotation from a Zen text, or some simple but challenging invitation. It might be, for example, 'Have a cup of tea!', to make the point that the empty circle resembles a cup when you look down on it from above.

In all its variations, however, the point remains that those who penetrate through the superficial appearance realise that there is nothing for them to be except the Buddha-nature. For that reason Gibon Sengai (1750–1837) used to merge calligraphy and painting into one, in order to emphasise that all things are equal since all things are devoid of differentiating characteristics (*shunyata*). In his 'Frog and Snail', for example, the frog and the calligraphy become part of each other, and the text reads, "Swallow the Three Buddhas, Past, Present and Future, in one gulp": like the well-known command of Linji Yixuan, "Kill the Buddha!", this command implies that since all things are the Buddha-nature, all things are equal and there is no hierarchy of respect or of authority.[18]

THE INTERNALISATION OF CONSTRAINTS AND THE CREATION OF RELIGIOUS ART

Those examples of the way in which religious beliefs constrain both the form and content of art show why the art of each religious tradition is so recognisable, and why also it is so stable through time. Of course it may also change greatly in detail as at least some of the artists of any generation make their own interpretation of the tradition. Artists working in religious traditions have been as capable as any others of challenging or of developing the conventions and codes. The reason for that is not surprising given what we now know about the liberating importance of constraint: religions offer (and sometimes impose) the constraints which, if they are internalised, can lead to greater freedom.

That can be seen in the art of all religions, but once again India offers a particularly clear example. That is so because the internalisation of constraint is tied to the obligation to observe Dharma (roughly in this context 'appropriate behaviour':). There is Dharma (appropriate behaviour) for every aspect of life, and it therefore follows that there is particular Dharma for artists of every kind, whether they are painters, dancers, sculptors, architects or those involved in the many forms of craft and skill.

Many of the rules and traditions are passed on in families (the Bhangora family, for example, were architects and builders for the royal family in Mewar, in Rajasthan, from the fourteenth to the seventeenth centuries) and also in well-organised guilds (*śreṇi*), but equally many of the rules were gathered at a very early date in texts including the works mentioned already, *Viṣṇudharmottara* and Bharata's *Naṭyaśastra*. It is not possible to become an artist or a craftsman without first internalising the constraints derived from Dharma, but that of course means at once that all art is fundamentally a religious act.

For that reason, when a craftsman is about to begin a particular piece of work, he lays out the tools that he is going to use and offers worship to or through them. Similarly, those who are patrons of art are also performing a religious act. To commission the building of villages, or temples, or palaces, or pools for immersion is regarded as undertaking a religious duty. Indeed, from early times a person who did this was known as *yajamana*, one who performs sacrifice.

In general, therefore, the importance of the internalisation of constraints is clearly fundamental in religious art. It does not, however, lead *automatically* to freedom and creativity in the way that constraints so often do. Instead, it may lead to painstaking imitation, and much religious art is indeed repetitive. But the fact remains that those who work within the boundary of constraint can be even more creative than those who ignore or even destroy the boundary. It is, yet again, the point made earlier by Stravinsky and de la Mare that constraint is the necessary condition of creative freedom, and that is as true of art as it is of music and poetry. A particularly striking example can be seen in the work of Barnett Newman.

Barnett Newman (1905–76) was an American painter from a Jewish background (his parents were Jewish immigrants), but he was not a conventional or traditional believer – any more than he was a conventional or traditional painter. Nevertheless, his Jewish background remained a profound constraint on his work. The Jewish reluctance to allow art to come anywhere near the making of idols meant that the move away from representational art during the twentieth century created great opportunities for Jewish artists like himself. His ambition as a painter was to create in those who saw his work an exaltation of the human spirit which, in his view, traditional religions were increasingly failing to do. When he was asked to design a synagogue in 1963, he wrote ('Recent American Synagogue Architecture', pp.181f):

> In the synagogue ceremony nothing happens that is objective. In it there is only the subjective experience in which one feels exalted. 'Know before whom you stand,' reads the command. But the concern now seems to be not with the emotion of exaltation and personal identity called for by the command but with the number of seats and clean décor.

His art joined the whole process of deconstruction referred to earlier in its attempt to escape from the cultural and religious past, from what Newman called "the weight of European culture", and from "the impediments of memory, association, nostalgia, legend, myth or what have you". He therefore sought to build 'the new cathedrals of the human spirit'. He produced images that he intended to be as self-evident as revelation, real and concrete, which anyone can understand who will look at them "without the nostalgic glasses of history". He was making a direct appeal to what he called "the absolute emotions", and he sought during his life to reveal the conducive properties leading to those emotions.

In Newman's view (quoting a phrase from the Jewish writer and commentator, Rashi, 1040–1105), artists ought to be, like God, "the Creator of worlds". As God (according to the opening chapter of *Bereshith/Genesis*) created order out of chaos, so artists create by separating order from chaos, light from darkness, colour from the absence of colour in order then to hold the opposites together. As a result, Newman's paintings became increasingly large fields of colour separated by thin lines which he called 'zips'.

The chaos and darkness which Barnett Newman faced were real and not imagined. They were the Nazis, the bombs on Hiroshima and Nagasaki, the many different totalitarian regimes of his time: "We now know the terror to expect. Hiroshima showed it to us" (O'Neill, p.164). In response, he began to paint 'The Fourteen Stations of the Cross' in 1958, shortly after he was released from hospital following a heart attack. He was not invited or commissioned to paint them, nor did he initially have any idea of a sequence. He gave them the title *Lema Sabachthani* (from the cry of Jesus from the Cross, '[My God, my God,] why have you forsaken me?' Matthew 27.46, Mark 15.34) in order to focus on 'the unanswerable question of human suffering': to what purpose? So he wrote (O'Neill, pp.187f):

> Can the Passion be expressed by a series of anecdotes, by fourteen senti-mental illustrations? Do not the Stations tell of one event? The first pilgrims walked the Via Dolorosa to identify themselves with the original moment, not to reduce it to a pious legend; nor even to worship the story of one man and his agony, but to stand witness to the story of each man's agony: the agony that is single, constant, unrelenting, unwilled – world without end.

> > The ones who are born are to die
> > Against thy will art thou formed
> > Against thy will art thou born
> > Against thy will dost thou live
> > Against thy will die.

> Jesus surely heard these words from Pirqe Abot,[19] 'The Wisdom of the Fathers'. No one gets anybody's permission to be born. No one asks to live. Who can say he has *more* permission than anybody else?

Barnett Newman illustrates how the internalisation of constraints can be, not limiting, but liberating. The constraints derived from Judaism and from the Jewish figure of Jesus did not restrict Newman; they set him free to create. But Newman also illustrates one particular way in which that freedom has to be exercised, namely in the *choice* of constraints. That in itself can be a demand-ing and contested process, and it returns us to the paradox of religion. Who (if anyone) in the protected circle of a religion decides whether a particular work of art counts as a true or legitimate expression of that religion? "Oh God, oh Montreal!" as Samuel Butler exclaimed on discovering that a statue of a nude discus thrower had been banished from a museum display to a basement.

But the issue for understanding religious art is much more serious than that. The nineteenth century, as we have just seen, was a time in the history of art of dramatic changes. In his book *The Invisible Masterpiece*, Belting showed how great the challenge was for artists in that century to create new worlds of imagination as a result of those changes. Prominent among them was the erosion of traditional constraints derived from two long-standing traditions, from Christianity on the one hand and from the classical tradition on the other:

> The search for a subject became an additional burden for artists. What sub-jects could still satisfy the public, given that every theme seemed to have

become either dated or hackneyed? An artist now needed to devise new topics if he was to make an impact. Implicitly the future of art itself hung in the balance, because artists continually had to prove that art could still maintain its credibility. And so once again the subject became a test, for it had to be one that could be made into art. Géricault had ventured to portray events from contemporary history [particularly in 'The Raft of the Medusa', 1819], but this was not a sure road to success, for people wanted painted dreams that offered an escape from the narrowness of everyday life. (Belting pp.106f)

One answer was to seek new constraints derived from different sources and to combine them with the old. That process was occurring in all parts of the world. An example occurring at much the same time can be seen in Japan in the Nanga (Southern) school and, after the Meiji restoration, in Nihonga painting, especially that of Kobayashi Kokei (1883–1967) and Maeda Seison (1885–1977). In Europe it meant new sources of constraint being identified alongside Christianity, as, for example, in exploring the opportunities of 'the Orient' and later of other religions. Belting (p.107) took as an example Delacroix's 'The Barque of Dante' (1822):

> "The picture released all the fantasies that the reading of Dante set free. This time they were transported not to an imaginary Orient but into another world – the Underworld – that was even more a matter for imagination. What subject could be greater than Dante's poem, which was indubitably art? Delacroix chose art itself to be the subject of art by painting literature. He was showing not so much the Underworld through which Dante travels, as the imaginative world of a poet who had turned an impossible subject into art."

By taking that example of a particular painting, Belting has made clear that the artistic creation of an imagined world is not contradicted, but rather is enabled, by the internalisation of constraints. There is nothing here of "unfettered flights of imagination". Those could, of course, be created: the subversion of realism into surrealism began very early in the nineteenth century, as Roberts-Jones's superb survey, *Beyond Time and Place*, makes unmistakably clear. His survey begins, almost inevitably, with Goya's passionate and angry revolt against "the bloody insanity of man": "Absurdities, bestial vices, agonies, and dreams are here engraved for ever in the imagination."

But Goya, in creating such a vivid and terrifying world of imagination, did not abandon the constraints of the recognisable. It was he who warned against 'the sleep of reason', not just in monitoring the brutal excesses of humanity, but also in the work and imagination of the artist himself. No. 43 of 'The

Caprices' shows the artist slumped in sleep losing control over his creations: a flock of nightmare birds overwhelms him, and one of them even seizes his pen. The inscription in the etching reads, 'The sleep [or 'dream'?] of reason produces monsters.'

So the constraints of reason and tradition were explicitly important for Delacroix when he placed Virgil and Dante realistically in their imagined barge, but they were no less important for Goya when he exhibited 'the disasters of war' epitomised in his ominous 'Colossus'. Whether realistically or surrealistically, both artists were able to create worlds of *shared* imagination precisely because *in both cases* they internalised the constraints which then set them free. As Roberts-Jones put it succinctly (p.7), "Goya with his extravagance was a contemporary of Louis David; the visions of Blake date from the same period as Canova's marbles."

Artists, therefore, in many different cultures, styles and traditions, have created worlds of imagination far beyond illustration. By the internalisation of constraint, they have made the invisible visible, and in more general terms they have helped to create and endorse those shared worlds of religious imagination.

SYMBOLS AND SIGNS

Among the constraints derived from religions, symbols and rituals have been of particular importance. The stability of religious art (in each of the many religions), persisting even through the long process of change and innovation, has happened in part because so much of religious belief and practice has been compressed or condensed into symbols and rituals.

The word 'symbol' comes from the Greek *sumballein*, 'to throw things together'. What symbols do is to 'throw together', or put into a compressed and brief form, information or instruction that people need to know. Thus symbols, and not long lists of printed instructions, tell you at once when a road in front of you is a dead end, or is 'One Way', or is 'No Entry'. In the same way, there is no need (at least for Hindus) to have a long list of instructions telling them that two hands placed together in front of the forehead is a greeting, that the figure seated on a tortoise is Kurma (the second incarnation of Vishnu), that the figure painted dark blue or black dancing on the snake is Krishna (the eighth incarnation of Vishnu), or that the figure dancing in a circle of flames and holding a drum is Shiva as Nataraja, the Lord of the dance of the universe.

Symbols do very much more than condense information, but in the case of religious art one of their most important roles is to condense beliefs and express them in ways that believers can recognise, and to which they can respond. Thus symbols are particularly powerful conducive properties which create that two-way interaction (described earlier) between an image and those who see it.

Religious artists respect and internalise constraints of that kind. They may attempt to bring them into visible form, or they may even be content simply to illustrate them. But equally the internalisation of those constraints may lead them into dramatic innovation, as it did in the case of Stravinsky in music or of Newman in art. We return yet again to the same point: where constraints exist, advantage can be taken of them; to which we may add, the more stable the constraints are, the greater the degrees of freedom may be.

To give a well-known and familiar example: the Cross is an instantly recognisable symbol generated within the circle of coherence that we call Christianity. The Cross is a symbolic constraint that acts conducively to bring believers into a deeper awareness of suffering, sin and redemption, but it does not have a single or simple meaning. It compresses a rich complexity of beliefs that characterise Christianity in distinction from other religions.

To be more specific: crucifixion was used by the Romans to inflict the death penalty for many offences, ranging from theft to terrorism. It helped them to establish the famous *pax Romana*, the peace and security which prevailed in the Roman Empire. It was a horrific execution of those regarded as the worst of criminals. And Jesus was crucified on the hill called Golgotha, meaning 'a skull'.

Yet that grotesque and criminal death on a cross became for Christians the foundation of their faith that God has broken into the world in order to rescue them from sin and from death, the consequence of sin. The death of Jesus on the Cross shows to Christians that God was prepared to go to the furthest limit to face the worst that humans can do, and to defeat it. Criminal crosses established the *pax Romana*, but this cross establishes the *pax Christi*, the peace of Christ which, as Paul wrote, "surpasses all human understanding" (*Philippians* 4.7).

So the Cross in Christian belief becomes the key that opens the door through which humans can move from their present condition of corruption and death to a new life in which they are made at one with God. That is why this act of rescue on the Cross is called by Christians 'the at-one-ment'.

How does it happen? Early Christians had many pictures to describe it: for example, slaves ransomed from bondage, debtors redeemed from what they owe, lambs sacrificed at Passover to ward off evil and death, the price that has to be paid to buy a precious object. There are many pictures, and Christians today add others derived from their own time and experience.[20] The Cross as a symbol compresses all these into a single conducive form.

As a result, the Cross in any particular work of Christian art frequently exhibits only one of the many ways in which the consequence of the Cross has been understood – as ransom, as redemption, as sacrifice, as victory and so on. Two of the best-known paintings of the crucifixion are those of Mathias Grünewald (d.1528) and Salvador Dali (1904–89), and they represent two extremely different ways of understanding the basic symbol – indeed, Dali wrote that he painted his picture in deliberate opposition to that of Grünewald.

Of Grünewald's paintings of the crucifixion four survive which are believed to be his work. They resemble each other in the way in which they portray the grim reality and the distortions of agonising pain, but the one that Salvador Dali seems to have had in mind was the Isenheim altarpiece.

The conducive properties in Grünewald's altarpiece were intended to evoke from those who see it horror at the suffering, grief at the human sin which brought it about, and a return to the mercy of God in penitence. In order to achieve that, Grünewald made the conducive properties extremely specific. The altarpiece was commissioned for a monastery of the Antonites, so called because they derived their order from St Antony. Antony (c. 251–356) was one of the most famous of those who went into the desert in order to live and pray away from the temptations of the world. In fact, temptations continued to assail him (often portrayed in Christian art), depicted in Grunewald's paint-ing in the form of grotesque monsters. But in that same panel, there is, in the bottom left-hand corner, a quite different creature, a more human person suffering from grievous illness. His heart-rending cry is painted on the scroll to the right, *Ubi eras Jhesu bone, ubi eras, quare non affuisti ut sanares vulnera mea?* 'Where were you, good Jesus, where were you? Why did you not come and heal my wounds?'

The cry is specific because the Antonites devoted themselves to the care and cure of those suffering from blood and skin diseases and especially from the one known as 'St Antony's fire': this was brought on by flour made from rye affected by the fungal disease known as ergot, hence ergotism. Sufferers who were being brought to this monastery for care were taken first into the chapel where Grünewald's altarpiece stood. If they did not receive an imme-diate cure, they could still identify with the Christ who suffers so grievously on their behalf, and also with the particular suffering of his gangrenous skin and broken body.

The brutality and pain of the crucifixion were portrayed differently but with equally savage power by Stanley Spencer (1891–1959) in his 'The Crucifixion' of 1958.[21] Spencer chose an unusual viewpoint. The observer is looking into the scene from behind the Cross on which Jesus is crucified, and is looking therefore at the two thieves, one of whom lunges ferociously toward the figure of Jesus. What is portrayed here is not only the suffering of Jesus but the cruelty of those who are nailing him to the Cross.

Spencer in his paintings often followed the lead given in the prayer of imagination (a long-standing tradition of prayer in Christianity, and one that is connected, as we have seen, with visualisation), and set the New Testament scenes that he was painting in his own world, especially in Cookham, whose High Street forms the background of this painting. It is one of the conducive properties that draws the observer into the scene.

Another is the fact that the 'soldiers' nailing Jesus to the Cross are wearing the caps of the Brewers' Company who had commissioned the painting for the Chapel of their school in Elstree. Catherine Martineau, a close friend of Spencer, recalled the reaction of the boys when he spoke about the picture at the school Rothenstein (p.131):

> He stunned the boys at Aldenham School, talking of his *Crucifixion* (which Jack [Martineau], a brewer, had commissioned for a Brewer's School), when he said: 'I have given the men who are nailing Christ to the Cross (and making sure that they make a good job of it) – Brewer's Caps – because it is your Governors, and you, who are still nailing Christ to the Cross.'

In different ways both Grünewald and Spencer have used conducive properties to lead the observer into a personal involvement in the horrific pain of the crucifixion. There is, however, an entirely different understanding of the cross summed up in the phrase 'Christus Victor', Christ the conqueror of sin and death. That is the theme portrayed by Salvador Dali in his famous and often-reproduced painting which, like that of Spencer, adopts an entirely different viewpoint: in his painting, the observer looks down on Christ on the Cross suspended above the world (or more specifically above Dali's own home village) as the one who has conquered the worst that sin and death can do.

Dali's point of departure was a small sketch in pen and ink, attributed to John of the Cross (1542–91), one of the great pioneers and guides in Christian prayer. Dali saw this sketch when he visited a convent in Avila in Spain. Not long afterwards he had a dream about it, in which he heard voices saying, 'Dali, you must paint this Christ.' His aim was to show Christ supreme and transcendent over the world. He wrote in *The Unspeakable Confessions of Salvador Dali*: "I want to paint a Christ that is a painting with more beauty and joy than had ever been painted before. I want to paint a Christ that is the absolute opposite of Grünewald's materialistic savagely anti-mystical one."

From even as few as those three artists it can be seen that a symbol, however much it compresses information, can be almost limitlessly rich. Symbols act as constraints, but where constraints exist, advantage can be taken of them. This means that the recognition of symbols can be as demanding, but also as rewarding, as the search for meaning in hermeneutics. Recognising symbols is known technically as 'symbolic cognition', and it is a massively important part of human learning and living. Without symbolic cognition we would be lost. We would, for example, have no advance warning whether a road is no-entry, one-way or a dead end – until we hit something. Religions map the world in easily learnt and recognised symbols, and thus help people to live successfully. But they also enrich those symbols, particularly through the process of art. It is simply not possible to understand religions without understanding the importance of symbols in general, and the particular symbols of each religion.

RITUALS AND SYMBOLS

Just as important in human life are rituals, and that again is why we find them in the non-religious as much as in the religious world. Rituals, as we will see in more detail in Chapter 9, are actions which are repeated regularly in a common form (and are therefore widely recognised and known in any group or society), and which hold organisations together as well as giving public expression to our deepest needs and feelings.

A familiar example of this is the way in which we use rituals to mark with significance important moments in life – such moments as birth and death, the transition from one year to another, graduating from university, opening a Parliament or Senate, celebrating a wedding. There are some particular moments or events which stand out as different from everyday life, and ritual is a massively important way in which we mark them out as having significance for us.

Rituals thus compress into action our rational understanding of what is happening in the world around us, and they combine that understanding with our emotions (for example, of happiness or of sadness, depending on the occasion) especially by connecting them with appropriate symbols. In other words, rituals are combined with all that we have learnt through symbolic cognition.

What this means in practice is that rituals are combined with symbols and symbolic displays in such a way that our rational understanding is experienced and felt emotionally with great power, not as one brain event followed by another, but as an immediate and integrated experience. We use signs and symbols (such things as words, pictures, costumes, actions, decorations, gestures) to construct and share our public understanding of what is happening in the world or in particular events. Symbols are then attached to rituals in order to express, or reinforce the expression of, the feelings and emotions which are appropriate to them (such things as mystery, awe, solemnity, authority, fear, grief, sadness, joy, and so on). Which feeling or emotion it is depends on the occasion, whether, for example, it is a wedding or a funeral.

Both rituals and symbols are immensely important in religious art, as is this whole 'way of seeing' in which reason and emotion are combined. In the case of rituals, it is art that clothes them with appropriate dress and with such things as masks, and also portrays what they purport to be about; it decorates objects used in ritual; it also often marks out in elaborate ways the arenas of ritual and symbolic action; and it choreographs the actions in order to give them formal recognition and thus to empower them. Art makes use of symbols and rituals as a condensed and coded (but well-understood) language through which beliefs are put into accessible and visible form, and in which they are evoked, endorsed and shared.

Not surprisingly, it is through art that our religious emotions, understanding and memories are most powerfully captured and expressed. Religious art may be used for many purposes – for leading into meditation, for example, or for instructing those who cannot read. When Europe was mostly illiterate, carvings, murals and stained glass conveyed the Christian message, and have indeed been called 'the villein's Bible', the title of a book by Brian Young illustrating this theme. It is important, however, to remember that they were equally powerful in evoking through their conducive properties an emotional and religious response – a fundamental purpose, as we have already seen, in many forms of religious art. That is a point made strongly by Michelle Brown in her introduction to the Folio Society edition of *The Holkham Bible* (pp.9f):

> To view it merely as a religious picture book, designed to help instruct an illiterate audience in the basics of Bible stories, is to miss the point of the work that marks a radical shift in modes of communication. It is to mistake an early *Flash Gordon* comic strip for George Lucas's *Star Wars* epic. For during the early fourteenth century, when the book was made, artists and spiritual directors were taking art into spheres as innovative as film would prove to be seven centuries later.... Art, like music, can provide an immediacy and profundity of access to the senses and to emotional response.

So art has its uses in the life of all religions, but beyond those uses, art brings into being what humans aspire to but otherwise find so difficult to achieve or to express – the imagination of God or of holiness, for example, or such things as praise, worship, thanksgiving, penitence, sorrow, hope, trust, joy – and vision. A work of art extends to others what it already is in its own meaning and integrity.

From all this it can be seen why the characteristic beliefs of any religious tradition create such distinctive forms of art. Art may of course illustrate a tradition, but far beyond that it can be 'the life and soul of the party'.

ARTISTS AND BELIEF

Does that mean that religious art can be produced only by believers? Clearly not. Rituals and symbols exist independently from the beliefs or opinions of the participants, and as a result it is entirely possible for religious art to be produced by artists who do not share the beliefs of the religion in question. On the other hand, they can still internalise the relevant constraints with at least some degree of understanding even if it falls short of belief. As Promey wrote (p.29) of John Singer Sargent's controversial *Triumph of Religion*,

> Though his [Sargent] experiences and attitudes were heavily informed by Western Christianity and its symbols, religion was an idea to which the artist more or less subscribed, not a practice or a community to which he committed himself. If Sargent was not an orthodox believer, however, he was certainly a fascinated and not entirely disinterested onlooker.[22]

Even so, it remains as essential now as it has always been for artists, whether they are believers or not, to understand the symbols they are using, and what they have meant, not least as a kind of conventional code, in the tradition. Religious art may be content to illustrate religious themes, but it can also be very much more than that: it can become the religious fact.

The key issue and challenge to an artist is the extent to which he or she can internalise the constraints in order to move beyond them into a new freedom, into a new work of *art*. To make that move beyond the facile and repetitive requires an immense struggle of discipline, feeling and understanding, particularly for those who do not share the beliefs of the religion in question. There are many examples of this struggle in recent years. One such is Henry Moore. Despite a profound experience of God when he was confirmed, Henry Moore did not remain a participant member of any Church. When, therefore, he was commissioned to make a Madonna and Child for the church of St Matthew in Northampton, he had to ask himself what the difference is between the sculpture of a mother and child and that of a Madonna and Child. He wrote:[23]

When I was first asked to carve a Madonna and Child for St Matthew's, although I was very interested, I wasn't sure whether I could do it, or whether I even wanted to do it. One knows that religion has been the inspiration of most of Europe's greatest painting and sculpture, and that the church in the past has encouraged and employed the greatest artists; but the great tradition of religious art seems to have got lost completely in the present day, and the general level of Church art has fallen very low (as anyone can see from the affected and sentimental prettiness sold for church decoration in church art shops). Therefore I felt it was not a commission straight-away and light-heartedly to agree to undertake ... I began thinking of the 'Madonna and Child' for St Matthew's by considering in what ways a Madonna and Child differs from a carving of just a Mother and Child – that is, by considering how in my opinion religious art differs from secular art. It's not easy to describe in words what this difference is, except by saying in general terms that the 'Madonna and Child' should have an austerity and a nobility, and some touch of grandeur (even hieratic aloofness) which is missing in the everyday 'Mother and Child' idea. Of the sketches and models I have done, the one chosen has I think a quiet dignity and gentleness. I have tried to give a sense of complete easiness and repose, as though the Madonna could stay in that position for ever (as being in stone she will have to do).

Another example of this struggle to enter into the code and to internalise the constraints is Stanley Spencer. Spencer had an unshakeable belief in God and Christ, but despite attempts to convert him to Roman Catholicism when he was young, he remained suspicious of organised and institutional religion. Nevertheless, his art remained deliberately rooted in God and Christ, and he had to wrestle all his life with the difference between ordinary and spiritual painting. So he wrote in 1926 (Rothenstein pp.21f):

What a funny thing it is, as soon as I contemplate the doings in the Gospel, I am fired at once, and yet I am not entirely in love with Christianity. I think it's this, that one can love Christ without fearing that one is going to be brought up with a sudden jerk, whereas with any other passion one fears a coul-de-sack [sic] ... It is strange that I feel so 'lonely' when I draw from nature, but it is because no sort of spiritual activity comes into the business at all. Its this identity business. There are certain things where I can see and recognise clearly this spiritual identity in something, but if I am drawing and dont see this clearly, its all up. In fact the only impulse I have to draw or paint is that I know that somewhere in all these things there is that miraculous spiritual meaning that just in a flash of a second could change boredom of drawing into a tremendous experience.

A third example (among many) is Henri Matisse. Matisse remained what his biographer, Hilary Spurling, called "a completely secular person". Nevertheless, when he asked himself in 1947, "Do I believe in God?", he answered: "Yes, when I am working. When I am submissive and humble, I feel as if some-one is helping me to exceed my powers." What he could not do was feel any gratitude: "I am remorselessly ungrateful." So when a former model, Monique Bourgeois, told him why she had decided to become a nun, Matisse tried to dissuade her, and he wrote to her:

> I do not need any lectures about religious calling. I've not needed the sacra-ments to glorify the name of God throughout my life. I went as far as Tahiti to admire the beauty of the light he created so I might share it with others through my work.

In that way the constraint of God persisted, and that 'sharing' of imagination he achieved supremely when he responded to the request of Sr Jacques-Marie (as she had then become) to design a chapel for her order at Vence in the South of France. The resulting Chapel of the Rosary (consecrated in 1951) was his attempt "to inscribe a spiritual space, one whose dimensions are not lim-ited by the objects represented" (Chipp p.142). The result is a profoundly Christian work which he regarded as the supreme achievement of his life, and one for which his whole life had been a preparation: "This is not a work that I have chosen", he wrote. "It is a work for which I have been chosen."[24]

There is, therefore, a sense in which religious art takes on (or can take on) a life of its own which is independent of the beliefs, or absence of beliefs, of the artist, but is never independent of the inherited and conducive constraints. Just as the building of a temple or a cathedral does not depend on the beliefs or absence of beliefs of the individual carpenters or sculptors, so it can be with any work of art. The constraints, if they are respected, can work, and the code can be transmitted – even by those who do not share the message.

There was a dramatic illustration of this in the Edinburgh exhibition of work by David Mach, *Precious Light (King James Bible, A Celebration, 1611–2011)*. Commenting on the exhibition, Lawson wrote:

> Although Mach is not himself a religious believer, he told me, in an inter-view for BBC Radio 4's *Front Row*, that he intended his pieces to be 'respect-ful'. And he confirmed that a sight I was surprised to witness during my afternoon at the gallery – visitors openly weeping as they stood beneath *Golgotha* – has been regularly repeated.[25]

This means that even works which were not specifically intended to be reli-gious can be seen by others in a religious way if the relevant conducive prop-erties are recognised or felt – that fundamental recognition of the code in a connection between reason and emotion. Such works give visible form to the beliefs of those who use them or see them, and they are thus the incarnation of the otherwise invisible, in any of the many senses of 'incarnation' in the religions of the world.

It is this which gives to art such high and precious value that it can be, in some circumstances, immensely threatening and dangerous. That is so because it carries interior and important beliefs in a visible and public form. That is why works of art have been burned and destroyed in the wars and conflicts of religion, from the destruction by Akhenaton (ruled c. 1350–1534 BCE) of images of rival gods in Egypt and the burning of the books of Confucius in 213 BCE, to the destruction by the Taliban of the massive images of the Buddha at Bamian in 2001 and the burning of manuscripts by the Muslim Ansar Din in Timbuktu and Mali in 2012.[26]

To approach, therefore, the understanding of religions through art does not lead us into an enchanted land far removed from the conflict and violence with which this book began. It makes visible the reasons why religions matter so much to believers. To understand the beliefs that underlie the religious art of the world is to begin to understand the conflicts because it is also to begin to understand the imagination and vision which have sustained humans at all times and have given direction and meaning to their lives.

That point, therefore, can be put the other way round: it is not possible to understand the world of the past or of the present without at least some understanding of religious art. Religions are communities of shared imagination, in which the internalisation of religious constraints sets free the imagination of the unseen, and indeed of the unseeable, in vivid ways. Few people have expressed this more eloquently than the artist and poet William Blake for whom the ultimate blasphemy is the denial of imagination. In 1799, he wrote (Keynes p.605):[27]

> I know that this world is a world of imagination and vision. I see every thing I paint in this world, but every body does not see alike. To the eyes of a miser a guinea is far more beautiful than the sun, and a bag worn with the use of money has more beautiful proportions than a vine filled with grapes. The tree which moves some to tears of joy is in the eyes of others only a green thing that stands in the way. Some see nature all ridicule and deformity, and by these I shall not regulate my proportions; and some scarce see nature at all. But to the eyes of the man of imagination, nature is imagination itself. As a man is, so he sees.

And in a famous passage he also wrote:[28]

> This world of imagination is the world of eternity; it is the divine bosom into which we shall all go after the death of the vegetated body. This world

of imagination is infinite and eternal, whereas the world of generation, or vegetation, is finite and temporal. There exist in that eternal world the permanent realities of every thing which we see reflected in this vegetable glass of nature ... 'What,' it will be question'd, 'When the sun rises, do you not see a round disk of fire somewhat like a Guinea?' O no, no, I see an innumerable company of the Heavenly host crying, 'Holy, Holy, Holy is the Lord God Almighty.' I question not my corporeal or vegetative eye any more than I would question a window concerning a sight. I look thro' it and not with it.

By seeing and understanding the religious art of the world we can begin to share the vision that endures even when we and the artists are dead. We can begin to see everything around us in new ways. As people see, so they are.

And as people are, so they act – the fundamental observation of character and virtue moralities with which this chapter began. Constraints internalised from religions are not restricted to particular and specific outcomes in ethics and in art alone. In an earlier draft of this book, many detailed examples were given of the difference that constraints derived from religions have made in recent years, but for reasons of space they could not be included. We can at least look at one particular example in the ways in which humans have used rituals in relation to their understandings of death.

9

Understanding religions

III Ritual and the human imagination of death

THE POET GEORGE BARKER ONCE OBSERVED: "THERE ARE TWO THINGS a poet can write about, death and sex – some call it love. No one knows anything about death, so I write about sex."

Religions, on the other hand, often give the impression that they know all that needs to be known about sex and prefer to talk about death. From their point of view, it is not true that 'no one knows anything about death'. In Asian religions the belief in rebirth means that a memory of previous lives and deaths is unsurprising. It is, for example, taken for granted in the Tibetan Book of the Dead (*Bardo Thödol*):

> In contrast to the assumption that no one can tell us anything about what happens after death because no one has ever come back from death, *Bardo Thödol* (and Tibetan belief in general) insists that everyone has come back from death, or at least come through death, and that consequently there is much that we know about it. Part of that knowledge is contained in *Bardo Thödol*. (Bowker 2011, p.285)

Short of remembering the experience of death, there is still much that we know about death. We know, for example, a great deal about the statistics and the distribution of death; we know much more than we did in the past about the many different ways in which death brings life to an end. For that reason alone we can postpone the occasion of death far more extensively than any generation before us.

In fact, it may well be true to say that we actually know *more* about death than we do about sex, given how little we understand of what actually happens in the human brain in that attraction between two people which evokes the word 'love'. We can scan and image activity in the brain very effectively, and we can map consistent correlations, but we understand virtually nothing of how it comes about that Jane Austen's Isabella and Catherine differ in what attracts them – in what, in more colloquial language, 'turns them on' (p.42):

> 'By the bye, though I gave thought of it a hundred times, I have always forgot to ask you what is your favourite complexion in a man. Do you like them best dark or fair?'
>
> 'I hardly know. I never thought much about it. Something between both, I think. Brown – not fair, and not very dark.'
>
> '…Well, my taste is different. I prefer light eyes, and as to complexion – do you know – I like a sallow better than any other.'

Of course, Barker may have had in mind the rather different point that we know nothing much about what may be the case *after* death. But on this side of the grave, there is much about death that we comprehend. Not surprisingly, therefore, the poetry of death is at least as extensive as the poetry of sex or love, maybe more so.

And that, quite simply, makes the point: humans, while they are alive, live in the domain of death. They live there, not in the form of ghosts, but in the power of imagination. "Death is," as Wallace Stevens observed (O. Williams, p.281), "the mother of beauty, mystical …" It is the mother also of films about vampires, zombies and the living dead. The truth is that the human imaginations of death affect profoundly the way we live our lives. As Dag Hammarskjold put it in his diary (p.136), "In the last analysis it is our conception of death which decides our answer to all the questions that life puts to us."

It is not that humans are unique in their awareness of death. Many animals recognise the singularity of death: elephants, for example, gather round a dead member of their group and often stay with it for days. There is among them a coded recognition of at least the disruptive difference which death brings about. But in the human case, it is the imagination which invades the domain of death with even greater apprehension – as in the familiar words of Keats 'On Seeing the Elgin Marbles':

> My spirit is too weak – mortality
>   Weighs heavily on me like unwilling sleep,
>   And each imagined pinnacle and steep
> Of godlike hardship, tells me I must die
> Like a sick eagle looking at the sky.

Death, for humans, is no longer *simply* disruption: it is disruption bearing cargoes of consequence and emotion, hence the equally well-known words inscribed on the tombstone of Keats in Rome:

This grave contains all that was mortal of a young English poet, who, on his death bed, in the bitterness of his heart at the malicious power of his enemies, desired these words to be graven on his tombstone, 'Here lies one whose name was writ in water.'

It is the conscious knowledge of death – the fact that in this sense death is extremely *well* known – which makes the imagination of death so prolific in the human case. As I wrote in *The Meanings of Death*, virtually everything that *can* be imagined about death *has* been imagined. When Guthke asked the question, "Is Death a woman?", in order to explore the gender of death in the iconography of Western art, he wrote (pp.8,10):

Imagination, being the elementary urge to visualise, does not stop short of the 'unimaginable.' It gives shape to the shapeless by approximating it to the familiar, thereby endowing it with meaning.... In this manner, death, rather than remaining shapeless and chaotically threatening, is made concrete and visible by our creative imagination. Such image-making, such interpretation through personification, occurs on all levels of consciousness, in all cultures, in all times that have left records. Many mythologies, including the fall of Adam and Eve that brought death into the world, all but define humans by their knowledge of death, their awareness that they are destined to die. Where there is life, there is its opposite, demarcating the border that circumscribes and, literally, defines it.

It has, however, not been imagined in disconnected or random fashion: the shared imaginations of death are highly stable, both creating and reflecting the differing styles of human cultures and civilisations, as Giedion showed spectacularly in the architecture of Mesopotamia and Egypt.[1] Where the temples of Egypt are concerned, the ways in which death-beliefs constrained architecture into its characteristic forms, and in which (reciprocally) developments in architectural possibility constrained beliefs, are made extremely clear in two symposia on religion and temples in ancient Egypt.[2] Those constraints interacting in both directions produced great stability even in the process of development and change.

Stability of that kind helps to bring into being, not just in Egypt but throughout the world, the extensive and enduring religious art of death. Amidst all that religions code, protect and transmit from generation to generation prominent and pervasive are the achieved imaginations of death which give to death its particular meanings. Religions then become the resource from which the human dealings with death are both internalised (giving individuals the means to interpret death) and also made public (so that death is understood in shareable ways). For that to happen there has to be stability, both in concepts and practices.

But although the imaginations of death are indeed highly stable, they nevertheless do change. That again is described at length in *The Meanings of Death*. The clearest and most striking example lies in the way in which all the major, continuing religious traditions of the world, both Asian and non-Asian, had in origin no belief that there would be some worthwhile life after death. They could not deny that there is a continuity of some sort after death: they could observe that the dead continue in the memory of the living (and continue to appear to the living at least in dreams), and they could observe that children often bear a resemblance to their parents or grandparents. As early as the Neanderthals, bodies were being given careful burial – even the body of 'the cripple of Shanidar' who cannot have given much help to the group in the search for food and survival. To the body of that man, broken from use, who could not extend territory, who could not stun prey, who could not heave fuel and defence, the group made his burial, to judge from the remains, a significant occasion:

> He died where we had given him
> Occasion to continue.
> Where we bury him
> The ground will signify:
> More than aggression, more than territory,
> We belonged in this cave together,
> And to him we gave occasion.[3]

So the dead in some sense have not gone to immediate or complete oblivion. But the state they are in was believed to be one of vague and insubstantial shadows, not at all to be compared favourably to the robust values of the living. It is, as Sophocles put it, *ton apotropon Haidan*, Hades to be shunned. There was definitely no future in dying.

And yet religious history shows how that virtually universal imagination of death was changed. In both East and West, it came to be believed that there is either that which subsists through the process of death (as, for example, in the case of soul, *nafs, atman, jiva* and the like) or that has consequence through the process of death, even though there is no subsistent self (as in the case of Buddhists).

That massive change in the human imagination of death, with its vast consequences for morality, ritual, architecture, poetry and so much more, came about for a complicated tangle of reasons. No doubt they included, as Marx and Freud proposed, the abject fears of humans who could not face the prospect of annihilation and who therefore invented a life after death, which some then exploited to maintain class inequalities. But much more than that, the change came about because of long and winnowed reflection on human experience of the persistent self and its possibilities within the boundaries of this life.

This means that the widespread assumption commonly made about the origin of religions is completely false – the assumption that religions came into being in order to offer spurious consolation to those who could not face the fact of death and of oblivion. That is simply wrong. However, given that there has been such a huge change in the human imagination of death in the past, the question for us now is whether an equally massive change is in the process of coming into being.

The issue facing us now is whether the human imagination of death is going to have to change in the new century, not as a matter of arbitrary decision, but because the evidence – the changes in our knowledge of death and of the human self – require it, just as changes in understanding demanded so immense a change about three thousand years ago. More particularly, what will be the implications of this for the imagination of death in the different religious traditions, and to what extent will religions continue, if at all, to supply the forms and symbols and concepts of an imagination of death in the millennium before us?

That question, of course, cannot be answered: none of us knows for certain what will happen in the next minute, let alone a thousand years from now. But what we can at least attempt is not so much an exercise in prediction as a reflection on the implications of the changes in the modalities of death which we can already begin to observe. So the questions are: What changes are we already in the midst of? And what consequences for the imagination of death might they have?

THE NATURALISATION OF DEATH

The most immediate change is the naturalisation of death. Of course, in the most basic sense, death *is* natural – in the sense, that is, of death belonging to the process of nature and of evolution in a universe of this kind. But the human imagination, while accepting that indeed all must die, has also repeatedly protested against the view that death is natural, claiming instead that life is the natural condition which death disrupts. As Simone de Beauvoir wrote sharply of the death of her mother (p.106),

> There is no such thing as a natural death: nothing that ever happens to a man is ever natural, since his presence calls the world into question. All men must die; but for every man his death is an accident, and even if he knows it and consents to it, an unjustifiable violation.

The point here is that while everyone accepts that death must surely happen, it is inevitably an event out of the ordinary: death is a literal 'once in a lifetime' event (except for those who are resuscitated after they have been pronounced clinically dead). In that respect it is exactly like birth; and both birth and death have been surrounded, historically, by reverence, awe, superstition and tabu.

Some 'natural' events, like the passing of the seasons or the alternation of day and night, can be reliably predicted. Birth and (even more) death cannot be predicted in every instance so reliably, nor can they be brought under human control, except in a limited sense on a few occasions. As Mrs Gamp observed to Mr Pecksniff of death, "It's what we must all come to. It's as certain as being born, except that we can't make our calculations as exact."

Consequently, the belief has been widespread that these events belong to some other power – for example, that they belong to *karma* or to God: it is God or *karma* that determines when a birth or a death occurs. By an extension of that belief, it was widely held (as by many it still is) that humans should not interfere with the dispositions of God in relation to life and death. As a result, we are often told that people in general and doctors in particular should not 'play God'.

The persistence of the attitude (which oscillates between reverence and superstition) that we should not 'play God' extends far beyond occasions of birth and death. A current example is gene modification. Thus the International Bioethics Survey of 1993 asked people in ten different countries for their opinions on various issues in bioethics: given that genes from most types of organisms are interchangeable, would potatoes made more nutritious, or chickens made less fatty, through such biotechnology be acceptable? Those opposed annotated their opposition with comments like: "God made all things good for us – we are not God"; "It's wrong because it's playing with God's nature".

In a second example (perhaps more pertinent to the issues of death), the same underlying attitude can be seen in the policies of the Vatican on birth control by artificial means (every sexual act must be open to life in order not to frustrate the purposes of God) and on voluntary euthanasia or on suicide. As the *Catechism of the Catholic Church* puts it (§2280), "It is God who remains the sovereign Master of life ... We are stewards, not owners, of the life God has entrusted to us. It is not ours to dispose of."

That kind of understanding of the disposition of death is what we may call a *super*natural imagination of death: the occurrence of death is outside the controls of either humans or of nature in its own right. It then seems obvious to some (in fact, still to many) that it *is* in the control of God or of *karma*, and that it is wrong or even impossible to interfere.

To think of God in that way destroys the recognition that God to *be* God simply is, whether this or any other universe happens to exist. It reduces 'god' to the status of a human-like agent within the universe who intervenes and interferes now and then, rather than being (as God must be to be God) the Creator and constant constraint, the source of all causes including those brought about by human agents – as we have already seen.

In contrast, therefore, to theological self-contradiction, the naturalisation of death means that death is brought increasingly into human responsibility and control. That does not entail a denial of God's authority (of God as the author of all creation, including life and death). It is, rather, a recognition of God as Creator without whom neither life nor death nor anything else can exist. It is thus a responsibility derived from that creative and sustaining purpose.

In the context of that understanding of agency, it is clear that conception and birth are much further on in the process of naturalisation since they are now so much better understood, and both are brought much more into human control and management. Death is further behind in that process, but clearly death is also being naturalised in that sense: it is being brought increasingly under human control and management.

The two are not symmetrical: intervention in relation to conception and birth is intended to be life-conferring; in relation to death it may be life-ending and is clearly irretrievable. Thus there is a proper resistance to all except pre-indicated euthanasia (and perhaps even to that), and there is still a considerable reluctance on the part of many to intervene in the moment of death (for example, in making the decision to turn off a life-support machine). In the United Kingdom it became a major issue whether the Liverpool Care Pathway, which began in a Hospice to assist people in dying, has been converted in hospitals to a form of euthanasia.

But those examples alone make it clear that the naturalisation of death has begun and is as inevitable in the case of death as it has proved to be in the case of birth – indeed, so much so that some have argued that we are moving even beyond that, into what we may call the *de*naturalisation of death: the argument is that because we can already postpone the occurrence of death, and are likely to do so even more extensively in the future, we are removing the human species from the natural context of evolutionary process, that is, from what is called 'natural selection'.

It is, of course, trivially true that human intervention is simply a new mode of natural selection, but what is meant here is that the conditions of natural selection, which have prevailed so far, are being altered radically by the human postponement of death. While this at present is on so small scale (postponement for a matter of decades at most) that it cannot yet be called 'denaturalisation', it may become so if the scale is greatly extended by the medical innovations which are likely to occur.

How will the naturalisation and denaturalisation of death affect the human imagination of death? And how will religions react? As we have seen repeatedly, religions phenomenologically (as a matter of observation) are conservative information systems. On the one hand, therefore, some people will resist the extension of human management and control because it will involve making decisions which they believe belong to *karma* or to God, but making them without the knowledge or the moral consistency of either. The naturalisation of death will for them be yet another instance of what Schiller called, in a graphic phrase, *die Entgotterung der Natur,* the 'ungodding' of nature.

But others will see this simply as an extension of the issues of choice and responsibility which humans have to make in the created order. They will emphasise that longevity and life on earth were the *earliest* considerations of excellence in religious history, both East and West, as, for example, in the three score years and ten of the Psalmist, the hundred years of the Vedas, or the postponement of death in the Immortality cults of China. To intervene responsibly to attain that kind of excellence will not seem irreligious, nor will the relinquishing of life for the sake of others when it is a matter of personal and uncoerced decision.

Important in that consideration is the understanding of agency and 'stewardship' (see p.155)– or its equivalent in other religions: the cultivation of *li* and *jen,* of *dao* and *de* in China, the association of *ṛta* and *dharma* in India, *khalifa* in Islam, *buddhata* and *bussho* in Buddhism, and so on. The naturalisation of death (including the extension of human control and management of death) will not be Promethean in its invasion of the domain of God if it is understood as an exercise of the human responsibility to cooperate with God, or with the cosmic order: indeed, the effect of the Vatican attitude quoted earlier would be to diminish or undermine the meaning of the word 'stewardship'.

So in this understanding, it is predictable that the religious imagination of death will increasingly reinforce the worth of the naturalisation of death (although there will be resistance to this), but it will emphasise that this is not an end, but a means to other ends which will still be religiously defined. Or to put it more specifically, the extension of life will always be subordinate to the attainment of the human potentials which have been discovered in the course of religious history; which means that there will not be a reversion to the earliest religious belief, that the extension of life is the *only* excellence open to us. The specifically religious goals, both immediate and ultimate, will persist.

THE TRIVIALISATION OF DEATH: DEATH AS ENTERTAINMENT

The fact that religions may well endorse the naturalisation of death does not mean that *none* of their anxieties about the naturalisation of death is valid. One unmistakeable consequence of the naturalisation of death against which religions are right to protest is the trivialisation of death. The longer we are able to postpone death, and the more we take it into our own control, the greater are the chances that we, or at least some of us, will reduce the significance of death and will turn it into entertainment.

That is a process which is accelerating already. In 1934, the *Daily Express* published a book called *Covenants with Death* (Innes and Castle) whose purpose was, through graphic photographs, "to reveal the horror, suffering and essential bestiality of death". The photographs in the main part of the book are grim enough (including some which have become icons of the horror of trench warfare). But the final section of the book contained pictures of death so barbaric that the book was sold with a red seal on those pages so that no one would have to look at them, and in order that they should not inadvertently be seen by children.

Now, in contrast, television, books, films, newspapers and computer games portray death in manners far more horrific and explicit than anything in those pages; and they do so, often, for entertainment. Death as spectacle and death as entertainment are a trivialisation of death which is unlikely to recede, given the commercial returns.

What effect will this have on the imagination of death? It may certainly reduce the fear of death: death may become so familiar that we worry about it less. One of the more misleading clichés of our time has been the opinion that death is the new taboo subject: we are told repeatedly that, whereas we used not to talk about sex, now we are afraid to talk about death. In fact it is hard to know how we could bring death much more into the public domain than we are now doing. We may not so often witness death at home and in the bedroom, but we witness it repeatedly at home and in the sitting room, whenever we turn on the television. And as the Romans before us knew well, "nimia familiaritas parit contemptum"[4] – familiarity breeds contempt.

Contempt of that kind can then lead to a casual indifference, an emotional reductionism which regards death (and by implication the worth of the person) as trivial; and this will show immediately (as it is already doing) in the treatment of the dead or of their remains:

'Due to lack of caskets ashes will be delivered in polythene bags.' This announcement is not some sort of sick joke, but appeared not so long ago on the door of a crematorium in the Ukraine.

So Vitaly Vitaliev tells us (in Porter), and he went on to give another instance of this contempt, recording how a funeral procession arrived at a cemetery only to be told that a huge boulder had suddenly appeared in the grave, and that the grave-diggers would need 100 roubles to remove it. "Since it seemed hardly proper to haggle at a cemetery, they agreed, and the boulder presumably moved on to another grave." Vitaliev commented on this:

> There are two conditions of human existence which none of us can avoid: birth and death, joy and grief, creation and extinction. We have learnt to measure a society's economic growth by means of figures, percentages and statistics. But what about our moral development? The best criterion for this may perhaps be our attitude to the dead ... I don't want to demand punishment for slapdash cemetery attendants, or to make suggestions as to the reorganisation of the 'ritual service', or even to name the crooks who profit from human grief (for those who speculate in death beyond reach). I simply want to say: indifference to the dead is a terrible disease. Unless we root it out we shall never build a genuinely democratic society. For democracy means compassion, and compassion means respect for the dead.

But if that general argument is correct, and if we wish to express our respect for the dead, then we will most certainly have to think carefully about what is required for the ritual occasions that accompany death. It is here that religions should have much to contribute because of their long experience in ritual and in the 'rites of passage'.

DEATH, RITUALS AND THE RITES OF PASSAGE

In 1909, Arnold van Gennep published his book, *The Rites of Passage*. In it he showed that there is a distinct pattern in certain rituals which have to do with moments of important transition in human lives, moments like birth, puberty, marriage and death – hence the look's title. The pattern, he argued, is made up of one condition, two categories and three stages. Put into ritual practice, that pattern often takes the form of separation from an existing condition, followed by transition, followed by incorporation into a new state. Thus if we take the example of marriage, the pattern is particularly clear: all people begin in the one condition of being unmarried. That one condition implies two categories: single and married. Those who wish to move from one to the other have to pass through three stages: being single, leading to the transition of betrothal or engagement, leading to incorporation in the married state.

van Gennep's achievement was to identify the same pattern in other 'rites of passage', including those concerned with death.[5] The one condition of being alive implies two categories: being alive and being dead. Those who move from the one category to the other have to make the transition and have to be incorporated in the new state of 'being among the dead'. Funeral rites effect the transition and the incorporation. The emotional response of humans to death means that those rites have been of paramount importance to them. What van Gennep also recognised is the fact that rites of passage focus mainly on the transition. The most important rituals help people (in this case the dead) to move over a threshold from one category to another. From the Latin word *limen*, 'a threshold', he coined the term 'liminality' to describe these rites of passage from one category to another – as in the Maori word *wheiao*: "*Wheiao* is the state between dark and light. This is a universal term used to describe the transitional condition between polar states: birth and death, night and day, sacred and profane, pleasure and pain." (Mataira in G. Harvey, pp.99–112).

Mataira went on to show how fundamental this is in the shared imagination of the Maori world:

> Life, to the Maori, is predicated on the understanding of connectedness, that all things have rhythm, shape and form, and are woven and patterned together in a pre-determined design created in the heavens. The traditions of the Maori embrace the acceptance that chaos and change, order and stability are conjoint processes held in tension by the existence of each other. Life as such is bound to the dynamic of shifting states between sacred and ordinary.... Through the actions of the Gods, all living things are given their opposites and the potential to procreate their own species. We are subject to the dichotomy of opposing forces: pleasure and pain, vice and virtue, good and evil, health and sickness.... [W]ere it not for the separation ... and the presence of all opposing forces, life would be void of learning, and thus absence of choice (agency) and experience.

Familiar examples closer to home in the United Kingdom are the great occasions of State funerals, as in the case of Winston Churchill in 1965 or more recently of the Queen Mother in 2002 or of Princess Diana in 1997 (see, e.g., Cohan in Richards). There was a prolonged and ritualised leave-taking of the deceased; ritual then moved them from life to death; and van Gennep's pattern of three stages was clearly visible: separation from the condition of being alive, transition to their new state of being dead, and commitment to a last resting place.

But the funerals themselves were very different, and the contrasts illustrate a growing crisis for rites of passage in our time. As the human imagination of death changes, so also the nature of the associated rituals is beginning to change, even to disintegrate and fall apart. At the very same time, our understanding of ritual has been changing greatly, but little of that change has affected as yet the human responses to death. In that understanding there have been four great changes in particular. What are those changes and what do they imply for the human responses to death?

FOUR RECENT CHANGES IN THE UNDERSTANDING OF RITUAL

1. The first change has been the correction of Freud's account of ritual and religion. Two years before the appearance of van Gennep's *The Rites of Passage,* Sigmund Freud published a brief article, 'Obsessive Actions and Religious Practices' (1907). In his view, ritual is a pathological form of obsessive behaviour. Obsessive behaviours are those in which people cannot function unless they repeat particular actions over and over again – as, for example, washing their hands many times, or returning again and again to make sure that they locked the front door, or performing the same actions before boarding a plane in order to make sure the plane flies.

Those examples make it clear that there is in all of us a certain amount of obsessive behaviour. That, in Freud's view, is what religions exploit in their development of ritual. Rituals, according to him, are obsessive behaviours, doing the same thing over and over again, but in religion those obsessionally repetitive actions are made socially acceptable. That is why, according to Freud, rites of passage enable us to deal with the great crises of life, like getting born or dying. In the words of Chapple's summary, "During the struggle life crises occur and, afterward, rites of passage ... are necessary mediators to reestablish the equilibrium of the group."

Of course, rituals as obsessions might be harmless, liking touching wood. But in Freud's view they are never harmless if they take people over and enslave their lives. According to Freud, that is exactly what rituals in organised religions do. So he concluded that they are therefore as destructive as any other kind of *compulsive* obsession because they prevent people from growing up and seeing life as it really is. So he came to his famous conclusion (IX.126f.):

> In view of these similarities and analogies one might venture to regard obsessional neurosis as a pathological counterpart of the formation of religion, and to describe that neurosis as an individual religiosity and religion as a universal neurosis.

So widespread did this view of Freud's become that 'ritual' or 'ritualistic' has often been the definition of obsession. Here, for example, is *The Encyclopedia Britannica* defining compulsive obsessions:

These are urges or impulses to perform repetitive acts that are apparently meaningless, unnecessary, stereotyped, or ritualistic.

So much for religious ritual! It is, to say the least, a negative view of ritual and of rites of passage. But Freud was wrong, and one reason why he was wrong was because he did not know – indeed, he *could* not know – the positive virtue of redundancy.

As a word, 'redundancy' does not sound either virtuous or positive, as it clearly is not for those who lose their jobs and are made redundant. But in the very different context of information theory, redundancy is extremely important.

The point is this: we need redundancy if we are ever going to communicate with each other. We need redundancy in order to make sure that information is protected and that it 'gets through'. To make the point, consider the riddle with which a child's guide to punctuation (*Punctuation Personified*, 1824) opens:

> Ev'ry lady in this land
> Has twenty nails upon each hand
> Five and twenty on hands and feet
> And this is true without deceit.
>> But when the stops were plac'd aright,
>> The real sense was brought to light.

Correct punctuation is essential in order for sense, rather than nonsense, to be conveyed. But punctuation in itself does not convey additional information. Consider the sentence familiar from childhood: the teacher said that that that that that boy had used was wrong. Punctuation does not add information; it simply makes the sentence intelligible (that that 'that', that that boy ...). Punctuation and spaces between words do not convey information: they protect information and make sure that the meaning 'gets through'. In the sense, therefore, that punctuation is not conveying any new information; it is redundant. But equally it is vital because it is helping information to get transmitted.

Redundancy is also necessary and essential in repetition. If I repeat something, or if I say it in a slightly different way, or if I add another version of it, there is a far better chance that you will understand the point I am trying to make. And that is exactly what has happened in that previous sentence: the same point has been repeated three times, not in order to convey new information, but to make sure that the basic information is transmitted.

Those may seem trivial examples, but the general point about redundancy is not trivial at all. In fact, our lives depend upon it – literally – because if there were not sufficient redundancy in the DNA, its code could never be transmitted. Take a familiar example: one of the agents of evolutionary change is mutation. If every mutation affected a single site of functional DNA, the code would immediately disappear into confusion and noise. But because DNA has redundancy built into it, it follows that a harmful mutation will not automatically and always affect the underlying function. That is why a potentially harmful mutation can persist from one generation to another as a harmless variation because it is not actually doing anything. Redundancy supplies back-up so that not all mistakes are lethal. Meaning does not get lost.

Back to Freud and ritual: in 1978, Gay wrote an article on 'Reductionism and Redundancy ...' in which he made the point against Freud that rituals are in fact highly redundant ways of protecting and transmitting information, above all the ways in which people have learnt through successive generations to negotiate the transitions of time. Rituals make public in enacted form what the meaning of the event is in any particular society (in the case of rites of passage, the event of birth or puberty or marriage or death), and they do so with enough repetition in the ritual action for the meaning not to get lost.

It follows that rituals do almost exactly the opposite of what Freud supposed. Freud believed that rituals help us to avoid and evade the reality of death. But ritual does exactly the opposite. It insists on the reality of death, where words so often duck and weave and run away from the truth of death. Think of the many different words and phrases we use in order to avoid saying that someone is dead of which at least some are gathered in this poem, 'Death, be not proud, for thou art not even to be mentioned':

> She has not died, she is not dead,
> Forbid the fact by what is said!
> He is not dead, he has not died,
> Let any other word be tried!
> She has wicked out, as candles do, He's kicked the bucket, gone
>   napoo, She's finally laid down her pen
> And he his hoe, his knife and fork, and then
> She's made her final exit, taken her last bow,
> While he's gone home, gone six feet under, and now
> She's popped her clogs and gone to sleep,
> While he has cast his anchor deep;
> She's in that happy hunting ground, and there
> She rests in peace, no time to stand and stare
> While he is backed on six men's shoulders, parked
> In that celestial multistorey, thence embarked

On the last voyage, crossing o'er the bar,
Welcomed by angels as weary travellers are.
She too casts off, winds up the ball,
Drops her last stitch to answer the last call.
In the grand secret now she finds her place,
While he, athletic in his time, has run his race,
Cashed in his chips, thrown in the sponge and dropped his cue,
Pegged out, struck out, as all must do:
Like many Achaians, he must bite the dust,
Like many a this-year's model, go to rust,
Go to the breaker's yard, turn up his toes,
Be food for worms and bait for crows,
Check in, sign off and pay the final bill.
As for the inconvenient, say not 'kill':
We cull, take out, put down and disappear
The excess baggage, the 'unwanted here'.
But truth be told and truth be said,
She has died, and he is dead. (Bowker pp.70f)

So this has been a major gain in the understanding of ritual. Rituals do not exist simply because they are a form of pathological behaviour. They are the most important way in which humans protect and transmit the meanings they give to the events, circumstances and people that matter most to them.

That is why rituals are not simply something that people do in the context of religion, as for example in Temple or Church. They are all over the place: at the opening of an Olympic games, at graduation ceremonies, at parties from the coming of age to retirement, on the occasion of silver, ruby and golden weddings, and so on. Rituals are celebrations – even at death there can be a party. Rituals are so important to us that we keep inventing new ones: among the parties for which new rituals have been invented are divorce parties with their own rituals. The truth is that we have no other language so powerful as ritual to express the meaning of the events that matter to us.

"No other language so powerful", but is ritual a language? Must we not say that myth is the language and ritual a relatively unimportant acting out of the language? Or might it not be the other way around, that ritual is the event in action, bringing something about, with myth the relatively unimportant explanation of what is going on? Which way round is it? It may seem odd, but that was a major and passionate battle in the 'myth and ritual school' of the mid-twentieth century. Does it matter whether myth is more important than ritual, or ritual more important than myth?

2. It was that debate which led into a *second* major advance in the understanding of ritual. The word 'myth' in this context does not mean even remotely what we mean by it today. For us, as we have already seen (in Chapter 3), it has come to mean 'something false', 'something invented', something that we have to explode or contradict. But for most of human history, myth has been the way in which people have shared in story or in narrative, in art, music and architecture, their most important insights into their own nature and history and world. Myth is the narrative that brings into being ritual as the enacted expression of its meaning. Or should it be the other way around, that ritual is the enacted truth that myth comes into being to explain?

The early 'myth and ritual' arguments were then taken further into the often acrimonious debates in anthropology between structuralists and functionalists, with Leach (a leading structuralist) insisting that "myth, regarded as a statement in words, 'says' the same things as ritual regarded as a statement in action." On that basis, myth controls ritual: as he put it, "rite is a dramatisation of the myth, the myth is the sanction or charter for the rite" (Leach, p.13).

It seems a remote point of only academic interest. How can it possibly matter whether myth controls ritual or ritual controls myth? In the rites of passage it matters a great deal: if the narrative subordinates the ritual, we end up with the false sentiment of Hollywood productions (or, for that matter, with the liturgical revisions of the Church of England), but if the ritual controls the narrative, we end up with the perfunctory formalism of parade ground drill.

Those academic battles, however, were a classic example of a falsely dichotomous question: *either* myth *or* ritual, when what we need is both. And that is what the great debate in the interwar years of the twentieth century taught us: we need both, both words and actions, illuminating and reinforcing each other.

3. So that was the second gain in the understanding of ritual. The next gain, the *third* gain, came more recently, and this was the exploration of the politics of ritual. This means, quite simply, looking at the ways in which ritual is used as a means of political and social control. For example, in a book called *The Politics of Reproductive Ritual*, Paige and Paige showed, as anthropologists, how men in small-scale societies use the rituals surrounding human reproduction to keep control over the lives of women; and another anthropologist, Bloch, wrote a book on early human development called, *Prey into Hunter: The Politics of Religious Experience*.

But we surely are more familiar with this on the much larger scale of totalitarian societies. Here is a verse from a hymn that few of us are ever likely to have sung:

> Mothers, your cradles
> Are like a sleeping army
> Waiting for victory -
> They will never more be empty. (Weyrauther p.162)

That verse is part of a hymn which was written for the ritual introduced by the Nazis in Germany on the 10th of May. It was the day they called 'The Day of the German Mother', the day when the Mother's Cross was awarded to those 'rich in children' – provided of course that none of the children was in any way dysfunctional, and provided that the mother herself did not smoke or drink, did not sleep around and ran an orderly home. When that 'sleeping army' awoke and joined the Hitler Youth, it entered with an enthusiasm into the ritualisation of politics so dramatically evident in the Nuremberg rallies: ritual as politics by other means – as frequently it is in organised religions.

What that example makes clear is that the rites of passage are needed for the politics of ritual in order to express the interests of society in what is going on, not least to express the tenacity of the legal at the moments of birth, coming of age, marriage and death.

4. Those three new ways of understanding the rites of passage have been important enough. The *fourth* is even more important. It is the way in which recent and continuing research in the neurosciences is throwing entirely new light on what can best be called 'the ritual brain' – on what is happening in the brain when we engage in ritual behaviours.[6]

From that research it has become clear why we need rituals for our own good and for the good of our humanity, not least because rituals lock reason and emotion together at the most important moments of our lives, and they do it in ways that we can rely on, because rituals are repeated in predictable and well-tested ways over and over again – exactly that good sense of redundancy.

Rituals are thus repeated patterns of action and behaviour undertaken for an immense number of purposes – for example, to celebrate the birth of a child or to lament the passing of the old; to give thanks for the life-giving presence of food and water or to bring a death-dealing disaster on enemies; to express praise or penitence; and also, certainly, to recognise and come into the presence of God.

It follows that rituals in their own way are as important as words in the building of a world in which we can live. As we saw in the case of art and symbols, so also rituals bring to the rational text of our lives the feelings that are appropriate to them, so that the occasions in which we are involved are indeed experienced rationally, but they are also at the same time felt emotionally. The result is that we live immersed in a rational world of symbols, but we live immersed also *and at the same time* in the emotional experience of symbols.

That is why rituals are so carefully and deliberately created, whether by religious or by secular authorities. They are created in order to evoke and satisfy the appropriate emotions: of pride and patriotism at a military parade, for example, of grief at a funeral, or of joy at a wedding – or of reverence in the case of worship. Art and music can do that. But so too can liturgy and ritual.

All this is so deeply embedded in our brains and bodies that we diminish our humanity if we do not treasure the ritual opportunity that helps to make us human. This is so profound within us that our earliest ritual experiences as children remain resonant within us, particularly if the early ritual experience has been good. People may abandon religious belief as they grow up and yet still retain the resonance of those early ritual experiences. Throughout life the resonances of ritual will continue to be powerful in memory and association.

The reverse, however, is also true. Just as there can be 'bad art' and 'bad music' (with plenty of debate, no doubt, about what constitutes 'the bad'), so for sure there can be bad ritual. If in early life we have been involved in bad ritual experience, that too will not be erased. And instead of deep satisfactions in the brain, there will be the opposite. That is why it is so devastating that within the Christian Churches so much liturgical revision in the last fifty years has been concerned with words and not with actions.[7]

This is predictable on the basis of Whitehouse's characterisation of the 'doctrinal' mode of religiosity (p.192) and of what the historian Collinson called "the logocentric iconoclasm" of the second English Reformation. We have seen an example earlier of too exclusive a concentration on language in liturgical revision.

That in itself is not surprising, bearing in mind that those in charge of the revisions are highly verbalised people. They have received exactly that kind of education. But the result is terrible. Take as another example the widespread liturgical revisions amongst Anglicans in the last half of the twentieth century. It produced *Common Worship* in 2000 and *Common Worship: Daily Prayer* in a preliminary version for use from 2002. It is true that *Common Worship: Daily Prayer* has a section called 'Deciding How' (p.x) which emphasises that "the way in which these orders [of prayer] are celebrated helps or hinders the prayer of the worshipping group", and it states that "all of the orders lend themselves to the use of symbols and simple actions" – note the word 'simple'!

Similarly, the earlier *Common Worship* contains the striking sentence (p.x), "Just as *Common Worship* is more than a book, so worship is more than what is said; it is also what is done and how it is done." That certainly sounds promising. But what does it mean? It means, to quote the Preface, that the texts provided in *Common Worship* should be known by heart, so that "the poetry of praise and the passion of prayer can transcend the printed word."

That is a good example of a religion encouraging the internalisation of constraint, but it hardly addresses the importance and practice of ritual. What actually 'transcends the printed word', or any word, is ritual, because actions speak, if not louder than words (remember the debate about myth and ritual), then certainly at least as loud. In contrast, what has happened in those recent revisions is that ritual actions are left to the leaders of any particular act of worship. The revisers of liturgy have concentrated so much on words that they have left ritual to chance by offering nothing, even in the form of guidance and advice beyond repeating the instructions in the old *Book of Common Prayer*. This is a tragic denial of the importance of ritual, all the more of a disaster because *Common Worship* (p.ix) makes this claim:

> In the worship of God the full meaning and beauty of our humanity is consummated and our lives are opened to the promise God makes for all creation – to transform and renew it in love and goodness.

"Our humanity": *that* is what is being neglected and ignored in these revisions, because ritual belongs to 'the full meaning and beauty of our humanity' as profoundly and powerfully as do words.

This is not to suggest that Liturgical Commissions should draw up a new edition of *Ritual Notes*, that late Victorian 'guide to the ceremonial of the Church' which went through many editions during the twentieth century, and which begins with the sentence (p.1), "The *High Altar* may be 3ft. 6in. high, or at the most 3ft. $7^1/_2$ in., and $7^1/_2$ft. long, or longer if in a large Church...." What is needed is that revisions of liturgy should be made by people who understand ritual, understand how it is embodied in our humanity, understand what it has meant to us and to our ancestors throughout the whole of our history. The human imagination of death is expressed at least as much in ritual as it is in words.

IMPLICATIONS FOR RITES OF PASSAGE

Looking now at those four major ways in which our understanding of ritual has been changed, we can see how little effect this has had on the rites of passage associated with death in most postmodern societies.

The changes were initiated by van Gennep, who established that rites of passage are not for the benefit of the living; they are for the benefit of the dead. Rituals do things for people that they cannot do for themselves. Rituals associated with death have historically done things primarily for the dead, not for the living. That is a far cry from the current wisdom that funerals enable people to deal with death, to give expression to their feelings, to weep without shame and to start their moving on.

The first of the changes was the correction of the 'redundancy' critique of Freud, which showed how important it is for rituals to be well known and well established in any society if they are to protect the well-winnowed experience of the generations that have gone before. That is a far cry from the modern (or rather, postmodern) wisdom that there is no privileged point of view, least of all that of the past, and that redundancy, therefore, has far less value than innovation and novelty.

The second change came from the myth and ritual debate which established that both narrative and ritual belong together, and that ritual enacts the narrative in a way that can speak louder than words. That is a far cry from the current wisdom in secularised parts of the world that the inherited narratives are completely implausible, so that the inherited rituals are no longer connected to any public narrative. The result has been the increasing privatisation of ritual, not least at funerals.

In the third change, the 'politics of ritual' established that society has an interest in the legal boundaries of death, not least because the rites of passage bind death to a common estimate of the worth of all citizens. That is a far cry from the current wisdom that in a plural society, all or nearly all narratives are permissible, so that each family has 'rights to rites' of its own choosing, so that value lies in idiosyncrasy, not in a common social action.

In the fourth, the exploration of the ritual brain has established that rituals cannot be erased from the deepest needs and satisfactions of our humanity because they engage so profoundly the kinds of brains and bodies that we happen to have – or be. That is a far cry from what has become a current wisdom that ritual may be pomp and ceremony, but you only have to look at it to see that it is really ridiculous pomposity and sanctimonious humbug.

Strangely, this dramatic devaluation of ritual *in practice* has been happening at exactly the time when we have been learning *in theory* what the indispensable values of ritual actually are. Why has this happened? For many reasons, of course. But at the heart of it is the way in which the naturalisation of birth and death has been gathering pace. One major consequence of this is that the narratives we now tell about death are different from the ones which were tied into the rituals that gave them vitality and meaning. The naturalisation of death is a new context, and the old rituals may not function any longer in the ways in which they did.

That is a major reason why the rites of passage in the case of death are coming into crisis, because, as we have just seen, ritual works by binding together the rational and the emotional ways of understanding and dealing with death. Rituals cannot survive any widespread crisis of plausibility, even though bits of them continue. Think again of the funerals of the Queen Mother and of Princess Diana. In the first, the tradition was completely intact, and rightly so for someone of her age and beliefs. But in the second, the crisis of plausibility was as obvious as were the reasons for it: many bits of the traditional ritual survived, but the improvisation was equally if not more obvious.

Rituals need narratives to make sense and to be engaging in the brain-body ways that we are now beginning to understand, just as narratives need ritual to catch hold of the attention and feelings of a congregation. That is the necessary conjunction between myth and ritual. Terence Deacon, a biological anthropologist, has called us 'the symbolic species' because we need symbols and we need rituals to undertake and share our constant quest to know and understand the meanings of our world. But the price to be paid for that is a high one. If a cultural form like a ritual is no longer coherent with our world pictures, it falls into crisis, no matter how vivid and compelling its sensory and emotional aspects may be. Old rituals continue, but in an increasingly filtered form – exactly as we saw in the case of Princess Diana's funeral, and as tourists see all around the world when ritual is enacted as a performance for entertainment and display.

This means that there is a fundamental contradiction in the increasing privatisation of rites of passage, those for marriage just as much as those for funerals. The privatisation of ritual has been liberating in the way in which it allows a personal and individual connection with the person or people involved. But on the other hand, we are in danger of losing the public language on which the power of ritual depends in the case of brains and bodies of the kind we happen to have. That is why liturgical commissions and the like need far more urgently to return to the consideration of ritual. Words can be revised forever, but unless the words are connected to ritual as we now understand it, the liturgies lie stranded on a beach of artificiality from which the tide of truth has gone out.

And what exactly *is* that truth? It is the truth, in the case of death, that whereas the privatisation of ritual does much to help the living but little or even nothing for the dead, the rites of passage in the past were primarily doing something for the dead, and only then doing something for the living. In the Muslim ritual of *talqin*, for example, the *shahada* is carefully recited over the body of a dead person so that when the messengers of death, Munkir and Nakir, visit him in the grave he will be able to prove that he is a true

believer. He is also told what he must say to them in order to avoid punishment.[8] What is being expressed here does not depend on correspondence but
on coherence, on the extent to which it is an enacted language (of both myth
and ritual) of care and concern.

Or to take another example, the Christian rites of passage. In 1911, van
Gennep's book, *Rites of Passage,* appeared in English, and in that same year
John Masefield published his poem, *The Everlasting Mercy.* In it he explored
the meaning and possibility of redemption, even for the worst of sinners, the
most stubborn clay. He wrote of old Callow at his autumn ploughing (p.12):

> Slow up the hill the plough team plod,
> Old Callow at the task of God,
> Helped by man's wit, helped by the brute
> Turning a stubborn clay to fruit.

Callow is, in Masefield's poem, the mediating symbol of the rituals through
which Christ enacts the everlasting mercy, forgiveness not as an aspiration
but as an accomplished, because enacted, fact:

> And as I drove the clods apart
> Christ would be ploughing in my heart,
> Through rest-harrow and bitter roots,
> Through all my bad life's rotten fruits.

That is what the Christian rites of passage in the case of death were created to
convey, the continuing and unceasing action of God in Christ in and for this
person. That is why the Viaticum for Catholics and the Ministry at the Time
of Death for Anglicans (both of them, incidentally, liminal rites of transition)
place such emphasis on the forgiveness and absolution of the dead person.
The Apostolic Pardon, for example, reads robustly:

> Through the holy mysteries of our redemption, may almighty God release
> you from all punishments in this life and in the life to come. May he open to
> you the gates of paradise and welcome you to everlasting joy. By the author-
> ity which the Apostolic See has given me, I grant you a full pardon and the
> remission of all your sins, in the name of the Father and of the Son and of
> the Holy Spirit.

Aristotle, as we saw earlier, quoted Agathon as saying, "Even God cannot
change the past." But in what I have called elsewhere 'retrogressive rituals',
that is exactly what God, in Christian belief, does do.

In the human imagination of death, it is only in ritual that the changing of
the past becomes objectively a fact, a new fact, because ritual creates a new
circumstance. It is ritual that makes the transition from single to married,

from alive to dead, from sinner to forgiven. In Christian belief, for example, rituals are the means chosen by God to make those transitions, just as ritual action is the means chosen by Christ to make the transition from bread to body. The human imagination becomes incarnate in the objectivity of ritual.

DEATH AS FINALITY

We looked earlier at the way in which the trivialisation of death can lead to death being treated with contempt, and we have seen that ritual is a profoundly religious rejection of that first sense of 'contempt' in relation to death (summarised earlier). There is, however, a second and different sense of contempt in relation to death that religions would certainly endorse. It is the sense of transcendence, of rising above something, of holding something in contempt because one sees something else, in a larger or wiser perspective, as being far more important. All religions have encouraged their adherents to develop that kind of contempt for death: in all religions the preparation for death, far from being morbid, gives meaning and purpose to life.

To give an example: *aniccanupassana* in Buddhism is the practice of deliberately contemplating the impermanence of all things, including one's own brief appearance. It is one of the single most important practices leading to enlightenment, and within that general cultivation of contempt for the world there are even more specific ways in which the mindfulness of death is developed. Mindfulness of death is a contemplation (summarised in Buddhaghosa's *Vissudhimagga* 8.1–144), which is undertaken in solitary retreat, concentrating on the ways in which death (*marana*) is approaching me personally: as appearing like a murderer, sword in hand, the invariable companion of birth ("as budding toadstools always come up lifting dust on their tops, so beings are born along with aging and death"); as the ruin of success ("all health ends in sickness, all youth ends in aging, all life ends in death"); by comparison with those who have been great in the world, but who nevertheless are all equally dead; by reflecting on the deaths which are already occurring in the body, inhabited as it is by many short-lived parasites ("here they are born, grow old and die, evacuate and make water: the body is their maternity home, their hospital, their charnel ground, their lavatory and their urinal; through the upsetting of these worms the body itself can be brought to death"); as always close because of the vulnerability and weakness of the body; as being usually unpredictable; as putting an inevitable limit on even the longest of lives; as in any case being related to the fact that a human does not exist for longer than a single instant (there being no self, *anatman*,), as when the rim of a turning wheel touches the ground only for an instant.

That is only one example of what is common in all religions, a cultivation of a healthy contempt for death, while at the same time recognising how close death is to *me*: I may watch death every night on TV, but the one death I will never watch is my own. Will religions be able to contribute to a future imagination of death *that* kind of transcendent contempt, in contrast to the other which trivialises death in so demeaning a way?

It may be difficult for them to do so, for two reasons. First, because that healthy contempt for death is, in the religious case, usually instrumental: it is tied to a belief that death is not an end but a beginning, not a conclusion but an opportunity (and without that specifically religious belief, it is much harder to regard death with that same healthy contempt); and second, because it was the religions themselves which trivialised death in the first place: once religions came to the hard-won and much contested belief that there is some kind of worthwhile continuity through death, then it became possible to think of death as an event on the road to life – or, to quote Bonhoeffer more accurately (p.163), "Death is the supreme festival on the road to freedom." While that kind of contempt for death may make heroes of us all, it may also make death *so* unimportant that it loses significance: religions can then use death (as they have) in campaigns of persecution and spiritual terrorisation, or in making this life trivial compared to the next.

The consequences here for the imagination of death are immense, and they point in two different directions: if death is *not* regarded as an event on the road to life, then the imagination of death will have to deal with it as finality; but if death is not regarded as the end of personal continuity or being, then the imagination of death will have to offer some account of what that continuity may be.

If we take the first of those (death accepted as finality), we need to bear in mind that this is nothing new. Early religions, as we have seen, did not have and did not depend on an expectation of a worthwhile life beyond death. The death of an individual was usually regarded as final with only the vaguest shadow being thrown forward in memory and descendants; and continuity in the memory of others has continued in the human imagination of death to the present day. But now, of course, the liveliness of memory has been transformed: whereas in the past we could only paint a portrait, we can now film and tape those whom we love, and we will shortly be able to recreate them in virtual reality. Furthermore, that virtual reality will be so interactive that it will be as though the dead person is still alive. We already have tapes and videos at funerals; All Souls' Day, or an equivalent occasion of commemoration of the dead in other religions, will, in the future, be a far more virtually lively occasion.

Yet it will still be of no moment to the person who has died. And religions will not relinquish their belief that the dead in some sense continue, since there is sufficient warrant for their affirmation that this is so. Therefore, in the second direction of imagination, there will continue to be an insistence that, as Emily Dickinson put it, "This world is not conclusion"; and the religious imagination will draw on contemporary phenomena as a base for at least analogical speculation. Thus the transference of programmes from one computer to another, so that the programme outlives the hardware in which it was first expressed, has become a commonplace of the religious imagination of death.[9] As Polkinghorne summarised the point (p.11), "Such meagre understanding as we have from science of the nature of humanity (which I think is best phrased in terms of psychosomatic unity) does not seem to make incoherent the notion of resurrection (the recreation of the 'information-bearing pattern' that is me in some new environment of embodiment)." That is clearly moving in a very different direction from the development of virtual reality.

The two directions seem at first sight to be irreconcilable. But there is, perhaps, a meeting-place in the consequence that arises from them both, that what happens in the present moment becomes all-important, both because what goes into the programme now becomes the character of whatever it is that survives and continues, and also because each moment is the opportunity for the enacted affirmation of value, no matter what the future may or may not hold.

RELIGIOUS AND MATERIAL ANTHROPOLOGIES

That suggested meeting-place, however, leads to a major challenge at present to the imagination of death: it lies in "the assertion and the affirmation of value up against the boundary of death."[10] It carries with it the challenge to traditional anthropologies – that is, to traditional accounts of what constitutes the human person. Material anthropologies insist that we *are* our brains and our bodies, and that when these cease, so do we: for them language of 'the soul' is meaningless because no such entity can be located.

Spiritual anthropologies, in contrast, insist that we are more than the sum of our parts: there is about us that which is the agent of our actions and the subject of the brain's activity yielding experience. Or to put it in other words, whatever is identifiable as the enduring and characterised individual who is the subject of its experiences and the agent of its actions is what is meant by the word 'soul'.

Material and spiritual anthropologies have been in opposition and conflict for millennia. They have even been a matter of contest within religious traditions, as one can see in the Lokacarya and Buddhist dissent in India, or in the Biblical literalism of the Sadducees in Judaism, which created tension at the time when Jesus was alive.

But here it seems unlikely that there will be a conclusive demonstration one way or the other. It so happens at the moment that the arguments (lucidly surveyed and summarised by Goetz and Taliaferro) in favour of mind and soul are far stronger than the arguments in favour of materialism, despite popular assumptions to the contrary. The arguments are vigorous and increasingly sophisticated; but even so, what could possibly count as a conclusive demonstration one way or the other? We are in the domain of abductively inferential arguments which, as we have seen, yield, not certainty, but degrees of probability.

Much the same is true of speculations surrounding spiritualism and near-death experiences. In the case of the former, it has been demonstrated that at least some claimed communications from the dead are fraudulent (and Huxley's opinion is often quoted, that he would rather live as a crossing sweeper than die and be made to talk twaddle by a 'medium' hired at a guinea a séance), but how can the opposite be demonstrated? Or again, descriptions of near-death experiences will continue, but are we likely to find a way of deciding between claims, either that these are insights into what awaits us after death, or that they are the last activities of some brains already suffering from oxygen deprivation?

No matter what the outcome of the arguments may be, people will continue to attempt to communicate with the dead because it is deeply embedded in human nature to seek the best we can for those who have died, especially for those whom we have loved. This may arise from feelings of guilt, but far more it is a continuing expression of involvement, care and love. That is why any changes to the rituals supporting the dead are usually opposed with a fierce tenacity – as this report from China makes clear (*The Times*, April 19, 1978):

Old customs die hard in China, if a radio broadcast from Mao Tse-tung's native province of Hunan is to be believed. The local Communist Party Committee has 'dealt seriously' with the case of a local official who performed religious rites and spent lavish sums for his father's funeral. The denounced man, named as Liu Hsin-hsing, was a party member and a deputy head of a country labour wages bureau. [According to the report],'On the evening his father died, Liu invited a Taoist priest to set up a tablet worshipping his father, to calm the spirit of the dead, and to choose an auspicious date and hour for the temporary burial. The next day, he invited a geomancer to check the wind and water, to choose the burial site and to fix an auspicious date and hour for the temporary burial.' The report is in itself an astonishing admission of the persistence of religious practices in China 28 years after the communist victory there.... The broadcast said that the late Mr. Liu's coffin was preceded by mourners carrying fifty or sixty wreaths, with musicians playing drum and gongs in front and behind. About three hundred people attended. A funeral feast of 112 tables was arranged, with expenses estimated at over £200.

Mr. Liu was sentenced to a year's probation in the party, and to dismissal from his job; and no doubt he thought it a small price to pay for doing all that he could for his father.

Even if material anthropologies become more widespread than they already are, the commitment of the living to the dead will continue. The challenge now, in rapidly changing and far less homogenous societies, is to find ways in which we can give shared and public expression to what Davies has called (p.13) "the covenant of mutual loyalty between the living and the dead." In using that phrase Davies was drawing on the work of Lloyd Warner and Lunt, *The Living and the Dead: A Study of the Symbolic Life of Americans*, part of the 'Yankee City' series on the social life of a modern community. Davies commended its argument "that the life of a community is comprehensible, subjectively and objectively, only when it is understood as grounded in a covenant of mutual loyalty between the living and the dead." He then commented:

> This covenant with the ancestors is the covenant which, beyond all others, makes sense of, makes moral and validates all the lesser covenants and contracts within which our communal life is enmeshed. Religion, for example, is never communally experienced as 'theology', but as the record of a religious historical journey, expressed in the lives of men and women no longer with us in the flesh, but speaking to us in handed-down and handed-on hymns, ceremonies, buildings. These hymns, ceremonies and buildings endlessly, insistently and helpfully present to the living the authoritative transcendental ideas and example of the dead. Cities may seem busy; but the busy life goes on in streets named after the ancestral dead ...

But life in the city, or anywhere else for that matter, is changing so rapidly that adequate rituals in such an entirely new context are extremely hard to envisage. The Internet will play its part, but how more publicly can the human imaginations of death devise rituals through which that covenant can be adequately expressed?

Part of this major challenge, therefore, lies in the fact that rituals inherited from the past are tied closely to the belief that death either is, or is the threshold of, a judgement of the person who has died. If that belief is eroded, will the commitment to the dead lose its urgency? When it was proposed to stage a play in London in 1774 called 'The Day of Judgement', John Wesley promptly drew up a playbill for an alternative production, which put a stop to the play completely:

By Command of the King of Kings,

And at the desire of all those who love His appearing

At the Theatre of the Universe on the Eve of Time will be performed

The Great Assize, or

DAY OF JUDGEMENT.

There then follow the scenery, the principal performers and a description of the three acts, ending:

To conclude with an Oration by the Son of God

After which the curtain will drop.

Schall has pointed out, in *The Politics of Heaven and Hell*, how extensive the consequences of this erosion of the traditional imagination have been for political life (p.101):

> What we believe about hell remains the touchstone of what we believe about politics. The mystery of evil, . . .of hell, its consequence, is neglected at a very high cost. The value of medieval theory was that it never ignored this . . . What made it all finally fit together was when men learned that there were in fact things that did not belong to Caesar. And the first of these is precisely hell, the doctrine of eternal punishment.

An urgent question for the imagination of death in the twenty-first century (and one which has immense implications for education and society) is clearly this: in what ways, apart from those of textual literalism, will the human imagination of death connect death with accountability, or more specifically with judgement, if at all?

THE CULTURE OF DEATH

The issue of literalism, linked as it is with fundamentalism, will clearly dominate the unfolding of the religious imagination of death in the immediate future. The point has already been made and emphasised that religions are necessarily conservative information systems. Nevertheless, the status of doubt in religions, as we saw in Chapter 4, makes it clear that they are, at least potentially, open to change when evidence and experience demand it. The example given earlier was of the change two millennia ago from a virtually universal belief that there will be no worthwhile life after death to a belief that there will be continuity through death. This allowed the possibility that the outcomes beyond death are the locus of accountability and judgement. That was a total change, with immense consequences for individual behaviour and social organisation.

So change is always possible, and indeed has always been a dynamic part of religious history. But on the other hand, religions (or rather many religious people and religious leaders) are inclined to resist change, since it seems to call in question the worth and validity of what has been believed and practised in the past and has been inherited from it. In the case of religions the issues are not just those of life and death, but also of life and life beyond death.

It is predictable, therefore, that the changes being brought about in relation to death will evoke two contrasting responses: on the one hand, a defensive opposition to change, and on the other, a critical appropriation.

Of the first, a defensive opposition to change, there is a sharp and clear example in the letter of Pope John Paul II, *Evangelium Vitae* which is addressed precisely to the issues raised earlier in this chapter by the naturalisation of death:

> In relation to life at birth or at death, man is no longer capable of posing the question of the truest meaning of his own existence, nor can he assimilate with genuine freedom those crucial moments of his own history. He is concerned only with 'doing', and, using all kinds of technology, he busies himself with programming, controlling and dominating birth and death. Birth and death, instead of being primary experiences demanding to be 'lived', become things to be merely 'possessed' or 'rejected.'

The Pope, in this Letter, was attacking what he called 'the culture of death', which to him was unmistakeably evident in the twentieth century. But despite the widespread occurrence in that century of death in brutal and savage ways, it would be equally true to recognise in the twentieth century 'the culture of life.' The development of the United Nations may have been no more successful than the League of Nations in preventing wars, but through its agencies it has been unequivocally committed to life. So too have the many smaller organisations which became prolific in the twentieth century: Amnesty International, the Samaritans, Oxfam, Médicin sans Frontieres, CND and many others are committed to a culture of life.

What this means, of course, is that the Letter has fallen into the fallacy of the falsely dichotomous question. The Letter scarcely considers the possibility that the twentieth century exhibited 'both/and', both a culture of life and a culture of death. One sees the same error in the paragraph just quoted: a wedge is driven between 'the quest for meaning' and 'technology', whereas many people engage in both. 'Man' is capable of doing both, and in any case the commitment to technology in relation to birth and death has been over-whelmingly a commitment to life.

In fact, of course, the Letter was a protest against specific targets: abortion, contraception (which are closely connected, p.24), artificial reproduction, prenatal diagnosis (where this leads to eugenic abortion, p.25) and euthana-sia. By summarising these as "an objective 'conspiracy against life'" (pp. 22. 30), *Evangelium Vitae* was able to conclude that this objective conspiracy has produced in the twentieth century a culture of death, which has been made manifest in its history: "The twentieth century will have been an era of mas-sive attacks on life, an endless series of wars and a continual taking of inno-cent life" (p. 29). We therefore end up with a dualistic "struggle between life and death" (p. 37; cf. pp. 43, 50, 154, 178), in which only those who agree with the Pope can be counted as being on the side of life (p. 50):

> This situation, with its lights and shadows, ought to make us all fully aware that we are facing an enormous and dramatic clash between good and evil, death and life, the 'culture of death' and the 'culture of life'. We find ourselves not only 'faced with' but necessarily 'in the midst of' this conflict: we are all involved in and we all share in it, with the inescapable responsibility of *choosing to be unconditionally pro-life.*

The disaster of this rhetoric is that it demonises the opposition and relies on a conspiracy theory, exactly those strategies which other totalitarian regimes in the murderous twentieth century employed when they set out to engage in war and in the slaughter of the innocent. But even more fatal is the cavalier way in which the Pope assumed that there cannot be genuine dissent on the part of those who may be equally pro-life and that those who take a different view from his own cannot ever be doing so on pro-life grounds. To give only one example: turning to the Word of God (Scripture), the Letter observes (pp.77f.):

> Although there are no direct and explicit calls to protect human life at its very beginning, specifically life not yet born ... this can easily be explained by the fact that the mere possibility of harming, attacking, or actually deny-ing life in these circumstances is completely foreign to the religious and cultural way of thinking of the People of God.

But among the People of God are the Jews (the Letter goes on to quote pas-sages from what it calls the Old Testament), and Jews read their own Scripture with some attention. It is unequivocally clear to them that abortion is allowed if the life of the mother is in danger, and there has been continuous debate about whether abortion is permissible for other reasons, at least in the first forty days of gestation (see Bleich). It is grotesque to suppose that only the Pope is capable of reading the Old Testament, and that the Jews who read their own scripture differently belong to an objective conspiracy and that they are on the side of the culture of death.

This demonising of the opposition made it impossible for the Pope to do justice to the fact that there was much about the twentieth century which made it a culture of life (for example, in its commitment to medicine and education, and in many of its applications of technology) at least as much as it was a culture of death in much of its history. In other words, it is indeed "a situation with its lights and shadows", as the Letter states (p.50). But the recognition of the twentieth-century "movements and initiatives to raise social awareness in defence of life" (p. 48) takes up only two pages in the Letter, of which increasing opposition to war and to the death penalty and growing attention to ecology take up one.

It is this lack of charity in acknowledging the strong commitment to life in much of post-Enlightenment culture which defeated the Pope's purpose in issuing the Letter. There are many who would share his opposition to instrumental evaluations and uses of death (and who might well remind him of the frequency with which the Church used death as an instrument when dealing with heretics and unbelievers), but who would nevertheless disagree about particular issues – whether, for example, assisted dying, in specific and controlled circumstances, far from being 'a thin end of a wedge', might more wisely be considered a voluntary laying down of one's life for the sake of others in an understanding of 'sacrifice' examined in the last chapter of my *The Meanings of Death*; or whether the Pope is correct in defining the moment of personhood at the moment of conception (in itself, incidentally, another example of religious change, since that understanding of ensoulment became widely accepted only in the nineteenth century). Those are open issues, and to demonise those who take a different view is to betray those lives which the Pope intended to defend, because he made his voice incredible.

But there is also that second and contrasting way (just referred to) in which the religious imagination of death may work its way into the more general imagination, the way of critical appropriation. It is, yet again, the issue of the protected circle. The first way maintains the boundary and resists change unless it is coherent within its own circle. The second way maintains coherence but is open to interactive communication with the world in ways which will include correction and change.

An example of what that means lies in the way in which an inherited tradition can be clarified and better understood. Take the Buddhist understanding of Karma/Kamma. A survey of the attitudes of Thai Buddhist students toward genetic disorders and death showed that "54% believed that the scientific view of disease in terms of physical cause (e.g., bacteria, virus) was not in congruence with the Buddhist teaching of karma" – and a further 35% did not know "whether such conflict existed". The point here is that *all* the respondents "agreed that genetic diseases were caused by karmic force, i.e., bad past deeds", but they disagreed about the worth or efficacy of gene testing and therapy (Ratanakul, p. 200):

> 60% believed that though it was theoretically impossible to treat these diseases, in practice these genetic diseases should be regarded as curable as long as there is life, because the karmic forces which cured them depended for their manifestation on present psycho-physical conditions (20.4%) and the operation of this force was a mystery (40%) – no one knows when the force will exhaust itself; 40% considered such testing and therapy useless because ultimately it could not interfere with the working of karma.

Is that opposition well grounded in Buddhist terms? Certainly it shares some of the entirely proper concerns of *Evangelium Vitae* for the defence of the weak, though not entirely for the same reasons (*op.cit.*, p.200):

> The negative feeling of [these] respondents reflects the general attitude of Buddhists who, strongly believing in karma, accept the shortcomings as a part of human existence in the endless life cycle of birth and death (samsara). In their thought, all human life is important and even the damaged life has sanctity and integrity as normal life. Handicapped fellow-men and women need sympathy and practical care from all of us though they are inflicted with incurable diseases and suffering from the consequence of their own misdeeds in their previous lives. To make mistakes is one of the frailties of human nature. The Buddhist way of dealing with these diseases is to make merits of various types, e.g., offering food to monks, observing the basic five precepts ... learning about the Buddhist truths of existence (i.e., impermanence, unsubstantiality and suffering), and practising meditation. All these activities are believed to have a calming effect on those inflicted with genetic diseases and consequently rid them of anxiety, for they realise that these diseases are the result of their own misdeeds in the past and that by the performance of good and meritorious deeds they can convert a bad destiny into a good destiny.

But as the author of the survey pointed out, the belief that there is a conflict between Buddhism and science concerning the aetiologies of disease and death rests on an inadequate understanding of Karma. He drew attention to the distinction between Karma as it answers the questions of 'why', and science as it answers the questions of 'how'. But perhaps even more to the point is the fact that Buddhism has an extremely sophisticated analysis of causality, which refuses claims to single causes in complex events. In other (less Buddhist) words, it is recognised in Buddhism that it is wiser to look for multiple constraints rather than a single cause. In one such analysis (of *niyama*), five possible contributions to causality are identified: (1) *bija-niyama*, biological or hereditary constraints; (2) *mano-* or *citta-niyama*, the unwilled operations of the mental order; (3) *kamma-niyama*, the consequences of volitional dispositions; (4) *uti-niyama*, constraints in the physical environment; and (5) *dharma-niyama*, constraints derived from the transcendental order.

If we apply those to an example: a bus crashes and all the passengers are killed. An over-simple understanding of Karma might suppose that the accumulation of bad Karma in each case brought all those individuals onto that particular bus in order to punish them for bad deeds in previous lives. In fact, however, if we follow the five possibilities above, it might be (1) the sudden death of the driver from a heart attack (which in itself may or may not have been the consequence of karma); or (2) an unwilled error on his part caused by his being dazzled by the sun; or (3) by his deliberately drinking while driving; or (4) by a failure in the braking system; or (5), by the malice of Mara distracting the driver's attention. In the case of some of the passengers (but not necessarily in the case of all), the eventuality might be the working out of Karma.

It follows that there is potentially a far greater congruence and coherence between Buddhism and science in the occurrence (and treatment) of genetic illness and death than the students in the survey had supposed. That is also true of other religions. What is clearly required is a far more careful and deliberate exploration of the issues as they are, or can be, understood by religions and by the sciences, if there is to be an imagination of death which does justice to the whole of human experience thus far. It is an exploration which requires the cooperation of sciences and religions, working together. That exactly was the purpose of the book, *The Meanings of Death*, which drew attention to the way in which the theme of sacrifice lies profoundly in both the religious and the scientific understandings of why death is necessary in a universe of this kind.

It is the precise opposite of the strategy adopted by *Evangelium Vitae*, with its demonising of those who think differently from itself. In this other and contrasting strategy, there will still be issues of truth and morality; there will be many points at which religions will protest against the trivialisation of death, whether, at one extreme, in the 'violence for entertainment' of films and video games, or, at the other, in the instrumental and ruthless genocides of 'death as politics by other means'. But those protests will be made in a context where their voice will be listened to instead of ignored. Religions will continue to point to consequence beyond and through the fact of death.

That is why the Christian rites of passage in relation to death begin in the rites of passage associated with birth and with baptism. In baptism, in Christian belief, people are transferred into death, into the death of Christ, so that they are, as Paul put it, already dead, "because my life lies hidden with God in Christ". In his end is my beginning. The Christian rites of passage in relation to death simply make real and manifest that which was hidden, the truth that in Christ enacted through ritual our death has happened and we are already risen from the dead. John Masefield, in another poem, 'Man is a Sacred City', wrote, "Death opens unknown doors. It is most grand to die." But the religious rites of passage in relation to death open a known and familiar door, and as a result it is most safe to die.

Understanding religions

IV Religions and imagination; communities of shared exploration and discovery

*T*HIS BOOK BEGAN WITH ANGRY CONDEMNATIONS OF RELIGION, FROM the anger of Marx and Engels at the suffering implicit in statistics and explicit in what they saw around them, to the anger of more recent critics at what religions (or at least some of those who belong to religions) believe, say and do.

There is no doubt that much of the anger against religions is justified. But in this book it has been argued that it is only one part of the story. The paradox of religions explored in this book is that religions can indeed be extremely bad news, but only because they have been and can still be very good news. To believers they matter too much to be left to chance. The internalisation of constraints derived from particular religions can produce terror and violence, but it can produce lives of extraordinary beauty and goodness: the achievements of religions include their explorations into a more profound understanding of ourselves as individuals who live in social organisation, and of the universe.

In order, therefore, to understand religions we have to recognise the truth of *both* sides of the paradox. When Christopher Hitchens launched his 'case against religion', *God Is Not Great*, he regarded as his most damaging criticism his claim that religion is man-made. No doubt (to judge from his opinion quoted on p.2) he thought that humans in their evolutionary infancy invented God and Enlightenment to fill the gaps in their ignorance. Therefore he wrote (p.10): "The mildest criticism of religion is also the most radical and the most devastating one. Religion is man-made."

But what else could it possibly be? Religions are the consequence of human explorations of themselves and of their environment (including the foundations of what we now call 'science'), and those explorations led them eventually, not just to science, but to God and to Enlightenment. Religions are a consequence also of their determination to protect and transmit to others (including the next and subsequent generations) their achievements and discoveries. It is not surprising, therefore, that religions emerge as protective systems with boundaries to maintain and if necessary to defend.

Among those 'achievements and discoveries' was the realisation that while *religion* is clearly man-made, it is much more than a *human* achievement. That is why Karl Barth, a highly influential Christian theologian of the twentieth century, equated religion with unbelief (*Unglaube*): he agreed with Hitchens that "religion is man-made", and for that reason he regarded it as under the judgement of God (p.314): "It is only by the revelation of God in Jesus Christ that we can characterise religion as idolatry and self-righteousness, and in this way show it to be unbelief."

To find an orthodox theist and a militant atheist in agreement that religion is man-made and a human invention is striking, and they are of course correct. But that observation does not in itself adjudicate on the issue of the truth or otherwise of what has been invented. Certainly, God was invented and states of Enlightenment were invented. But so were atomic theory and quantum mechanics. The procedures and objectives are surely different, however much they may be interconnected. But the fundamental point is that the Latin word *invenio* means 'I come into'. To invent something does not necessarily mean 'to make up some kind of falsehood'. It may mean to come into something that was waiting to be found.

In that sense, Columbus invented America, but the land mass now named America was there waiting for him to come into it. The same is true of scientific invention. What our ancestors found, and what we can still find today, is that in the discovery of God or of Enlightenment, God and Enlightenment are already there waiting to be discovered. There have been folly, falsehood and fraud in the religious explorations, just as there have been in the scientific ones, but there has been true discovery as well:

> It was easier as a dream,
> As a guilt, as a compensation.
> Then I could cultivate God as a garden,
> Lay down paths and weed the theology.
> But what if the dream outlines the shape,
> Creates what was there before the creation,
> Imagines what was there to be imagined?[1]

That leads at once to an unending engagement with the ontology of what has been discovered (what we can truthfully say about a land mass now known as America, what we can truthfully say about God). In the case of

God, that includes the overwhelming sense, not so much of 'discovering God' as of 'being discovered by God' in the creative initiative that works, as we have seen (p.155), in and through human beings. God is certainly 'man-characterised' and invented in that sense, but God is not in any way 'man-made'.

Any attempt to understand what religions are and why they matter has to begin at this point: religions are a consequence of those explorations and experiments by humans of their own nature, of their relationships and of their varied environments, and a consequence also of the determination of humans to preserve what has been discovered in order to transmit it to succeeding generations.

The underlying achievement of our ancestors worldwide, as much in Asia for example as in Europe, was the way in which they held all parts of their explorations together. Throughout human history, the explorations and experiments were not divided into isolated, let alone antagonistic, compartments, of 'science' and 'religion'. They were held together in ways that inspired and corrected each other.

Some attempt has been made in this book to show how that can still be attempted today. But it may perhaps be easier to see what it means in practice and why it is so important for the understanding of religions if we look back at an earlier example. It can be seen with particular clarity in the seventeenth century in Europe, and in the life of Thomas Browne in particular.

RELIGIONS, EXPLORATION AND DISCOVERY

Thomas Browne was born in 1605 and died in 1682. He lived therefore during one of the greatest centuries of European exploration and discovery. It was an exploration *externally* of the universe and the planet (the latter combined often with trade: the East India Companies of the Dutch and of the Merchants of London were founded in the years immediately before his birth), and *internally* of the composition and character of human nature. It was the century of Bacon's 'Great Instauration', the century therefore of Galileo and Newton, of Harvey, Boyle and Culpeper. But it was also the century of Shakespeare (just), Milton, Pascal, Molière and Descartes, and of George Herbert, John Donne, Traherne and Vaughan.

Bacon's *Magna Instauratio* was his great project of which the second part, *Novum Organon*, appeared when Thomas Browne was fifteen years old. Webster chose it for the title of his landmark book, *The Great Instauration: Science, Medicine and Reform, 1626–1660*, in which he described the period (p.xiii) as one of "a spectacular phase of creative work in experimental science, the rapid development of scientific organisation, and a major philosophical reorientation."

Thomas Browne was typical of the way in which he saw that *both* explorations belong together. He had, as Coleridge observed, "a feeling heart and an active curiosity" (reason *and* emotion as we discussed them earlier), and he was a cosmographer of the two related worlds. In the words of Webster (p.146), he "exploited his enjoyment of the minutiae of the natural world to the advantage of his metaphysical ideas." In his own words (p.19),

> I could never content my contemplation with those general pieces of wonder, the flux and reflux of the sea, the increase of Nile, the conversion of the needle to the North; and have studied to match and parallel those in the more obvious and neglected pieces of Nature, which without further travel I can do in the Cosmography of my self; we carry with us the wonders that we seek without us: there is all Africa and her prodigies in us; we are that bold and adventurous piece of nature, which he that studies wisely learns in a compendium what others labour at in a divided piece and endless volume. Thus there are two books from whence I collect my Divinity; besides that written one of God, another of his servant Nature, that universal and public manuscript, that lies under the eyes of all; those that never saw him in the one have discovered him in the other.

Thomas Browne had originally regarded his idea (of an internal world to be explored with as much enthusiasm as the external world) as a rhetorical device. He came to realise that it corresponds to the reality of what there is (p.40):

> We are only that amphibious piece between a corporal and spiritual essence, that middle frame that links those two together, and makes good the method of God and Nature, that jumps not from extremes, but unites the incompatible distances by some middle and participating natures. That we are the breath and similitude of God, it is indisputable, and upon record of holy Scripture; but to call our selves a Microcosm, or little world, I thought it only a pleasant trope of rhetoric, till my nearer judgement and second thoughts told me there was a real truth therein.

Religions are a consequence of 'the real truth' of both explorations – not just of the oceans and continents of the Trading Companies, or of the planet and the universe, but also of what Thoreau called (p.321) "the private sea", the inner ocean of our being:

> Is it the source of the Nile, or the Niger, or the Mississippi or a North West Passage around this continent, that we would find? Are these the problems

which most concern mankind? Be rather the Mungo Park, the Lewis and Clarke and Frobisher of your own streams and oceans ... Nay, be a Columbus to whole new continents and worlds within you, opening new channels, not of trade, but of thought.

Thoreau then went on to warn us:

It is easier to sail many thousands of miles through cold and storm and cannibals in a government ship with 500 men and boys to assist one, than it is to explore the private sea, the Atlantic and the Pacific Ocean of one's own being alone.

In making that addition, Thoreau may well have been accurate in describing his experience of solitude in Walden Wood, but he was nevertheless missing the reason why religions exist. In commenting on those observations of his, I wrote in *Licensed Insanities* (pp.8ff.):

The basic reason why religions exist, is that we *never* have to make those explorations of our own nature and possibility alone. In fact we cannot do so, because we would have to invent and discover everything for ourselves. In that case life in each generation would have to begin *de novo*: each of us would have to invent the wheel and discover fire all over again. The point is obvious but it is, all the same, important. The point is that information does not float around the universe at random: information to *be* information has to be coded, channelled, protected and received. Between humans it can then be shared and transmitted from one life, or from one generation, to another. And since information can also be stored, it is for all these reasons that John of Salisbury could report (in a quotation much appreciated by Isaac Newton): 'Bernard of Chartres used to say that we, like dwarfs on the shoulders of giants, can see more and farther, not because we are keener and taller, but because of the greatness by which we are carried and exalted.'

The huge advantage of this is obvious: none of us, to adapt the Zen image of *The Gateless Barrier*, has to spend a lifetime trying to find fire because we already have a lighted lantern in our hand. *Mumonkam* (*The Gateless Barrier*) 7 makes the point that the enlightening truth is sometimes so well established and obvious that we fail to see it:

It is so clear that it is difficult to see.
A fool searched everywhere for a fire with a lighted lantern.
If he had only known what fire is
He would have cooked his rice much sooner.

One result of shared exploration and discovery is that religions pioneered the way into forms of association that are now being transformed by the IT and media revolution. In more ordinary words, they offered, not least with powerful and controlling metaphors of association, a *social* answer to the question, where do people end?

The immediate answer is of course that they end at the boundary of their bodies, at the skin. On the other hand, they live in the middle of many other bodies with whom they are interrelated in many ways, ranging from violent aggression to altruistic love. An individual can only be a self in a field of selves. It is the quality of *ubuntu*, as Desmond Tutu put it in relation to the pursuit of truth and reconciliation, a person being a person through other persons. In an interview for the magazine *Third Way* in May 1994, Tutu observed:

> We have a thing called *ubuntu* – it's difficult to render into English – which speaks about the essence of being human; and central to it is that we say a person is a person through other persons. I am human only because I am part of community and I have to do all I can to maintain the harmony and interdependence that are so critical for community.

As a result, people live in many different forms of association and society which develop a life and a history of their own. Social organisations, such as societies, families, institutions or religions, are obviously made up of individuals, but they have a life and history of their own: Parliament is made up of individual MPs (members of Parliament), but there is a history of Parliament that is independent of particular members at any one time. And Parliament as a social organisation with its staff, traditions and regulations is far more than the sum of its parts.

It was this basic point that gave such impetus to the development of sociology during the twentieth century. It led also to this further speculation: if societies have a life and history of their own, perhaps they should be understood as having a mind of their own, and many attempts, going back to the very early days of Durkheim and of McDougall, were made to describe the group or social mind. However, the conclusion became increasingly inescapable that the attribution of mind to society was a metaphor too far: like the ill-judged metaphor of memes, it became clear that there are no structures in society in which anything like mentality, as it was then understood, could occur. It seemed to be the end of the debate about whether 'mind' or mentality extends realistically beyond the boundary of the skin.

Now, however, the debate has been reopened in a different way as a consequence of the IT revolution and of the cognitive sciences regarding key aspects of cognition as computational. Computational cognition simply means that the relevant computations occur outside the immediate boundary of the individual and yet are completely integrated into the neural basis of cognition. Thus Malafouris has put forward, in his material engagement theory (MET), the argument that human cognition and intelligence spread out "beyond the skin" into the material world and into culture. An example he gives is that of a blind person using a white stick. For the brain, the stick is much more than a register of obstacles: it becomes (where the brain is concerned) a part of the body so that Malafouris called it "a cognitive prosthesis". The brain thus extends its cognition, not just through, but also with the material environment.

Another example among many is the work done by Hutchins on navigation at sea. Individual sailors on a boat in the middle of the Atlantic in the sixteenth century could very easily get lost. In the twenty-first century, it would still be possible to get lost, but it would be much harder to do so because of the development of so many technological aids which are performing the computations that could not be performed by the human mind without its extension into materiality.

This extension of the self through the material has been of paramount importance in religions, as indeed it still is. It can be seen in the creation of ritual objects, in the orientation of sacred architecture, in the development of those formal actions summarised in the word 'sacraments'. That word has different meanings and applications in different religions (on the basic meaning, see Bowker 2014, p.107), but they include the enactment of intention and belief in ways that words and reflection cannot do. One particular definition of a sacrament as "an outward and visible sign of an inward and spiritual grace" recognises the actualised connection between the exterior and the interior realised through the material.

An issue in the debate in the cognitive sciences about what is called 'individualism and externalism' is whether those external computations are nevertheless only significant when they are internalised by individuals, or whether those computations are a supplementary system in which individuality is embedded and by which it is in part constituted. Hutchins therefore argued (p.xiv):

> [H]uman cognition is not just influenced by culture and society, but ... is in a very fundamental sense a cultural and social process. To do this I will move the boundaries of the cognitive unit of analysis out beyond the skin of the individual person and treat the navigation team as a cognitive and computational system.

To the extent that cognition is understood as computational, the computations of individuals in a population are occurring outside the individual in a real, and not just in a metaphorical, way, so that the boundary of the individual is set far beyond the skin. There has always been a strong intuition of this in the observation of organisms that live in colonies, such as ants, bees or wasps. It can be observed in the coordinated and apparently instantaneous movement of flocks of birds and shoals of fish. It is the group, and not the individual organisms constituting the group, that functions as a unit.

Shared computation and cognition is thus a specific example of 'no man being an island', and it underlines how important in human history religions have been in organising and making foundational the forms and rules of social sharing. It can be seen in the powerful and controlling metaphors of interdependence in all religions – the body, for example, in Christianity, the *umma* in Islam, the Jewelled Net of Indra in Buddhism, the temple in Indian religion, Tian and its link to *li* as both ritual and natural principle in China. Tian is understood in different ways in China, but even in the works of those like Xunzi, who emphasised an impersonal and non-normative understanding of Tian, the connection is retained between Tian and *ritualised* social action in creating the interdependent Trinity of Heaven, Earth and humanity. Thus Eno's detailed and illuminating study concludes (p.169):

> The overriding point about the role of T'ien [Tian] in the *Hsun Tzu* [Xunzi] is that regardless of whether T'ien is pictured as nonpurposive Nature, as a normative natural force, as fate, or as a purposive deity, its instrumental function remains always the same – to legitimise ritual forms, ritual study, and ritual society.

There are many other examples. Religions are not an aggregation of individuals but are socially organised and therefore shared explorations of possibility.

This means that religions have played a decisively important role in the evolution of human beings and social groups because their success in creating coherent and cohesive societies has been rewarded in the terms of group selection discussed earlier. To some extent, of course, all animals explore their environments and do so on the basis of their innate and inherited competence, and to some extent also they learn and experiment. In the human case, the explorations, the learning and the experiments were utterly transformed by the ability to share them with each other and with succeeding generations, especially through the development of symbols and language. "Evolution", as Terence Deacon put it (p.412), commenting on the evolution in humans of symbolic communication, "has widened the cognitive gap between the human species and all others into a yawning chasm."

In that process of exploration and experiment there is for all animals, including humans, an inbuilt corrigibility set by natural selection. That is why any understanding of human life has to begin at the level of genes, proteins, evolution and natural selection. Without that natural correction there would be no humans to be religious or anything else. Life is constantly threatened by death, so if we are to live and grow, our lives, especially those of our children, have to be protected. Religions, to repeat the point already made repeatedly, are the earliest protective systems of which we have evidence that create the circumstances in which people are more likely to survive, to have children and to bring them up to be adults.

PROBLEM-SOLVING AND THE COMPOUNDS OF LIMITATION

This means that religions are addressed to the many constraints that delimit human possibility. Death is the ultimate constraint, but there are many others. In *The Sense of God*, they are discussed at greater length where it is suggested (p.66) that

> it may be possible to gain a better understanding of religions ... from an anthropological point of view, if religions are set in the context of human endeavours to find a way through the limitations which circumscribe their projected activities or which ultimately circumscribe their lives as such. The suggestion is, therefore, that the identification of the compound of limitation is the correct general context of explanation: it explains nothing in itself, but it makes explanation of detail more possible.

The phrase 'compounds of limitation' summarises the critical importance of problem-solving in evolutionary history. It is indeed the second of the five basic principles of evolutionary psychology in the understanding of Cosmides and Tooby (although their use of the word 'designed' makes the same elementary error as Dawkins): "Our neural circuits were designed by natural selection to solve problems that our ancestors faced during our species' evolutionary history."

In that respect, 'the compound of limitation' resembles 'natural selection' which does not in itself explain anything but which, as a constant constraint, makes explanation more coherently possible. In his book *Climbing Mount Improbable*, Dawkins has a chapter entitled 'Silken Fetters'. In it he contrasts the ways in which, through natural selection, spiders evolved into net-spinning creatures, with computer modelling designed to produce a comparable effect. The chapter begins (p.33):

> A good way to order our understanding of any living creature is to imagine, fancifully and with something more than poetic license, that it (or, if you prefer, a hypothetical 'designer' of the creature) faces a chain of problems or

tasks. First we pose the initial problem, then we think of possible solutions that might make sense. Then we look at what the creatures actually do. That often leads us to notice a new problem facing animals of this kind, and the chain continues.... Notice that the progression of problem leading to problem is not to be thought of as marching through one animal's lifetime. If it is a temporal progression at all the time scale is evolutionary, but it may sometimes be not a temporal but a logical progression.

If, in that paragraph, we substitute 'religion' for 'creature', 'religious believers' for 'creatures' and 'individuals' for 'animals', it becomes an excellent description of religions as problem-solving organisations addressed to the compound of limitations in which at any time they are set – but with one important difference. Dawkins surely had in mind the importance of correcting his 'fanciful poetic license'. His intention was to show that on the way to becoming 'net-spinners', spiders do not purposefully "face problems", but rather that they are either equipped by random mutations to deal with the threats to their survival and gene replication, or they go to extinction. As he put it succinctly (p.64), "Real life is starkly simple in this sense: some animals are more likely to die than others."

On that basis Dawkins believed that he could eliminate teleology (as he somewhat naively understands it). But, as we have already seen, there is no possibility at all that we can eliminate teleonomy in evolution in general, and certainly not in the case of humans. Humans actually *do* "notice problems", they have a shared perception of the compounds of limitation that surround them, and they address themselves to them. The consequences emerge in what we understand as 'culture' and in religions as organised systems that protect identified solutions – hence (to repeat the vital point once more) their decisively important role in evolution in creating the conditions for group selection of such a kind that particular gene selection is rewarded.

An immediate consequence of this is the fact that different communities of shared understanding may and often do develop and then transmit entirely different proposals or even solutions to comparable compounds of limitation – hence, yet again, the often radical differences of religions in which divergent 'solutions' have been tested and winnowed through time. A succinct example of this can be seen in the Bemba response to an English folktale (Hunt p.10):

> Dr. Aubrey Richards, an anthropologist who lived among the Bemba of Northern Rhodesia in the 1930's, once related to a group of them an English folk tale about a young prince who climbed glass mountains, crossed chasms, and fought dragons, all to obtain the hand of a maiden he loved. The Bemba were plainly bewildered, but remained silent. Finally an old chief spoke up,

voicing the feelings of all present in the simplest of questions: "Why not take another girl?" he asked.

Religions have thus created cultural systems able to endure through time, however much those systems evolve and change. Culture and religions belong closely together, and it is evident historically how closely related they are. Even the word 'culture' is connected with religion since it comes from the same Latin word *cultus*, which refers to the worship of a supreme being, or of gods and goddesses.

NEUROSCIENCE AND THE PREPARATION FOR BEHAVIOURS

Thus far the argument has been that at the most basic level of human survival, it was advantageous for human beings to devise systems in order to help to protect themselves. Having observed at the beginning of this book that animals, birds and fish gain protection by living in social organizations without saying their prayers (though actually in some religions it is thought that they do), we then asked the question: Why *religious* systems?

That led us to the way in which religions are a consequence of those two directions of exploration, the external and the internal. People living successfully within the constraints of protective systems are able, not just to survive, but to do many other things as well. Religions were successful in creating and sustaining the beliefs and practices that provide a secure context. As a result of those constraints, at least some people were – and still are – set free to explore their own nature and the family or society in which they live, as well as the world around them.

The human ability to make those far-ranging explorations is rooted in an inheritance with which we are endowed when we are born with the kind of brain and body that most humans have. When the genes and proteins build our brains, they build them, not in a random way, but with great consistency from one generation to another.

As a result of that gene-protein process humans and all other animals are prepared for particular (albeit extremely varied) outcomes. In the context of the compounds of limitation, the most important consequence is the way in which we and other animals are prepared for *competence in problem-solving*. It is literally vital, because without it survival would not be possible.

It is, therefore, the gene-protein process that prepares us for our characteristic human behaviours. There are certainly many differences among human beings, even though they come from much the same gene-protein process (for example, skin pigmentation, colour of eyes, average height), but there is much more that we all have in common. We are prepared, for example, in much the same way for face recognition of emotions such as rage, surprise or happiness with an 80 per cent (but not, as Ekman showed long ago,[2] *complete*) cross-cultural accuracy. We are prepared for eating and drinking, for sleeping and waking, for sexual development and behaviours, for speaking languages – indeed, Deacon has argued (p.412) that in the case of symbol learning and the use of language the human brain is *over*-prepared in the sense that its restructuring has driven symbol-learning abilities to such 'fixation' that it has become a universal trait of the species. It is clear from recent brain research that we are prepared also for those behaviours that we call religious – maybe even over-prepared as Deacon understands it, in the sense that 'religion' is a universal trait of the species.

The way in which we are *prepared* for those and other behaviours does not in any way dictate or determine what we do with our 'preparedness'. Biology does not dictate what language we speak, let alone what we will say, nor does it dictate what food we eat, let alone what we will have for breakfast tomorrow.

So also with religion: biology does not determine what we do with our religious preparedness. We can decide, if we want, to give up religion, just as we can decide to give up sex or (for short intervals) food. But to abstain altogether from something so fundamental as religion would be to make oneself less than fully human – as research for the Oxford Cognition, Religion and Theology Project concluded (CRT Project Summary, p.2):

> New empirical research is demonstrating that impulses to religion are part of the most basic ways the human mind works. Religion has always been a basic feature of human life and is always likely to be. Atheism is as sophisticated a response to this fact as any theology. Which is right cannot be settled by empirical discovery, but religion cannot be dismissed as the private preoccupation of a few. Religious responses to the world, right or wrong, are part of what it is to be human.

The recognition that we are prepared for particular behaviours is an example of what are known as 'innateness theories' of explanation. They correctly identify *first-level constraints* over outcomes derived from the gene-protein endowment and from the consequent architectures of the human brain and body. But they tell us very little about the ways in which particular people appropriate and express those opportunities, still less about the ways in which social groups construct their consequences. As Deeley has put it, in an article summarising the contribution of current advances in neuroscience to the understanding of 'the religious brain' (2004, p.249),

> Yet we still have to explain why some kinds of conceptions and behaviour are widely distributed (such as religious beliefs and behaviour), and also

why these conceptions are regarded as real and motivating. To address these questions, we must go on to consider the relations between symbolic culture and individual cognition. A fundamental question for anthropology and cognitive science concerns how the extrapersonal realm of symbolic culture influences intrapersonal cognition – processes such as learning, reasoning, emotion, and motivation.

That question has been addressed by those cognitive anthropologists who are known collectively as 'neo-associationists' by using "models derived from cognitive psychology in an attempt to characterize how the public forms of symbolic culture (such as objects, actions, words, songs, smells) are interpreted by individuals, through processes that both render symbolic culture meaningful, and constrain its development" (*op.cit.*, pp.249f).

The 'public forms of symbolic culture' create *a second-level of constraints*. They are derived from the contexts in which individuals and groups live. In an IT world, the boundaries of those contexts are now changing, often dissolving, so rapidly that the range of constraints has expanded correspondingly; that creates immense problems for religions, or for religious groups, for whom the maintaining of boundaries is important.

Even then, Deeley's question (how do specific conceptions come to be regarded as real and motivating?) has not been answered. Part of the answer, in Deeley's view, lies in the ways in which religions as organised systems *enculturate* and make coherent a particular and shared (and maybe, in the case of world religions, a *widely* shared) interpretation of endowed opportunity. Religions as coinherent communities of meaning and practice (in, for example, symbolic communication and ritual performance) then offer *third-level constraints* over the formation of human lives in both beliefs and practices.

Those three different levels of constraint offer in combination a naturalistic, even a reductionist, explanation of religious beliefs and behaviours. But there are then *fourth-level constraints* derived from the evaluation of the adequacy, even indeed of the truth, of what those beliefs and practices purport to be about. It is a point that Deeley makes strongly and emphatically: having surveyed the research and arguments summarised in the preceding paragraphs, he then states (*op.cit.*, p.264):

A religious sceptic might take the arguments here as a form of eliminative reductionism, which account for religious belief in naturalistic terms without a need to invoke the existence of the objects of religious belief. By contrast, I suggest that the programme here can be understood as a social neurocognitive extension of the sociology of knowledge, in which the existence of all beliefs is taken as equally problematic (in the sense of equally requiring explanation). The focus of inquiry is the Kantian question of 'what cognitive capacities are presupposed by, and necessary for, the existence of beliefs'? This question can be asked of any beliefs, including those of scientists. The sociology of knowledge does not obviate the need to determine the conditions under which, and senses in which, a given belief or web of beliefs can be judged to be true or false.

Religions are the consequence of those levels of constraint being recognised and at least to some extent understood (in however approximate a way) so that shared responses can be developed. Within those recognitions and responses are the explorations that humans make of what their bodies are able to experience and understand. That is what I have called, in summary, 'somatic exploration' (from the Greek *soma*, 'a body'). Religions are a consequence of the discoveries they have made as well also of their ability to interpret those discoveries and to share them with each other in what I have called 'somatic exegesis'. There is a perfect illustration of what that means in practice in Flood's *The Tantric Body*, since in his argument (p.185), "the tantric body has been established within traditions of specific revelation, ritual practice and initiatory teachings from which it cannot be separated." His book also makes clear why the internalisation of constraint in a disciplined way is indispensably important (p.ix):

> The specificity of the claim is that in the Hindu tantric traditions focused primarily on the deities Viṣṇu and Śiva in the early medieval period, the practitioner becomes divine through the internalisation of the text, through the inscription of the body by the text, and learns to inhabit a tradition specific subjectivity. The text is mapped onto the body.

The universality of constraints and the diversity of possible responses to them explain why there is much that is common in religious behaviour and belief, but also why, nevertheless, there are many different religions and why there are radical contradictions and differences between and within them – of which the following gives some examples (Bowker 2003, p.6):

> It [religion] can mean believing that God is the source and the goal of life, or that belief in God is at best a juvenile distraction; it can mean loving one's neighbour as oneself, or excommunicating him or her to a fate far worse than death; it can mean consulting witches for wisdom, or burning them alive; having a soul, or not having a soul; obeying the command to be fruitful, or taking a lifelong vow to be celibate; withdrawing into silence, or speaking in tongues; it can require shaving one's head, or never cutting one's hair; going to mosque on Friday, synagogue on Saturday, or church on Sunday; it can mean praying, meditating, levitating, worshipping, entering into trance and ecstasy; building St Paul's Cathedral, the Golden Temple,

and the Great Pyramid; crossing oceans and continents to go on pilgrimages to holy places; to convert others; to fight crusades, holy wars, or jihads; it has also meant the inspired creation of music, art, icons, symbols, poetry at the very farthest stretch of human imagination, and yet it can also reveal itself as trivial sentiment.

Variety and contradiction of that kind are inevitable because what people do with their somatic preparedness, either individually or in their societies and cultures, is (to repeat the point yet again) constrained but not determined. It also means that religious belief and practice will endure among humans unless there are major alterations in the human DNA.

The consequence is, of course, immense. It has enabled humans to move far beyond the contingent and restricted circumstances of the time and space they happen to inhabit. A religious humanism (the account religions give of what it means to be human) is rooted in a recognition of the ways in which humans embody truth and values that must of course arise in contingent and transient circumstances, but which transcend contingency: humans are the place where values that are unchanging (or, in other words, that they regard as absolute) are embodied in the midst of time and space. Humans are the living point where eternity and time intersect. They are astonishingly, in the old phrase, *capax veritatis*, but far beyond that they are also *capax caritatis*, even *amoris*. True, they often fail to be what they are capable of being, and religions offer different accounts of why those failures occur and of what can be done about them. But beyond failure and beyond contingency, humans are capable of receiving the help or grace they need in order to arrive in eternity and live in truth. Here, supremely, as Blake observed (p.151), "Eternity is in love with the productions of time", but equally the productions of time can be in love with the Eternal.

EXPLORATION AND EXEGESIS

We can now see how the paradox of religions is rooted in the nature of religions as protective systems safeguarding the massive achievements and consequences of exploration and discovery. For many centuries, indeed for millennia, religions have coded and protected the consequences of those explorations and discoveries. Religions, whatever else they are (and they are much else), are organised systems for the coding, protection and transmission of information. They have, therefore, been able to offer to one generation after another the opportunity of entering into the achievements and discoveries of those who have gone before them. Some religions have concentrated on exploring inward and on finding truth within the body in Enlightenment, peace, emptiness, the Buddha-nature, and for that reason they are known as 'introversive systems'. It is the exploration of Thoreau's 'private sea', and it has led to such religions as Jainism and Buddhism.

Other religions looked outward and discovered the substantial (emphasising the underlying Latin *substantia*) importance of our context – hence the conjunction until very recently between 'religion and science'. They have emphasised the importance also of our relationships with each other and with One far greater than ourselves. This has produced religions like the Abrahamic religions (Judaism, Christianity and Islam) in which the One greater than ourselves is recognised as God and as the uncreated Creator of all that is, the One who continues in being whether this universe happens to be here or not. The systems which explore the truth and value in relationship of that kind are known as 'extraversive systems'.

It is important not to drive too hard a distinction between them, because all religions are concerned with both the inside and the outside. To give only one example: in Buddhism, there is a strong emphasis on the practice of meditation, of which one part is known as *samatha-bhavana*, often translated as 'calming meditation'. Fundamental in *samatha-bhavana* is an attempt to put discursive thought to rest by entering into the stages of absorption known as *jhana* (Pali; Skt. *dhyana*). The aim in this has been effectively summarised by Kenneth Ch'en (pp.350f):

> *Dhyana* ... refers to the religious discipline aimed at tranquilizing the mind
> and getting the practitioner to devote himself to a quiet introspection into
> his own inner consciousness. He is made to feel an interest in things above
> the senses and to discover the presence of a spiritual faculty that bridges the
> gap between the finite and the infinite. When he is thoroughly disciplined
> in *dhyana*, he can keep the serenity of mind and cheerfulness of disposition
> even amid the world of turbulent activity ... Continuous practice of *dhyana*
> exercises enables him to attain to the higher ecstatic trances or to the blissful
> state of equanimity and wisdom.

That certainly illustrates the purpose of an introversive system. As progress is made, the various stages drop away, leading to complete absorption in the object of meditation. But it is not the only kind of meditation in Buddhism. There is another discipline known as *vipassana-bhavana*, usually translated as 'insight meditation'. Here the purpose is to develop insight and awareness of awakening in the present moment in which discursive rationality is clearly involved.

It is true that some commentators on Buddhism have felt that the relationship between the two is one of stages, with *vipassana-bhavana* being a first stage or foundation for the higher and ultimate goal of *samatha-bhavana*. But that would be to drive too hard a distinction between them, because *both* are routes and methods leading to the same goal but dealing with different obstacles or compounds of limitation. It is exactly as Keown has concluded (pp.79f): "[T]he obstacles to enlightenment are themselves twofold, both moral *and* intellectual.... This is why two meditative techniques are required for the eradication of the roots of evil and the attainment of the ethical and intellectual perfection which is *nibbana*."

It would be absurd, therefore, to describe as 'nothing but' introversive a religion derived from the compassion (*karuna*) of the Buddha and founded on the ethical precepts of *sila*. It would be equally absurd to think of Islam as 'nothing but' extraversive simply because it places great emphasis on deeds and actions on the Day of Judgement, as though it is not also the home of Sufis.

Nevertheless, differences of emphasis and priority, of advice, instruction and practice, do obtain. They produce different and often contrasting ways of speaking and acting. Flood, for example, has described the two kinds of spiritual languages that result from this difference in emphasis, the languages of unsayability (apophatic discourse in relation to God) and languages of inner ascent. He then commented (2012. p.91):

> They [the languages] are not merely intellectual curiosities or leftovers from the past that we have gone beyond after the retreat of religion from cosmology with the rise of science. They are still with us in contemporary traditions, albeit in altered ways, and we can trace trajectories of these languages into modernity, particularly in poetry and philosophy.

The differences in emphasis produce also the varying practices that are characteristic of different religions – such things as worship, prayer, meditation, sacrifice, yoga, annicanupassana, zazen and many more. Such practices, when they are undertaken with good faith, can lead people into experience and insight so real to them that all else in life becomes totally unimportant in comparison.

And far beyond that, far beyond the explorations of spirituality they undertake, comes the realisation in all religions that human effort and human initiatives cannot achieve the furthest goals. They can only be attained with a profound help that is not of human making: God and Enlightenment invite volition and effort, but in the end they are not achieved by effort; they can only be received as gift. On that basis, religions take people far beyond what Freud used to call "our abject points of departure". On the foundation of faith, they take them to goals and behaviours far beyond anything that can be predicted from an analysis of brains and biology. To quote the summary in *The Oxford Dictionary of World Religions* (p.xxiii),

> Faith, as trust in the tradition and the teacher, then sets out on journeys which for many (not inevitably, and certainly not for all) reveal the truth of that for which it yearns. 'Eternity in time', to quote the phrase of Henry Vaughan, is no longer a puzzle but a persuasion.
>
> Meditation enters into meaning far beyond common senses, and rests in that supreme condition which leaves behind it even such treasures as beauty, excitement, and delight.
>
> Prayer is presence, before One who elicits praise, thanksgiving and joy, as well as penitence and sorrow. Because prayer is the greatest of the human languages of love, it connects others to God as well.

We have moved here far beyond the baseline of biology. Not surprisingly, therefore, the far-reaching consequences of somatic exploration were not left without interpretation, and that is the role of somatic exegesis, the interpretation of what has been discovered. Somatic exploration and exegesis are combined in teaching and instruction so that others can move in the same direction by internalising the well-winnowed constraints.

From this come the elaborate belief systems and world pictures that we associate with religions. They are well-winnowed traditions, protected in both literal and metaphorical boundaries – and protected also in some cases by the kind of fundamentalist appeal described earlier. That in itself makes a massive contribution to the paradox of religions because it means that for some people their beliefs and practices are so immune from challenge or criticism that they act as a specific and non-negotiable constraint over their thought and behaviour. It is an important reason why, to come back to the beginning of this book and to the paradox of religions, religions can be such a dangerous threat to each other and to us all: they include people who live, literally, in disjunctively different worlds of imagination, and any one of those worlds may contain an obligation to maintain the boundary to the exclusion of others.

So is conflict inevitable? At the beginning of this book I asked whether the dangers inherent in the protected circles of religion can be averted. I answered, Probably not – unless we understand much better why religions matter so much to their adherents that they will do both good and evil in the name of their belief, with 'good' and 'evil' being defined both in and outside the systems.

This book has been an attempt to offer at least a little of that understanding. Applying that understanding to conflicts, both between religions and often within religions, it is clear that the divisions are utterly serious because they relate to the diverse consequences of somatic exploration and exegesis, and thus they relate profoundly to issues of truth.

GUIDELINES IN CONFLICT

Given that issues of life-saving truth are involved, it is not surprising that conflicts involving religions are often so intransigent and long-running. The immediate and challenging question is whether ways can be found in which religions can engage more dispassionately, or at least with greater detachment, with each other and with the non-religious world. But how?

In the case of the three Abrahamic religions (Judaism, Christianity and Islam), a detailed and pioneering answer to that question is being given in the work of Miroslav Volf. His explorations are constantly applied to practical issues and opportunities. Thus at the end of his book, *Allah; A Christian Response*, he offers "ten ways in which major strands in the book contribute to combatting extremism", and he concludes (2012b p.262):

> The main thrust of all ten suggestions is this. The claim that Christians and Muslims, notwithstanding their important and ineradicable differences, have a common and similarly understood God (1) delegitimises religious motivation to violence between them and (2) supplies motivation to care for others and to engage in a vigorous and sustained debate about what constitutes the common good in the one world we share.

In a comparable way, I included in *Is God a Virus?* eight 'elementary guidelines in conflict'. Now I would add a ninth in large letters: REMEMBER HALDANE'S BEETLES. Haldane observed that 'the Creator, if he exists, has an inordinate fondness for beetles'.[3] If there are abductive inferences to be drawn from creation to a Creator, one such would have to be an overwhelming preference for diversity without which a universe of this kind and human life within it are impossible. Religions, on the other hand, tend to go in the opposite direction and look for uniformity and conformity in belief and practice. In conflicts, the value of diversity has to be treasured.

The other eight guidelines in conflict came from experience and they too suggested practical steps.

The first is to establish who is actually involved, and who, in the background, is offering support. In a general way people may regard themselves as 'Muslims', 'Christians', 'Hindus', but in practice and in detail they belong to far more specific parts of the whole, as the earlier discussion of subsystems has indicated, and as recent events in Lebanon and Syria have shown. On the other hand, however, if the conflict is inter-religious, those involved will often identify themselves with the entire system, and think of themselves as

Muslims, Christians, Hindus and so on. The actual relation between subsystem and system may well be decisive in suggesting appropriate action, and it needs to be carefully established.

So the second point is to ask (and find out) how the issue in question looks from within the subsystems of the religions involved and to bear in mind how it looks from the viewpoint of the overarching system, which may offer, at least theoretically, some controls. Thus, the IRA, despite the context and affiliations of its members, became increasingly distanced from the Roman Catholic Church. For the outsider, there is no Archimedean ground on which to stand in order to issue overriding or superior judgements. The nearest approach to that lies in the increasing consensus concerning human rights, particularly when that consensus is translated into declarations and courts of law. Religions, however, may regard them as human constructions compared with their own sources of authority, and are unlikely to regard them as absolute.

The third point, therefore, is to learn to argue within the logic of the systems involved, particularly of a system other than one's own. From the point of view of the earlier discussion of the importance of context in understanding what other people say and mean, it is clear that 'to argue within the logic of the systems involved' requires a great deal more than a knowledge of the relevant languages – although it is a necessary condition of any conversation. If, however, one goes that 'second mile', it becomes possible to see what the logic of each system demands – *or forbids* – in relation to a particular issue. Logic rarely wins an argument, but it establishes what ought to be relevant to it.

The fourth point is to define, from the respective points of view of those involved, what the point or purpose or cause of this particular issue is, remembering then to set it in a wider network of constraints, since it is often *there* that the true root of conflict or of intransigence is to be found.

The fifth is to bear in mind that many people, as we have seen, would rather die than abandon their faith, and that they are consequently prepared to die, and carry others with them into death, in ways that may seem incredible to an outsider. Differences are profound and cannot be negotiated away as semantic inadequacies. They are literally matters of life and death. When Cynthia Cockburn made her brilliantly helpful analysis of initiatives made by women's groups in Northern Ireland, Israel/Palestine and Bosnia-Herzegovina, she offered six 'tools' that clearly helped them: the first of these was, to *affirm difference* (her italics), to "resist the temptation of erasing it, of collapsing mixity into mere heterogeneity or, worse, a pretended homogeneity" (p.224). It is, therefore, essential to understand how a religion (or a subsystem within a religion) arrives at non-negotiable truth (i.e., at what counts as non-negotiable truth from its own point of view) according to the limits set within that tradition on legitimate or appropriate utterance, since otherwise, all that will be heard will be either the vague expressions of goodwill which bring inter-religious meetings into such disrepute; or nothing. The challenge here is so great that those in dispute cannot persuade each other to agree. This means that we have always to look for ways in which people can live together even in disagreement. What are the terms that might allow the sharing of both literal and metaphorical space?

The sixth point addresses that question. It is to establish, in any conflict in which religions are involved, what the perceived conditions of continuity are for the participants involved: on what terms do they perceive that there is a reasonable chance that their grandchildren might grow up as Shia Muslims, Vaishnava Hindus, Orthodox Jews or whatever (bearing in mind the first point above about the relation between subsystems and systems)? No one knows the future. But this is not an exercise in exact prediction. Rather, it is a way of eliciting participant perception by asking the following question in a practical way: What do you think you need in order to secure the continuity of your lifeway, not just for tomorrow but into some reasonable future? Usually when this question is asked, the answer comes back, 'Everything'. But, at the other end of the spectrum, the Jews in the Nazi camps of Europe required virtually nothing to retain their Jewish identity and their faith. Somewhere between the two extremes, between everything and nothing, there will be a compromise which is worth the risk for those involved; and if the word 'compromise' is an unhappy one – a good umbrella but a poor roof, as Lowell called it – then take instead Samuel Johnson's 'reciprocal concessions'.

The seventh point is to think in terms, not of causes, but of constraints, for all the reasons put forward in this book. This removes from the arena contest about 'who caused' the conflict: in a network of constraints, responsibility is diffused and face is saved. On the other hand, it is essential to be generous (and often compassionate) in the specification of constraints.

The eighth point is to remember, in the midst of religious conflict and challenge, always at some point (preferably early on) to follow Thomas Hardy's advice and take a full look at the worst. Religions can be extremely bad news, especially for those of whom they disapprove. At the same time, however, they are the source of immense goodness: faith is constantly moving mountains a little to the left or a little to the right, making the possible happen and the impossible take a little less long. The aim has to be to get the virtues within a system to engage with the evils that the system is endorsing, or allowing, or ignoring, or setting forward – goodness and evil, that is, on its own terms of

reference. What rapidly becomes apparent is that the definitions are not actually relative, and that there is a very extensive religious consensus concerning
both good and evil. Religions *can* be allies in healing the Earth.

Religions, therefore, offer powerful resources in the enterprise of being
good, generous and just, despite all there is in their present behaviours and
past histories which contradicts that. Those involved in conflicts, not least
politicians and diplomats, need to know what those resources are and how
they can be mobilised. *Conflict and Reconciliation: The Contribution of World
Religions*[4] offers a summary of what those resources are that religions must
bring to the process of reconciliation after conflict. The word 'must' is derived
from what each of the traditions requires as a matter, not of goodwill or of
concession, but *of obligation* according to its own authoritative logic.

Since offering those eight guidelines, the revolutions in communication
and technology have completely changed the ways in which we interact with
each other: communication can be immediate and direct, and it can break
through or ignore the boundaries of protected circles, including those of religions. The use of mobile phones, for example, can work in opposite directions: they can be used to assemble and organise people in riots and violent
protests, but, as Bock has shown in his book, *The Technology of Nonviolence*,
they have the potential to organise interventions to defuse violence and turn
it into non-violent protest.

In a more general way, it is obvious that the IT revolution will make a dramatic difference in the religious world. Since religions create communities of
shared imagination, there is now an entirely new opportunity for religions to
explore the consequence of sharing their imaginations with each other without in any sense betraying what is true or valuable to themselves.

To do that would be to take a hint from what James Joyce once called "intersecting fictions". Instead of leaving the narratives of religions and theologies
in isolation, it would be wise to examine what the extent and consequence of
intersecting narratives might be.

If we think yet again of religions as 'protected circles', they cannot be
merged into each other in any form of syncretism that would entail losing
their identity or what they hold to be true. But religions have much in common, and they may (and frequently do) overlap. They intersect in ways that
can and should be formally and deliberately explored. Instead of a row of
adjacent circles side by side, the exploration would be of the extent to which,
by intersecting, they actually reinforce each other: we would have a row of
overlapping and intersecting circles as in the Olympic symbol. The advantage
of that model is that it also forms a chain, and a chain will be much stronger
in bearing the weight of the world. The model, however, is only a start: if

a one-dimensional model sufficed, we would still be living on a flat earth. Instead, we live in a multidimensional universe, and in the case of religions we know that each intersects, not just with its neighbours, but with many others, and we do not yet understand, despite many interfaith endeavours, how to engage with that complexity.

So issues of space, truth, enlightenment and salvation will certainly remain. But that does not prevent or prohibit the enrichment of one's own imagination from that of others, not least through art, music, dance, storytelling and the care of those in need. In that extension of imagination, schools can, or at least should, play a massively creative part: at their best, they are already creating 'the Olympic chain'. In the so-called global village and in any multicultural country, the study of religions should be a highly important part of education. Apart from being interesting in its own way, it contributes immensely to the ways in which schools are able to create in miniature what religions are in general – communities of *shared* imagination. But what does it actually mean to think of religions in that way, as communities of shared imagination?

RELIGIONS AS COMMUNITIES OF SHARED IMAGINATION

As I walked through the wilderness of this world, I lighted on a certain place where there was a Den, and I laid me down in that place to sleep; and as I slept, I dreamed a dream.

With those famous words, John Bunyan began his book (1678), *The Pilgrim's Progress from This World to That which is to Come; Delivered under the Similitude of a Dream, Wherein is Discovered the Manner of his Setting Out, his Dangerous Journey, and Safe Arrival at the Desired Country.*

Bunyan was described by Robert Blatchford as "a man of abnormal imagination; his imagination was vivid, active, flaming Dantean; it gave light – often lurid light – and heat, and form, and colour, to all he saw."

That may well be true. What is not true is that his imagination was abnormal. The word 'abnormal' rests basically on a statistical observation: it means 'standing away from the statistical norms' of some or other opinion or behaviour. It follows that, far from being abnormal, humans almost without exception create and live in worlds of imagination. They have their own imaginative ideas and understandings of the world and the circumstances in which they live (they can 'imagine the unimaginable', as Guthke put it, p.24). Or, better, 'worlds', since people live in several different worlds at once. They may, for example, live in a particular society and they will have their own ideas of what that society is and of what it means to belong to it; or they may live in a family and they will have different ideas of what a family is and of what it means to belong to a family; or they may live through a computer in the imagined worlds of virtual reality.

Most of us live also in worlds created by our work or play. Thus scientists, far from living in 'the real world' (whatever that might be), create their own imagination of the universe or of that part of the universe with which their research is concerned. Indeed, the programmes made in 1982 by the BBC, in which scientists described the nature and the implications of their current research, were called 'Imagined Worlds'. One of the contributors, Roger Penrose, described how the theory of twistors, a speculative idea of how mathematical geometry might relate to physics, changed his imagination of how and what the universe is (p.180):

> So really the theory has changed my view of nature, finding new instances of such a close unity between the real world and the mathematics. In a sense what appears to be physical reality all around us is deceptive. In my view, the deeper reality is actually the underlying abstract mathematics.

But which then is the real world?

The example of science illustrates the way in which imagined worlds (in this case of cosmology) are *shared* imaginations. They may be private in the sense that each individual appropriates them in an idiosyncratic way, but they are public in the sense that there is sufficient consensus about them for people to understand each other and to participate together in a shared imagination – however much its details may be contested or changed as a consequence of further reflection and research.

People live in many more imagined worlds than those of science alone, including much of what has traditionally been described as culture. We have already seen (Chapter 8) an example of this in the way in which art creates imagined worlds (including those of religions) and makes the invisible visible. But religions, with or without art, are in themselves worlds of shared imagination: they are the context in which most human lives have been lived and have been given order, meaning and significance.

The 'worlds' they create are extremely varied and diverse. They are certainly varied and different in the content of what they imagine to be the case. They may, for example, create what Hall called 'a world of wonders' and 'an enchanted universe' which is simply unbelievable to others. He was writing about one particular 'shared imagination', that of people in seventeenth-century New England (Hackett p.29):

> The people of seventeenth-century New England lived in an enchanted universe. Theirs was a world of wonders. Ghosts came to people in the night,

and trumpets blared, though no one saw from where the sound emerged. Nor could people see the lines of force that made a 'long staff dance up and down in the chimney' of William Morse's house. In this enchanted world, the sky on a 'clear day' could fill with 'many companies of armed men in the air, clothed in light-colored garments, and the commander in sad [somber].' Many of the townsfolk of New Haven had seen a phantom ship sail regally into the harbour.... Voices spoke from heaven, and little children uttered warnings. Bending over his son Joseph's cradle one evening, an astonished Samuel Sewall heard him say, 'The French are coming.'

All of these events were 'wonders' to the colonists, events betokening the presence of superhuman or supernatural forces. In seventeenth-century New England it was common to speak of the providence of God as 'wonder-working.' Some wonders were like miracles in being demonstrations of God's power to suspend or interrupt the laws of nature. Others were natural events that God employed as portents or signals of impending change. The events that Cotton Mather described in *Wonders of the Invisible World* were the handiwork of Satan and his minions. A wonder could also be something unexpected or extraordinary, like a sudden death or freak coincidence.

From that particular example it can be seen how easily the shared imaginations of a particular religion identify and deal (often savagely) with a supposed enemy – with supposed witches, for example, in that same New England. That is one half of the paradox of religions, that religions can be extremely bad news for those of whom they disapprove.

At the same time, however, the shared imaginations of religion create effective, stable and thus 'liveable' communities, not least in dealing with what at any particular time is unknown and inexplicable. As Hall went on to point out of that period in New England (p.46),

> The plan and order of the universe was, after all, not always visible or readily deciphered ... there was mystery at the heart of things. Death could strike at any moment, the devil could mislead, the earth begin to tremble. In dramatising all these possibilities, the wonder tale evoked the radical contingency of a world so thoroughly infused with invisible forces.

As a historian, Hall was writing of 'a world of imagination' in the past. But in the case of religions those past imaginations will for some people be the world in which they live. They remain in those familiar worlds even to the extent of resisting change. It is an instance of what is known as 'cultural lag' which has a profound effect on the practice and organisation of religions. It may, for example, produce the contrast between magic and science on which Wittgenstein commented (p.37) in his assessment of Frazer's *The Golden Bough*: "Simple though it may sound, we can express the difference between science and magic if we say that in science there is progress, but not in magic. There is nothing in magic to show the direction of any development."

There is thus an inevitable contrast in religions between conservation and change. When Berlioz arrived in Rome in 1831, he observed with contempt the numerous clergy well adapted to a straightforward nineteenth-century life, but, as Barzun put it (pp.122f), when Berlioz saw a peasant kiss the toe of a statue of St Peter, "he envied the 'happy biped' who had 'faith and hope', for to the educated mind historical criticism stood in the way of literal belief: 'This bronze that you worship and whose right hand holds the keys of heaven was once a *Jupiter tonans* holding lightning. But you know it not, lucky biped!'"

Which then is the real world? Where is the truth of practice and belief to be found? In circles of coherence, it is possible for many different domains of imagination to coexist, and there are no general agreements about whether change is desirable or not. Some, like the Amish in Christianity, are extremely reluctant to change; others, like Anglicans/Episcopalians in Christianity, seek to integrate both the opportunities and the challenges of change – though often in the face of extreme resistance.

There may thus be serious and even violent tension between the two, and there is certainly no general endorsement of 'progress' except towards the attainment of goals specified in the circle. As Bernard Nightingale says in his argument with Valentine, in Tom Stoppard's *Arcadia* (p.87), "Don't confuse progress with perfectibility. A great poet is always timely. A great philosopher is an urgent need. There is no rush for Isaac Newton. We were quite happy with Aristotle's cosmos. Personally, I preferred it. Fifty-five crystal spheres geared to God's crankshaft is my idea of a satisfying universe."

In creating such vivid (though sooner or later vulnerable) worlds, religions have had enduring and extensive importance throughout history. They have been the defining context in which virtually all people have lived their lives – irrespective of what their individual beliefs (or unbeliefs) and practices may have been. In particular, religions are the context in which collective memories are shared and justified, and also are given expression in narratives, practices, beliefs, the organisation of social groups and so on. "The sociology of memory", as Misztal put it, "asserts that the collective memory of the group is quite different from the sum total of the personal recollections of its various individual members" (p.11):

> Memory is social because every memory exists through its relation with what has been shared with others: language, symbols, events, and social and cultural contexts.

The paramount importance of collective memory in religions is obvious. What is missing in Misztal's list is ritual, although Connerton, exploring 'how societies remember', had already before him emphasised the importance of bodily gestures, not least in ritual, in "silting" (to use his word) the contents of collective memory into conscious awareness and behaviour. With that addition it can be seen how central religions have been and still are in the creation of communities of shared imagination.

Not surprisingly, therefore, the ways in which people create and live in their worlds as they imagine them to be, including those of religion, have been an increasingly important subject for anthropologists in recent years. A focal study in that regard has been Benedict Anderson's book, *Imagined Communities*.

Anderson's goal was to explore the ways in which people have come to form their sense of belonging to a particular nation or nationality. What does it mean to someone, or to a group of people, to be Irish/British/Japanese and so on? And to what extent are those 'meanings' identifiable and shared – a question not infrequently asked by politicians? In the case of religions it becomes a question of asking what it means to belong to a particular religion, to be Daoist, Muslim, Christian or whatever; and usually that involves the further question of what it means to be a Protestant Christian, a Catholic Christian, an Orthodox Christian; and usually that involves the further question of what it means to be a Catholic Christian in Lagos or in Rome, and so on.

Anderson argued that in the past the two major cultural systems were the religious community (a coherent imagination created and sustained by sufficiently shared language, beliefs, practices and authority) and the dynastic realm ("a world in which the dynastic realm appeared for most men as the only imaginable 'political' system"; p.19). They were, in what Anderson calls "their heydays", taken-for-granted frames of reference. Religions were communities in which a shared imagination produced "unselfconscious coherence" (p.16). They have been displaced by the rise of nation states and the consequent overriding sense of nationality and national identity

Anderson then argued that those earlier coherent and taken-for-granted communities of shared imagination went into a long decline and fall when 'sacred languages', offering "privileged access to ontological truth", were displaced by print and vernacular languages, and when in consequence the shared imaginations of authority, cosmology and history disintegrated.

There is much in his argument that can be illustrated, but where religions are concerned, it is less successful because religions have proved to be far more resilient as communities of shared imagination than he supposed. Sometimes, indeed, they contradict what he says. For example, when in the nineteenth century Japanese leaders wanted to create a nation state to rival those of Europe, they had to go in exactly the opposite direction to that described by Anderson: they had to create from virtually nothing "a particular script-language [that] offered privileged access to ontological truth", and they had to go back to much earlier ideas about the link between the ruler and cosmological dispensation and to "a conception of temporality in which cosmology and history were indistinguishable". That is the all-important connection between Kokugaku and the Meiji restoration. Far from there being a wedge, harsh or otherwise, between cosmology and history in the Japanese creation of a modern nation state, exactly the opposite was the case.

In any case, it is certainly not true that, as a generalisation, the old sacred languages have been "fragmented, pluralised, and territorialized" as a result of printing. Latin may have declined but Arabic has not (just as Sanskrit has declined but Hindi, with its powerful relationship to the Indian imagination of Hindutva, has not), Nor is it true that the imagination of the world community as a single Ummah is in "slow uneven decline" – distant though it remains as a dream. As a result, far from moving into the acceptance of the nation state, many Muslims reject it with great passion as something imposed by colonial powers. As Saddam Hussein once put it, "The spiteful pencil and scissors of imperialism began to draw up maps, based on ensuring that every part of the Arab homeland ... will remain weak and ineffective towards Arab awakening [i.e., 'urubiyya] and unity as a whole [i.e., Ummah]." When I made the BBC World service series 'What Muslims Believe', one Muslim put it very clearly (Bowker 1995 p.77):

> The biggest obstacle to the realization of the dream of umma is this whole business of national sovereignties. We now have these nation-states. Of course, there are already pan-Islamic, or universalistic, movements, made up of people who want to put the fact of their being a Muslim above the fact of their being an Egyptian or of their being a Pakistani, and so on. So this is clearly something that is going to be on the agenda indefinitely, because it hasn't been achieved yet. But I think there is a potential for it to be achieved. It depends on whether or not the Muslims are prepared to subdue the cultural details of their religion to the scriptural details of their religion. If they say, 'Look, my being a Pakistani or my being an Egyptian is in some sense an accident of birth and biography, but my being a Muslim is a matter of God's grace,' then I think it's quite easy to see that there is real potential for universal community.'

There is no doubt that the ways in which religions create a shared imagination among their adherents are affected greatly by change and especially by secularisation understood, not as a competitive ideology, but as an endorsement of options, freedom (within limits) and choice on the part of relatively autonomous individuals. Wherever the 'preferential option for options' is endorsed politically and socially, it usually results in religions and religious belief becoming optional.

Nevertheless, even in changed circumstances of that kind, religions still create imagined worlds in which many individuals and societies live, and unquestionably they remain axiomatic. One of the ironies, in the light of Anderson's argument, is that many believers (some of them highly organised) in virtually all religions reject modernity. They aspire to recreate a golden age of the past when (so they think) all people believed and acted as they should. It might be the age of the Apostles for some Christians, or the age of the arRashidun (the first four caliphs after Muhammad) for some Muslims, or of the Vedas for some Hindus. That those imagined 'ages of perfection' did not ever exist does not affect the fact that for such believers the way forward has to be the way back to 'the golden age', and on that basis they create strongly bounded communities of shared imagination.[5]

Quite apart from those extreme examples, religions continue to play an immensely important part in creating the imagined worlds of today. The endurance of religions in doing this was well caught by Kamen in his book *Imagining Spain: Historical Myth and National Identity*. Accepting the view that "the myth of Spain as a nation was born around 1808 or 1812" (i.e., in the struggle against the French and the resistance to Napoleon), he argued that modern Spanish nationalism nevertheless created its identity from the past. He therefore began his book with the words (p.ix), "One of the most extraordinary aspects of Spain's sixteenth century is that many Spaniards are still living in it. In a sense they have never left it." They have created an imagined community out of what Kamen calls 'the myths of history' – his seven chapters are called 'The Myth of ...', of the historic nation, of the failed monarchy, of a Christian Spain, of an empire, of the Inquisition, of a universal language, of perpetual decline.

Kamen has a confused, and in some respects factually false, understanding of myth, since in answer to his own question, 'what is a historical myth?', he answers (p.ix), "The first and most obvious definition is that it is not based on reality, and it is in essence a product of the imagination. In that sense, it lacks any empirical evidence to support it. It is, historically speaking, false." Myth, as we have seen, is often based on reality, may have empirical evidence to support it, and will in any case contribute to historical truth. The importance of myth does not rest on it interpreting history rather than legend, but on the way in which, as a product of the imagination, it helps to create our sense of the world or worlds in which we live.

But Kamen's totally mistaken understanding of myth does not affect his basic point that religious beliefs and practices (in this case those of Christianity) are still powerful in creating the worlds of our imagination. Or to be more precise, religions create worlds of shared imagination in which people 'live and move and have their being', and in which they can identify who and what they are, from what origin they come and to what destiny they are going, who belongs to their community and who does not, what they should believe, how they must live and what they must do in order to secure approval and avoid condemnation,

Anthropologists and sociologists have therefore focused on a range of interconnected questions: what kinds of world have the religious imaginations created? What account do these shared imaginations give of the cosmos, of time, of human nature, of appropriate behaviour, or of any other aspects of the experienced world? How have those accounts been made manifest in cultural forms? How have they been translated into practice? How have they been remembered and transmitted through time? In what ways and in what circumstances have they been changed during the course of time, and how have any resulting conflicts been handled? How do authority figures deal with dissidents or with delinquents – with those, in other words, who challenge or subvert the shared imagination? How are the communities of shared imagination sustained and perpetuated particularly in the face of change?

DESCRIPTION AND TRUTH IN THE
UNDERSTANDING OF RELIGIONS

Those are not new questions, and answers to them have been offered, not just by anthropologists and sociologists, but by many others as well, not least by historians. If, however, one addresses the questions in the context of religions as communities of shared imagination, it becomes possible to integrate the answers in a new way in order to understand what it is that creates and sustains the religious communities of shared imagination.

In that context it becomes possible to draw the many different resources together in order to help us to understand how any particular community of shared imagination comes into being and how it sustains itself through the process of time. In addition to the answers offered by anthropologists, sociologists, historians and others, it becomes, not just desirable, but actually necessary to include the answers that arise within the communities themselves. From that it follows that specific answers arise uniquely within the discipline of Religious Studies, and that these too have to be integrated.

Consider, as an illustration of this, the question of how particular beliefs in Christianity led to the persecution of Jews and to anti-Semitism. Historians, sociologists and psychologists give their own important answers to that question. But some equally important answers arise within the religions themselves and within the terms of their own discourse, since those unquestionably act as a constraint on beliefs and behaviours. Religions, for example, generate the powerful and enduring metaphors by which people live – to use once more the title of the book by Latoff and Johnson. Conflicting metaphors can all too easily be translated into destructive action as one can see, by way of example, in the binding of Isaac by his father Abraham in obedience to God's command to sacrifice him (*Bereshith/Genesis* 22.1–19). In Judaism it is the binding, 'Aqedah, that has entered into the Jewish imagination of its own vocation and suffering.[6] Christians, however, take Jewish Scripture as the Old in relation to their own New Testament, and read it as a revelation of God's purpose, culminating, not in Torah, but in the person of Jesus as Christ. For them, therefore, the sacrifice of Isaac prefigures the crucifixion of Jesus understood as the supreme and consummating sacrifice. The Jewish understanding has been displaced by the Christian, and that displacement became increasingly aggressive in a way that, in general, the New Testament is not, even though the theme of displacement is present.

This means that, in addition to the reasons offered by historians and sociologists, there are also powerful constraints derived from the religions themselves – as here from the Christian imagination of itself, of its relationship with the Jews and of God's relationship to both. There is no access to those constraints through the analysis of individual or social behaviour. As Auerbach observed (p.64) of the Christian use of the binding of Isaac, "a connection is established between two events which are linked neither temporarily nor causally – a connection which it is impossible to establish by reason in the horizontal dimension.... It can be established only if both occurrences are vertically linked to Divine Providence, which alone is able to devise such a plan of history and supply the key to its understanding."

The paralysis that has occurred in the study of religions arises from our inability thus far to connect beyond the level of description the accounts offered by anthropologists, sociologists, historians and others with those that function creatively within the communities of shared imagination. For the critics of religion with whom this book began, the religious communities of shared imagination are so clearly 'not true' (as we have seen in Kamen's understanding of myth) that they cannot enter into 'scientific' explanations of cause.

If, however, we remember that what we should be seeking in our attempts to understand human behaviour is not an isolated cause but a multiplicity of constraints (as we have seen repeatedly throughout this book), then it is no longer a competition between the most probably true and the obviously false. In other words, it cannot be a matter of history versus myth, or of truth versus invention, or of fact versus fiction. What we need to identify are the ways in which the past, however it is understood, enters into, informs and nourishes (i.e., constrains) the shared imagination of any particular community, and how the opportunities of that shared imagination are appropriated by individuals in their own particular ways. But that, of course, requires a serious understanding of what religions actually are. How can that be done?

The immediate answer is, With difficulty. This book alone, even though it has been focused on a particular question, will have indicated how much is involved in the study and understanding of religions, both in content and method. How can we study something that cannot even be defined? Strictly speaking it is not the case that 'religion' *cannot* be defined, because very many attempts have been made to do so. It is, rather, that no definition can ever catch anything as complex and diverse as religion. That is why, as we saw earlier, Jonathan Smith argued that those studying religion must have their own imagination of what religion is, and Wittgenstein insisted that we should look, not for definitions, but for family resemblances.

So what are the resemblances that allow us to speak of 'religions' as forming a family? They are far too many to summarise in a book. Hastings' Encyclopaedia of Religion (and Ethics) ran to twenty volumes, Eliade's to eighteen. In fact, Encyclopaedias of that kind are immensely helpful because the study and understanding of religion must rest on clear and (so far as possible) dispassionate accounts and descriptions.

That is the work of phenomenology at the first level: it sets out to describe the phenomena of the religious world – so far as possible in a value-free way. That in itself is no easy task given how many different methodologies of description there are, how vast and immensely detailed the worlds of shared imagination are that religions create, and how many of them have persisted through millennia. Religions as communities of shared imagination bring into being the metaphorical and literal constraints which, when they are internalised, create lives of brilliant, though sometimes equally terrifying, consequence. They enable people to tell the stories of their lives in ways that make sense – and in ways also that unify the narrative of the present with the past and the future.

This means that the shared imagination of any particular religion is in itself (in its own constructed circle) coherent and comprehensive, even though its adherents may dissent in detail or may have major differences among themselves, and even though it changes greatly in the course of time. To put it more jargonistically, a religion is neither synchronically nor diachronically immutably the same, and yet its adherents (no matter how much they reject, or for that matter murder, each other) can be picked out through the family resemblances they share.

What that means in less jargonistic terms (to revert, by way of example, to the imagined world of John Bunyan and *The Pilgrim's Progress* above) is, first, that the world constructed by Christian imagination in the seventeenth century is very different from the world constructed by Christian imagination in the twenty-first century; and second, that at any particular time those identifying themselves as Christians disagree (often violently) about the imagined world in which they live: the Thirty Years War ended when John Bunyan was twenty years old, and the imagined world in which he lived was very different from the world of Urban VIII who was Pope in Rome at the time. Yet they both belong, at least in a descriptive sense, to the same 'family'.

It follows that the challenge to phenomenology at the first, descriptive level is formidable because there is so much to be described. But there is then a further challenge to phenomenology at the first level – the attempt to describe *in a value-free way* the phenomena of the religious world. It is of course true that a 'value-free' description of virtually anything is impossible because we carry our values with us in everything we do. Nevertheless, the attempt must be made at this first level to suspend (or, as Husserl would have said, 'bracket out') our own beliefs and value judgements of the worth or truth of what we are describing.

But questions of value or truth do not go away simply because they are suspended. That is why there is (and has to be) a *second* level of phenomenology, a level that is often ignored in the study of religion. On the basis of first-level description, it is essential then to ask: What is it that has brought those phenomena into being? Given that x presents itself evidentially and given that we have tried to describe x as dispassionately as possible, we are then entitled to ask: What may we (and on occasion what must we) infer as a *sufficient reason or reasons* for the appearance of x? It is the immense merit of Deeley's work on 'the religious brain' and of Flood's work on 'the importance of religion' that they keep *both* levels in play together.

Here, as so often, the importance of abductive inference returns. We have already seen how much we rely on abductive inference in the sciences as well as in the humanities. At the second level of phenomenology, we are asking what it is that has brought into being the phenomena we are trying to understand: what ontologically has evoked the words and language that we use? Frequently such questions cannot be answered except by abductive inference. Those answers are rarely certain, as we have seen: they have to be held in a tentative and cautious way, or indeed with trust and faith.

It remains the case, therefore, that although the answers to the second-level question will be approximate, provisional and corrigible, they must nevertheless be attempted since without them there cannot be any serious appreciation of what religions are and why they matter so much. Husserl glimpsed this long ago and opened the way to a far more profound understanding of how questions of truth can be related to value-free description.[7]

The interlocking conjunction between the two levels of phenomenology means also that we are rescued from the impoverished and reductionist explanations of religion which, as we saw in the case of Wilson, Dawkins, Jones, Hitchens and the other critics with whom this book began, cannot engage with questions of truth (however approximately expressed) in the case of religions. Wilson and Dawkins in particular are surely correct in their claim that religions have been decisively important in protecting human life, but the success of religions in doing that cannot be accounted for in terms of structure and function alone. In part it rests on the adequacy and truth of their beliefs (however approximately expressed), and in particular on their beliefs about the nature and opportunities of human life – beliefs that have been tested *and winnowed* through long periods of time, as we saw (albeit briefly) in Chapter 2.

When we put the two levels of phenomenology together, we achieve a far richer and more accurate understanding of religions because the foundation in dispassionate description gives rise to abductive considerations of truth and value. Inference in general, and abductive inference in particular, form a bridge between correspondence and coherence. Always we are asking what it is that has evoked the vocabularies of human discourse. As a result, we can see at last how Religious Studies and Theology (often uneasy partners at best) must necessarily belong together.

That immediately makes possible an understanding of why religions matter from the point of view, not just of the outside observer, but also and at the same time of the participant and believer. On that basis we achieve a clear understanding, as this book has tried to show, of the paradox of religions: why it is that religions can be such a bad news only because they are such good news. It *then* becomes possible to do something together about the dangers that confront us. We can observe and attempt to describe with detachment (in the context, usually, of theory), and we can equally enter into the circles of religions in order to understand what it is that has evoked their own descriptions of what matters to them and why. We then have some chance of applying *together* the fundamental principle of maximising the good and minimising the damage.

The familiar questions which we have encountered repeatedly in this book do not disappear: who defines the good? What happens when those definitions are so different that they lead to contest and conflict? Those and the many other questions raised in this book have not changed. What *has* changed by holding together the two levels of phenomenology is the style and purpose that we bring to them: we now have a new and entirely different *context* in which those divisive and intransigent issues can be addressed. In that context there is just a chance that we might defuse the anger and avert the dangers with which this book began. And even beyond that we might begin to share and take delight in the imaginations that have made us what we are.

A final word: the original draft of this book included two chapters showing how in practice this understanding of religions was applied in recent years to specific issues ranging from the beginnings of the Hospice movement to the United Nations Declaration on religions and apartheid. The chapters were dropped because they made the book far too long, but in any case they come from a vanished world. The IT revolution has created vastly different opportunities to develop together this new understanding of religions and apply it in practical ways. So the next stage belongs to those who know and live in the IT world and have scarcely known any other. I am sure that enough of them will see the point and the urgency, and I wish them well.

Notes

1 INTRODUCTION

1   In Marx and Engels, *On Britain*.
2   *Introduction to a Contribution to the Critique of Hegel's Philosophy of Right*, in Marx and Engels, *On Religion*, 1958.
3   Hindutva, 'the quality of the Hindu way' found in the entire entity of land, people, beliefs and practices, was introduced by Savarkar in 1923: "A Hindu is he ... who above all addresses this land, this Sindhusthan, as his *punyabhu*, as his Holyland – the land of his prophets and seers, of his godmen and gurus, the land of piety and pilgrimage."
4   Juergensmeyer (1993), p.195. See also *Terror in the Mind of God: The Global Rise of Religious Violence*, 2003. There is now extensive research and publication on religions and violence. See especially Juergensmeyer (2013), and also for further reading Hinnells and King; de Vries; Lorimer.
5   The essays are collected in Lorimer, and they contain extremely helpful material relating to Christianity, Islam, Buddhism, Hinduism and New Religious Movements. They are a response to the criticisms of Hitchens and his claim that "religion poisons everything. As well as a menace to civilisation, it has become a threat to human survival." In response to the question, "Are the world's major religions the root cause of terrorism?", the book answers 'no' (p.143). But it can only do so on the basis of two different assumptions. The first is that the authors can base their work on an agreed definition of terrorism (the Academic Consensus Definition which first appeared in 1984: see Schmid & Longman, pp.1f.). But that leads to strange conclusions: for example, it enables one contributor to conclude that traditional Christianity condemns violence and with it terrorism without mentioning the Inquisition or the Christian pogroms against the Jews. The second assumption is that there are single or root causes of complex phenomena. The mistake in that assumption is the reason for the analysis in this book of the relationship between causes and constraints.

2 THE PARADOX OF RELIGIONS

1   *Prejudices*, 1923, pp.232ff; see also Bowker, 1978, pp.1–3.
2   For a fuller account of this, see 'Sex and Safety: A New Crisis Facing Religions', in Bowker 2007, pp.149–70.
3   George, p.26.
4   For a summary see Bowker 2002, pp.32–35.

5 On the importance of language in the creation of communities of shared imagin-ation, see further p.280

6 See Bowker 2011, pp.167f.

7 For a summary of the issues involved, see the Introduction to Flood (2012), and in more detail 'The "Idea" of Religion', in Flood 1999, ch. 2; see also Bowker, 1997, Introduction.

8 Turner in Volf, 2012b, p.22: "It is obvious, I suppose, that the category of 'religion' is a taxonomic term of principally academic provenance. I mean, I know of no one at all who actually practises 'religion'. For sure I don't. I am a practising Catholic Christian." That observation, however, becomes untrue as soon as a pronoun is added to the word 'religion'. People practise 'their religion', just as I may practise 'my religion'. Turner practises his religion as a Catholic Christian.

9 This is from the heading to chapter 16 in *Daniel Deronda* (ed.cit., p.160): "Men, like planets, have both a visible and invisible history. The astronomer threads the dark-ness with strict deduction, accounting so for every invisible arc in the wanderer's orbit; and the narrator of human actions, if he did his work with the same complete-ness, would have to thread the hidden pathways of feeling and thought which lead up to every moment of action."

10 See, for example, Kar, 1978, esp., pp.99, 110.

11 The distinction is well expressed by Walker, 1989, pp.2ff "The coherence theorist holds that for a proposition to be true is for it to cohere with a certain system of beliefs. It is not just that it is true if and only if it coheres with that system; it is that the coherence, and nothing else, is what its truth consists in. In particular, truth does not consist in the holding of some correspondence between the proposition and some reality which obtains independent of anything that may be believed about it. This is a radical thesis."

12 For a fuller discussion of coherence and correspondence, see Bowker 2009, pp.118–133.

13 In their account of evolutionary psychology, Cosmides and Tooby take that phrase to imply that those early theologians (they mention Aquinas specifically) held the view that "the human mind resembles a blank slate, virtually free of content until written on by the hand of experience." Whether or not they held that view affects, but is nevertheless independent of, their account of intellectual activity. Aquinas in particular has a far more subtle understanding of *intellectus*, and he is certainly not a precursor of John Locke and later British empiricists.

14 Polanyi, 1958, p.17.

15 That particular comment was made of Chinese art in Bowker 2007, p.66.

16 Thackeray, *Pendennis* (1848–50), Preface.

17 For a clear discussion of the issues raised by abductive inference, see Shepherd 1975.

18 Bowker 1973, pp.119f, discusses this and Freud's misuse of Vaihinger.

19 The titles of these books (details in the Bibliography) exemplify the point: Broad and Wade, *Betrayers of the Truth: Fraud and Deceit in Science*; Waller, *Fabulous Science: Fact and Fiction in the History of Scientific Discovery*, 2002; Gratzer, *The Undergrowth of Science: Delusion, Self-deception and Human Frailty*, 2000.

20 Statement issued by the Director of the Institute, *The Chronicle*, 16.5.11.

21 There are more than 20,000 scientific journals with an electronic data base of at least forty million items to which additions are being made at the rate of about two per minute.

22 The refusal of drug companies to publish negative results was attacked by Goldacre in *Bad Pharma: How Drug Companies Mislead Doctors and Harm Patients* (2012). In February 2013, GlaxoSmithKline agreed to release thousands of items of unpublished data online. A spokesman said: "We are committed to being transparent about clinical trial data to advance scientific understanding and inform medical judgement" (*The Times*, February 6, 2013). Yet on January 3, 2014, Richard Bacon (a UK MP and member of the Public Accounts Committee) observed in an interview on the BBC Today programme that "for years and years drugs companies have been able legally to withhold from the public domain information about their clinical trials." He argued that the companies should publish the many millions of pages of data as yet unpublished on the grounds that negative results are important, and that published data may be seriously distorted when related negative results are not published. It remains to be seen whether anything will change.

23 *PLoS [Public Library of Science] Medicine*, 30 August 2005. This article was received with considerable anger, but more recently Ioannidis has claimed, not only that the situation has got worse but that is now compounded by repeated publication of the same results: see, e.g., Sionitis *et al.* 2013, f4501.

24 'BBC Trust Review of Impartiality and Accuracy of the BBC's Coverage of Science', July 2011.

25 *The Daily Telegraph*, 14 December 2011, p.31. For the theory, see Margulis 1992.

26 In *Dandelion Days* (p.204), Mr Rore of Colham School encourages his pupil Maddison to work harder – *ad astra per aspera* – and not to be content "to lie on his back in the sun all day and let ripe bananas drop into his mouth: overcome that banana inclination!"

27 See Moore 1989.

28 On one occasion the physicist Landau put forward one of his ideas to Pauli, and when he sensed that Pauli was not convinced, he asked with some asperity whether Pauli thought that his ideas were nonsensical. Pauli replied, "Not at all, not at all. Your ideas are so confused I cannot tell whether they are nonsense or not."

29 In the *Blue Book* Wittgenstein suggested that we would be wise to curb our craving for generality, our tendency, that is, to look for something in common in all the entities which we describe under a general term. The example which he gave was the word 'games'. The word is often used as though there are features common to all games (for example, competition or rules) from which a definition of the word 'games' can be derived. Against this, Wittgenstein argued that what games have in common are not single, universal properties, but many resemblances that characterise certain very diverse activities as 'games'. He called those resemblances 'family resemblances'. In *Philosophical Investigations* 66–67 he wrote:

> Consider for example the proceedings that we call 'games'. I mean board-games, card-games, ball-games, Olympic Games, and so on. What is common to them all? – Don't say: 'There *must* be something in common, or they would not be called 'games'' – But *look and see* whether there is anything common

to all. For if you look at them you will not see something that is common to *all* but similarities, relationships, and a whole series of them at that. To repeat: don't think, but look! ... And the result of this examination is: we see a complicated network of similarities overlapping and criss-crossing: sometimes overall similarities, sometimes similarities of detail. [67] I can think of no better expression to characterise these similarities than 'family resemblances'; for the various resemblances between the members of a family: build, features, colour of eyes, gait, temperament, etc. etc. overlap and criss-cross in the same way. And I shall say: 'games' form a family.

30 Cyprian wrote originally (*Ep.*72), "Salus extra ecclesiam non est." The application to others, both Christian (i.e., heretical or schismatic people outside a particular 'inner circle') and non-Christian, has often been made – for example, at the Council of Florence in the Decree for the Jacobites, 1442:

> She [the Holy Roman Church] firmly believes, professes and preaches that no one who remains outside the Catholic Church, not only pagans but also Jews, heretics and schismatics, can become partakers of eternal life but will go to the everlasting fire prepared for the devil and his angels [*Matthew* 25.41] unless before the end of their life they are received into it.

31 Newman (1845), pp.93f. According to Newman, the mind must be broken in and reason must submit to believing all or nothing: reason, in other words, must not engage in selecting on its own terms which of "the mysteries of faith" in the protected circle of Catholicism it will believe or not believe (1861, pp.274f):

> I come then to this conclusion; if I must submit my reason to mysteries, it is not much matter whether it is a mystery more or a mystery less, when faith anyhow is the very essence of all religion.... When once the mind is broken in, as it must be, to the belief of a Power above it, when once it understands that it is not itself the measure of all things in heaven and earth, it will have little difficulty in going forward.

32 Huxley, 1870, p.viii.

3 RELIGIONS AND SCIENCES
I MYTH AND MEANING: 'THE WARFARE BETWEEN SCIENCE AND RELIGION'

1 In *Lectures* II §39 he condemned "the Pride of Faith" which leads believers to "withdraw from all such true services of man, that they may pass the best part of their lives in what they are told is the service of God; namely, desiring what they cannot obtain, lamenting what they cannot avoid, and reflecting what they cannot understand." When he revised the lectures in 1887, Ruskin realised that he had been too severe and he added a note: "This concentrated definition of monastic life is of course to be understood only of its more enthusiastic forms." By then he had seen a better side of Roman Catholicism, having had lunch with Cardinal Manning. He wrote afterwards in a letter, "I lunched with Cardinal Manning, and he gave me *such* a pie. I never tasted a Protestant pie to touch it. He gave me lovely soup, roast beef, hare and currant jelly, puff pastry like Papal pretensions – you had but to breathe on

it and it was nowhere – raisins and almonds, and those lovely preserved cherries like kisses kept in amber."

2   *Praeterita* 2.2.24.

3   Ruskin was at least even-handed between Protestants and Roman Catholics. He had left the Protestants in 1858 after his experience in the Turin Chapel listening to (as he put it in his diary) "a poor little wretch in a tidy black tie … expounding Nothing with a Twang."

4   Elementary Education Act. 1870, 14.2.

5   It published its report in 1970 as *The Fourth R* (i.e., in addition to the three Rs, reading, 'riting and 'rithmetic), a title that reflected the acceptance in the far-reaching 1944 Education Act that Religious Education (or Religious Instruction as it was often called) should be compulsory, as in practice it already was.

6   "One day a friend put *The Origin of Species* into his hands. This wrecked his faith; chiefly because it was not reconcilable with the biblical account of creation, and as the biblical revelation hung together and was all of one piece, if part of it fell out, the rest would fall out too. If Adam never existed, he did not sin; if he did not sin, man was not fallen; there was therefore no need for Christ to come. If the Bible was wrong in science, how could we be sure it was right in Theology? We fail in justice and in sympathy if we make light of the real agony of mind through which he and many of his contemporaries passed" (Leeson, pp.97f).

7   Arnold wrote those words originally in 1880, in the Introduction to T.H. Ward's *The English Poets*, reprinted as 'The Study of Poetry', in *Essays in Criticism*, Second Series, 1888.

8   The reaction of Christians to Darwin and the theory of evolution was extremely diverse. There is an excellent introductory survey of that diversity in Brooke, 'Christian Darwinians', in Robinson 2012.

9   The extent and detail of this pre-Darwinian work on geohistory has been described and analysed in Rudwick's two superb volumes (2005, 2008).

10   For some examples of attempts at definition, see Bowker 1997, pp.xvf. The difficulty is why Smith argued in his book, *Imagining Religion* (1982), that academics engaging in the study of religion have to create their own imagination or understanding of what it is they are studying.

11   Maxwell 1876, p.2.

12   *Works* 5.133. On Victorian attitudes to myth, see Kissane, pp.5–28; see also Landow 1971.

13   The shift in meaning of the words 'myth' and 'mythology' can be seen, by way of example, in the title of the book by Roberts, *The Mythology of the Secret Societies*: in earlier times the book would have recorded and examined the myths those societies told and preserved, but in fact the book is about the false beliefs ('myth' is equated with 'nonsense' on p.15) held *about* those Societies by others – including what we would now call conspiracy theories.

14   In 'A Garland of Precepts':

> Pressed for rules and verities
> All I recollect are these:
> Feed a cold to starve a fever.
> Argue with no true believer.

Think too-long is never-act.
Scratch a myth and find a fact.

15 See Beckett, especially ch. 6. She accepted, of course, that Wagner drew on many
    sources (well reviewed in ch. 1), but for her the work remains profoundly and
    "properly Christian" in its essential theme of Redeemer and redemption: "It ... is
    properly Christian, even if its Christianity is sometimes overlaid by remnants of
    Schopenhauer which Wagner saw no more cause to expunge than the remnants of
    pagan magic" (p.136).

16 Tanner 1979. Tanner argued that while *Parsifal* is clearly a work *about* religion, it is not a
    religious work. It is an exposition of "the psychopathology of religions belief" (p.209).

4 RELIGIONS AND SCIENCES
II DOGMATISM AND DOUBT

1 Newman, *Apologia pro Vita Sua* (1864), 1959, p.132 – committing, ironically, the fallacy of the falsely dichotomous question.

2 Bierce, *The Devil's Dictionary, ad loc.*; in the recovered and original work, *The
   Enlarged Dictionary*, he also defined religion as "A goodly tree, in which all the foul
   birds of the air have made their nests."

3 Mencken, 1942. Mencken was making a cross-reference to Pascal, "People never do
   evil so completely and cheerfully as when they do it from religious conviction."

4 This is discussed briefly in Bowker 2014, ch. 1.

5 There is a clear account of the methods of argument underlying 'disputation' and
   'determination' in Chenu ch. 2, 'The Procedures of Exposition'.

6 For a description of Hadith and for further reading, see Bowker 2011, pp.133–7.

7 The three gates are *kama* (desire), *krodha* (anger) and *lobha* (greed).

8 See further Bowker 1987, pp.46ff.

9 For a brief account of the way in which the work of Husserl lends itself to the understanding of religion and of Theology, see Bowker 1995, pp.158–80.

10 See 'Narrative Theory' in Flood 1999.

11 The examples are given in Bowker 1978, p.62 from Colenso pp.33, 61, 128. Colenso
   made the calculations because they involved a deep pastoral problem, the veracity
   of the foundations of the faith which he was encouraging among the Zulu people:
   "My heart answered in the words of the Prophet, Shall a man speak lies in the name
   of the Lord? I dared not do so [Zechariah 13.3]." Colenso was bitterly attacked and
   was deposed as bishop and excommunicated, although he continued to exercise his
   ministry.

12 1871, I, p.163.

13 For a brilliant summary of this transformation and of the reasons for it, see
   Harvey 2012.

14 For an account of this exploration of empiricism in a Muslim context, see Bowker
   1978, pp.192–243.

15 Roland. What's the desert made of?

> Gavin. Well ... I've never been there.
> Some deserts are made of sand and some are made of grit but –
> Mother (as if to herself).
> This one is made of doubts and dried-up hopes.

16 Sloterdijk, p.48.

5 RELIGIONS AND SCIENCES
III THE SELFLESS GENE: GENETIC DETERMINISM
AND HUMAN FREEDOM

1 The study of 'implicit religion' was pioneered and developed by Edward Bailey in his Centre for the Study of Implicit Religion and Contemporary Spirituality. In a personal communication he summarised his understanding of implicit religion:

> The concept of implicit religion took shape as a way of encapsulating the question, What does he stand for?, or, What makes her tick? ... The concept of Implicit Religion invites us to consider whether talk of people's "devotion" to their children, the "sacrifices" they make in order to "better" themselves, or the "spiritual" benefits of undergoing the "rituals" of a health centre, might be closer to what is conventionally called religious than we may sometimes think. We ask whether there might be a religious dimension to ordinary life (even if the religion is of a kind we've never met before), in order to enhance our overall understanding, both of others and of ourselves.

2 See, e.g., *Social Science, ...* 1959.
3 Halsey, *Oxford Dictionary of National Biography*, 2004, *ad loc.*
4 For the importance of this in understanding secularisation see Berger pp.1ff, Bowker 2002, pp.316–17.
5 Coniff and Foster, June 25, 2006. In the human case, however, it is not a matter only of subordination. There may be specific gene contributions to cooperative and altruistically supportive behaviours, not least through satisfaction systems.
6 In *Consilience* (1999), Wilson defined consilience as "literally a 'jumping together' of knowledge by the linking of facts and fact-based theory across disciplines to create a common ground work of explanation" (p.7).
7 See Bowker 1990, pp.7–22.
8 *prasada* comes from *pra+√sad*, 'brightness', 'clarity'. By bringing light to bear and by thus clearing away ignorance and anxiety, *prasada* brings 'serenity' and 'a calm disposition'. It is thus an act of kindness and generosity. As such, it refers particularly to the offerings made by a worshipper and to the part left generously for the worshippers. It thus comes to refer to the generous kindness of God which is not earned or merited. See Sharma and Hejib, pp.18f.
9 "The principle of *adhikara* or eligibility refers to the fact that human beings differ in their taste and capacities, needs and aspirations and, therefore, no single rule of life can help all alike" (Warrier, p.418).
10 The distinction between teleology and teleonomy, and its decisive importance in understanding evolution, is described and discussed in Bowker 1981, pp.98–126.
11 It may seem frivolous to use these terms in such an inexact way, but the purpose is to draw attention quickly and briefly to a difference in emphasis on the effect of seminal/genetic inheritance.
12 The debate about altruism, kinship altruism and reciprocal altruism is summarised in Bowker 1995a, pp.33f.

6 RELIGIONS AND SCIENCES
IV CAUSES AND CONSTRAINTS

1 'Newton's sleep' is the phrase through which William Blake is supposed to have attacked Isaac Newton. When the new British Library was opened, it featured

Paolozzi's sculpture based on Blake's supposed ridicule of Newton portraying him at the bottom of the sea stooping over geometrical designs. So the sculpture was criticised at the time on the ground that it celebrated the Romantic contempt for science (as at Haydon's "immortal evening" in Elwin, pp.316f). The criticism was misplaced. Blake admired the genius of Newton and called him "a mighty spirit". He placed him, at the climax of *Jerusalem*, along with Bacon and Locke among the Chariots of the Almighty. What Blake wished to convey was his belief that 'a mighty spirit' attending only to analysis would be asleep to the additional and much wider concerns of humanity. He therefore placed in the Chariots Shakespeare, Milton and Chaucer. Blake would have criticised 'Dawkin's sleep' for the same reason, while still admiring the achievements of genetics.

2 See Bate 1969, p.112.

3 The Greek word *adutos* means literally 'not to be entered', hence, and usually, the innermost sanctuary and shrine: see, e.g., Homer *Iliad* 5.448, 512.

4 Bodley manuscript Shelley d.1.

5 On the focus of 'Newton's sleep', see note 1 to this chapter.

6 See W.T. Jones, p.126.

7 For the correspondent breeze as a romantic metaphor, see Abrams, pp.37–54.

8 Koubeissi's research, for example, on epilepsy and consciousness "suggests that a single area, the claustrum, might be integral to combining disparate brain activity into a seamless package of thoughts" (Thomas, p.10), but this research, as Thomas comments, "is incredibly intriguing but it is one brick in a large edifice of consciousness that we're trying to build" (p.11).

9 Bowker in Watts 2008, quoting Fraser, p.24.

10 See Bowker 2007, pp.101–2.

11 The quotation and its relevance to individual intention and action are discussed in Bowker 1995b, pp.18ff: "No one presumably doubts that even the will of Caesar is constrained. Let us even say, for the moment (in order to avoid being diverted into arguments about free will), that his will is *wholly* constrained; let us, in other words, agree with Caesar: 'What can be avoided/ Whose end is purposed by the mighty gods?' Even then, the means through which those constraints are brought to bear which take him to the Senate (the dreams of Calpurnia, the auguries, the persuasions of Brutus, Artemidorus, the soothsayer – and these are only the most immediate) are innovatory in the sequential construction of Caesar's action. Yet if that is so, then it would be quite impossible, on behavioural grounds alone, to exclude an effect within the individual of the reality (supposing there is one) of the objects of his belief."

12 Darwin to Lyell, 28 September 1860, Darwin Correspondence Project, No.2931.

13 For a fuller discussion of the frame problem and of its importance, see Bowker 1995a, pp.54, 252–54.

14 p.86. Pattee p.262 makes the same point that "someone or something must choose what to ignore about the system."

15 For an example of this, see 'In sheltering flame' in Bowker 2010, pp.19f.

7 UNDERSTANDING RELIGIONS
I ISSUES OF TRANSLATION AND INTERPRETATION

1 Jeffery (1937) gathered many in preparation for a critical edition of the Quran. For an introduction to the field, see Jeffery 1952.

2 Many are described in Bowker 2011.

3 Letter to *The Daily Telegraph*, 26 September, 2011, p.25.

4 *The Tablet*, 19 January 2013, p.9.

5 *The Tablet*, 31 October 2009, p.29. Taylor (2010), President of ICEL from 1997, recorded how the Vatican Congregation for Divine Worship overruled the agreed ICEL translation and imposed what he called "a disciplinary Exocet missile", insisting on extreme literalism instead of the previously favoured 'dynamic equivalence'.

6 On Targums, see Bowker 1969.

7 There is a clear example of this in Jeremiah 4.24 where, in the context, the Hebrew can only mean, "and I not make a full end of it? [I most certainly will]. Therefore ...".

8 For this episode, see Bate 1967, pp. 84–89.

9 The word 'tendency' may of course be used, not of doctrinal changes, but of consistent reasons why the text of a document was changed over time. For examples, see Sanders.

10 Bettelheim 1991, p.vii. On Freud's ambition to become 'the Newton of the human head', see Bowker, *The Sense of God*, pp.5f, 121–27.

11 Even so, it is important to remember that 'wrong' translations can have a life of their own and can have enduring importance. A good example of this is the translation in the Authorised Version of Job 19.25-7:

> I know that my Redeemer liveth,
> And that he shall stand at the latter day upon the earth:
> And though after my skin worms destroy this body,
> Yet in my flesh shall I see God,
> Whom I shall see for myself,
> And mine eyes shall behold, and not another.

Once Handel had used those words in his oratorio *The Messiah*, they became the constantly renewed and inspiring meaning of the text. The Hebrew text, however, is extremely uncertain, although it does make clear that Job is using the common biblical theme of the law court, insisting that he is innocent and that God will come as his defending counsel to prove it. A possible translation is:

> I know that the one who takes my side [or 'is my advocate'] is active, and that as the final speaker he will stand up in court. I will see my witness standing beside me, and my defending counsel I will see to be none other than God.

In this instance a translation that can be said to be wrong is of far greater consequence than any other suggestions.

8 UNDERSTANDING RELIGIONS
II BEING RELIGIOUSLY HUMAN: THE INTERNALISATION
OF CONSTRAINT IN ETHICS AND ART

1 Whitehouse 2000. The two 'modes of religiosity' are proposed in his *Inside the Cult* and applied in *Arguments and Icons*.

2 For the Ikkarim (Thirteen Principles) of Maimonides, and for Creeds and Confessions in Christianity, see Bowker 2011, pp.38, 69–72.

3 In 'Religions as Systems' (p.179), I drew attention to the problems faced by Taylor and Fayol when they tried to incorporate into their system design theory what they called "unanticipated mean behavioural patterns."

4 The treatment of Curran and others by the Congregation for the Doctrine of the Faith (CDF) under Cardinal Ratzinger before he became Pope Benedict is described (with interviews) in Collins.

5 Beliefs as constraints over outcomes are equally obvious in architecture. For an example in the case of Egypt, see p.241.

6 Sabartés pp.147–49. Picasso was responding to the question whether artists should paint from life: "People think that bullfights in my pictures were copied from life, but they are mistaken. I used to paint them before I'd seen the bullfight so as to make money to buy my ticket ... The important thing is to create. Nothing else matters: creation is all; ... The value of a work resides precisely in what it is not."

7 See Bowker 2007, pp.85–95.

8 "The danger and evil of their [Roman Catholic] church decoration, altogether, lie ... in its tinsel and glitter, in the buildings of the shrine and painting of the image, in embroidery of dingy robes, and crowding of imitated gems."

9 Mather, p.100: "With appalling monotony, ten thousand times ten thousand, she, for it was always she, appeared and reappeared on Salon walls. When her nudity had been approved by a medal, she was transferred to a public museum."

10 In his poem 'Terra Incognita', Lawrence sought escape from known and inherited tradition into a new world of direct and immediate experience:

> There are vast realms of consciousness still undreamed of
> vast ranges of experience, like the humming of unseen harps,
> we know nothing of, within us.
> Oh when man has escaped from the barbed-wire entanglement
> of his own ideas and his own mechanical devices
> there is a marvellous rich world of contact and sheer fluid beauty
> and fearless face-to-face awareness of now-naked life ....

11 See Britt 1995.

12 The title of his book published in Munich in 1932.

13 Op.cit., p.5.

14 On the similarities as well as distinctions, see Clark, pp.73–74.

15 On the importance of storytelling in India in which a storyteller is "a conduit for ultimate truths" (Narayan, p.246), see Bowker 2011, p.183.

16 For a comparison in another tradition, see Brown on the Holkham Bible, pp.9f.

17 The words are not exact synonyms but come from different areas of Australia giving priority to different aspects of 'The Dreaming'.

18 This scroll is in the Sanso Collection in California. It is reproduced in Stanley-Baker p.184.

19 An early Jewish text in the Mishnah, more usually called The Chapters [or Sayings] of the Fathers. The quotation is from R. Eleazar haKappar, 4.22.

20 See, for example, the poem 'Atonement' in Bowker (2010), p.80.

21 It is reproduced in Hyman and Wright, p.235.

22 The controversy focused on his depiction of Synagogue and on whether he was depicting traditional bigotry and anti-Semitism. The question, in other words, was whether he had attempted to understand the symbols that he used. Promey's book is an illuminating study of the artist's role and responsibility in public art.

23 In a leaflet for the Jubilee Festival at St Matthew's in 1943. It is quoted here from Read, p.154.

24 "Ce n'est pas un travail qui j'ai choisi mais bien un travail pour lequel j'ai été choisi par le destin sur la fin de ma route, que je continue selon mes recherches, la chapelle me donnant l'occasion de les fixer en les réunissant."

25 Lawson, p.9. Lawson then added the comment that in this respect, Mach's pieces "executed by a sceptic, but affecting the devout … are part of a new cultural trend." There is nothing new about it; and when he also wrote, "I believe that Mach's work is part of a new – and, in many ways, counter-historical – artistic re-examination of sacred images", he is equally wrong about history and religious art.

26 On the burning of books (and works of art), see the Conclusion to Bowker 2011.

27 Letter to DrTrusler, 23 August 1799, in Keynes, p.793.

28 Blake, 'A Vision of the Last Judgement', in Keynes pp.605, 617.

9 UNDERSTANDING RELIGIONS
III RITUAL AND THE HUMAN IMAGINATION OF DEATH

1 Giedion 1964. Having summarised Egyptian and Mesopotamian attitudes toward death, Giedion pointed out (pp.11f.):

> Unlike Egypt, in Mesopotamia there could be no impetus to create an architecture based on such vague and intangible convictions and such an abysmally pessimistic approach to life after death. The dead had to rest beneath the earth. There was nothing for them in heaven. Everyone must descend to the nether world to the 'land of no return.' It would thus be senseless to erect permanent dwelling places for the dead. So Mesopotamian graves were simply covered with earth, and thus it remained.... Architecturally, Mesopotamian tombs were without significance. Yet this was the period when the great pyramids of Cheops, Chephren, and Mycerinus were storming the heavens.

2 See Shafer 2005.

3 On the Shanidar burials, see Solecki, pp.389–425. On the crippling injury, see Stewart, pp.274–78. The poem is from Bowker 1995b, pp.57f.

4 Publius Syrus, *Sententiae*, 463.

5 The same pattern has subsequently been discerned in other momentous and socially significant transitions, as, for example, the movement from peace to war: see, e.g., J. Smith (*Tapu …*), pp.11–13.

6 For an introduction to this research, see Deeley 2004, and for a much briefer summary, see Bowker 2007.

7 This is predictable on the basis of Whitehouse's characterisation of the 'doctrinal' mode of religiosity (see p.192) and of what Collinson called "the logocentric iconoclasm" of the second English Reformation.

8 See, e.g., Granqvist, pp.82–84.

9 For an example, see Tipler.

10 Bowker 1991, p.39.

10 UNDERSTANDING RELIGIONS
IV RELIGIONS AND IMAGINATION; COMMUNITIES OF SHARED EXPLORATION AND DISCOVERY

1 'The Future of an Illusion', in Bowker 2010, p.94.

2 Consistency in recognition of six common facial expressions (happiness, surprise, fear, disgust, anger, sadness) led to the drawing up of FACS, Facial Action Coding

System. Subsequent work, however, has questioned the extent to which this is truly cross-cultural (see, e.g., Jack *et al.*), but that does not affect the fact that we are 'prepared' for facial recognition. See also the discussion of epigenetic rules in Bowker 1995a, pp.47–51.

3 'Haldane's beetles' are quoted in different forms. Haldane's friend, Kenneth Kermack, wrote (*The Linnaean*, August 1992): "What he actually said was: 'God has an inordinate fondness for beetles.' . . . More often then not it had the addition: 'God has an inordinate fondness for stars and beetles'. . . . Haldane was making a theological point: God is most likely to take trouble over reproducing his own image, and his 400,000 attempts at the perfect beetle contrast with his slipshod creation of man. When we meet the Almighty face to face he will resemble a beetle (or a star) and not Dr Carey [at that time the Archbishop of Canterbury]."

4 Gresham College in London sponsored a working party that produced the Report published in Bowker 2008.

5 For Muslim statements of this, see Bowker 1995c, pp.38–42.

6 See, for example, my translation of poems by Ephraim of Bonn and Greenberg in *Before the Ending of the Day*, pp.133–35.

7 For a summary of this, see my article 'Phenomenology' in *the Oxford Dictionary of World Religions*, and also chapter 8 in *The Sense of God*.

Bibliography

This Bibliography is of books and articles quoted or mentioned in the text; the abbreviated references in the text are to this Bibliography.

Abadia-Barrero, C., *et al.*, 'Errors in Medical Interpretation', *Pediatrics*, 111, 2003, pp.1495f.

Abercrombie, L., *Emblems of Love*, London, John Lane, 1912.

Abhedananda, Swami, *The Sayings of Sri Ramakrishna*, New York, Vedanta Society, 1903.

Abrams, M.H., 'The Correspondent Breeze: A Romantic Metaphor', in ed. Abrams, *English Romantic Poets*, Oxford, Oxford University Press, 1960, pp.37–54.

Addiss, S. and Loori, J.D., *The Zen Art Book: The Art of Enlightenment*, Boston, Shambhala, 2009.

Altman, L., 'When Peer Review Produces Unsound Science', *New York Times*, 11 June 2002.

Andersen, P. and Cadbury, D., *Imagined Worlds: Stories of Scientific Discovery*, London, Ariel Books, 1985.

Anderson, B., *Imagined Communities: Reflections on the Origin and Spread of Nationalism*, revised and extended edn., London, Verso, 2006.

Arnold, M., 'The Study of Poetry', in *Essays in Criticism*, Second Series, London, Macmillan, 1888.

Ashby, W.R., *An Introduction to Cybernetics*, London, Chapman & Hall, 1964.

Ata urRahim, M., *Prophet of Islam*, Wood Dalling, Diwan, 1977.

Auerbach, E., *Mimesis: The Representation of Reality in Western Literature*, New York, Doubleday Anchor, 1957.

Austen, J., *Northanger Abbey*, Oxford, Clarendon Press, 1948.

Austin, J.H., *Zen and the Brain*, Cambridge, MA, MIT Press, 1998.

Badayuni, A.alQ., *Muntakhab atTawarikh*, Lucknow [Lukhnaw], Nuwal Kashawr, 1867.

Barash, D., *Sociobiology and Behaviour*, Oxford, Elsevier, 1978.

Barbour, I., *Religion in an Age of Science*, London, SCM Press, 1990.

Barloewen, C., ed., *Der Tod in den Weltkulturen und Weltreligionen*, Munich, Diederichs, 1996.

Barth, K., *Church Dogmatics*, I.2, Edinburgh, T. & T. Clark, 1963.

Barzun, J., *Berlioz and His Century*, Cleveland, Meridian, 1956.

Basalla, G., Coleman, W. and Kargon, R.H., *Victorian Science: A Self-Portrait from the Presidential Addresses to the British Association for the Advancement of Science*, New York, Doubleday, 1970.

Bate, W.J., *John Keats*, Oxford, Oxford University Press, 1967.

Coleridge, London, Weidenfeld & Nicolson, 1969.

BBC Trust Review of Impartiality and Accuracy of the BBC's Coverage of Science, July 2011.

Beckett, L., *Richard Wagner: Parsifal*, Cambridge, Cambridge University Press, 1981.

Believing in the Church, London, S.P.C.K., 1981.

Bellak, L. *et al.*, *Ego Functions in Schizophrenics, Neurotics, and Normals*, New York, Wiley, 1973.

Belting, H., *The Invisible Masterpiece*, London, Reaktion Books, 2001.

Berger, P., *The Heretical Imperative*, London, Collins, 1980.

Bernard, C., *An Introduction to the Study of Experimental Medicine*, New York, Schuman, 1949.

Bettelheim, B., *The Use of Enchantment: The Meaning and Importance of Fairy Tales*, London, Penguin, 1976.

Freud and Man's Soul, London, Penguin, 1991.

Bierce, A., *The Devil's Dictionary*, in *Collected Works*, VII, New York, Neale Publishing, 1911.

Blake: see Keynes.

Blatchford, R., *My Favourite Books*, London, Clarion, 1900.

Bleich, J.D., 'Abortion in Halakhic Literature', in Rosner, *qv.*, pp.134–77.

Bloch, M., *Prey into Hunter: The Politics of Religious Experience*. Cambridge, Cambridge University Press, 1992.

Blumberg, B., 'Foreword' to Coveney, *qv.*, pp.xi–xiv.

Blythe: see Goddard Blythe.

Bobbitt, H.R., *et al.*, *Organizational Behaviour: Understanding and Prediction*, Upper Sadde River, Prentice-Hall, 1978.

Bock, J.G., *The Technology of Nonviolence: Social Media and Violence Prevention*, Cambridge, MA, MIT Press, 2012.

Bonhoeffer, D., *Letters and Papers from Prison*, London, Fontana, n.d.

Bowker, D.C., 'Meteorology and the Ancient Greeks', *Weather*, 66, 2011, pp.249–51.

Bowker, J.W. 'Intercession in the Qur'an and the Jewish Tradition', *Journal of Semitic Studies*, 11, 1966, pp.69–82.

The Targums and Rabbinic Literature: An Introduction to Jewish Interpretations of Scripture, Cambridge, Cambridge University Press, 1969.

Problems of Suffering in Religions of the World, Cambridge, Cambridge University Press, 1970.

'Merkabah" Visions and the Visions of Paul', *Journal of Semitic Studies*, 16, 1971, pp.157–73.

The Religious Imagination and the Sense of God, Oxford, Clarendon Press, 1978.

'The Aeolian Harp: Sociobiology and Human Judgement', *Zygon*, 15, 1980, pp.307–33.

'Religions as Systems' in *Believing in the Church*, *qv*, 1981a. pp.159–89.

'Did God Create This Universe?', 1981b, in Peacocke *qv*, pp.98–126.

'Religious Studies and the Languages of Religions', 17, 1981c, pp.425–39.

'Only Connect: A Reflection on the Importance of Understanding Religions in Making Decisions Today', *Christian*, 7, 1982, pp.59–66.

Licensed Insanities: Religions and Belief in God in the Contemporary World, London, Darton, Longman & Todd, 1987.

'The Religious Understanding of Human Rights and Racism', 1988, in Honoré *qv*, pp.153–73.

'Cosmology, Religion, and Society', *Zygon*, 25, 1990, pp.7–22.

The Meanings of Death, Cambridge, Cambridge University Press, 1991.

Is God a Virus? Genes, Culture and Religion, London, SPCK, 1995a.

The Sense of God: Sociological, Anthropological and Psychological Approaches to the Origin of the Sense of God, 1973; 2nd edn., Oxford, Oneworld, 1995b.

Voices of Islam, Oxford, Oneworld, 1995c.

'Die menschliche Vorstellung vom Tod', 1996a, in Barloewen *qv*, pp.406–31.

'World Religions: The Boundaries of Beliefs and Unbelief', 1996b, in Gates *qv*, pp. 3–8; Broadbent and Brown, 2002, pp.210–17.

The Oxford Dictionary of World Religions, Oxford, Oxford University Press, 1997.

The Complete Bible Handbook, London, Dorling Kindersley, 1998a.

'Science and Religion: Contest or Confirmation?', 1998b, in Watts *qv*, pp.95–119.

'Morality, Tradition and Global Community', 1998c, in Yao *qv*, pp.14–27.

God: A Brief History, London, Dorling Kindersley, 2002.

World Religions, London, Dorling Kindersley, 2003.

'God, Spiritual Information, and Downward Causation', 2005, in Harper *qv*, pp.479–83.

The Sacred Neuron, London, I.B.Tauris, 2007.

Conflict and Reconciliation: The Contribution of Religions, Toronto, Key Publishing, 2008a.

The Aerial Atlas of the Holy Land, London, Mitchell Beazley, 2008b.

'Creation, Law and Probability: A World Religions' Perspective', 2008c, in Watts *qv*, pp.181–88.

Knowing the Unknowable: Science and Religions on God and the Universe, London, Tauris, 2009.

An Alphabet of Animals, Toronto, Key Publishing, 2010a

Before the Ending of the Day, Toronto, Key Publishing, 2010b.

The Message and the Book, London, Atlantic, 2011.

God: A Very Short Introduction, Oxford, Oxford University Press, 2014.

Boyer, P., *Religion Explained: The Human Instincts that Fashion Gods, Spirits and Ancestors*, London, Heinemann, 2001.

Brecht, B., 'On Chinese Acting', *Tulane Drama Review*, 6, 1961, pp.130–36.

Britt, D., ed., *Art and Power: Europe under the Dictators, 1930–45*, London, Hayward Gallery, 1995.

Broad, W., and Wade, N., *Betrayers of the Truth: Fraud and Deceit in Science*, Oxford, Oxford University Press, 1982.

Broadbent, L., and Brown, A., *Issues in Religious Education*, London, Routledge, 2002.

Brooke, J., 'Christian Darwinians', in ed., A. Robinson, *qv*.

Brown, M., *The Holkham Bible*, London, Folio Society, 2007.

Browne, T., *Religio Medici*, in *The Voyce of the World: Selected Writings of Sir Thomas Browne*, ed. G. Keynes, London, Folio Society, 2007.

Burbridge, P., and Sutton, R., eds., *The Wagner Companion*, London, Faber, 1979.

Burleigh, M., *The Third Reich: A New History*, London, Macmillan, 2001.

Burnyeat, M.F., 'Can the Sceptic Live his Scepticism?' in Schofield, M., *qv.*, pp.20–53.

Bussey, G.C., trans. La Mettrie, *Man a Machine*, La Stalle, Open Court, 1943.

Butler, S., *Samuel Butler's Notebooks*, ed. G. Keynes and B. Hill, London, Jonathan Cape, 1951.

Calow, P., *Biological Machines: A Cybernetics Approach to Life*, London, Arnold, 1976, p.120.

Campbell, D.T., 'A Naturalistic Theory of Archaic Moral Orders', *Zygon*, 26, 1991, pp.91–114.

Caplan, A.L., ed., *The Sociobiology Debate*, New York, Harper & Row, 1978.

Carothers, J.C., 'Culture, Psychiatry and the Written Word', *Psychiatry*, 22, 1959.

Catechism of the Catholic Church, London, Geoffrey Chapman, 1994.

Ch'en, K., *Buddhism in China: A Historical Survey*, Princeton, Princeton University Press, 1972.

Chapple, E.D., *Culture and Biological Man*, New York, Holt, Rinehart & Winston, 1970.

Chenu, M.D., *Toward Understanding St. Thomas*, Chicago, Henry Regnery, 1964.

Chesterton, G.K., 'The Eccentric Seclusion of the Old Lady', in *The Club of Queer Trades*, London, Hesperus Press, 2007, p.112.

Chipp, H.B., *Theories of Modern Art: A Source Book by Artists and Critics*, Berkeley, University of California Press, 1968.

Clark, T., *Art and Propaganda in the Twentieth Century*, New York, Abrams, 1997.

Cockburn, C., *The Space Between Us: Negotiating Gender and National Identities in Conflict*, London, Zed Books, 1998.

Cohan, A., 'The Spatial Diana: The Creation of Mourning Spaces for Diana, Princess of Wales', in J.Richards, *q.v.*

Colenso, J.W., *The Pentateuch and Book of Joshua Critically Examined*, I, London, Longman & Green, 1862.

Coleridge, S.T., *Biographia Literaria*, ed. G. Watson, London, Dent, 1965.

Collings, M., *This Is Modern Art*, London, Seven Dials, 2000.

Collins, P., *From Inquisition to Freedom*, London, Continuum, 2001.

Collinson, P., 'From Iconoclasm to Iconophobia: The Cultural Impact of the English Reformation, 1500–1640', in Marshall *qv*.

Colvin, S., *Letters of Robert Louis Stevenson*, I, London, Methuen, 1911.

Common Worship: Daily Prayer: Preliminary Edition, London, Church House Publishing, 2002.

Common Worship: Services and Prayers for the Church of England, London, Church House Publishing, 2000.

Coniff, R., and Foster, G., 'Discover Interview: E.O.Wilson', *Discover*, 25 June 2006.

Connerton, P., *How Societies Remember*, Cambridge, Cambridge University Press, 1989.

Cornford: see Jowett.

Cosmides, L., and Tooby, J., 'Evolutionary Psychology: A Primer', http://www.cep.ucsb.edu/primer.html

Coveney, P., and Highfield, R., *Frontiers of Complexity: The Search for Order in a Chaotic World*, London, Faber, 1995.

Crick, F., *The Astonishing Hypothesis: The Scientific Search for the Soul*, London, Touchstone, 1995.

Cronin, M., 'The Moral, Social, and Political Philosophy of St. Thomas', in Lattey, *q.v.*, pp.132–203.

CRT Project Summary: http://www.ox.ac.uk/research/cognition-religion-and-theology/project-summary/

Cushing, J.T., *Philosophical Concepts in Physics: The Historical Relation Between Philosophy and Scientific Theories*, Cambridge, Cambridge University Press, 2003.

Cushing, M.C., *The City Without Walls*, London, Cape, 1932.

Dakins, R., 'A Man for All Reason', *New Scietist*, 220, December 21/28, 2013, pp.40–41.

Danto, A.C., *The Transfiguration of the Commonplace: A Philosophy of Art*, Cambridge, MA, Harvard University Press, 1981.

Darwin, C., *The Expression of the Emotions in Man and Animals*, London, John Murray, 1872.

Davies, J., ed., *Ritual and Remembrance: Responses to Death in Human Societies*, Sheffield, Sheffield Academic Press, 1994.

Dawkins, R., *The Selfish Gene*, Oxford, Oxford University Press, 1976.

The God Delusion, London, Black Swan, 2007.

'Evolution? Yes, Children Can Adam and Eve It', *Eureka*, 24, September, 2011.

Dawson, C., *Gibbon's Decline and Fall of the Roman Empire*, 6 vols., London, Dent, 1954.

Day, C., *These Were the Days*, London, Reprint Society, 1946.

de Beauvoir, S., *A Very Easy Death*, London, Weidenfeld, 1966.

de George, R. and F., eds., *The Structuralists from Marx to Lévi-Strauss*, New York, Anchor Books, 1972.

de la Mare, W., *Sweet as Roses: A Little Treasury of Sonnets*, in ed. L. Russell, *The Saturday Book*, London, Hutchinson, 1950

de la Mettrie, J.O., *Man a Machine*, trans., G.C. Bussey, La Stalle, Open Court, 1943.

de Riencourt, A., *The Eye of Shiva: Eastern Mysticism and Science*, London, Souvenir, 1980.

de Vries, H., *Religion and Violence: Philosophical Perspectives from Kant to Derrida*, Baltimore, Johns Hopkins University Press, 2002.

Deacon, T., *The Symbolic Species: The Co-Evolution of Language and the Brain*, New York, Norton, 1997.

Deeley, P.Q., 'The Religious Brain: Turning Ideas into Convictions', *Anthropology and Medicine*, 11, 2004, pp.245–67.

'The Cognitive Anthropology of Belief', in Halligan and Aylward, *qv*.

et al., 'Using Hypnotic Suggestion to Model Loss of Control and Awareness of Movements: An Exploratory fMRI Study', *PLOS ONE*, 8(10), 2013.

et al., 'Modelling Psychiatric and Cultural Possession Phenomenon with Suggestion and fMRI', *Cortex*, Epub. Jan. 17, 2014.

Denis, M., 'Definition of Neotraditionism', in Chipp, *qv*.

Dennett, D., *Consciousness Explained*, Boston, Little, Brown, 1991.

Denvir, B., *Paul Gauguin, The Search for Paradise: Letters from Brittany and the South Seas*, London, Collins & Brown, 1992.

Descartes, R., *Essential Works of Descartes*, New York, Bantam Books, 1981.

Diamond, J.: see George, A.

Dickinson, E., *The Complete Poems of Emily Dickinson*, Boston, Little, Brown, 1924.

Dien, A., *The History of Chinese Civilization*, IV, Cambridge, Cambridge University Press, 2012

Donceur, P., *The Heart of Ignatius*, Baltimore, Helicon, 1959.

Dorsch, T.S., ed., *Essays and Studies, 1972, in Honour of Beatrice White*, London, Murray, 1972.

Dostoevsky, F., *The Idiot*, trans. E. Martin, Ebook 2638, 2013.

Drake, S., *Discoveries and Opinions of Galileo*, Garden City, Anchor, 1957.

Drees, W.B., *Religion, Science and Naturalism*, Cambridge, Cambridge University Press, 1996.

Dretske, F.I., *Knowledge and the Flow of Information*, Oxford, Blackwell, 1981.

Drinkwater, J., *Poems, 1908–1914*, London, Sidgwick, 1923.

Dumoulin, H., *Zen Buddhism: A History*, II, New York, Macmillan, 1990.

Duties in Aid of the Civil Power, Lagos, The Government Printer, 1945a.

Duties in Connection with Unlawful Assemblies and Riots, Lagos, The Government Printer, 1945b.

Ekman, P., *The Face of Man: Expressions of Universal Emotions in a New Guinea Village*, New York, Garland, 1980.

Eliot, G., *Middlemarch*, 1874, ed. cit., London, Folio Society, 1999.

  Daniel Deronda, 1876, ed. cit., London, Panther, 1970.

Ellis, G., 'Physics, Complexity and Causality', *Nature*, 435, 9 June 2005.

Elwin, M., ed., *The Autobiography and Journals of Benjamin Robert Haydon*, London, Macdonald, 1950.

Emon, A.E., Levering, M., and Novak, D., *Natural Law: A Jewish, Christian, and Islamic Trialogue*, Oxford, Oxford University Press, 2014.

Eno, B., *The Confucian Creation of Heaven*, Albany, SUNY Press, 1990.

Epp, E.J., *The Theological Tendency of Codex Bezae Cantabrigiensis in Acts*, Cambridge, Cambridge University Press, 1966.

Evangelium Vitae, London, Catholic Truth Society, 1995.

Feduccia, A., *Riddle of the Feathered Dragons: Hidden Birds of China*, New Haven, Yale University Press, 2012.

Fénelon, F.: see Whiston.

Ferguson, E., 'Inscriptions and the Origin of Infant Baptism', *Journal of Theological Studies*, 30, 1979.

Ferguson, N., 'The Darwinian Economy', www.bbc.co.uk/programmes/b01jmxqp/features/transcript

Feynman, M., *Perfectly Reasonable Deviations from the Beaten Track: The Letters of Richard P. Feynman*, New York, Basic Books, 2005.

Feynman, R.P., *Easy and Not-So-Easy Pieces*, London, Folio Society, 2008.

Finocchiaro, M.A., 'Science, Religion and the Historiography of the Galileo Affair: On the Undesirablity of Over-simplification', *Osiris*, 16, 2001, pp.114–33.

  The Galileo Affair: A Documentary History, Berkeley, University of California Press, 1989.

Fitzmyer, J., *Romans*, London, Geoffrey Chapman, 1993.

Flood, G., *Beyond Phenomenology: Rethinking the Study of Religion*, London, Cassell, 1999.

  The Tantric Body, London, Tauris, 2006.

  The Importance of Religion: Meaning and Action in our Strange World, Oxford, Wiley-Blackwell, 2012.

  The Truth Within: A History of Inwardness in Christianity, Hinduism, and Buddhism, Oxford, Oxford University Press, 2013.

Flores, G., 'Errors in Medical Interpretation and their Potential Clinical Consequences in Pediatric Encounters', *Pediatrics*, 111, 2003, pp.6–14.

Flores, G., *et al.*, 'Language Barriers to Health Care in the United States', *New England Journal of Medicine*, 355, 2006, pp.229–31.

Foucault, M., *Power/Knowledge*, New York, Pantheon, 1972.

Fowler, R.M., 'Post-Modern Biblical Criticism: The Criticism of Pre-Modern Texts in a Post-Critical, Post-Modern, Post-Literate Era', *Forum*, 5, 1989.

Fraser, G.M., *Flashman and the Mountain of Light*, London, HarperCollins, 2005.

Freud, S., *Standard Edition of the Complete Psychological Works*, Hogarth, London, 1953–74.

Fujiki, N., and Macer, D.R.J., *Intractable Neurological Disorders, Human Genome Research and Society*, Christchurch, Eubios Ethics Institute, 1994.

Gates, B., ed., *Freedom and Authority in Religions and Religious Education*, London, Cassell, 1996.

Gay, V.P., 'Reductionism and Redundancy', *Zygon*, 13, 1978.

George, A., 'The way we were', an interview with Diamond in *New Scientist*, 12 January 2013, p.26.

Gibbon, E.: see Dawson.

Giedion, S., *The Eternal Present: The Beginnings of Architecture*, New York, Bollingen Foundation, 1964.

Goddard Blythe, S., *The Genius of Natural Childhood*, Stroud, Hawthorne Press, 2011.

Goetz, S., and Taliaferro, C., *A Brief History of the Soul*, Oxford, Wiley-Blackwell, 2011.

Goldacre, B., *Bad Science*, London, Fourth Estate, 2009.

    Bad Pharma: How Drug Companies Mislead Doctors and Harm Patients, London, Fourth Estate, 2012

Gonda, J., *Die Religionen Indiens*, I, *Veda und älterer Hinduismus*, Stuttgart, 1961.

Gould, S.J., 'Sociobiology: The Art of Storytelling', *New Science*, 16 November 1978.

Granqvist, H., *Muslim Death and Burial: Arab Customs and Traditions Studied in a Village in Jordan*, Helsinki, Helsingfors, 1965.

Gratzer, W., *The Undergrowth of Science: Delusion, Self-Deception and Human Frailty*, Oxford, Oxford University Press, 2000.

Greene, M., ed., *Knowing and Being: Essays by Michael Polanyi*, London, Routledge, 1969.

Grene, D., *The Complete Greek Tragedies: Sophocles*, London, The Folio Society, 2011.

Griffiths, R., *Poetry and Prayer*, London, Continuum, 2005

Griggs, E.L., *Unpublished Letters of Samuel Taylor Coleridge*, I, London, Constable, 1932.

Grigson, G., *The Romantics*, London, Routledge, 1942.

Guthke, K.S., *The Gender of Death: A Cultural History in Art and Literature*, Cambridge, Cambridge University Press, 1999.

Hackett, D.G., *Religion and American Culture*, New York, Routledge, 1995.

Halio, J., *Understanding Shakespeare's Plays in Performance*, Manchester University Press, 1988.

Hall, D., 'A World of Wonders: The Mentality of the Supernatural in Seventeenth-Century New England', in ed., D.G.Hackett, *q.v.*

Halligan, P., and Aylward, M., edd., *The Power of Belief*, Oxford, Oxford University Press, 2006.

Halpern, P., *Edge of the Universe: A Voyage to the Cosmic Horizon and Beyond*, Hoboken, John Wiley, 2012.

Hamilton, P., *Coleridge's Poetics*, Oxford, Blackwell, 1983.

Hammarskjöld, D., *Markings*, London, Faber, 1966

Hanson, L. and E., *Necessary Evil: The Life of Jane Welsh Carlyle*, London, Constable, 1952.

Harper, C.L., ed., *Spiritual Information*, Philadelphia, Templeton Foundation Press, 2005.

Harris, J.V.C., *The Place of Human Sexuality in Four Religious Systems*, unpublished Ph.D. thesis, Lancaster University, 1982.

Harris, S., *Letter to a Christian Nation*, New York, Knopf, 2006.

Harvey, A., *Is Scripture Still Holy? Coming of Age with the New Testament*, Grand Rapids, Eerdmans, 2012.

Harvey, G., ed., *Indigenous Religions: A Companion*, London, Cassell, 2000.

Hatfield, G., and Pittman, H., eds., *Evolution of Mind, Brain, and Culture*, Philadelphia, Penn Museum Press, 2013.

Hava, J.G., *Arabic-English Dictionary*, Beirut, Catholic Press, 1951.

Hegel, G.W.F., *Hegel's Philosophy of Right*, trans. T.M. Knox, Oxford, Clarendon Press, 1945.

Hennecke, E., *New Testament Apocrypha*, I, *Gospels and Related Writings*, London, Lutterworth, 1963.

Hinnells, J., and King, R., *Religion and Violence in South Asia: Theory and Practice*, London, Routledge, 2007.

Hisao Inagaki, *A Dictionary of Japanese Buddhist Terms*, Union City, Heian, 1989.

Hitchens, C., *God Is Not Great*, New York, Twelve, 2007.

Hoijer, H., ed., 'The Sapir/Whorf Hypothesis', in *Language in Culture*, Chicago, Chicago University Press, 1959.

Holloway, K.W., *The Quest for Ecstatic Morality in Early China*, Oxford, Oxford University Press, 2013.

Holt, E.G., *From the Classicists to the Impressionists: Art and Architecture in the 19th Century*, New Haven, Yale University Press, 1986.

Honderich, T., ed, *The Oxford Companion to Philosophy*, Oxford, Oxford University Press, 1995.

Honoré, D.D., *Trevor Huddleston: Essays on his Life and Work*, Oxford, Oxford University Press, 1988.

Hunt, M.M., *The Natural History of Love*, New York, Knopf, 1959.

Hutchins, E., *Cognition in the Wild*, Cambridge, MA, MIT Press, 1995.

Huxley, T.H., *Lay Sermons, Essays, and Reviews*, London, Macmillan, 1870.
  Life and Letters of Thomas Henry Huxley, ed. L. Huxley, I, London, Macmillan, 1903.

Hyman, T., and Wright, P., eds., *Stanley Spencer*, London, Tate Publishing, 2001.

Innes, T.A., and Castle, I., eds., *Covenants with Death*, London, Daily Express Publications, 1934.

Ioannidis, J.A.P., 'Why Most Published Research Findings are False', in *PLoS Medicine*, 30 August 2005.

Jack, R.E., *et al.*, ' Facial Expressions Are Not Universal', *Vision Sciences Society*, Florida, 2011.

Jakobson, R., 'Linguistics and Poetics', in de George, *qv.*

James, W., *The Varieties of Religious Experience: A Study in Human Nature*, London, Longmans, 1922.

Jeffery, A., *Materials for the History of the Text of the Quran: The Old Codices*, Leiden, Brill, 1937.

The Quran as Scripture, New York, Moore, 1952.

Johnson, D.D.P., Price, M.E. and Van Vugt, M., 'Darwin's Invisible Hand: Market Competition, Evolution and the Firm', *Journal of Economic Behaviour and Organization*, XC Suppl., 2013, pp.128–40.

Johnson, S., *Lives of the English Poets*, Oxford, Oxford University Press, I, 1906.

Jones, S., 'The battle for your soul rages in your DNA', *Daily Telegraph*, 31 August 2005, p.14.

Jones, W., in ed. W. Stevens, *The Theological, Philosophical, and Miscellaneous Works*, X, London, 1801.

Jones, W.T., *The Romantic Syndrome*, The Hague, Nijhoff, 1961.

Jowett, B., *The Republic of Plato*, Oxford, Oxford University Press, 1955.

Judd, J., *The Coming of Evolution*, Cambridge, Cambridge University Press, 1911.

Juergensmeyer, M., *The New Cold War? Religious Nationalism Confronts the Secular State*, Berkeley, University of California Press, 1993.

Terror in the Mind of God: The Global Rise of Religious Violence, Berkeley, University of California Press, 2003.

Juergensmeyer, M., Kitts, M. and Jerryson, M., *The Oxford Handbook of Religion and Violence*, Oxford, Oxford University Press, 2013.

Kamen, H., *Imagining Spain: Historical Myth and National Identity*, New Haven, Yale University Press, 2008.

Kar, B., *The Theories of Error in Indian Philosophy: An Analytical Study*, Delhi, Ajanta Publications, 1978.

Keenan, J., *A History of Catholic Moral Theology in the Twentieth Century: From Confessing Sins to Liberating Consciences*, London, Continuum, 2010.

Kelly, J.D., *Early Christian Doctrines*, London, Black, 1977.

Keown, D., *The Nature of Buddhist Ethics*, Houndmills, Macmillan, 1992.

Keynes, G. *Blake: Complete Writings*, Oxford, Oxford University Press, 1972.

Kircher, A., *Misurgia Universalis*, Rome, Francisci Corbelletti, 1650.

Kissane, J., 'Victorian Mythology', *Victorian Studies*, 6, 1962–63.

Kramisch, S., 'Introduction to the *Viṣṇudharmottara*', in *Exploring India's Sacred Art*, Philadelphia, University of Pennsylvania Press, 1983.

La Mettrie: see Bussey.

Lakoff, G., and Johnson, M., *The Metaphors We Live By*, new edn., Chicago, University of Chicago Press, 2003.

Lancaster, L., *Masters of Political Thought, Hegel to Dewey*, London, Harrap, 1959.

Landow, G.P., *The Aesthetic and Critical Theories of John Ruskin*, Princeton, Princeton University Press, 1971.

Lattey, C., *St. Thomas Aquinas*, Cambridge, Heffers, 1925.

Lawrence, D.H., *Nettles*, London, Faber, 1930.

Lawson, M., 'Mundane? Sublime', *The Tablet*, 3 September 2011, pp.9–10.

Leach, E., *Political Systems of Highland Burma*, London, Bell, 1954.

Leeson, S., *Christian Education*, London, Longmans, 1947.

Lehrer, J., 'The Truth Wears Off: Is There Something Wrong with the Scientific Method?', *The New Yorker*, 13 December 2010.

Lenain, T., *Monkey Painting*, London, Reaktion Books, 1997.

Lindberg, D.C., and Numbers, R.L., eds., *God and Nature: Historical Essays on the Encounter between Christianity and Science*, Berkeley, University of California Press, 1986.

Lloyd Warner, W., and Lunt. P., *The Living and the Dead: A Study of the Symbolic Life of Americans*, New Haven, Yale University Press, 1959.

Longuet-Higgins, C.H., 'The Seat of the Soul', in Waddington (1970), *q.v.*

Lord, A.B., *The Singer of Tales*, Cambridge, MA, Harvard University Press, 1964.

Lorimer, L.J., *The Root of All Evil? Religious Perspectives on Terrorism*, New York, Peter Lang, 2013.

Lou Yulie, ed., *The History of Chinese Civilization*, IV, Cambridge, Cambridge University Press, 2012

Ludskanov, A., 'A Semiotic Approach to the Theory of Translation', *Language Sciences*, 35, 1975.

Mackay, A.L., *The Harvest of a Quiet Eye*, Bristol, The Institute of Physics, 1977.

MacNeice, L., *The Dark Tower*, London, Faber, 1979.

Magee, B., *Men of Ideas: Some Creators of Contemporary Philosophy*, Oxford, Oxford University Press, 1982.

Malafouris, L., *How Things Shape the Mind: A Theory of Material Engagement*, Cambridge, MA, MIT Press, 2013.

Mao Tse-tung, *Selected Works*, Peking, 1961.

Maquet, J., *The Aesthetic Experience: An Anthropologist Looks at the Visual Arts*, New Haven, Yale University Press, 1986.

Maraini, F., *Secret Tibet*, London, Hutchinson, 1952.

Marchl, H., ed., *Beitrage zur Sprachkunde und Informations Verarbeitung*, Munich, Oldenbourg, 1963.

Margulis, L., *Symbiosis in Cell Evolution: Microbial Communities in the Archean and Proterozoic Eons*, New York, Freeman, 1992.

Marshall, P., ed., *The Impact of the English Reformation*, London, Arnold, 1997.

Marty, M.E., and Appleby, R.S., *Fundamentalisms Observed*, Chicago, Chicago University Press, 1991.

Marx, K., and Engels, F., *On Britain*, Moscow, Foreign Languages Publishing House, 1962.

On Religion, Moscow, Foreign Languages Publishing House, 1958

Marx, K., *Introduction to a Contribution to the Critique of Hegel's Philosophy of Right*, in Marx and Engels, *On Religion* (above).

Mascall, E., *The Importance of Being Human*, New York, Columbia University Press, 1958.

Masefield, J., *Collected Poems*, London, Heinemann, 1923.

Mataira, P.J., 'Mana and tapu: Sacred Knowledge, Sacred Boundaries', in Harvey (G.), *q.v.*

Mather, F.J., *Modern Painting*, New York, Garden City, 1927.

Matilal, B., *Moral Dilemmas in the Mahabharata*, Shimla, Indian Institute of Advanced Study, 1989.

Matthews, J., 'Spelling Confusion for Foreigners', *The Guardian Weekly*, 28 January 1979.

Maud, R., *Entrances to Dylan Thomas' Poetry*, Pittsburgh, Scorpion Press, 1963.

Maxwell, J.C., *Matter and Motion*, London, SPCK, 1876.

McCaughlin, M., 'Battle of Words Threatens Chaos in the Courts', *Scotsman*, 1 November 1 2009.

McCoy, A., 'How to Be Happy', *The Tablet*, 30 November 2013, pp.6f.

McGinley, P., 'A Garland of Precepts', *The New Yorker*, 6 February, 1954, p.38.

McGinn, B., 'Three Forms of Negativity in Christian Mysticism', in Bowker 2009 *qv.*, pp.99–121.

Mencken, H.L., *Prejudices, Third Series*, London, 1923.

A New Dictionary of Quotations on Historical Principles, New York, Knopf, 1942.

Miller, D., Review in *The Times Literary Supplement*, 22 May 1987, pp.544f.

Miller, R.W., *Fact and Method: Explanation, Confirmation and Reality in the Natural and the Social Studies*, Princeton, Princeton University Press, 1987.

Misztal, B., *Theories of Social Remembering*, Maidenhead, Open University, 2003.

Moore, W., *Schrödinger: Life and Thought*, Cambridge, Cambridge University Press, 1989.

Nagel, T., 'Qualia', in Honderich, *qv.*

Narayan, K., *Storytellers, Saints, and Scoundrels: Folk Narrative in Hindu Religious Teaching*, Philadelphia, University of Pennsylvania Press, 1989.

Newman, B., 'Barnett Newman: The Stations of the Cross Lema Sabachtani', in O'Neill, *qv.*

'Recent American Synagogue Architecture', in O'Neill, *qv.*

'The New Sense of Fate', in O'Neill, *qv.*

Newman, J.H., *An Essay on the Development of Christian Doctrine*, London, Toovey, 1845.

Discourses Addressed to Mixed Congregations, London, Burns & Oates, 1861.

Apologia pro Vita Sua, ed. cit., London, Collins, 1959.

Newton, I., *Principia Mathematica*, trans. F. Cajori, Berkeley, University of California Press, 1947.

Nordau, M.S., *Entartung*, Berlin, Duncker, 1893.

Norio Fujiki and Macer, D.R.J., *Intractable Neurological Disorders, Human Genome Research and Society*, Christchurch, Eubios Ethics Institute, 1994.

O'Brian, P., *The Ionian Mission*, London, The Folio Society, 2012.

O'Neill, J.P., *Barnett Newman: Selected Writings and Interviews*, New York, Alfred Knopf, 1990.

Oettinger, A., 'The State of the Art of Automatic Language Translation: an Appraisal', in Marchl, *q.v.*

Ong, W.J., *The Presence of the Word*, New Haven, Yale University Press, 1967.

Pääbo, S., 'The Human Condition – A Molecular Approach', *Cell*, 157, 2014, pp.216–26.

Paige, K.E. and J.M., *The Politics of Reproductive Ritual*, Berkeley, University of California Press, 1981.

Pattee, H.H., 'Physical Theories of Biological Coordination', *Quarterly Review of Biophysics*, 1971.

Peacock, T.L., *The Four Ages of Poetry*, ed., J.E. Jordan, Indianapolis, Bobs-Merrill, 1965.

Peacocke, A.R., ed., *The Sciences and Theology in the Twentieth Century*, South Bend, University of Notre Dame Press, 1981.

Peacocke, A.R., *The Physical Chemistry of Biological Organisation*, Oxford, Clarendon Press, 1989.

Pearce, E., Stringer, C. and Dunbar, R.I.M., 'New Insights into Differences in Brain Organisation between Neanderthals and Anatomically Modern Humans', *Proceedings of the Royal Society B*, 280, online, 13 March 2013.

Penrose, R., 'Beyond Space-Time', in Andersen and Cadbury, *qv.*, pp.163–80.

Persson, P.E., *Sacra Doctrina: Reason and Revelation in Aquinas*, Oxford, Blackwell, 1970.

Picard, F., and Craig, A.D., 'Ecstatic Epileptic Seizures: A Potential Window on the Neural Basis for Human Self-Awareness', *Epilepsy and Behaviour*, 16, 2009, pp.539–46; *ibid.*, XVII, 2010, p.592.

Picard, F., Scavarda, D. and Batolomei, F., 'Induction of a Sense of Bliss by Electrical Stimulation of the Anterior Insula', *Cortex*, 49, 2013, pp.2935–37.

Piggot, C., *A Political Dictionary*, London, Eaton, 1795.

Polanyi, M., *Personal Knowledge: Towards a Post-Critical Philosophy*, London, Routledge, 1958.

'The Logic of Tacit Inference', in Greene *qv*.

Polkinghorne, J., guest editorial in *Science and Religion News*, 1990/91.

Porter, C., *The Best of Ogonyok*, London, Heinemann, 1990.

Prigogine, I., and Stengers, I., *Order Out of Chaos*, London, 1984.

Promey, S.M., *Painting Religion in Public: John Singer Sargent's Triumph of Religion at the Boston Public Library*, Princeton, Princeton University Press, 1999.

Quasem, M., *Salvation of the Soul and Islamic Devotions*, London, Kegan Paul, 1983.

Quine, W.V.O., *Ontological Relativity and Other Essays*, New York, Columbia University Press, 1969.

Radhakrishnan, S., *The Bhagavadgita*, London, Allen & Unwin, 1948.

Rahner, K., *Spiritual Exercises* London, Sheed & Ward, 1967.

Ratanakul, P., 'A Survey of Thai Buddhist Attitudes Towards Science and Genetics', in Norio Fujiki and D.R.J. Macer, *qv*.

Read, H., *Henry Moore: A Study of his Life and Work*, London, Thames and Hudson, 1965.

Remarque, E.M., *All Quiet on the Western Front*, trans. B. Murdoch, London, Folio Society, 2010.

Rescher, N., *The Coherence Theory of Truth*, Oxford, Clarendon Press, 1973.

Richards, J., Wilson, S. and Woodhead, L., eds., *Diana, The Making of a Media Saint*, London, Tauris, 1999.

Ripke, S., *et al.*, 'Genome-Wide Association Analysis Identifies 13 New Risk Loci for Schizophrenia', *Nature Genetics*, 45, 2013, pp. 1150–59.

Ritual Notes on the Order of Divine Service, London, Walker, 1913.

Roberts, J.M., *The Mythology of the Secret Societies*, London, Watkins, 2008.

Roberts-Jones, P., *Beyond Time and Place*, Oxford, Oxford University Press, 1978.

Robinson, A., *Darwinism and Natural Theology: Evolving Perspectives*, Cambridge, Cambridge Scholars Press, 2012.

Rosen, C., *Music and Sentiment*, New Haven, Yale University Press, 2010.

Rosenthal F., *Knowledge Triumphant: The Concept of Knowledge in Medieval Islam*, Brill, Leiden, 1970.

Rosner, F., and Bleich, J.D., eds., *Jewish Bioethics*, New York, Hebrew Publishing Company, 1985.

Rothenstein, J., *Stanley Spencer: The Man: Correspondence and Reminiscences*, London, Paul Elek, 1979.

Rudwick, M., *Bursting the Limits of Time: The Reconstruction of Geohistory in the Age of Revolution*, Chicago, University of Chicago Press, 2005.

Worlds Before Adam: The Reconstruction of Geohistory in the Age of Reform, Chicago, University of Chicago Press, 2008.

Rundle, B., *Why There Is Something Rather Than Nothing*, Oxford, Oxford University Press, 2004.

Ruskin, J., *The Queen of the Air Being a Study of the Greek Myths of Cloud and Storm*, New York, Crowell, 1869.

The Seven Lamps of Architecture, London, Dent, 1907.

Lectures on Art, London, Allen, 1910.

Praeterita, ed. A.O.J. Cockshutt, Keele, Rybun, 1994.

Sabartés, J., trans. A. Flores, *Picasso, an Intimate Portrait*, London, Allen & Unwin, 1949.

Sachs, C., *The History of Musical Instruments*, London, Dent, 1942.

Safadi, Y., *Islamic Calligraphy*, London, Thames & Hudson, 1978.

Sanders, E.P., *The Tendencies of the Synoptic Tradition*, Cambridge, Cambridge University Press, 1969.

Saunders, D., *20th Century Advertising*, London, Carlton, 1999.

Savarkar, V., *Essentials of Hindutva*, 1923; reprinted in 1928 as *Hindutva: Who Is a Hindu?* New Delhi, Hindi Sahitya Sadan, 2003.

Schall, J., *The Politics of Heaven and Hell*, Lanham, University Press of America, 1984.

Schimmel, S., *The Tenacity of Unreasonable Beliefs: Fundamentalism and the Fear of Truth*, Oxford, Oxford University Press, 2012.

Schmid, A.P., and Jongman, A.J., *Political Terrorism: A New Guide to Actors, Authors, Concepts, Data Bases, Theories, and Literature*, Amsterdam, North-Holland Publishing Company, 1988.

Schofield, M., *et al.*, eds., *Doubt and Dogmatism: Studies in Hellenistic Epistemology*, Oxford, Clarendon Press, 1980.

Schön, J.H., *Plastic Fantastic: How the Biggest Fraud in Physics Shook the Scientific World*, London, Palgrave Macmillan, 2009.

Schrickx, W., 'Coleridge and the Cambridge Platonists', *Review of English Literature*, 7, 1966, pp.71–91.

Schultze-Naumburg, P., *Kampf um die Kunst*, Munich, 1932.

Seidler, V.J., *Jewish Philosophy and Western Culture: A Modern Introduction*, London, Tauris, 2009.

Shafer, B.E., ed., *Religion in Ancient Egypt: Gods, Myths, and Personal Practice*, London, Routledge, 1991.

Temples of Ancient Egypt, London, I.B.Tauris, 2005.

Shah, P., *Vishnudharmottara-Purana*, Delhi, Parimal, 2002–05.

Sharma, A., and Hejib, A., 'A Note on the Word *Prasada* in the Bhagavadgita', *Journal of the Gujarat Research Society*, 39, 1977.

Shea, W., 'Galileo and the Church', in ed. D.C. Lindberg and R.L. Numbers, *qv.*, pp.114–35.

Shelley, P.B., *A Defence of Poetry*, ed., J.E. Jordan, Indianapolis, Bobbs-Merrill, 1965. Bodley ms. Shelley d.1.

Shepard, G., 'The Mark and Olly Follies: Reality TV Series Misrepresents Tribal People', *Anthropology News*, 52, 12 May 2011; http://ethnoground.blogspot.com/2011/05/mark-and-olly-follies.html

Shimamura, A.P., *Experiencing Art in the Brain of the Beholder*, Oxford, Oxford University Press, 2013.

Sionitis, K.C., Hernandez-Boussard, T. and Ioannidis, J.P., 'Overlapping Meta-Analyses on the Same Topic: Survey of Published Studies', *British Medical Journal* (Clinical Research ed.), 347, 2013, f4501.

Sjeklocha, P., and Mead, I., *Unofficial Art in the Soviet Union*, Berkeley, University of California Press, 1967.

Skya, W.A., *Japan's Holy War: The Ideology of Radical Shinto Ultranationalism*, Durham, Duke University Press, 2009.

Smith, J., *Tapu Removal in Maori Religion*, Wellington, The Polynesian Society, 1974.

Smith, J.Z., *Imagining Religion: From Babylon to Jonestown*, Chicago, Chicago University Press, 1982.

Solecki, R., 'Shanidar Caves: A Palaeolithic Site in Northern Iraq', *Smithsonian Annual Review*, 1954, pp.389–425.
   'Three Adult Neanderthal Skeletons from Shanidar Cave', *Smithsonian Annual Review*, 1959, pp.603–35.

Spadaro, A., 'A Big Heart Open to God', *America*, 30 September 2013.

Spotts, F., *Hitler and the Power of Aesthetics*, Woodstock, Overlook, 2009.

Stanley, A.P., *The Life and Correspondence of Thomas Arnold, D.D.*, London, Ward Lock, 1904.

Stanley-Baker, J., *Japanese Art*, London, Thames & Hudson, 2000.

Stevens, W.: see Williams and Honig.

Stevenson, R.L.: see Colvin.

Stewart, T.D., 'Restoration and Study of the Shanidar I Neanderthal Skeleton in Baghdad, Iraq', *Year Book of the American Philosophical Society*, 1958, pp.274–78.

Stone, J.I., 'Priest Nisshin's Ordeals' in Tanabe *qv.*, pp.384–97.

Stoppard, T., *Arcadia*, in *Plays* 5, London, Faber and Faber, 1999.

Stravinkas, P.M.J., ed., *Our Sunday Visitor's Catholic Encyclopaedia*, Huntington, Our Sunday Visitor Publishing, 1991.

Stravinsky, I.F., *The Poetics of Music*, Cambridge, MA., Harvard University Press, 1977.

Suddendorf, T., *The Gap: The Science of What Separates Us from other Animals*, Philadelphia, Basic Books, 2013.

Swearer, D.K., 'Fundamentalist Movements in Theravada Buddhism', in Marty, *qv.*

Tanabe, G.J., *Religions of Japan in Practice*, Princeton, Princeton University Press, 1999.

Tanner, M., 'The Total Work of Art', in Burbridge *qv.*

Taylor, M., *It's the Eucharist, Thank God*, Brandon, Decani Books, 2010.

Thompson, F., *Selected Poems*, London, 1921.

Thomson, H., 'Consciousness – We Hit Its Sweet Spot', *New Scientist*, 5 July 2014, pp.10f.

Thoreau, H., *Walden*, Princeton, Princeton University Press, 1971.

Thurber, J., *The Thirteen Clocks*, London, Penguin.

Tipler, F., *The Physics of Immortality: Modern Cosmology and the Resurrection of the Dead*, New York, Doubleday, 1994.

Traherne, T., *Centuries, Poems and Thanksgivings*, ed. H.M. Margouliouth, 1, Oxford, Clarendon Press, 1972.

Trefil, J., *Cassell's Laws of Nature*, London, Cassell, n.d..

Tucker, S.I., 'Biblical Translation in the Eighteenth Century', in Dorsch, *qv.*

Turner, D., 'Christians, Muslims, and the Name of God: Who Owns It, and How Would We Know?' in Volf, *qv.*, pp.18–36.

Tyndall, J., *Address Delivered before the British Association Assembled at Belfast with Additions*: see Basalla *et al.*, pp.441–78.

Unicode: The Universal Telegraphic Phrase-Book, London, Cassell, 1896 (ed. cit., 1927).

Vaihinger, H., *Die Philosophie des Als-Ob*, Berlin, Reuter, 1911.

Vasari, G., *The Lives of the Artists*, trans. G. Bull, Harmandsworth, Penguin, 1977.

Vitaliev, V., 'On the Soviet Way of Death', in Porter *qv.*

Volf, M., *Do We Worship the Same God? Jews, Christians, and Muslims in Dialogue*, Grand Rapids, Eerdmans, 2012.

  Allah: A Christian Response, New York, HarperCollins, 2012.

Waddington, C.H., ed., *Towards a Theoretical Biology*, I–IV, Edinburgh, Edinburgh University Press, 1970.

  'The Basic Ideas of Biology', in ed. Waddington, I, pp.42–54.

Wagner, R., 'The Music of the Future' in trans. E. L. Burlingame, *Art, Life and Theories*, New York, Holt, 1889.

Walker, R.C.S., *The Coherence Theory of Truth: Realism, Anti-Realism, Idealism*, London, Routledge, 1989.

Waller, J., *Fabulous Science: Fact and Fiction in the History of Scientific Discovery*, Oxford, Oxford University Press, 2002.

Walsh, E., *et al.*, 'Using Suggestion to Model Different Types of Automatic Writing', *Consciousness and Cognition*, 26 May 2014, pp.24–36.

Wang Jingmin, 'Education in Schools and in Society', in Lou Yulie, *qv*, pp.430–528.

Warneken, F., and Tomasello, M., 'Varieties of Altruism in Children and Chimpanzees' *Trends in Cognitive Sciences*, 13.9, 2009, pp.397–402.

Warneken, F., (2013). 'The origins of human cooperation from a developmental and comparative perspective', in Hatfield and Pittman, 2013, *qv.*

Warrier, A.G.K., *The Concept of Mukti in Advaita Vedanta*, Madras University Press, 1961.

Watt, W.M., *Islamic Creeds: A Selection*, Edinburgh, Edinburgh University Press, 1994.

Watts, F., ed., *Science Meets Faith*, London, SPCK, 1998.

  Creation: Law and Probability, Aldershot, Ashgate Publishing, 2008.

Waugh, E., *Decline and Fall*, London, Penguin, 2001.

Webster, C., *The Great Instauration: Science, Medicine and Reform, 1626–1660*, London, Duckworth, 1975.

Weil, S., *The Notebooks of Simone Weil*, I, London, Routledge, 1976.

Wensinck, A.J., *The Muslim Creed: Its Genesis and Historical Development*, Cambridge, Cambridge University Press, 1932.

West, M., *Children of the Sun: The Slum Dwellers of Naples*, London, Heinemann, 1961.

Weyrauther, I., *Muttertag und Mutterkreuz: der Kult um die 'deutsche Mutter' im Nationalsozialismus*, Frankfurt-am-Main, Fischer Taschenbuch, 1993.

Whiston, C.F., *Christian Perfection: Instructions from the Spiritual Writings of François Fénelon*, New York, Harper & Row, 1947.

Whitehouse, H., *Inside the Cult: Religious Innovation and Transmission in Papua New Guinea*, Oxford, Oxford University Press, 1995.

   Arguments and Icons: Diverging Modes of Religiosity, Oxford, Oxford University Press, 2000.

Whorf, B.L., *Language, Thought and Reality*, Cambridge, MA, MIT Press, 1969.

Wiggins, J., *Religion as Story*, New York, Harper Row, 1975.

Williams, C.S.C., *Alterations to the Text of the Synoptic Gospels and Acts*, Oxford, Blackwell, 1951.

Williams, O., and Honig, E., eds., *The Mentor Book of Major American Poets*, New York, New American Library, 1962.

Williamson, H., *Dandelion Days*, London, Faber & Faber, 1930.

Wilson, E.O., 'Group Selection and Its Significance for Ecology', *Bioscience*, 23, 1973, pp.631–38.

   On Human Nature, Cambridge, MA., Harvard University Press, 1978.

   Consilience: The Unity of Knowledge, New York, Vintage, 1999.

   The Social Conquest of Earth, New York, Liveright Publishing Corporation, 2012.

Windfuhr, M., ed., *Heinrich Heine: Historich-kritische Gesamtausgabe der Werke*, XII, Hamburg, 1980.

Wittgenstein, L., *Philosophical Investigations*, Oxford, Blackwell, 1958.

   'Remarks on Frazer's *Golden Bough*', *The Human World*, 3, 1971.

Woodhead, L., Survey: www.faithdebates.org.uk

Woodhead, L. and Catto, R., *Religion and Change in Modern Britain*, London, Routledge, 2012.

Woodhead, L.: see also Richards.

Wooton, B., *Social Science and Social Pathology*, London, Allen and Unwin, 1959.

Yandell, K.E., *The Epistemology of Religious Experience*, Cambridge, Cambridge University Press, 1993.

Yao, X., *Moral Character Education Facing the New Century*, 1998.

Young, B., *The Villein's Bible: Stories in Romanesque Carving*, London, Barrie & Jenkins, 1990.

Young, J.Z., *An Introduction to the Study of Man*, Oxford, Oxford University Press, 1971.

Young, M., *An Enquiry into the Principal Phenomena of Sounds and Musical Strings*, London, G.Robinson, 1784.

Yulie, L., *The History of Chinese Civilization*, IV, Cambridge, Cambridge University Press, 2012.

Zeller, E., *Ausgewahlte Briefe von David Friedrich Strauss*, Bonn, Emil Strauss, 1895.

Index